M000217089

Working *with* Student Writers

PETER LANG
New York • Washington, D.C./Baltimore • Bern
Frankfurt am Main • Berlin • Brussels • Vienna • Oxford

Working *with* Student Writers

ESSAYS *on* TUTORING *and* TEACHING

SECOND EDITION

Edited by Leonard A. Podis *and* JoAnne M. Podis

PETER LANG
New York • Washington, D.C./Baltimore • Bern
Frankfurt am Main • Berlin • Brussels • Vienna • Oxford

The Library of Congress has catalogued the first edition as follows:

Working with student writers: essays on tutoring and teaching /
[edited by] Leonard A. Podis and JoAnne M. Podis.
p. cm.
Includes bibliographical references.
1. English language—Rhetoric—Study and teaching. 2. Tutors and
tutoring. I. Podis, Leonard A. II. Podis, JoAnne M.
PE1404.W66   808'.042'07—dc21   98-36828
ISBN 978-0-8204-4032-3 (first edition)
ISBN 978-1-4331-0710-8 (second edition)

Bibliographic information published by **Die Deutsche Nationalbibliothek**.
Die Deutsche Nationalbibliothek lists this publication in the "Deutsche
Nationalbibliografie"; detailed bibliographic data is available
on the Internet at http://dnb.d-nb.de/.

The paper in this book meets the guidelines for permanence and durability
of the Committee on Production Guidelines for Book Longevity
of the Council of Library Resources.

© 2010 Peter Lang Publishing, Inc., New York
29 Broadway, 18th floor, New York, NY 10006
www.peterlang.com

All rights reserved.
Reprint or reproduction, even partially, in all forms such as microfilm,
xerography, microfiche, microcard, and offset strictly prohibited.

Printed in the United States of America

Once again to Lauren

Contents

Acknowledgments

This book would not be possible without the contributions of the students who have served as writing tutors—more recently called writing associates— at Oberlin College since the inception of the program in 1976. We thank them for the good they have done in helping others and for the intellectual climate and collaborative community they helped create. Whether or not their essays appear in this book, they have played a role in enabling it. In particular we thank David Plank, currently with PACE (Policy Analysis for California Education) at the University of California, Berkeley, who, during his senior year at Oberlin, suggested that a peer tutoring program in writing might be a workable idea and who subsequently became the first tutor.

We are grateful to all the students whose essays comprise the bulk of this collection, including the fifteen students whose work is new to this second edition. Special recognition goes to Katie Gilmartin, who wrote Chapter 1, "Working at the Drop-In Writing Center," and who first suggested that tutors' course papers might be written specifically to offer advice to future trainees. Her essay marks a watershed in the evolution of the program and the discourse that has grown out of it. We also want to acknowledge Noelle Howey for contributing two essays to our book and for her friendship and encouragement over the years. For this second edition, we give special thanks to Jeremiah Dyehouse, Tisha Turk, and Monica Bielski Boris—all of whom are now professors—for revising and adding epilogues to their chapters from the first edition. And once again we thank our daughter, Lauren Podis, for having the courage to enter curricular territory well trodden by her parents and also (as the saying goes) to "speak truth to power."

Thanks also to our colleagues at Oberlin College and Ursuline College for their support. Laurie McMillin at Oberlin and Beth Johnson at Ursuline offered us encouragement to pursue this revision. We are grateful to Kaye Donnelly of Ursuline for her savvy assistance in scanning documents.

Finally, thanks go to the good people at Peter Lang. We are immensely grateful to our editor, Mary Savigar. Astute, supportive, knowledgeable, and efficient, she has been a delight to work with. For help in translating the project into a product of which we are proud, we also thank the production staff, especially Sophie Appel.

Introduction

Who holds the pen? This is something I've been noticing lately in the writing center. Is it the tutee or the tutor? Does the tutee hand the tutor one of her own pens, or does the tutor produce one? Am I sharing the pen with her or do I have it the whole time? Who wants to write the corrections? Does one person ask for a pen if the other won't volunteer it? What happens if we both have pens—then who lays the boundaries? I think pens are power in this situation, and it's interesting [to see] which tutees w/ which papers volunteer or claim power. You would think, since she wrote the paper, the tutee would want control over the revisions & all the changes. You would think she would want to interpret my ideas and translate them into her own in the form of a note in the margins.

—Leslie Bosworth

Leslie Bosworth wrote the above as part of an informal journal entry in a course for students training to be teachers and tutors of writing. While she was, by almost any stretch of the imagination, a novice in the field, she raises issues worthy of serious attention by even the most experienced members of our profession. What does it mean to "hold the pen" in a teaching or learning situation? Should we as tutors and teachers keep the pen to ourselves, or does it make more sense to share it with our tutees? At the heart of this issue are questions about authority and how to empower the writers with whom we work, whether in the writing center or the classroom.

We decided to call this book *Working with Student Writers* to stress the inclusiveness of the audience to whom it is addressed. As the subtitle— *Essays on Tutoring and Teaching*—indicates, the text is aimed at tutors and teachers of writing, but it is also intended for a wider audience: namely, for anyone who is interested in helping students with their writing. This audience would include tutors and teachers, to be sure, but also teaching assistants, literacy program volunteers, specialists in rhetoric and composition studies, writing program administrators, and even professors of English literature who also teach introductory composition.

It is important to recognize that *Working with Student Writers* grows out of a specific context: the training course for undergraduate peer writing tutors and future teachers of writing at Oberlin College. As such, the essays collected here have been field tested as required course readings in one of the foremost tutor training programs in operation for the past thirty years. Moreover, as many of the essays were composed by students to address problems and issues arising from their practical work and from their reading of professional pieces and previous student essays alike, the book serves in part to chronicle the developing nature of knowledge and technique in composition over the past three decades. In most instances, the tutors—more recently known as "writing associates"—wrote their essays to clarify their thinking by offering advice to their classmates as well as future generations of writing associates. Thus, while providing an introduction to tutoring and teaching, the book highlights specific issues that arise when tutors and novice teachers actually attempt to work with student writers.

While the selections in *Working with Student Writers* reflect the specific context in which they were produced, they also speak generally to tutors and teachers of writing, not only because of the authenticity of the situations in which they were composed, but also because of their incisiveness. We believe the excerpt from Leslie Bosworth's journal entry (quoted at the start of this introduction) illustrates the quality, relevance, and timeliness of the student contributions featured throughout the book.

Tutoring as Collaborative Learning

> When I made the decision to tutor for a course, I assumed that I would be acting as a *teacher's assistant*. What I've discovered since then is that when I'm doing my job well, I'm really functioning more as a *writer's assistant*.
> —Jeremiah Dyehouse

Jeremiah Dyehouse is one of the writing associates whose work appears later in this collection. As the teaching and tutoring course in which he was enrolled progressed, Dyehouse developed a special interest in the authority dynamics of the writing classroom. It is apparent from his quotation that he, like many other students, initially conceived of tutoring as a form of intervention that would simply work to uphold the status quo in terms of power relations. That is, he assumed that his role would be to enforce what the teacher wanted by helping his tutees to figure out exactly what that was and how they could produce it. However, through reading the kinds of essays that are collected in *Working with Student Writers*, participating in discussions with other writing associates, and gaining on-the-job experience, he began to believe that his role as a tutor should more properly be that of a *collaborator* in the development of his tutees' writing.

In saying that the tutor's function is collaborative, we mean to stress the *social* nature of the interaction that occurs between tutors and tutees. As many scholars and teachers have observed in recent years, and as the proliferation of social networking websites has made abundantly clear, writing, although it often appears to be a solitary activity, is highly social. There are several factors that inevitably make writing a social behavior. First, the very language that writers use derives largely from their culture: for example, the English language comes to all its users already formed, as a gift of sorts. Second, the diverse forms and genres in which writers compose are at least partly determined by communal *conventions* that govern discourse. For instance, writers of textbook sections (such as this one) might use subheadings to help structure their work after seeing such headings used in similar books. Third, writers' creations are influenced not only by reading other texts, but also, ideally, by the input of actual people who discuss their writing processes with them, read their developing drafts, and offer advice on composing and revising specific papers. Within this context, tutors can be foremost among those who join in a conversation with tutees about their unfolding ideas and texts, serving as readers, advisors, and (to use Jeremiah Dyehouse's term) "writers' assistants." This collaborative aspect of the tutor-tutee dynamic is fundamental throughout *Working with Student Writers*.

Balancing Theory and Practice

In assembling this collection, we have tried to maintain a balance between theory and practice. In our experience, when novice writing associates are presented with theory and methods before being allowed to tutor real writers, they become frustrated by their lack of contact with actual tutees. In the absence of genuine tutoring or teaching situations, most trainees find the readings on theory and methods to be abstract, uninspiring, and even vague and perplexing. For instance, experience shows that talking about various theories and techniques of responding to tutees' writing by practicing with past sample texts (rather than by working with actual tutees' drafts) feels only marginally useful to trainees, as they are anxious to get on with the real business of helping people. Without an opportunity to apply the pedagogical approaches they are encountering, trainees often find it difficult to absorb the materials in a meaningful way.

By the same token, attempts to immerse new trainees in practical tutoring or teaching activities without exposure to theory and methods leaves much to be desired. In such cases, the trainees typically feel overwhelmed by the prospect of taking on significant responsibilities without the benefit of well-theorized models or approaches to guide them. "How are we supposed to know what to do?" becomes a familiar complaint. To avoid the problems associated with the extremes of "all theory" or "all practice," *Working with Student Writers* emphasizes the crucial interplay between pedagogical theory and practice. The book is constructed to support and enact the precept that theory informs practice even as practice gives life and immediacy to theory.

Concrete Advice and Conceptual Grounding

While *Working with Student Writers* balances theory and practice, it puts concrete, practical material before more conceptual and theoretical material. In our experience, most tutors and teaching assistants, while seeking theory and rich conceptual models for guidance and direction, generally feel most comfortable and confident about what they are doing if they are given ample practical advice on exactly what to do. To dispense heavily conceptual material before offering straightforward tips may frustrate both new writing associates anxious for guidance on how to interact with their first tutees and novice teaching assistants concerned with how to mark the first set of drafts they receive. Thus, although we strongly support a balance of theory and practice, we have set this book up so that concrete, practical advice on tutoring and teaching usually precedes related theoretical issues.

Organization of the Text

This Second Edition of *Working with Student Writers* comprises eleven sections containing a total of 37 chapters. In Section One, entitled "Tutoring Writing: Practical Advice," the first two chapters give direct guidance on tutoring in a writing center (Katie Gilmartin) and tutoring for a writing-intensive course (Tisha Turk). The third essay turns to a more conceptual kind of inquiry: exploring the role of the tutor in facilitating informal discourse about formal, academic discourse (Alicia Koundakjian), a topic that applies to tutoring for both drop-in formats and ongoing tutorial arrangements in courses. Chapter 4 reflects on the writer's (Franchesca Medina) experiences as a tutee in one setting and as a tutor in two other settings, stressing valuable lessons learned about the interpersonal dynamics of the tutor-tutee relationship.

Section Two, "Perspectives on Peer Tutoring and the Writing Process," steps back to look at some of the historical and institutional contexts within which writing associates operate, while Section 3, "Facilitating and Respond-

ing to Student Writing" offers concrete strategies for conferencing, responding to drafts, and evaluating tutees' writing. Section Four, "Writing in the
Classroom: Approaches and Methods," seeks to conceptualize both teaching
and tutoring of writing, while Section Five, "Writer's Block," offers practical
advice for dealing with writing blocks (Jenny Love) and a more theoretical
analysis of the causes of blocking in college paper writing situations (Miriam
Axel-Lute).

Section Six, "Challenging Traditional Approaches," offers a range of
essays that question accepted conventions of writing in the academy, focusing especially on the inclusion of personal writing in academic contexts.
Along the lines of challenging tradition, Section Seven, "Online Writing and
Electronic Communication," explores important influences of information
technology on writing and writing pedagogy.

Section Eight, "Discourse Communities: Issues and Problems," attempts
to lay the groundwork for a social consideration of writing by examining
aspects of diverse discourse communities, both within academia and outside
it. The introduction to that section provides a brief overview of the cross-
disciplinary movement in writing instruction that began three decades ago,
while the first article, Anita Stone's "Scientific Writing: What's So Difficult
About It Anyway?" takes a look at a particular kind of academic discourse:
writing for the scientific disciplines. The next two essays in Section Eight are
concerned with the relationship between personal and academic writing.
Elizabeth Schambelan's "Defining a Persona Within the Boundaries of
Academic Discourse, or God, I Sound Like a Pretentious Ass" discusses the
author's experiences with the restrictiveness of academic essay writing, and
Holly Thompson's "Traveling the Middle-Ground: Bridging the Dichotomies
Between Academic and Personal Discourse" focuses on the process of
establishing connections between the two types of writing. The final chapter
in that section, "Academic Papers Within the College Discourse," by Kanupriya Arora, critiques the "walling off" of student papers from the intellectual discourse of the classrooms for which they are produced.

Sections Nine, Ten, and Eleven are all concerned with tutoring and
teaching in alternative ways for nontraditional, non-mainstream, or marginalized learners. For example, Monica Bielski Boris's essay, "My Hidden Class
Consciousness and the Impact of Socioeconomic Class in Academia," raises
important issues about tutoring and teaching writing to students with diverse
class backgrounds. Monica Davis's "Caught Between Skin Color and Dialect" explores race and identity in relation to the required use of standard
English in academic discourse. Emily Ryan, in "Attention Deficit Hyperac-

tivity Disorder and the Writing Process," focuses on tutoring students who may have a learning disability. Pursuing the importance of identity issues, Rebecca Phares and David Schwam examine sexual orientation as it relates to writing instruction in their collaborative piece, "Writing Inside Out: Issues of Sexual Identity in the Writing Classroom." Section Eleven also contains two chapters that contextualize the work of writing associates and teachers within the fields of English studies and composition studies. To professionals familiar with the status of those who teach primarily composition courses, these essays will probably not be startling, but tutor trainees and new teaching assistants may be surprised to learn of the marginalized status of "compositionists" both within English studies and the academy at large. The drift of these pieces, which provide some historical overview (especially Grace Chang's "Contextualizing the Debates: A Historical View of Expository Writing," but also Lauren Podis's "No Voice, No Vote") is that tutors and teachers who help student writers may be in need of some help themselves.

Section One

Tutoring Writing: Practical Advice

In his widely anthologized "Politics and the English Language," George Orwell, after listing five rules for avoiding "bad English," gives some final advice: "Break any of these rules sooner than say anything outright barbarous." (91–92) In introducing this first section on the "nuts and bolts" of tutoring and teaching writing, we want to offer a caution as well. To be sure, the four chapters in this section offer a great deal of useful advice, a wealth of tips and suggestions that should prove helpful to just about anyone setting out to work with student writers, particularly in a college or university setting. However, to paraphrase Orwell, we would admonish teachers and tutors to be ready to ignore or reject any given piece of advice at certain times, "sooner than [do] anything outright barbarous."

In presenting this caution, we mean to remind those who work with student writers that so much depends on the particulars of a tutoring or teaching context: who are the tutees, what are their backgrounds, what contextual factors (e.g., gender, race, class) might influence their approaches to learning, what are their goals as students, and so forth. A technique or approach that works well for one tutee or for some students in a class might not work well for others. We think it is essential to consider all advice on tutoring and teaching from this basic standpoint, recognizing that it is inadvisable to look for absolute answers, fool-proof formulas, or neat fixes that supposedly apply in any and all situations.

The Articles

This first cluster of articles is aimed more directly at tutors than teachers, but it is important to acknowledge that, while not all advice on teaching writing is applicable to tutoring (for example, the design of course syllabi), most advice on tutoring writing is applicable to teaching. The reason why tutoring techniques are important to teachers, as well as tutors, is that most writing teachers will frequently find themselves in situations where they are essentially tutoring the students in their classes.

We have found that one of the major challenges facing any new writing associate (or teaching assistant) is handling the anxiety that accompanies the role of being responsible for helping tutees or students to produce quality writing. Often the best way to quell the fears and insecurities that go along with the territory is to recognize that (a) these feelings are totally normal; (b) it is probably a bad sign if tutors and teachers are *not* somewhat worried and anxious about the possibility of being ineffective or unhelpful; and (c) having a few easily remembered techniques or procedures for tutoring will be a source of aid and comfort.

The first chapter in *Working with Student Writers*, Katie Gilmartin's "Working at the Drop-In Writing Center," was written to identify and codify some of those "easily remembered techniques or procedures for tutoring." It is fitting that this piece opens the book because chronologically it is also the earliest of the student-authored pieces collected here, and many of the essays that follow it owe something to it in terms of its aims and techniques. Gilmartin set herself the goal of giving future generations a practical guide that would get them started, and the history of the program shows that she succeeded. Even though this essay was written in the 1980s, it remains a rich source of ideas for working with student writers. We would particularly underscore Gilmartin's reminder to start a session by asking the tutee questions about the context and the piece of writing, rather than just tearing into the paper without consulting the writer to learn about his or her views, concerns, or goals for the session. Gilmartin also makes excellent suggestions on "setting priorities," listening carefully to tutees, and asking them to read their drafts aloud. Her discussion of how to deal with papers on unfamiliar topics is as good as any we have seen, and her comments on "flexibility and versatility" are especially important for people working with student writers.

The next chapter, Tisha Turk's "'Tutoring' Beyond the Writing Center," attempts to provide for writing associates or writing consultants (tutors assigned to work with students in a particular writing-intensive course) what Gilmartin's essay does for writing center associates. For this Second Edition of *Working with Student Writers*, Turk, now a college professor and the director of her own writing center, has substantially revised the chapter to offer more context at the start of the piece and also added an epilogue to note some changes in her views over the years. The perspective lent by Turk's essay is essential in that tutoring or assisting in a course presents a different array of challenges and rewards from those encountered by writing center associates. The most notable differences are that course tutors work with the same group of tutees for a whole term, and they see papers covering a much more predictable range of topics drawn from a single discipline. Writing center tutors may only see a tutee once (often at the eleventh hour), and the range of topics is limitless.

Turk, like Gilmartin before her, wanted to record what she had learned in order to identify the most important issues and techniques and to establish a guidebook for future course tutors. Also like Gilmartin, Turk incorporated the views and ideas of others involved in the tutoring enterprise: fellow writing associates as well as the tutees with whom she worked. Among other issues, Turk's essay tackles the problem of the *stigma* often attached to being tutored. Since a common assumption is that the need for tutoring implies some inadequacy, tutees may sometimes be "dismissive or resentful." After reviewing various negative attitudes attributable to some tutees, she suggests how writing associates can best function within this context. She offers good suggestions for tutors hoping to join in class discussions. Her candid analysis of the difficulties a writing associate might face is balanced by discussions of successful techniques she used in working with individual student writers.

Chapter 3, Alicia Koundakjian's "Speaking the Written Voice," offers a helpful model for thinking about the role of the tutor. The essay positions the writing associate as an agent "in the middle," one with the potential to bridge everyday personal/social discourse and specialized academic discourses that many tutees are struggling with for the first time in their college courses.[1] More specifically, Koundakjian identifies the special contribution of writing associates as an opportunity *to engage students in academic discussions through the use of everyday conversational language.* Koundakjian sees the tutoring session as a unique rhetorical situation: one that revolves around an informal spoken dialogue about the production of a more formal, academic piece of writing. Writing associates, she believes, can use this situation to help students "personalize academic thought" more effectively.

Koundakjian's essay is noteworthy not only for her ideas about the writing associate's role, but for her mode of presentation, which combines personal and autobiographical writing with academic analysis, making use of the everyday personal/social language she applauds in her paper. Her piece, in short, enacts in its form the balance of the personal and the academic that she identifies as characterizing the ideal function of the tutor. Her success in crossing personal/academic boundaries raises an issue that concerns writers of later chapters of *Working with Student Writers*: the challenge of entering and negotiating diverse discourse communities. Her article also touches on two more themes that recur in many chapters. First, she discusses what she, as a writing associate, gained through the experience of tutoring. That is, she puts forth the idea that it is not only the tutee that profits from the tutorial exchange. Second, in her conclusion, she sketches her vision of the potential for the tutor-tutee relationship to serve as a model for the transformation of authority dynamics within the academy at large.

The final chapter in this section, new to this edition, is Franchesca Medina's "The Motives Behind Tutoring and Being Tutored." Medina, a writing associate assigned to tutor students at the local high school as well as in the college writing center, discusses a variety of experiences and perspectives, focusing on her changing roles as a tutee in certain educational settings and a tutor in others. By drawing on her experiences in these various contexts, she is able to offer lessons about how writing associates can motivate their tutees to engage in productive work. Realizing that she herself was at times a reluctant and resentful tutee, she analyzes the social and interpersonal dynamics that contribute to failed tutoring sessions. Medina cautions tutors against adopting—however unintentionally—an attitude of superiority toward their tutees. If the tutee perceives the writing associate as someone who views himself or herself as a savior figure, then the interaction may become tainted by an unhealthy atmosphere of condescension. An important message of Medina's chapter is that tutees will respond best when they feel that their tutors truly respect them and care about their welfare, not about grooming the tutor's self-image.

The Process Approach

The essays in this section often mention "process" instruction and the "New Paradigm." Many people may already be familiar with these terms, which refer to a system of teaching that tries to treat students as *writers*. In other words, students are encouraged to follow the types of processes that, according to research studies, practicing writers tend to use. This is to say that, under the "New Paradigm," students are generally asked to do multiple drafts and revisions, making changes in their developing texts in response to the discoveries they make while composing and to concrete suggestions from a network of readers and advisors. Such an approach, while not, strictly speaking, "new" at this point in time, represents a departure from the traditional mode of expecting students to produce first-draft-final copy based on a strict, immutable structural formula (such as the five-paragraph essay format). Whereas traditional or "Old Paradigm" methods, sometimes called product-based teaching, assumed that students already knew what they would say before they began to write, "New Paradigm" approaches operate from the view—expressed by many practicing writers—that writing itself is a mode of discovery.

There are many other features of New-Paradigm instruction, which we will not go into here. Indeed, within the field of rhetoric and composition studies, scholars have moved on to a phase known as "post process." Rather than focus on cutting-edge composition scholarship in this book, however, we wish to include pieces mainly intended to enable writing associates to infuse a process approach in their work with tutees, whether at the writing center, in writing-intensive courses, or both.

NOTES

[1] Another published expression of this view can be found in Muriel Harris's "Talking in the Middle: Why Writers Need Writing Tutors," *College English* 57 (1995): 27–42.

WORKS CITED

Orwell, George. "Politics and the English Language." In *Shooting an Elephant and Other Essays*. New York: Harcourt Brace Jovanovich, 1950: 77–92.

Chapter 1

Working at the Drop-In Writing Center

Katie Gilmartin

Working at the drop-in writing center presents writing associates with a variety of challenges. Some of the problems I have considered in this guide confront both course tutors and writing center tutors, but I have focused on aspects of tutoring that particularly concern the latter. I have drawn on the class readings for English 481 ("Teaching and Tutoring Writing") as well as on the experiences of other writing center tutors and tutees that I surveyed in preparation for writing this paper.

Helping Writers Get Started

One of the most common problems for which tutees seek help is getting started on papers. Some tutees simply need someone to listen as they clarify ideas for themselves or mentally work through what they will write; in such cases, it may be best to keep your own input to a minimum, perhaps asking questions if ideas are unclear. More often, however, tutees come for help because they are having trouble getting their ideas down on paper. A good antidote to this—if it's not so serious that the tutee is incapable of writing— is freewriting. It's important to emphasize that this is a preliminary type of writing, during which writers should not concern themselves with form or organization, spelling, grammar, or style. Many writers (myself included) are terrified of writing the momentous First Word, so it may help to stress that tutees need not begin their drafting process with the introduction but should initially write on any idea that interests them.

If a tutee is utterly incapable of writing, talking about his or her ideas or about writing in general—perhaps some of your own struggles with it—may help. Discussing the "New Paradigm" approach to writing is often beneficial, especially for writers who mistakenly believe that they *should* be able to create a perfectly organized outline and then sit down and write their papers effortlessly from start to finish. Such convictions can lead to feelings of inadequacy and to writer's block. Compassion is important. It may help simply to acknowledge that the writing process is not neat and organized;

that writing is, in fact, usually difficult; often agonizing; occasionally even excruciating; and, at times, heart-rending.

Preliminary Questions

Most tutees who come to the writing center bring a draft of their paper; because drop-in tutors usually see papers in isolation, it's a good idea to begin by asking for some background information. Some important things to inquire about are the following:

- The Course: Information about the class in which the paper is due may give you some idea of what to look for in the paper, especially if you are familiar with the expectations of the professor who teaches the course.
- The Assignment: This knowledge will enable you to advise the tutee as to whether or not he or she has fulfilled the professor's expectations. For example, I've gone over several papers which were supposed to include both factual material and the writer's analysis of that material, but which were noticeably lacking in the latter.
- Length Requirement: Having a sense of the paper's ideal length will let you know whether to look for areas of the paper that might be expanded upon, or whether to focus on clarifying, tightening up, or condensing what has already been written.
- Special Concerns of the Writer: Often writers are particularly concerned about certain aspects of the paper, such as organization or clarity. You would probably be looking out for such problems anyway, but knowing the tutee's concerns can help you to set priorities.
- The Due Date: Vital information! Depending on when the paper is due, you'll want to focus the tutee's attention on further exploration or on tightening, sharpening, and clarifying what is already present. (Murray, 3–20)

Setting Priorities

Your priorities will probably depend somewhat on the answers to all of the above questions, but especially on your consciousness of the due date. If the writer has several days in which to continue working on the paper, you can view it as an early draft and suggest areas of the paper that the writer might want to expand upon or delve into in greater depth, emphasizing how he or she might continue to explore the topic. You might encourage the writer to rework certain areas or sections of the paper; you might look out for especially lively parts of the paper where it seems the writer could have more to say, or for connections that are lacking or might be developed more fully. On the other hand, if the paper is due soon (as is usually the case), you'll want to focus more on organization, clarification, and finer details such as grammar, spelling, and typos (although, of course, further development might still be possible, depending upon the tutee's attitudes and goals).

Reading the Paper

So, after you've thoroughly interrogated your tutees, you can horrify them by asking them to read their papers aloud to you. Most of the writing associates have found this technique very helpful (the reading aloud, not the horror); it usually helps writers to catch some of their own mistakes— especially incorrect or awkward sentence structures. You'll probably want to ask the writer to read fairly slowly as you follow along by looking at the text as it's being read and to be prepared to stop and ask questions about the piece. If tutees appear exceedingly nervous or distraught, you might forego asking them to read aloud.

If a writer registers extreme surprise when I ask him or her to read the paper aloud, I usually explain that this is often a good way for both of us to find out what works and what doesn't. I've occasionally had writers refuse my request if they felt especially uncomfortable or had been working on the paper a long time; in such cases I've asked them to stay with me and follow along as I read the paper. It's generally preferable for the tutees to participate in this way, if at all possible, for it allows you to make sure you are focusing on what they wish to do in the paper and to draw ideas, possible revisions, and corrections out of them rather than just scribbling comments yourself. Furthermore, problems that could be cleared up in a moment by talking about them with the writer may take a good deal of time to explain in written comments.

Often tutees will correct mistakes as they read, without realizing that they have done so; as you read along, keep an eye out for such corrections, which should be pointed out and recorded. If a paper has many complex and awkward sentences, it may be helpful for you to read parts of it aloud, so that the writer can hear how these sentences come across. This approach is especially helpful if you spot a sentence that may be unclear depending upon how it is read; reading the sentence with the unclear or incorrect inflection can quickly help the writer to understand why the wording doesn't work.

Listening

According to one of the writing associates I surveyed, perhaps the "most helpful, important, and difficult task [of a tutor] is careful listening. A tutor has a limited amount of time to absorb a lot of information regarding a paper and its context, and in order to be helpful [the tutor's] perception of the paper and the assignment must be accurate."[1] When listening to a tutee read aloud, keep in mind the broader aspects of the paper, and try not to get too bogged down in sentence-level problems, especially if you're dealing with an early draft. Focusing on a paper sentence by sentence while simultaneously trying to absorb the overall meaning and structure—or lack thereof—is difficult, particularly if the subject matter is unfamiliar, if the paper is very long, or if the writing is disorganized. Note-taking helps. Scribbling down a summary sentence or a few words at the end of each paragraph or making a rough outline based on what the tutee has written can help you to keep track of the general movement of a paper so that you can help the tutee to improve the organization and development of the piece.

While we have been indoctrinated through our teaching and tutoring class readings with the process-oriented model of writing, which tends to be anti-outline, most of the tutors have found that outlines can be helpful if they are made *after* a draft of the paper has been written. Sometimes it is useful to encourage writers to make outlines of their completed drafts; when doing so, I stress that the writer should not let an outline *limit* the writing process to come.

Error

As Joseph Williams has pointed out in "The Phenomenology of Error," it is often difficult to determine whether or not a particular usage is absolutely wrong. I have often found myself "correcting" things that weren't exactly "incorrect" to begin with. Here are some questionable errors (or non-errors) in usage and style that I've come across:

- Repeated use of "I" in an academic paper
- An abundance of sentences beginning with "It is"
- Introductory paragraphs that begin with "In this paper I will" and concluding paragraphs that begin, "In conclusion"
- Sentences that begin with "and" or "but," but not necessarily for stylistic effect
- The use of a plethora of clichés

As a tutor who is also an English major, I've found that writers of papers which are not for English classes often feel that I'm being persnickety and hypercritical when I point out such usages as problems. Their feelings may result in part from their realization that professors in, for example, political science and biology, tend to regard such stylistic nuances as less important than English professors do. I am generally more insistent that such usages are likely to be considered wrong when I am tutoring people on papers for English classes; in the case of papers for other disciplines I am more likely simply to inform the tutee that such usages may raise a red flag for some professors.

Approach

Because it is often difficult to determine whether an "error" is absolutely incorrect or whether it is used for stylistic effect, it may be hard to draw the line between correcting a paper and imposing one's own style on it. I generally try to lessen such imposition by emphasizing that many of my suggestions are, in fact, merely suggestions for improvement. I try to phrase my advice accordingly: "Maybe you should . . . "; "You might consider . . ."; "Have you thought about trying. . ."; and so forth. I also try to elicit the ideas of tutees as much as possible, rather than jumping in and suggesting explicit revisions. Often, drawing out the ideas of writers helps them to clarify those ideas and to play a more active role in revising their papers. For example, if a transition is needed between paragraphs, instead of suggesting a possible transition sentence you might help the writer to create his or her own by asking how the ideas in the two paragraphs are connected. If a paragraph lacks some kind of clarifying statement, an obvious but often very helpful question is, "How would you summarize the ideas of this paragraph?" If a sentence or paragraph is confusing, it may help simply to ask, "What are you saying here?" Ideas are often communicated much more simply and clearly in spoken words, words that can then be scribbled down and added to the paper; this seems to be especially true if the writer has been laboring over the paper for a long time. This type of advice is particularly helpful because it may give writers an idea of how to go about creating transitions, providing summary statements, and clarifying sentences on their own.

Unfamiliar Topics

Since writing center associates work with a variety of students, you may find yourself faced with a complex paper on a subject with which you are completely unfamiliar, and which is therefore difficult for you to understand. Advising the tutee on the more superficial aspects of language, style, and structure is usually possible in such instances, but you should probably let the tutee know that you are having difficulty—and acknowledge that your difficulty might not be the result of problems in the paper. Sometimes unfamiliar terms or seeming "leaps" in logic may be quite clear to someone familiar with the field. On the other hand, the paper might actually need work to make it clearer. If I suspect that perhaps it is a problem of my being an outsider with regard to the subject matter, but I'm not certain that that's the problem, I generally ask the writer whether such terms are common jargon in the field, and whether the "leaps" I see would seem logical to someone with a basic grasp of the subject area. Simply raising the question for yourself and the tutee to mull over should prove helpful.

Encouragement and Process

Many tutees come to the writing center because they are upset with the quality of their writing; anxiety is, obviously, not only no fun—it can also seriously impede writing. Sometimes tutoring mainly entails providing encouragement and moral support. Positive feedback is important; remember to look not only for problematic aspects of a paper, which will allow you to perform your critical "tutorial duties," but also for strengths, potential strengths, and positive aspects. (Podis, 252–257) Commenting on promising areas, as well as those that need work, is vital; the majority of the tutees I surveyed wrote that they were thankful for encouragement and motivation, as well as criticism. If tutees appear to be particularly distraught, and their papers to be especially poor, I try to emphasize the "process" model of writing and encourage them to view their writing as "discovery drafts" which they can expand and improve. And I encourage them to come back. Of course, it's best to avoid unfounded praise; still, most papers have *some* redeeming qualities, although once in a while you may have to be resourceful in order to ferret them out.

The process model of writing is a good one for tutors to keep in mind as well; many of the papers brought to the writing center are, in fact, discovery drafts and should be viewed as such. For instance, to borrow an example from an article by Podis and Podis, if a writer has included a good deal of plot summary in a literature paper, in the course of pointing out that he or she will want to eliminate much of it from the final draft, the tutor might emphasize the heuristic value of such plot summary for clarifying the development of the story and the student's ideas about it. (93–94)

Flexibility and Versatility

It's often necessary to modify your tutoring style, depending on the tutee and his or her needs. If tutees ask for factual information that they might need again, such as documentation forms, you should probably show them where to find it rather than just giving it to them. If writers seem to be blindly accepting your suggestions for improving a paper, try to shift more of the responsibility for revision onto their shoulders by asking what *they* think needs improvement. If tutees are extremely panicky or on the verge of tears, you'll probably want to press them as little as possible. If writers have severe writing problems, you should recommend that they visit a writing instructor and enroll in a composition course. Tact may be necessary in making such recommendations; one tutor suggested to me that tutees are less likely to be offended if you point out that getting further help with their writing is "a way to do justice to good ideas."

Trust your instincts; they are usually dependable. If you are having difficulty understanding a paper, it is probably because the paper is unclear (except as discussed above, under "Unfamiliar Topics"). Talking with other writing associates about your tutoring experiences can be very helpful. Try to view tutoring as helping people to write better, not just to improve one paper; this may be easier to do if you try "to make sure people don't consider [you] an expert—only someone who has learned tools and can help people to use them."[2]

NOTES

[1] Kelly Pfeifer, response to writing associate survey. I have drawn on Kelly's thorough and enthusiastic survey responses throughout this paper.

[2] Pfeifer, writing associate survey.

WORKS CITED

Murray, Donald M. "Writing as Process: How Writing Finds Its Own Meaning." *Eight Approaches to Teaching Composition*. Edited by Timothy R. Donovan and Ben W. McClelland. Urbana, IL: NCTE, 1980: 3–20.

Podis, Leonard A. "Training Peer Tutors for the Writing Lab." *Rhetoric and Composition: A Sourcebook for Teachers and Writers*. Edited by Richard Graves. Upper Montclair, NJ: Boynton/Cook, 1984: 252–257.

Podis, Leonard A., and JoAnne M. Podis. "Improving Our Responses to Student Writing: A Process-Oriented Approach." *Rhetoric Review* 5 (1986): 90–98.

Williams, Joseph M. "The Phenomenology of Error." *College Composition and Communication* 32 (1981): 152–168.

Chapter 2

"Tutoring" Beyond the Writing Center: Peer Consulting in the Classroom

Tisha Turk

I wrote the original version of this essay at the end of my first semester as a tutor or writing consultant for a writing-intensive course; my goal was to synthesize what I'd learned from reading composition theory in our teaching and tutoring course with what I'd learned from working with student writers and talking with my fellow tutors. I wanted to focus particularly on the experience of working with a class—that is, on the whole experience as opposed to the more widely discussed process of responding to paper drafts. I drew heavily on my own experiences as well as those of fellow tutors, and I asked for feedback from the people who were most directly affected by my efforts: the English literature students with whom I worked.

As a junior in college, I enrolled in a class called "Teaching and Tutoring Writing," which featured a course reader put together by the professor. This reader was primarily a compilation of articles from scholarly journals in the fields of composition theory and pedagogy, but it also included the work of previous students, whose final papers for the course contained insights and practical information relevant to our fledgling attempts at tutoring—a sort of insiders' guide. For me, at least, these student essays were some of the most valuable parts of the reader, since the other part of the class was not theoretical but hands-on: we were given the title of "tutor" and sent forth to figure out where theory and practice overlap. Some class members worked at the writing center in the main library; others, including myself, were assigned to writing intensive classes and worked with all the students in that class.

As the semester wore on, I became increasingly frustrated with the articles in our reader, most of which failed to account for the experiences I was having as a classroom-based tutor. The "peer tutoring" I read so much about related to me insofar as it described students helping students, but the circumstances of that interaction as I read about it and as I experienced it were quite different things. The first paper in our reader, Katie Gilmartin's

"Working at the Drop-In Writing Center" (Chapter 1 in this volume), was useful as far as it went. But Gilmartin didn't address the particular *context* in which I was supposed to do whatever it was I was supposed to be doing. My practical experience was informing me of possibilities (and difficulties) that nobody seemed to be talking about. Those of us based in the classroom are in a position to offer help to people who might not otherwise take advantage of our services, or even be aware of them; we have opportunities that a tutor at a writing center does not. On the other hand, we're also in the potentially awkward position of having to negotiate a nebulous space somewhere between Teacher and Student while in a classroom with both.

This process of negotiation has involved, for me, a rejection of the term "tutor" for my role in other people's writing processes. "Tutor" implies someone who helps remedial students so they can keep up with the rest of the class; it suggests a one-way flow of information. As such, it doesn't describe my idea of my role or what I want writers to expect from me. I have therefore chosen to adopt for myself the more neutral term "writing consultant": my role is to ask questions and to model a reader's responses, not to tell the writer what to do.

A consultant, like a tutor, is "a middle person [...] who inhabits a world somewhere between student and teacher" (Harris 27–28). In the case of a consultant, however, the situation becomes a little more complicated. Moving tutors into the classroom can shift perception of us too far to the teacher side of the continuum. We run the risk of being seen as "little teachers," to use Kenneth Bruffee's term (446): because our work in the class is not writing papers but reading them, we may seem more closely aligned with the teacher than with our fellow students. This isn't the case—or at least it shouldn't be. But authority is conferred on us by writers and by the academic situation itself whether we like it or not, and we have to think about what we want to do with that authority.

In my view, a consultant should try to have something to offer all the students in a course, at whatever level their writing may be. In some ways, the more advanced writers in a group—the ones who know perfectly well that they don't need remediation and who therefore aren't likely to frequent the writing center—are the ones who can most benefit from feedback and conversation and the occasional reminder that, sure, the paper's probably fine, but it could still be better.

Our Role in the Classroom

Before the class begins, professor and writing consultant need to have a conversation about their expectations for each other and the class. It's particularly important for us to find out what the professor expects in terms of writing, which is, after all, our primary area of responsibility. For example, are drafts required? Will meetings with the consultant be mandatory? Will they be mandatory all semester or only for the first paper or two? Will writers be given the opportunity to workshop each other's papers in class, or should such sessions be set up outside class time? Will writers have the option of further revision after the paper is graded? How will such revision affect the grade? This initial conversation is also a good time to negotiate the role of the consultant in class discussion. I feel very strongly that consultants should be absolutely clear on the professor's expectations so we can answer writers' questions accurately and fairly, and also because—as with writers!—asking professors to articulate expectations may help them clarify those expectations. "Good writing" or "clear expression of ideas" is not a useful description of an expectation; writers will just ask what that means—and they will often ask us rather than the professor. Such questions should, however, be passed on to the professor; consultants can, in this way, provide the professor with valuable information on what's really going on with the members of the class.

Because we work with everyone in a course rather than those who self-identify as wanting feedback, some of the writers in a given class may not be naturally enthusiastic about the presence of a "writing tutor." Reactions in my section of "Approaches to Literature" ranged from indifferent ("I didn't really expect anything."[1]) to dismissive ("That's nice, but it's probably not for me.") to indignant ("I thought Oberlin College was small enough not to use teacher assistants.") to dismayed ("What do I need a writing tutor for, when my writing is perfectly acceptable?!") to simply suspicious ("I thought the relationship between student and tutor might be forced. [...] I had heard stories of bad writing tutors."). Several students seem to have expected the tutor to force their writing into some sort of pre-determined structure: "I expected her to get in my way, that we'd disagree greatly on points of style and format"; "I expected a great deal of hassle with very little benefit, if any at all." How can a consultant overcome such reactions and expectations?

In my experience, the first and most important thing to do is to get to know the writers, typically by attending the class as often as possible. This advice may seem really obvious, but I have yet to talk to a writing consultant who wishes she'd spent *less* time with her class. Some consultants set up office hours of their own; others work things out more informally—meeting with writers for lunch, or over coffee. Informal sessions tend to be less intimidating and more flexible, and have the added benefit of helping to reinforce the consultant's difference from the teacher. Whatever the system, writers need to feel welcome to come talk. Being accessible, however, does not mean being pushy. Some writers are simply unwilling to meet with us, and it's my opinion that forcing or pressuring them to do so is unwise; fostering resentment is not productive for anyone, including us.

In class, I've found that it's not enough to just sit there and observe. There needs to be some real interaction for writers to get comfortable with the consultant and vice versa; writers will feel better about coming to a consultant if they have a sense of her as a person rather than an authority figure. So how exactly does classroom interaction work? Eliza, a fellow consultant who told me she thinks it's "crucial [...] to get involved as much as possible" said that she regretted not having been "more vocal in class at the outset."[2] As in any class, the habit of silence is hard to break; it's difficult and potentially awkward to start contributing in mid-semester. Besides, sitting in class listening to other people speak (or not speak, as the case may be) can be really frustrating. As a member of the class, I exercise my right to bring up things I find interesting and to introduce new topics of discussion if the current one is going nowhere. I have learned to verbalize the observations that run through my head as I sit waiting for someone else to say something, the observations I am often too scared to bring up when I am just another student; paradoxically, participating in student discussion is easier exactly because in this class I'm not "just another student." In the academic hierarchy, being in between Teacher and Student means I have been moved up a notch. The belief of the class that I am, in whatever small way, an authority, literally empowers me. It's a great feeling, especially for those of us who have struggled with class participation in the past.

The flip side of this empowerment is the danger of talking too much. After all, the class is for the writers; I'm just there to consult. Having learned to speak up, I must now resist the temptation to jump in immediately to answer the professor's questions. Molly, a fellow consultant, had this to say:

> I need to remember to be a better listener and ask more questions. [...] I often try to restate what I think the students are saying in a more academic manner, and then it sounds like me, not them.

In other words, one function of a consultant in a classroom setting is to try to get *other* people to speak. Asking questions is one way for us to balance the need to be an active presence with the equally important need to not dominate discussion. Asking questions can be frustrating, particularly when writers seem to be on the way to making a potentially interesting point but are having such difficulty getting the words out that the idea isn't coming across; often it seems that it would be easier just to say it for them. But for most students, the struggle to express ourselves coherently is usually more valuable in the long run than having someone speak for us: finding the right words for a thought may make that thought clearer in our own minds, in speech as well as writing.

Our Role in the Writing Process

Like those who work in writing centers, classroom-based consultants meet with writers one-on-one. But instead of being handed a draft when the writer walks in the door and having to provide instant feedback, we may have time to read a draft thoroughly, even to read it several times, and to write comments in response to it before the conference takes place. End comments or notes in margins can help us make points we don't get to in conferences, or prioritize the points that need the most time and attention; they also provide writers with a written record of our responses.

Much has already been written about dealing with drafts; Muriel Harris suggests ways to go about everything from "translating" professors' assignments to helping writers learn to proofread, and Katie Gilmartin's hints (Chapter 1, "Working at the Drop-In Writing Center"), while directed at writing center tutors who tend to see papers in isolation, are useful for classroom-based consultants as well. I will not rehash their points here, except to emphasize that comments on and conferences about the paper should generally focus on ideas rather than sentence-level technicalities; trying to deal with content and mechanics will only confuse both of the issues. In my experience, grammatical problems often (though of course not always) stem from a writer's uncertainty about how to communicate an idea or lack of clarity in the formulation of the idea itself. Asking writers to clarify ideas rather than fix grammar generally produces a stronger draft; once the ideas are less confused the grammar often fixes itself. In cases where that approach doesn't work, the consultant can schedule extra meetings to work on editing.

But if we're serious about treating writing as a process, we need to be willing to deal not only with drafts but also with the messes that precede a draft; we need to help writers through the Horror of Getting Started. Setting up group brainstorming sessions before the first paper can be a valuable way both to work with individual writers and to remind those writers that other people have trouble getting started too. Such sessions might begin by asking about what kinds of writing people have done prior to the present course or what their writing processes have been in the past, and then move on to discussing the assignment at hand. The subject of the paper may have been covered in class, but examining it in light of the particular assignment is often useful.

Writers struggle with getting started for a variety of reasons, including not understanding the assignment: writers in their first year of college, especially, may never have written on narrative point of view or been expected to base a five-page paper on the close analysis of a single quotation, or they may be used to being assigned a very specific topic and just not know how to choose their own. And although the professor will, one hopes, have provided some guidance in class, it may very well emerge in the course of a conference about ideas for a draft (or even about an actual draft) that a writer simply has no idea what is expected. I used to dismiss as shameless manipulators or sell-outs those writers who complained that they didn't know what the teacher wanted. It took me a while to figure out that when writers say they are perplexed about what they are expected to write, they don't *necessarily* mean that they want me to tell them what angle will get them an A; they may just need to do some talking about, for example, what it means to use one's sociological imagination or analyze the structure of a novel or review a popular work of scientific nonfiction as a microbiologist would. This type of confusion is another reason why consultants need to establish a close working relationship with the professors who will be grading the papers. Certainly our goal is not to train writers to cater to the whims of a particular instructor, and we can (and, I think, should) refer specific questions to the professor directly, but it's important that we at least know enough to not mislead a writer.

Some writers may have difficulty articulating their ideas or may simply have no idea of what to write about; they may be uncomfortable with writing; they may lack confidence in their ideas. As consultants, we need to be creative in finding ways to help writers get started, especially if they're anxious about writing—as was Emily, a student in the literature course with which I worked: "The first paper we had to write, I completely freaked out because I had literally forgotten how to write a paper." She gave me a draft in class, and I read it through, but when she showed up for our first conference, it became very clear that she disliked what she had written. She obviously wanted to abandon it and start over but was afraid to do so because she still had no ideas about the story that was the topic of the first paper. I proposed freewriting, but her reaction was unenthusiastic, largely (as we determined later) because of her conviction that writing a paper meant beginning with Sentence #1 (the thesis), perfecting that, then moving on to Sentence #2, perfecting that, and so on. The problem, it seemed, was the rigid structure and equally rigid process she had been taught to associate with paper writing.

So I asked her what kind of writing she did on her own, what kind of writing she enjoyed; it turned out that she liked writing letters. I asked her whether there was anyone at home with whom she used to discuss books in an informal way, and she mentioned her former English teacher, with whom she had kept in touch. I asked whether it might help to think about writing a letter to this person about the story we had just read: Had she liked it? Why? Would she recommend it? Of course I was really just asking her to write a draft, but this way of approaching a draft allowed her to "explore ideas, rather than just pick an easily proven topic," as she put it; it helped her to stop thinking of the paper as a version of the five-paragraph essay that she had, predictably, loathed in high school, in which, as she put it, she "basically labored from beginning to end." She ended up writing the letter (although I don't think she ever mailed it), and it really did get her started in earnest on a completely new approach to the short-story analysis. The resulting paper was perhaps not brilliant (as Emily herself was the first to admit), but the process of writing it "de-paralyzed" her, so to speak, and the experience dispelled some of her illusions about writing papers. Her next two essays involved substantially less trauma.

Different writers have different needs and require us to play slightly different roles. Caroline, a self-professed "non-English person," liked conferences because, she said, they offered "the opportunity to work through my ideas orally, which helped to make them more concrete in my mind." I read her drafts beforehand and formulated lists of questions for her. Our meetings generally consisted of my asking these questions for thirty minutes and listening to her responses. As she felt her way through the answers, she scribbled notes in the margins of her own copy of the draft.

Brian, on the other hand, was an accomplished writer when he arrived in class (a fact of which he was well aware), and, as he put it, "I didn't expect to be asking her to tell me how to write my papers. [...] I figured she would be just one more person to talk about books with." This is, in fact, more or less what happened. He always dutifully presented me with about half a draft: a beautifully written, well-thought-through draft that stopped abruptly in the middle with a long list of possible points to make next. So we generally spent our conferences discussing where he might take the draft, although because of his self-confidence I could, when necessary, critique the actual written part quite rigorously without worrying about discouraging him or bruising his ego. Thus, although I didn't really play a huge part in Brian's writing process, he notes that "the discussions I have had with her have been not just interesting but quite valuable in terms of finding topics and writing good papers on them. [...] I am assured of having a thinking individual with whom I can discuss ideas."

George was in a fairly similar situation; he adds that the consultant's "receptiveness to my work has helped me stay enthusiastic about and really put myself into papers consistently." The particular paper of which I suspect he's thinking is one for which he presented me a draft that had, as he characterized it, "a unique structure." He was obviously excited about the paper and, at the same time, worried that it was, well, too weird. We discussed it for a while and came to the conclusions that a "normal" paper (i.e., a paper that follows the conventions of academic discourse) is intended to facilitate clear expression of the writer's ideas, and that if this not-normal format was the clearest way for George to express his ideas, he should just go with it. Writers usually appreciate being shown how their own ideas can be made into viable papers; it gives them a certain amount of authority (and therefore confidence) which has frequently been denied them in their high school English classes. Helping writers see the legitimacy of their own ideas requires a certain amount of enthusiasm on the part of consultants: a willingness to really get involved in the drafts with which they're presented—to be, as Peter Elbow discusses in "Ranking, Evaluating, and Liking," excited about the draft's possibilities.

As far as drafting itself goes, Paul's comments expressed the sentiments of most of the class: "The expectation of a draft is really great. […] It leaves more time for reflection on a topic. The longer it's swimming around in the back of my head, the more chance for some revelation to resurrect my lame critical thinking." This is, of course, exactly what we would all love to hear, and most writers really did seem to feel this way (although most of them grumbled about drafting anyway—which, come to think of it, so do I).

But what about the people who disagree? John expressed it this way:

> I just cannot get used to turning in a draft a week before the paper is due. Because I work well under pressure, I don't like these imposed time constraints. In a sense, we are being forced not to procrastinate. Yet, much of my best work came at the "eleventh hour" in high school and I work well that way. Working under pressure is how I like to work […] Why should I need to use someone else's method?

This kind of attitude is a common difficulty of working with a class.

Problems

There are plenty of writers who reject their consultant, at least initially; they didn't ask for us, they don't want to talk to us, and they wish we would go away. Dealing with dismissive or resentful writers is a prime frustration of consulting; among other things, it can undermine our self-confidence. As a brand-new writing consultant with no prior experience, I had certain reservations about the whole endeavor anyway: Here I am, barely two years older than these people (if that), having written just a few more papers than they have; how am I qualified to do what I'm supposed to be doing? As Eliza points out, the situation is especially nerve-wracking when the consultant is a junior and the class is one in which there are other juniors or even seniors as well as the usual first-years and sophomores. It's easy to feel overwhelmed. This is another reason why it's good to feel comfortable with the professor: consultants with more official backing are likely to be granted more authority and respect.

Authority itself can be a problem, of course, if it results in writers who simply want to be told what to do, but it can be very helpful when dealing with writers who are reluctant to make use of the resources available to them. I've found it useful to reiterate periodically that writers can come to me for feedback as well as for help, for conversation rather than remediation; but for those who are unmoved by this reminder, asking the professor for help is often useful. Writers who might not visit a consultant on their own are more likely to do so if the professor recommends it. I stress the word "recommends"; required conferences may produce nothing but resentment, monosyllabic responses to the consultant's questions, and a lack of real involvement in the conference in which the writer is supposedly participating. For the consultant, this going-through-the-motions usually creates more frustration than it's worth. As Joanna, another consultant, remarked,

> [M]y sessions with students who show resentment towards those attempting to help them [...] appear to be wastes of my time. One student in particular regularly disregards both my and [the professor's] comments on her drafts, then [is surly and upset] when she gets [poor] grades.

Ah, yes—grades. As a consultant, I advise students on their papers, but what role do I have in grading them? None. Some students won't see this as a problem. Some will. Ideally, of course, nobody would care about their grades, only about their learning and their progress. At selective colleges, however, and particularly when working with writers fresh out of high school who may be used to getting A's on everything, grades can be very much a reality. In our tutoring class we discussed Process vs. Product and the grading system itself at length—to the point of abstraction, in fact. And because in the class I worked with I read and discussed just as the rest of the class did, but didn't have to write the papers they wrote, it was easy for me to lose track of what for some of the writers was clearly a big deal. John, the same student who was so annoyed at being expected to hand in drafts, described his consultant (that would be me) as lacking in the sense that she does not know what the professor wants in a paper. Her comments about the papers have been helpful and insightful in their own right, but have not helped me to make the papers more "palatable" to the teacher.

While it is easy to dismiss this writer as grade-obsessed, or maybe just a jerk, it's important to recognize that his expectation of increased palatability is not at all uncommon. That said, it is also not an expectation to which we must cater. As Joanna pointed out, writers (and, I would add, consultants too) need to be aware that "[the writers] have to do the work, and the grade, in the end, is the result of their thoughts and ideas and work." At some point consultants must accept that not everyone is going to want the kind of help they have to offer. This acceptance can be difficult, particularly when a consultant knows that someone who needs help isn't getting it.

There is, on the other hand, the problem of parasitic writers, the writers who seem incapable of writing a paper if the consultant isn't holding their hands every step of the way. Eliza describes such a situation and her solution: "I finally had to curtail his consulting time, because he was robbing others of time and not really using our sessions productively." It's nice to feel needed, but there's a limit to everything. Still, there may well be some writers who will need a lot of the consultant's time for very legitimate reasons: writers with dyslexia or other learning disabilities, ESL writers, some first-generation college students and those whose high schools have not adequately prepared them for college-level writing all may require a great deal of time. Those of us who don't have the time to commit should, for the writer's sake, recognize that fact and encourage the writer to find a personal tutor or make some other arrangement in addition to their regular work with us. If we're truly swamped with our own work and cannot possibly go over one more draft, encouraging writers to get additional and possibly specialized help is the best thing we can do for them.

Conclusions

Classroom-based consultants can help writers in ways that writing center workers often can't. Because we don't see papers in isolation, we may be able, particularly as the semester goes on, to refer to writers' past problems, solutions, strategies, and so on. By doing so, we can give writers a sense of continuity and help them see the places where superficially different assignments overlap. We can also, because of our familiarity with the subject of a paper and its context within the class, deal with content in a particularly thoughtful way: recognizing a paper that merely rehashes class discussion, an insight that's so original it really should be part of the thesis, an argument that's based on only one part of a text without consideration of its other aspects. A tutor in a writing center, who may or may not have read the text, heard the lecture, or participated in the discussion, is not always equipped to offer feedback on these aspects of a paper.

Working with a class has advantages for consultants as well. As a result of being located between teacher and student, we are free to observe both: How does the teacher teach? How do the students respond? Which questions stimulate discussion? Which stop it dead in its tracks? How gracefully does the professor handle her authority, and how does she help us establish ours? Since many of us become consultants with the goal of trying our hand at some form of teaching, this opportunity to observe a classroom as both a member and a distinctly separate part of the class is enlightening. Balancing our insider and outsider roles allows us to observe and learn in ways we otherwise might not.

But ultimately, the experience isn't really about us; it's about the writers. Having an entire semester to watch writers make progress (we hope!) not only on specific papers but on their writing more generally has given me a particular interest in the writers with whom I've worked. It is this opportunity to care about writers, to know their work well, to empathize with their struggles and celebrate their successes that I find most fulfilling about working with a class.

Epilogue

In the years since this piece was written, I've had the opportunity to learn a lot more about writing centers and to work with hundreds of writers as both a writing consultant and a teacher. I want to extend my particular gratitude to Brad Hughes of the University of Wisconsin, the best boss and mentor a graduate writing center employee could hope to have; to the UW Undergraduate Writing Fellows Program, with which I was affiliated for three very happy years; to the Fellows themselves, who were a constant joy to teach, to work with, and to learn from; and to the University of Minnesota, Morris, where I now teach a class very much like the one for which I wrote the original essay, and where I hope in the near future to start a classroom-based consulting program to complement our writing center.

For the second edition of *Working with Student Writers*, I've been unable to resist the urge to tinker with this chapter, mostly by adding some context at the beginning and reorganizing the paragraphs a bit. I think differently now about a few of the ideas in this piece; for example, I'm no longer convinced that consultants need to attend the class to which they're assigned, at least not as often as I did (though it sure was a great excuse to audit some terrific classes!)—I think there are other ways of getting to know writers and of establishing a presence in the class, mostly through the aid of the professor. But as a gesture of respect for the student I was, and remembering how much I liked reading essays by students as well as professors, I've left the essay and its ideas largely as they were.

NOTES

[1] All student quotations are taken from written responses to questions distributed to the introductory literature course with which I worked. Names have been changed.

[2] Consultant quotations are drawn from written responses to questions distributed to members of the Fall 1993 Teaching and Tutoring Writing class at Oberlin College. The questionnaires were administered only to those who worked with a course (rather than the writing center). Thank you, Eliza, Molly, and Joanna (and while I'm at it, thank you to everyone else in the class for being so helpful and supportive and just plain great).

WORKS CITED

Bruffee, Kenneth A. "Training and Using Peer Tutors." *College English* 40 (1978): 432–49.

Elbow, Peter. "Ranking, Evaluating, and Liking: Sorting Out Three Forms of Judgment," *College English* 55.2 (Feb 1993): 187–206.

Harris, Muriel. "Talking in the Middle: Why Writers Need Writing Tutors," *College English* 57.1 (Jan 1995): 27–42.

Chapter 3

Speaking the Written Voice

Alicia Koundakjian

I remember the dinner table growing up: my older brother sitting in between my mother and father, all eyes glued to his electric smile, roars of laughter bursting forth at the completion of each of his gripping stories, me sitting on the other side, spitting broccoli into my paper napkin while no one was looking. I loved Martin's stories as much as my parents did. They usually consisted of exaggerated recountings of his day or of illustrated synopses of movies—the best were his new ideas for inventions that could make him a millionaire. It was truly an exhilarating experience to watch him in action.

At the time, I was content to sit on the other side of the table—we were a great team; he pitched, I caught. In fact, that is the structure most of my social interactions took on for a very long time. I would sit back and observe, soak it all in, while the fast-paced world went about its business, unbothered by my presence. People who didn't know me very well thought I was just being shy or that I was quiet by nature. Others thought I was passive, boring, shallow. Those whom I did let in were always people who needed someone else to listen. Regardless of their interpretations of who I was or why I acted as I did, I believed I had mastered the art of "silent language." I was empowered by my ability to keep everything inside: my thoughts, my feelings, my theories. During junior high school, I came across a quotation by Graham Greene that became my motto: "How they defeat us with their silences, for one cannot throw back a silence as one can a word or phrase." I have no idea where I found it. I am sure I do not even remember it correctly, and I'm certain I have seriously distorted its original meaning by taking it out of context. But I wanted so much to justify my silent approach to life. I didn't want to admit to myself that I just didn't know how to speak: I couldn't tell stories; I couldn't paint pictures with words; I couldn't influence people.

And I didn't want to miss anything, either. After all, if I was wasting time talking, I might not hear what someone else had to say. For me, "learning" translated to "listening." I wanted to hear everything there was to hear.

At the same time, my own silence didn't strike me as a problem because I believed in the power of non-verbal communication, and I convinced myself that my voice was being heard through a glance or a handshake.

I continued on like that all through my childhood. It wasn't until I started college that I realized how limiting my life of silence had been. I finally reached a point of resenting the way I let other people construct my identity, as well as my own complicity in the process, my behaving according to how I saw them seeing me—perceptions of perceptions. I felt like a mess of external influences, a malleable blob of nothingness that found her shape by reacting to her surroundings—clearly, if I had mastered silence, I had also mastered assimilation, the art of adjustment, and it was at the expense of my selfhood. In college I gradually began forcing myself to make a statement, to ask questions, tell jokes. I wanted to be the kind of person other people wished would just shut up, or at least would feel compelled to respond to in some noticeable way. If I spoke before being spoken to, I reasoned, my true self would burst forth. If I claimed the spotlight, people would not have a choice but to see who I really was. And I would learn by listening to myself.

My plan seemed relatively simple at the time. Unfortunately, it didn't actually work, and I quickly resorted to my familiar ways. But it did begin what has become a three-and-a-half year struggle with my identity, with the notion of a true self, and with a passion for language and silence, and their respective roles in human communication.

What I hadn't realized in that supposed moment of enlightenment as our car rolled up to my first-year dorm, is that the silence I sought to banish had been selective and hardly the result of shyness or insecurity. By the end of freshman year, I understood that my silence had been part of a trade-off I had unconsciously made. I may not have been vocal with my friends or family, but academically I had been one of the most talkative, engaged students in my high school. In fact I had found a balance of sorts: socially, I was re-served and kept to myself, but in an academic context I was outspoken, expressive, *loud* even. Clearly I had taken that for granted. I was not a social person; I was an "intellectual." I watched people the way I read books, engaged but not interactive. In high school I had resigned myself to the idea that it was necessary to give up one aspect of my vocal faculties in order to indulge another. The absurdity of this theory did not occur to me until I had already taken it too far in college.

I was a second semester junior, I had just spent five months studying in France, painfully trying to express myself in a foreign language, and I came back to find myself thoroughly paralyzed in all of my classes by the clash of my desire to speak with my extreme discomfort at the sound of my academic voice. I was instantly aware of the fact that I hadn't really spoken in the classroom for my entire college career. I was no longer the socially quiet listener type, but I had lost that quality of speaking my mind, of expressing my intellectual side, and perhaps the most frustrating part was that I still couldn't claim to know who I was.

I am interested in this tension between the academic voice and the everyday personal/social voice. It is not the written voice that concerns me so much, for in academia that voice is so often restricted in its expression to the eyes of one professor per paper. I am troubled by the out-loud voice, the one everyone hears and sees. It seems that this voice is one of the fundamental routes to successful process learning in the "New Paradigm" approach. It is a voice that I had tucked away for three years, a voice that many students hide for numerous reasons—fear of exposure, inability to access their unwritten selves, need to avoid visible mistakes. For me it was a combination of these as well as a resistance to exclusive (and sometimes pretentious) high academic discourse. I would like to explore the way that has changed for me in my role as a writing tutor this semester.

In studying alternative approaches to teaching and thinking about writing, the tutor or writing associate, for various reasons, often employs these methods with tutees without explaining the theories behind them or even putting them directly into practice. Ironically, a writing tutor frequently has little to do with writing at all. The basic premise of a tutoring session is oral communication, talking about writing rather than participating in the act itself. My success as a writing associate depended entirely on the development of this skill. For the first time, I had no choice but to reconcile myself to academic discourse, to appropriate its components and features within a more social context to achieve my pedagogical goals.

I want to emphasize here the importance of *context* in my argument. I am not devaluing the power of silence in either academic or social development. I do not think my college education has been less valuable because of my failure to contribute to class discussions; I have certainly learned to engage my course work in other ways. Nor am I placing more value on academic knowledge than social know-how, because I believe if a trade-off had to be made, I would be much happier to feel capable of interacting with people outside of class than I would be by confining my self-expression to the safety of academic subject matter. The context to which I am referring is specifically the peer tutorial session, where I believe that the boundaries between everyday personal/social and academic discourse are blurred and that education can result from a transgressing of predetermined, diametrically opposed forces: teacher/student, high/low, silent/articulate, pitcher/catcher. The tutor-tutee relationship has the potential to be liberating and empowering for both parties involved, a space for a new form of academic discourse to flourish.

The nature of a tutoring session by definition personalizes academic thought and individualizes the learning process. Writing associates function as an ear for students to direct their ideas toward and a mouth for those ideas to become valuable and significant topics for academic study. For those students who are intimidated in varying degrees by the atmosphere of the classroom, such a private space can become a safer place to give voice to their thoughts. Moreover, the tutoring space also provides something for students who are accustomed to talking in class: They can begin to understand their academic voice in a more relaxed, social context.

As a tutor, one of my primary tasks was to uncover what issues were important to each student as well as how he or she could then write about them in a way that would validate them. Part of my method relied on establishing a social context in which academic matters could be talked about indirectly, in informal or unconventional ways. In bringing their attempts at academic discourse into the realm of everyday discourse, students are almost immediately forced to raise their stake in their written work; their interest level heightens and their capacity for clarity increases. When students are facing a peer who is receptive and responsive to their ideas, they are more apt to believe that their ideas truly warrant serious attention and to challenge themselves to convey them accordingly.

The writing associate's challenge, then, is to act as an interpretive audience while still allowing the student to be the authority over his or her own work. In my experience tutoring for a section of "Introduction to Narrative Fiction," this goal was easier to accomplish once students saw our sessions as informal private meetings that were flexible and loosely structured. We would often begin with a reading of their draft or rough outline and then lead into a discussion of their concepts or arguments. It is these discussions that I found to be a basic element in the process approach to writing. By giving my tutees the time and space to play with their knowledge, I was generally able to increase their confidence to the point that they felt compelled to explain their arguments on paper.

This kind of verbal exchange of academic discourse cannot take place with the same flexibility in a classroom. A notable difference between tutoring session and classroom would be the kind of language used. If students are asked, for example, to explain what they mean orally in class, their assumption would generally be that they are expected to sound more "academic." However, in a tutorial session, the object is to move away from academic language in order to solidify a student's understanding of his or her own point. By forming thoughts in a language with which they are comfortable, students become better grounded in their conceptual analysis and lose the weight of intimidating terminology. For the thoughts to truly be their own, they must first own the language that shapes them.

In light of all this, it seems to me that the ideal outcome of the new pedagogical approaches to the teaching of writing would be a redefinition of the role of the student writer to incorporate within it the functions of the writing tutor as well. My own experiences this semester, for example, have dramatized for me the impact that tutoring can have on the *tutor's* own writing and level of participation in academic activity. My input in the "Teaching and Tutoring" course, in particular, has been intensely concentrated compared to the back-desk, outside-observer persona I have habitually taken on for my other college courses. I did not view this course as one to passively learn from—without full participation from everyone, without input from all members of the group, the class simply would not have worked. It is rare for students to feel such authority over their own education. We not only were responsible for teaching ourselves, but each other. My attitude carried over into other courses as well: Friends would ask me to read their essays before turning them in; I would discuss my ideas for a paper's thesis with a peer. I find it remarkable that this semester I read more works written by fellow students than by published authors, and that in consequence I learned more about my own writing than ever before.

Education has for too long been stuck in a one-way conversation. No one should forever be stuck on the opposite side of the dinner table. We all have the capacity to be our own storytellers, to speak about our lives, our writing. I am, in closing, calling for more interaction in education and for more alternative sites where this interaction can take place. The old system is not going anywhere, for old traditions and expectations are still very much alive in academia. As students, as writing associates, we cannot deny or ignore or wish away the existence of the old, but we must also find room for the new, and I do believe there is a place for both. This improved new space for education can come from claiming our own place and location within the tutorial session and the classroom. In the process we can achieve, through dialogue, a heightened sense of our identity as both teachers and students.

Chapter 4

The Motives Behind
Tutoring and Being Tutored

Franchesca Medina

A key element in holding a successful tutoring session is having a receptive tutee who is eager to participate in the partnership as well as a tutor who is just as willing to please. This design is both ideal and reasonable, yet the complex reality of the situation is that not every tutee wants to be tutored, and, to make matters even worse, not every tutor wants to tutor. In my experience, there are those tutees who want to learn because they are genuinely interested in working on their writing. By contrast, there are the tutees that sit with you because they have no other choice, forced to do so for a grade, as a requirement, or even as punishment. Tutors, of course, may also be to blame for unsuccessful sessions. Some may employ ineffective techniques, but beyond issues of pedagogy, some fail for more basic personal reasons: perhaps they are tutoring mainly for the recognition or because they need the money. Moreover, tutors who are also students may periodically experience severe pressure due to their own strenuous workloads and feelings of academic insecurity, pressure that can undermine their resolve and reduce their effectiveness. To ensure success, the motives on either side of the partnership must be sincere; the desire to help and be helped must be present. In this essay I explore several of my experiences as both tutor and tutee, identifying the reasons behind failed meetings and proposing strategies for more successful sessions.

At the tender age of three, I entered elementary school and was enrolled in pre-kindergarten class. Actually my mother had brought me to the school merely to check out the facility and the teachers for the following year, but when the teacher saw me joining the other children in solving puzzles, she was so amazed at my assertiveness and eagerness to learn that she asked my mother to let me stay. I attended class for the rest of the year, and although I had to repeat the course the following year because I had started in the middle of the term and because I was so young, the experience was a preview of my intensity in the classroom. As the years passed, I adapted well to the public school system and excelled in my studies. In fact, I did so well that I was asked to be a special tutor for the ESL (English as a second language) students in the upper grades. I accepted the offer and was hired, received bi-weekly paychecks with my own name on them, and earned the respect of the faculty and staff—managing to accomplish such a sterling reputation by the age of eight.

Working as an ESL Tutor

In retrospect, I believe my public school tutoring was bound to be successful because all my tutees had volunteered to be in the program to receive extra help and were more than eager to learn the material. These students did not have bad study habits or records of delinquent behavior. They were simply the children of immigrants, thrown into a new country with a foreign language and expected to reach the same reading and writing levels as the native students as soon as possible. Many of these students came from my own country of origin, the Dominican Republic, and so I felt both obligated and proud to help them excel. Although some were initially hesitant at seeing that their tutor was so young, most were relieved to find that I was a peer with a background similar to theirs. I taught them the English alphabet, moved on to basic vocabulary words, and spent most of the tutorial sessions on dialogues and conversation.

One student named Roberto, an immigrant from the Dominican Republic, came into the fifth grade class when I was in third grade. The first time I met with him, he seemed aggravated at the idea of having a younger student tutor him. He was brilliant in science and mathematics yet sat in complete silence during social studies and English. His classmates laughed at his silence and perpetuated his failure by negatively reinforcing his anxieties. He feared being labeled "dumb" or "slow" due to his inability to communicate in English. Consequently, instead of welcoming me as a resource, he pushed me away as he did with his classmates. He saw me through the wrong lens, as someone who would belittle him, not someone who would encourage his advancement and promote his development. Yet how could he know I was trying to help him when it seemed everyone else was not? Regrettably, he eventually dropped out of school because he continued to fall further behind.

The tutoring program was not as academically effective as the school system had hoped, but at least some of the students were able to communicate better with their teachers and peers by the end of the semester. The majority of my tutees were appreciative of my efforts to support their learning, and I was grateful for the opportunity to change people's lives at such an early time in my own life. The main problem was that the school system expected the ESL students to be as fluent as the native students, not taking into consideration the challenges of learning a new language and being a foreign-born minority student adapting to an entirely new way of life.

These students knew I was not tutoring for any personal recognition or even for the money—what could an eight-year-old girl do with the money anyway? I was able to reach them because I actually took the time to get to know their individual stories. They knew I was sincerely interested in their academic development, while at the same time I knew they were concerned about their academic and social advancement in the new system. The sessions were successful because the tutees actually wanted to learn and because I sincerely wanted to help them.

With an impressive academic record behind me, I graduated as valedictorian of my fifth grade class, and I was ready to begin a new life at a private middle school. Sitting on top of the world, or so I thought, the academic adjustment was the least of my worries. Instead, I focused on the fact that I would be the only student of color in my sixth-grade class and apparently the only student from a working-class background. As it developed, I was also at a lower level in math than the rest of the class. While my classmates were already adding and subtracting fractions, I was still trying to figure out what fractions were. Gradually, I fell behind in my schoolwork and completely withdrew from the social scene; the once proud and self-confident valedictorian began her slow descent.

The Former Tutor as Reluctant Tutee

The teacher decided to keep me in class after school with a tutor to help me catch up to the proper math level. I hated the teacher. I hated school. Ironically, I also hated being tutored. As a veteran tutor myself, how could I reject a tutor who was trying to help me? The answer is that I suddenly felt stupid. I could not believe that I, of all people (especially considering my previous academic experience), was now the slow one. Given my attitude, the tutorial sessions were unsuccessful. I came into each meeting feeling vulnerable, hurt, and disenchanted. The tutor did not add to the partnership because it seemed that an important goal for her was to flatter her self-image. I think she envisioned herself as "the great white hope" who would easily solve my problems. However, upon confronting my hostile indifference, she quickly burned out. She would speak down to me, as a parent with a toddler, and would make me feel inferior. She was never intentionally mean to me, but her tone made me act defensively because I did not want her to think she was "making" me a better student. I was not dumb. I was not lazy. I was educationally disadvantaged and was now suffering the consequences.

Eventually, I took it upon myself to catch up with the rest of the class because I could no longer deal with having to meet my condescending tutor every day. Unfortunately, most children who are behind in many of our public school systems lack the same sense of drive. I did it because I knew it was my only ticket out, and I had the proper support at home encouraging my development. The tutorial partnership failed because there was no understanding between the tutor and me. She had no idea about the socio-economic adjustment I was dealing with or the psychological effects I suffered in reaction to the public school-private school transition. I wanted to learn, but I was too overcome with emotion to allow myself to do so. My tutor made the effort to teach me, but she failed because she was too unaware of who I was and of the internal struggles I was going through. I don't mean to suggest that tutors need to be "shrinks," but rather that they need to commit themselves to understanding and respecting their tutees' unique circumstances. My tutees in elementary school had learned from our sessions because they felt comfortable with me and were able to lower their defenses; yet I was unable to do the same as a tutee at my private school because I felt vulnerable and violated and could not, first and foremost, relate to the tutor as a person.

The transition to high school was much easier for me because of the intense drive to succeed that I developed in junior high. After struggling with feelings of being a fraud who needed intensive tutoring to function in private school, I finally felt deserving of my private school privilege. Everything went smoothly in high school, and I was neither a tutor nor a tutee. Soon, college applications were due, and the next phase of my life beckoned. The next stop on my academic journey was a private and highly selective liberal arts college.

Admittedly, my freshman year was a little shaky, but I never attributed my bad grades to my inner city background, my first-generation status, or my membership in the low-income bracket. Instead, I believed I was doing poorly because I attended a lot of parties, had many late-night conversations about nothing, and relied on last-minute cramming. By the end of first semester, I started feeling guilty. I had worked so hard throughout my school career and done well enough to make it to a prestigious college. Why was I floundering? I decided to re-prioritize my activities and enrolled in a course called Practicum in Tutoring as a way of giving back to those in need, as I had done years before. Tutors in the practicum would work with struggling students from the local public schools. I figured that the opportunity would force me to reflect on how far I had come and motivate me to push myself further. The professor of the practicum warned me, "These students you are about to work with need help, a lot of help [...] Approach this position with love, support, and patience [...] We're in a state of emergency." I kept that in mind as I approached my first tutoring session at the high school.

Tutoring at the Local High School

"Who the hell is this bitch?"

That was the disconcerting welcome I received on my first day of tutoring at the high school. Everyone stared at me as I entered the classroom. It was a scene from a classic movie about students running wild, where the teacher is writing on the board as students sit on top of their desks or roam the aisles, throwing paper wads at each other, talking, singing, rapping, or play-fighting in the corners.

I took a deep breath and introduced myself to the teacher and the class. The teacher tried to offer me some backup. "Oh, everyone, please pay attention, the new Spanish tutor is here," she begged in a sweet little voice that was quickly lost in the air of delinquency. I was escorted to the back of the classroom where a separate room was hidden. I took another deep breath, amazed that I could breathe at all in that atmosphere, and prepared myself for the worst.

My first tutee was a quiet young man who had problems with Spanish grammar. The teacher asked me to make up a couple of quizzes to assess his problem areas. He was obviously not interested in learning the material at all and begged me, with tears in his eyes, to help him get an A because he was on academic probation and his possibilities of graduating were looking dim. We ended up sitting there for the entire hour, just talking about his problems with school and troubles at home.

I suddenly felt the weight of the world on my shoulders. "I understand how important it is for you to pass this class, but I can't help you pass all by myself." I made up some review sheets, put them in his hands, and begged him to help me. He sensed my sincerity and carefully put the papers in his bag.

The next day he came back to see me, and we reviewed the sheets before he took the quiz. He just barely passed the quiz, but it seemed a promising start to our tutorial relationship. We worked together for the next couple of weeks, and he gradually let down his guard. I would tell him stories of my hard, yet successful, journey through the educational system and exhort him to keep pressing forward. I would say, "You can go to a good college, too— if you work hard enough." He felt comfortable with me as a person and consequently put more effort into the work he did with me. He felt bad coming to see me if he had not completed his assignments. In my experience, if a tutor can establish a supportive and trusting relationship with a tutee, it helps motivate the tutee to perform well for fear of letting the tutor down.

My second student was a girl named Monique. She was only fourteen and was very petite, yet she used the foulest language I had ever heard. I soon discovered that it was she who had so rudely welcomed me with that outburst on my first day of tutoring. In fact, she proudly informed me of this. Obviously hostile to the idea of seeing a tutor, she whipped her notebook out of her bag and slammed it on the table. I noticed there were several pictures of a beautiful little boy chaotically taped to the cover.

"Awwww, is that your little brother?" I asked.

"Hell no," she quickly retorted, "that's my son."

This exchange created an awkward tension between us as we sat and tried to review some grammatical rules, so I put the books aside and decided to inquire about her life. She thawed out and began to ask me lots of questions about living in New York, and before I knew it, we sat and talked about what life was like for a fourteen-year-old mother of a one-year-old boy.

As with the first tutee, Monique gradually let down her guard. One day when I walked into the school, someone ran over to her and said, "Hey, your cousin is here!" I smiled, a bit puzzled, but I realized that through our companionship she had come to view me as family. This relationship allowed us to work well together. I realized that these students needed someone to talk to. The way they poured out their feelings happened so naturally and spontaneously, as if no one had ever taken the time to just listen to them.

It reminded me of the students I tutored in elementary school. They allowed me to help them because I had made the effort to reach out to them. Tutoring the ESL children had also been successful because they needed English in order to survive. The high school students did not need to learn Spanish, per se, they needed to graduate, and the Spanish class happened to be in the way. So tutoring them was less successful academically because deep down they just did not care about the material. They did the bare minimum, enough to pass. However, I did not feel as if I had failed them. I did what I was supposed to do, and more. I got to know each one of them. I listened to their stories, and not only was I able to assess and help them with their Spanish grammar, I was able to comprehend the issues preventing their overall advancement: a strategy more professors might look into.

Tutoring at the College Writing Center

As I write this essay, I am a junior in college and approaching graduation. I find myself in a tutoring program yet again. However, this program is completely different. The students I tutor do not need help learning the basics. Only rarely are they students transitioning from inadequate schooling or suffering from socio-economic side effects. Indeed, they are not even in a tutoring program as such. Rather, these students voluntarily come in to the Writing Center for extra help.

Ironically, although these tutees are highly skilled and generally create admirable pieces of writing, many of them continue to feel inadequate. This low level of confidence apparently stems from the heavy doses of criticism they receive from their professors. While those criticisms are no doubt well intended, they are not constructive. Comments on papers I have seen are mostly negative and seldom offer praise for stronger sections or suggestions for improvement. These students come into the Writing Center with great papers; I read them, make a few comments and offer the positive reinforcement they yearn for.

My tutees take the time from their hectic schedules to come to the Writing Center to improve their work, and they deserve to be commended for it. It is a humbling experience to show your paper to others and allow them to dissect it. I believe this tutoring program is successful because both parties have a more mature understanding and appreciation of academic work and what success entails. In light of my earlier experiences with tutoring, I don't even think of my present job as a tutorial position; instead, call me a "refiner" or a "motivator."

My peers are amazing writers and thinkers. They have a skillful way of integrating academic theory with personal interpretation and creating substantial texts of their own. However, my position as a writing associate has shown me that they struggle with insecurities that can be overwhelming. Often, professors leave students feeling inadequate, and this can give rise to overachieving and hypercritical students. One young man, for example, came to the Writing Center with a paper that was perfectly structured, coherently organized, and properly edited. Truly, there were no apparent weaknesses in the paper, nothing that needed to be fixed. However, when he observed my motionless pen as we read over his piece, his eyes became wild and filled with rage.

"You're not going to fix it?" he demanded incredulously.

"There was nothing to fix," I replied.

He quickly stood up, tersely thanked me, and nervously shuffled out. I later found out that he had returned to the Writing Center later that night with the same paper, no doubt hoping to find a more critical writing associate. Why was he hoping for things to be wrong?

I will never forget the disturbed look that tutee gave me when I disclosed my delight at having read his paper. It's extremely sad to contemplate the pained faces of distraught Writing Center tutees, not only those who need the most help, but those with outstanding pieces that need only minimal changes. Why do we college students crave negative reinforcement? Do we inherently desire it, or is it a vicious circle of conditioning?

No Bad Tutors

There is no such thing as a bad tutor or writing associate, but it is important to have the right motivation. One needs to reflect: Why do I want to be a tutor? Is it for the credit? The recognition? As I mentioned earlier, I now call myself a motivator because I spend lots of time giving encouraging words to my tutees who come into the Writing Center feeling disheartened. Honestly, in retrospect, I've been something of a motivator for my whole tutoring career. In elementary school the ESL students needed someone on their side, someone with their best interests at heart. At the high school, my tutees were able to learn because I let them know it meant the world for me to see them succeed, not merely to pass a Spanish quiz.

Tutoring is more than helping people to revise their papers or teaching grammatical rules. Tutoring is at its most successful when it takes on aspects of a friendship. The students at the high school wanted to do well not only for themselves but because they knew it was also very important to me. Similarly, the college students who come back to consult me on every paper assignment do so because of the support I offer. Perhaps unconsciously, I fill a void, a void that might be filled by others in the educational system, but which apparently is not. As tutors and writing associates, how can we instill much-needed confidence in our tutees? Perhaps the words of my practicum professor bear repeating: "These students you are about to work with need help, a lot of help [...] Approach this position with love, support, and patience. [...]"

Section Two

Perspectives on Peer Tutoring and the Writing Process

I had a tutee approach me last fall and say, "Josh, I need to write a paper due tomorrow, and I still haven't finished the book. I want to read it, but I'm a very slow reader, and I just haven't been able to keep up." Why did this student come to me, rather than to his professor? Possibly because he realized—and helped me to remember—that I, even though a tutor, was still just a student. And I helped him—not by telling him to read faster next time, or by analyzing the book for him, but by [suggesting that he] pick a scene he'd already read, and focus on it exclusively.
—Joshua Kizner

In the presentation from which this excerpt is taken, Josh Kizner focuses on the unique role of the writing associate, who, in his experience, is a highly approachable and accessible source of authority and advice. When confronted with his tutee's admission that he simply couldn't finish the assigned reading in time to write his paper, Kizner avoided the kind of inflexible moralizing that he suspects the course instructor might have offered; instead, he gave the tutee some straightforward advice that he drew from his familiarity with a plight in which students commonly find themselves: being swamped with nearly impossible amounts of reading. Lamenting the fact that all too often the professor in a writing-intensive course may strike students as a remote and unsympathetic figure, Kizner concludes the presentation by looking hopefully towards a time when the spirit of collaboration that informs peer tutoring also "characterizes the majority of the professoriat.[...]"

This spirit of collaboration is a distinctive element of the *idealism* of the so-called New Paradigm in the teaching of writing, a pedagogical movement in which peer tutoring has played an important role. Since their inception, peer tutoring programs in writing have often been characterized by idealism in that their chief goal has been to help other students to negotiate the difficult demands of academic writing. However, in the early days, tutoring programs sometimes operated from an old-fashioned and somewhat unenlightened perspective in which tutees were stigmatized as being "sick" writers who needed "remediation." Such "afflicted" student writers, if they could overcome the stigma involved, would visit the drop-in center much as ill people would go to a "clinic"—often at the behest of faculty members who were dismayed by the poor quality of the students' writing.

With the development and refinement of the new pedagogy and with the growth of writing-across-the-curriculum programs, there was a tendency toward "mainstreaming" peer tutoring. While drop-in "clinics" and "labs" remained, tutors (often relabeled as writing associates) were also being used in writing-intensive classes to help students with their initiation into writing for various disciplines. With this mainstreaming, a degree of the stigma was removed, as institutions seemed to be saying that since so many writers could profit from tutorial assistance in writing, the aid would be provided to them directly. To pursue the medical metaphor, being tutored no longer implied that a student needed major surgery or powerful medications; rather, tutees could be seen as regular student writers benefiting from something akin to vitamins or good nutrition.

Furthermore, as the new pedagogy grew and changed in the direction of social constructionism (i.e., through the influences of Marxism, feminism, multiculturalism, and postmodernism), tutoring came to be seen as a catalyst in the communal building of knowledge from a diversity of cultural positions (e.g., gender, race, class, ethnicity, sexual orientation). Under this model, writing associates have increasingly taken on the task of recognizing and appreciating the strengths of the discursive backgrounds and strategies that tutees bring with them. Well-trained writing associates and teaching assistants can provide a well-theorized and intellectually rich culture of support, motivation, and guidance for students attempting to find their positions and voices within various academic and social discourses.

The Articles

The section begins with Chapter 5, Peggy Putney's "Working with Peers at the Writing Center: Tutoring for Diverse Disciplines." Putney, a physics major who worked at the writing center, was initially intimidated by the prospect of helping peers with papers from disciplines about which she knew little or nothing. However, the knowledge and support she gained from participating in her tutor-training course, coupled with on-the-job experience, gave her the confidence and the ability to succeed. In her essay she shares the attitudes and techniques that enabled her to be an effective writing center tutor, even though she was herself "hardly a perfect writer." Echoing advice from earlier chapters, Putney emphasizes the importance of establishing rapport with the tutee and describes the approaches she took in helping tutees with papers from disciplines in the humanities, social sciences, and sciences.

The second article (Chapter 6), Jeremiah Dyehouse's "Peer Tutors and Institutional Authority," discusses how writing associates participate in the power dynamics of the college classroom. Dyehouse raises several questions about tutor-tutee interaction with the aim of enabling himself and other writing associates to use their authority to "counteract hierarchy." A key question he explores is whether, in the eyes of the tutee, the tutor must inevitably be regarded as an institutional authority figure whose function is to serve as a "guide to a good grade." Dyehouse questions such a role, preferring instead to support the authority of the tutee and his or her writing. One recommendation that Dyehouse makes is that writing associates should be candid with tutees in discussing the authority relations that underlie the tutoring situation. In focusing on the issue of authority dynamics in higher education, his piece is itself a good example of candor. Despite his idealistic view of the tutorial role, he is far from naive, as he points out that working as a peer tutor is not like helping a friend with a paper because in the tutorial role, like it or not, he cannot help but be perceived as "the agent of the professors." Ironically, subsequent to writing the piece (1997), Dyehouse himself became a writing professor, and for this edition of *Working with Student Writers*, he has provided a brief epilogue to reveal how his thinking on the topic of his essay has continued to evolve over the years.

Chapter 6, the last essay in the section, is Polly Dondy-Kaplan's "Processing Writing." For this piece, which was her final paper for her Teaching and Tutoring Writing course, she decided to do a complete revision of her midterm essay for the course. To her surprise, the revised essay was vastly different from the midterm version, making use of only a small part of the original. Her recognition of this fact gives rise to a useful metaphor: the earlier draft, she observes, served as a kind of "fertilizer" for the final version. In conducting this close examination of her own writing process, Dondy-Kaplan makes a strong case for the importance of robust, ongoing revision in a writer's approach. Her essay also identifies an irony that may resonate with tutors and teachers of writing: at points in the piece she admits that she has not always practiced what she has preached with respect to the importance of viewing writing as a process. Still, her essay underscores the importance of understanding our own writing processes as a basis for improving our writing and the writing processes of our tutees.

Chapter 5

Working with Peers at the Writing Center: Tutoring for Diverse Disciplines

Peggy Putney

I have had the chance to work at the writing center during peak hours when a great variety of writers with a variety of assignments from diverse disciplines have sought help. I'll be the first to admit that I'm hardly a perfect writer. Yet things have gone surprisingly well. Frequently, the tutee has thanked me at the end of the session and then made a note about what hours I work. I now have a handful of repeat visitors, and I attribute this to my ability to take the tutoring theory I have learned and to apply it successfully.

It is not always one's own ability to write that makes her the best writing associate. I have found that, unfortunately, my ability to help others doesn't always translate into an ability to help myself. But therein lies a key point: no one is special enough to ignore help in writing, and those who seek help are not doing so because they are "bad at writing." What I have learned from working at the writing center that has benefited me most is that revision is key and that another set of eyes can make all the difference.

General Tips

In my experience, the main thing that determines how well the session goes is how I interact with the tutee. Every single session that went well featured my going through a specific social interaction that allowed me to weave composition pedagogy techniques into the conversation. If a writing associate is not very social or simply ignores the social dimensions of tutoring, he or she is unlikely to have an enjoyable or productive session, and neither will the tutee. As tutors, we are ideally investing our own time because we enjoy doing it, we want to be there, and we are genuinely interested in hearing what the person has to say and helping them to say it better.

Generally, there are a few techniques that have been useful for just about every session. I always first ask what the assignment was, and what the student wants to say with the paper—not what he or she is *supposed* to say, but what the student wishes to convey to the reader. This way I learned a lot more about the writer's interests and excitement about the topic at hand and avoided receiving only a recitation of what the teacher had dictated.

Next, having the person read their paper aloud has never failed to yield good results. By acknowledging the writer's own speech and where they are coming from, I avoid misunderstandings, and the tutee shows me where work is actually needed, often picking out the simple mistakes without my intervention. What I say to each of these tutees with their vastly different paper topics, writing levels, and personal investment in the papers has a lot to do with my own interest in the arguments they are presenting me and a recognition that they know more about the specific subject than I do.

After reading the paper aloud and going through its general theme and purpose, I set about determining priorities. I may only see this person once the entire semester, and their paper may also be due the next morning. For example, at one of my sessions, a girl had a paper due the next day. I was careful not even to mention the more complicated issues of content, style, and voice that could only be remedied by extensive reading and reworking of the prose but focused rather on urging her to make her point as clear as possible. This became a theme throughout my sessions with tutees. Our role as a writing associate is crucial. We must ask the right questions to determine what the student wants to say. If we find a paper dull, or even wrong, it is not our place to say (with the exception of morally repugnant topics; see next section). Rather, it is our job to help tutees get their point across clearly.

While we reworked the language of the paper, I made sure the tutee (a first-year) knew I was only a few years older and that I still struggled with some of the same issues. We worked together extensively to improve a certain problematic passage, a passage that would have most likely been scrapped if either of us alone had tried to tackle it. It is important to remind students that no paper is ever finished; it is just abandoned at that point, and there is always more than one way to say the same thing. What's most important is whether or not the paper makes its argument reasonably well.

Dealing with Papers on Ethically Troublesome Subjects

In class the consensus seemed to be that the best approach in dealing with uncomfortable or morally repugnant subjects was to take a distanced stance and focus purely on the writing. After all, it was not our place to judge the content, but only whether the argument was well made, with good writing techniques. After my tutoring experiences, I would partially disagree with this. At times it is not possible to ignore the subject, and you may have to bring in an outside example to reveal the weak spots in the argument.

One of my tutees came in with such a paper. It did not argue something totally outrageous, like reinstating slavery or some other truly appalling idea, but it did make me uncomfortable because it emphasized the writer's approval of physical violence. I found it impossible to address the problems in the paper without addressing the topic itself. Many times I find it's easy to put myself in the paper in order to test the hypothesis; in this case the writer was arguing that we will all at some point find ourselves in a situation where recourse to violence is the only answer. When I told the tutee I was an exception to his rule because I find the kind of violence he described to be impossible for me, it forced him to clear up his language and get rid of absolutes, to acknowledge exceptions or counterarguments. By engaging openly in a give-and-take discussion, I was able to get him to qualify his statements.

Writer's Block

As a writing center tutor, I find that I wield a surprising amount of influence over writing blocks students may face. It is always important to realize that the mere presence of the students in the writing center speaks to where they see themselves in the writing process, and how they view their problem. The advice and techniques I offer here can only be applied to those who come into the writing center and not to writers across the board.

My ability to help peers overcome a barrier seems to stem from the fact that I am not academically invested in the tutee's writing, so I can approach it with a clearer and more rational mindset. I have found that what tutees at the writing center need most is to talk out their ideas with the tutor and be shown what a wealth of information they already possess. This often gives them the confidence to continue with the writing process.

For example, one night a girl came in with a poetry analysis. I asked her to simply tell me what she had gained from the poem and what parts and aspects of the poem stuck out to her. As I listened, I remembered the different points and then repeated them to her in a more organized fashion. Here, as a physics major, I did not know anything about poetry analysis, yet I was able to help her formulate her thesis just by echoing what she had told me.

Going over ideas verbally with another person is an incredibly useful tool for any writer. It calms writers to discuss ideas with someone who does not influence their grade. Often they only need to be reminded of what they already knew to break through their block.

Longer Papers

Lengthy papers have always been intimidating to me, no matter if I'm writing them or helping someone with them. How do you grasp the idea and control the flow of a paper so long? I feel that the magnitude of the ideas dwarfs what I can physically hold in my brain. Nevertheless, I discovered a solution that is as old as writing itself.

A friend of mine came in with a 30-page paper for an economics class. After some discussion, we decided to physically cut it into sections, so that we could view it as a series of smaller papers. The physical act of tearing the pages up and cutting apart paragraphs was really satisfying and revved us up to work on it. Covering the entire table in the writing center, we solved a problem that computers have given us by enabling ourselves to see the bigger picture. We were going back to the original "cut and paste" functions in a literal sense. The cut and paste functions on the computer are wonderful, and certainly save time when it comes to moving pieces of writing around. Nevertheless, computers can't do everything yet, and the ability to see before you all the sections of your paper can be the key to overcome a structural block you were facing in finishing that longer paper. It certainly helped me to do a better job of tutoring my friend on that very long economics paper.

Working with Tutees on Narrative Nonfiction

Narrative nonfiction or creative essay writing is something in which I have had no classes and something that, with my scientific background, can intimidate me. The only way I could learn anything about helping with such a piece was to plunge right in and work enthusiastically with the first student who brought me such a paper.

One tutee who came to the writing center with a creative piece was extremely resistant when I suggested taking a closer look at her grammar. She believed her sophisticated style of writing precluded any need for help with "grammar." In fact, it turned out that the issue in her paper was really *voice*, or a type of discourse and rhythm in writing. I began to understand how the tutee wanted things to flow, yet she continued to react defensively to my suggestions, explaining the history of the genre of creative nonfiction and so on until she finally looked over the paper with me and saw I was not suggesting some basic arbitrary changes but simply a clarification of theme.

I was finally able to get her to listen to me when I changed how I phrased "grammar." I specifically told her that I had begun to understand her rhythm, especially as she read, and my goal was to ensure the rhythm came through. Essentially, that's what good grammar does, but the word has such a negative connotation for some people, that the tutee could no longer listen to anything connected to that word. I had to adopt her discourse—focusing on "voice" and not "grammar"—in order to help her with her writing.

This is pertinent to working with all kinds of writers, but especially those whose ideas about revision may conflict with the language we would normally use when tutoring. Creative nonfiction isn't too different from everyday writing. Ultimately it still needs to be clear and support a theme, with every sentence important to the message. Once the tutor and tutee get on the same page about what needs to be done, it resembles any other kind of revision. But it is very important to be flexible and adopt the writer's discourse in order to reach the person with whom we are working.

Science Writing

My primary training in writing has been for the sciences. I have read and written about complex phenomena in a language that is known for its denseness. Last year I struggled to get through the paper my own lab had just published. Scientific writing is a genre that is precise and yet can never explicitly state that something is known beyond a doubt. The tutee I had who best exemplifies this point came to the writing center with a paper for his archeology class. Archeology may be seen as a history or social sciences field in some respects, but it relies on principles of geology and biology and is recorded and researched in a strict scientific way.

In science writing, a careful balance between being assertive and being correct is essential. Normally, a writer should be assertive throughout the paper. I tell people who come in not to be "wishy-washy," and that a strong idea should be reflected in the writing. "Don't use 'I believe this is true'; instead say, 'this is true.'" Usually in science writing, however, you are not asserting your opinion but showing evidence for a physical truth. Because laws in science are specific and limited, writers should avoid absolutes. For example, one might write: "Evolution by natural selection is the dominant determining agent for traits in today's species." Better would be: "Evolution by natural selection is *thought to be* the dominant determining agent to present traits in today's species." It can be a tough job for the writing associate to help the tutee sort through what is opinion and what is fact.

Authority

Regardless of the genre of writing a tutee brings to the writing center, it is important to establish an appropriate level of authority. In my Teaching and Tutoring course, I read many theoretical articles on authority, on voice, on old theories and beliefs about grammar, writing, and how to teach writing, but I found it hard to connect that to what I have experienced, specifically on issues of authority. Do I have authority? Have I not been stressing my peer status? How do issues of authority connect with the actual tutoring process?

At first I resisted the idea that to sustain proper authority, tutors must remove themselves emotionally from the people they are helping. I would like to believe I am just as capable of helping my good friends as I am of helping someone I just met. I know now, though, that authority has a lot to do with the success of a tutoring session. I don't mean the true authority we wield as peer tutors (that's almost nil) but the perceived authority we have. The respect we get from our tutees is what counts when we are tutoring.

I have had successes in tutoring people I know, but they have consistently been those who look up to me in some way. At the opposite end of the spectrum, my most disastrous session came when a girl from my own year in school, who was in my same social circle and who knew a lot about my background and vice-versa, entered the writing center with her application letter to grad school. She consistently rejected all my suggestions for improvement, as though she felt I, as a lowly peer, couldn't possibly know what I was talking about, and it was extremely frustrating for both of us.

It became apparent that she was according me very little authority because of the history of our personal relationship. Peers with whom we are familiar, and who are familiar with our problems with writing (maybe friends who have read over our first drafts for us) may not be able to take us as seriously as they need to in order to benefit from our efforts. Indeed, having the ability to help tutees does not necessarily translate into making our own writing flawless. So sometimes working with those who know our faults can present special challenges to our authority. All we can do is offer our best advice and hope that its quality will speak for itself.

Conclusion

Tutoring at the writing center can be especially difficult if writing associates don't know what to expect and can't switch gears when confronted by diverse problems from assignments in diverse disciplines. In my experience, flexibility is crucial. There are many types of people and kinds of essays, each with their own needs that should be addressed. However, all types of tutoring sessions can profit from a tutor's use of basic tools. A comfortable atmosphere encourages tutees to open up, emboldening them to read their work aloud, which can highlight the writer's voice and insecurities as well.

I realize that reading this essay will not make one a good tutor. However, I hope it might help make the transition into tutoring easier. Unfortunately, advice alone will not provide magic tools to allow tutors to fix all problems. But advice combined with experience can give us the knowledge and techniques to help an array of tutees at the writing center, including those who are working on papers that fall outside of our disciplinary comfort zones.

Chapter 6

Peer Tutors and Institutional Authority

Jeremiah Dyehouse

Peer tutors are granted their authority by the academic institution to aid in the teaching of writing. What any particular tutor does with this authority is a matter of personal and institutional responsibility. I believe that questioning this authority is a crucial step towards becoming an effective tutor. This process can (and should) take many forms, but for the purposes of this paper I will focus on three questions that arise directly from my experience: What are the dynamics of tutor-tutee relationships that result from the authority of the tutor? What are some positive ways for the tutor to deal with authority? What are the possibilities for the authority of the peer tutor within the academic institution? In exploring the answers to these questions, I hope to address some of the implications surrounding peer tutors' authority. I think this process has consequences for each individual tutor, for the pedagogical paradigm that each of us adopts, and for the institution within which we act as tutors.

What Dynamics Result from the Authority of the Tutor?

My limited experience with peer tutoring has shown me that being a tutor is unlike engaging with a friend over writing. Although ideally I would like my conferences to proceed as though there is no authority barrier between the tutee and me, I have not been able to accomplish this. I have found that student-teacher authority patterns tend to be reproduced in the tutee-tutor relationship. This is particularly upsetting to me because I do not like the traditional student-teacher relationship and its related power dynamics.

I experienced some problems related to my authority as a peer tutor in a writing-intensive course when I tried to coordinate brainstorming sessions for paper topics. Invariably, I found that students talked directly to me (and only me) even though the sessions were set up as discussion groups. Moreover, the discussion of ideas seemed fixed in a rigid fashion on formulating "good papers," in direct contradiction to what I saw as the nature and purpose of "brainstorming," which should be informal and exploratory. Finally, I noticed that discussion among the tutees occurred only when I completely retreated from the conversation. Having sat through several such sessions, I wondered whether I should try to disrupt this dynamic or whether it was simply an unchangeable reality that I must accept and try to negotiate.

Although this is only one example of the authority dynamics in the tutor-tutee relationship, I think it is indicative of problems that tutors have to face. When I enter into a tutoring situation, I am the agent of the professors, the academic institution, and even of academic discourse itself. When I meet a student, I carry all of these roles within my greeting. Although I say, "It's nice to meet you," the situation says (for me), "I am an accredited authority on writing, and you can learn something from me to help you gain power in this institution." Many messages are sent, and many discourses speak through the situation of tutoring as a result of my having authority as a writing tutor.

I think that this authority is not so much given by the institution as it is given up within the tutoring situation. I don't necessarily demand power over a tutee, but my role as tutor carries power. Of course different tutees give up more or less power in a tutoring session, thereby giving me more or less authority. The specifics of the tutoring relationship affect the degree to which I can be more or less of a *peer* in the tutoring relationship. I have adopted this understanding of my own authority as a way to explain how different relationships generate different roles for myself and a tutee.

At one point during the semester, a tutee asked me, "What will Professor XYZ think about this paper?" I can't imagine that she knew that I have actually taken a number of courses with Professor XYZ, so I don't think her trust in my knowledge of Professor XYZ's preferences was based on her belief that I had first-hand experience in writing papers for him. Yet she wouldn't have asked me the question if she didn't think I had some special insight into the mysteries that would determine her grade in the professor's eyes. At the time, I sidestepped the question and tried to prompt her to say what she thought of her own paper. I also brought up my view of my own role as peer and mentioned that I felt it was my responsibility not to try to second-guess the professor. Thinking back now on this incident (ironically within the bounds of a course paper), I know that I could have answered her question with some accuracy. However, I did not want to align myself any more with the professor than I already was by virtue of being in the role of tutor to begin with. My responsibility in that situation was to distance myself from the evaluative function of the professor and the institution in order to get her to interact more fully with her own paper.

What Are Positive Ways for the Tutor to Deal with Authority?

In reflecting on the incident just described, I understand what transpired as the student's trying to identify me as a representative of the professor and my trying to escape from that role. In fact, in this instance I did succeed in escaping my institutional role as "the tutor" or "the teaching assistant" by redirecting her comment and foregrounding my sense of my responsibility in our relationship. It seems that the best way for me to address the authority dimension of the tutorial situation is to be candid about my own reservations and conceptions of my role.

I feel that it is important for me to discuss issues of authority with tutees explicitly as a way of initiating a tutoring situation with fewer "surprises." In short, it is crucial to engage the tutee in an open discussion about the nature of our relationship. With this shared understanding as the foundation of the interaction, perhaps some of the destructive assumptions about the tutor-tutee situation can be reduced.

One such assumption that I think might detract from the effectiveness of tutoring is that the tutor primarily serves as a guide to a good grade. This implicit assumption can undermine the New Paradigm writing process that peer tutoring is supposed to facilitate. As tutors, we are accordingly urged in our training course to ask questions that evade or forestall the inevitable question on many tutees' minds: "What does the professor think?" Indeed, many faculty members only give lip service to the process model of writing. Students and professors alike consider it uncouth for students to be explicitly concerned with grades. This situation is aggravated by the hypocrisy of instructors who often value the learning process in the classroom but reinforce the importance of the product in communication outside the classroom (i.e., the worship of the transcript). In many situations, I imagine that tutees would not directly ask me, "What will Professor ABC think?" but instead assume that our entire tutoring relationship exists to allow them to discover the answer to that very question.

Such an assumption can be explicitly dealt with in the beginning of the tutoring relationship. I think that it is the responsibility of the tutor to acknowledge the reality of the power dynamics in the institution and to be clear about the role that she or he wants to play. I imagine that this gesture could open up the possibility for "real" peer tutoring, where the student-teacher authority relations of the traditional classroom are not simply duplicated. When the tutor acknowledges that his or her function is not that of a *teacher's assistant* but really that of a *writer's assistant*, I think that some of the negative aspects of authority in tutoring can be reduced.

Another strategy that I have used in trying to reduce any possibly adverse effects of my authority is to bring my personal experience into the tutoring session. When appropriate, I try to reinforce the idea that I am but a peer of the tutee and that I struggle with some of the same issues in writing. Although I think that this strategy is often misused by authority figures who employ it in a deceptive and condescending manner, I still believe that it is not a bankrupt gesture. As a means of making this "gesture" more genuine, I bring myself into the discussion only when I legitimately have something relevant to add or reveal.

I have found that in recounting my own experiences of struggle or success with writing, I have actually built some bridges between myself and my tutees. I think that a personal relationship of this sort is entirely appropriate if it can facilitate trust and communication in talking about writing.

I also want to consider the possibility of transferring the authority of the situation to the student's writing itself. This idea, suggested in our teaching and tutoring course, seems very promising as a way for me to give more authority to the tutee. Such a transfer could locate the direction and purpose of the tutoring session within the draft being reviewed. In this way of thinking about tutoring, I could emphasize the tutee's writing as the focus of our work and de-emphasize the hierarchy of the institution. In addition, this explicit framework for the session would reinforce the authority of the writer and their stake in writing.

I know that many tutors employ such strategies in one form or another. What I am trying to do here is to explicate some of the possibilities for using the strategies. One of the most positive things that I can do as a peer tutor is to be explicit about my assumptions about the tutoring situation. Initiating the conversation about authority and related issues is central to this effort. In so doing, I will also be able to get a better sense of how the tutee wants the relationship to proceed. Having a tutee define the parameters of the tutorial interaction could be the best way of eliminating many of the adverse effects that accompany the tutor's mantle of institutional authority.

What Are the Possibilities for the Authority of the Peer Tutor?

The authority of the peer tutor can be used in a positive and responsible way. One of the unique aspects of peer tutoring is the possibility for discussing writing without an immediate evaluation. Also, peer tutors can use their individual authority to counteract the hierarchy and negativity that is so prevalent in today's college classrooms. This progressive reform can be accomplished, I believe, by being open and supportive of our tutees' ideas and concerns about writing. Also, the authority of the peer tutor allows for the propagation of a process model of writing in higher education, which I think is innately valuable.

In the tutoring situation, then, we have a great potential to affirm and empower our tutees. In whatever ways we can achieve this, our goal must be to give compositional and institutional authority back to the tutees. I believe that by being explicit about our roles and deferring to the needs of the tutees, we have the potential to empower student writers, including ourselves.

Epilogue

In their practice, peer tutors gain a special view on college writing, and it was this view—this particular perspective—that I explored in "Peer Tutors and Institutional Authority." Looking back on the chapter, from a desk in the Writing Center I direct, no less, I still appreciate the goal I articulated: "to give compositional and institutional authority back to the tutees." Now, I realize that there are multiple paths that lead toward this end. Sometimes, for instance, tutors can act authoritatively to guide writers to new insights. At other times, peers can simply be peers, working on writing together.

As a perspective, the peer tutor's view surveys two worlds at once: the world of the professors and the world of the students. This perspective is rich, although sometimes uncomfortable, for it shows writing education from two different sides. In my current work with peer tutors, I make an effort to attend to this view, in collaborative research on tutoring interactions, for instance. Yet, my contact with it must always be secondhand. Working in institutions, we can all expect as much: our views tend to change with the positions that we occupy.

Amidst institutional authority's shifting roles, the peer tutor's perspective can reveal learning dynamics of real consequence. Grasping these, understanding them, and making something out of them, peer tutors can certainly empower student writers, including themselves. Perhaps this is the way in which peer tutors make their own authority—an authority that doesn't fit in either students' or professors' worlds. Or, alternatively, this power over writing may not have much to do with "authority" at all, but rather with the people it affects and with the problems they solve together.

Chapter 7

Processing Writing

Polly Dondy-Kaplan

I am trying something new. I do not think that in my entire college career I have ever revised a piece by building upon an existing paper—in this case my midterm essay—as I aim to do with this final paper for our Teaching and Tutoring course. I always write drafts of papers for myself, and I have submitted chains of ideas and drafts to professors before turning in final copies. However, I have never turned in a piece I considered "final" and then reworked it later—and not only reworked it, changing paragraphs and word choice, but added to it and expanded upon it. In revising this paper to create something new and hopefully of better quality, I do not want to create a piece that would lead the reader to believe that my ideas occurred to me all at once, that they emerged from my mind and fell on the page in a way that was well formed and coherent. I do not want to create the illusion of seamlessness. Rather, I want the seams of the paper to show through so readers are aware of the stages this paper went through. I also want to make it clear that my thoughts will likely never be finished, for revision is an ongoing process.

When contemplating the journey I am about to embark on, I feel like I am reentering a conversation with myself that I had put on hold for a while. In my midterm paper I made many points, and most of them were valuable, but then I pressed the pause button. The ideas stayed there, and I had time to mull over them, churning them around in my head until I felt ready to continue the conversation initiated by the first paper. This essay, then, marks my reentry to the previous conversation.

Reentering the Conversation

In my midterm essay I tried to figure out why I love to write. It turned into a valuable paper for me because I was forced to thoroughly examine how I write, the process I go through. In the end, I came up with some reasons why I love writing and drew some relevance from my discoveries for my job as a writing associate. Just before I handed the paper in, however, I realized that I had forgotten to title it. "Shit," I thought to myself, "what is it that I say in this paper?" I glanced quickly through it, looked at the theme of each paragraph, read my conclusion and titled it "Processing Writing." A clever title, I thought, "processing" referring to my figuring out how I write, and also emphasizing that writing should be process- (not product-) oriented. I did not recognize this double meaning until after the title came to me. But once I became aware of it, I realized that the paper I really wanted to write, the paper that was trying to emerge from my midterm essay, was about the *process* of writing and how people feel about it. I realized that instead of the process being part of why I loved writing, my love for writing was in part due to my viewing writing as a process.

It is one thing to say that process is important, however, and another to incorporate a robust process into one's writing regimen. As a new college student, I was shocked to learn that some of my peers did not even read over their papers before handing them in. They said they edited as they wrote, as though that proved that they employed a thorough revision process. I could not conceive of such a truncated approach, for I always need to review what I've written, to rearrange paragraphs and fine-tune ideas. For me, writing a paper entails writing by hand, pouring out ideas onto the computer, shaping them into some form, rereading, taking time away from the project, showing the piece to others, and changing it according to their reactions and mine. Why am I receptive to reviewing and changing my papers, even when they apparently meet all requirements, when other people are not? I think a major reason is because I was taught to write that way.

Something Old

In elementary school, I learned to write using something called Writers' Workshop. In Writers' Workshop, we were supposed to write about autobiographical events. My classmates and I would all spread out to wherever in the school we felt like working on a given day and write for an hour or so. If we came to a point where we felt we had finished our pieces, we could partner with someone and share our work. After reading our writing to a peer, we would get comments about what they liked, what confused them, what they found funny. This happened until we were relatively happy with the piece. At that point we would read it to the entire group and get everyone's reaction to it. Each semester we had to pick one piece we had written and turn it into a book. This meant rereading, correcting grammar, and editing again. Once we had revised it, we had to type it up, paste it together, illustrate it, add a title and dedication page and sew it all together between covers that we had marbleized for the purpose.

This workshopping taught us, from the age of six or seven, that writing is a process and revising is a natural part of writing. In addition, it taught us that the process is never entirely complete. When we reread pieces months later, even those we had felt were finished seemed to need further changes. Sometimes we would struggle with a piece for a while, decide the time was not right for it, move onto something different, and maybe finish it weeks or months later, or simply leave it as a fragment. Writers' workshop gave us the confidence in our ability to write because the focus was not on the finished product or a grade, but on the process, which was ongoing.

Writers' Workshop also taught us to be keenly aware of the process we went through in writing. Becoming aware of how you write, the steps you go through, is an important part of viewing the paper as a process. In my case, I know that the first step in writing is always some form of procrastination. For example, for the first incarnation of this essay, it took me forever to put words onto the computer. Now matter what I tried to do, I was left looking at a blank screen. I got up from my comfortable chair, put down the laptop, and straightened up my room a bit. No luck. "Tea!" I thought suddenly, "that's the key." So I descended into the kitchen, waited for the water to boil, ate a cookie, threw some darts with my housemate, then returned to the essay. Actually, I just returned to my room. I let the tea cool and watered my plants. I paid my credit card bill and balanced my checkbook. I found the right radio station and set the volume level to my taste. I looked around and could find nothing else to do except write. Still I felt I had nothing to say.

"This is ridiculous," I thought, "you know that you always have trouble starting a paper; just put down your ideas, get yourself going." That that's what I did. For almost two hours straight I wrote about what I wanted and did not want to write about and about the problems I saw myself facing if I followed certain trains of thought. Everything from the actual form the paper would take to the ideas it would contain came to me in this outpouring of words. In the end, I had something that I was excited about and which I felt I could do: trying to communicate to another person my love for writing. And that is what I wrote about in my midterm essay. It did not end there for me, however. I finished that paper wanting to do more. Fortunately, I was given the opportunity to write this essay.

Another way I view writing is as an act of discovery. Tackling issues in political theory and grappling with different ideas about the real versus the ideal makes me wrestle with my own views, and when I finally emerge, I have a somewhat different outlook that I did before I began the paper. I do not always go into a paper knowing exactly what I want to say; I go in with a general idea and ways to express my point. Inevitably, as I write the paper, new ideas present themselves and my paper begins to shape itself. When I am finally through, what is on paper may be very different from what I set out to write. Sometimes I will have a draft that I think is great. However, when I read it over the next morning, I see that I am not saying what I want to say, and I end up changing around the paper, shifting some paragraphs and eliminating others in order for it all to make sense.

This part of the process is like a puzzle to me. I lay out my entire paper in front of me and rearrange it. I write cryptic notes all over it and sometimes literally cut it up. The feeling of figuring out how to create meaningful connections is wonderful. Once I establish the links I am able to see my paper more clearly. I can go through every part of it and determine how it fits into my overall thread of argument. If a part does not fit, I get rid of it, although it can be difficult to delete something I've written because I have become attached to it. I still have many files saved on my computer that contain paragraphs that were cut from a paper but which I really like. The challenge comes in letting go of whatever does not fit into the chain, and this can only occur after taking the paper apart to determine what it really says.

Something New

When I take the above advice about the writing process—which I adapted from my midterm paper—and try to apply it to this essay, I discover the need to push things a bit further. Some people view writing a paper as a process, but only up until a point. This attitude is something I encounter when I tutor people. I am the writing associate for a literature class in which the professor assigns drafts and revisions of papers. The students meet with me after they receive their first drafts back from the professor, and we discuss how they can rewrite their papers. It does not always end with the "final" draft, however. Sometimes the professor hands back papers to be rewritten again if she feels they need it. At this point many people come to see me voluntarily because they do not know how to rewrite under such circumstances. Many times all I do is assure them that they can still make structural changes even at this late point in the writing process because what they have written is not set in stone but is malleable.

The idea of process applies to more than simply rewriting a draft of a paper, however. It can also refer to the kind of revision I am doing now, expanding a paper I considered finished and final—a paper I felt (and still feel) proud of, yet one whose point I want to expand on in ways I could not have done had I not written the original. Through that paper, I was able to see my way to a fresh set of ideas.

Thinking about the process of incorporating and expanding on old ideas, I am surprised that I have not used more of that essay—a paper I felt, and still feel, proud of—in writing this new version. I have used three or four old paragraphs, but this essay contains more than twenty paragraphs, so the vast majority of the writing is new. When I envisioned writing this paper, I thought it would be about half and half. While I may not be transplanting words from the first paper into this one, however, I am using ideas from the first essay as fertilizer. Without the first paper, the second could not grow.

An Analogy

When trying to create an analogy for the process of revising this essay, I came up with an image of people needing to stand on blocks to enable them to look up and see the next higher block. Standing on the first block is necessary in order to see the second block, and one has to climb up to the second block in order to see the third, and so on. I realized I was picturing the writer as someone from a Nintendo game: Doing major revisions of papers is kind of like playing Super Mario Brothers. Your guy, Mario or Luigi, starts off and runs along, trying to stay alive. Eventually, he reaches the end. "Whew," you think, "glad I got to the end." Suddenly, however, your guy finds himself confronting the next level. It is a whole new world in this level, where the hero encounters different challenges. But he does not enter this world without skills. Everything he learned in the last level holds good in the new one.

I see this game as similar to the process of writing and revising a paper. For me the first stage in the writing process is the first level of the game. I have some ideas, I work with them, become frustrated with them, work with them some more, and finally, after a lot of effort, have a paper to submit. Then the professor returns my piece with comments, and I enter the next world. What facilitates this encounter with the next level? For me, it is often questions the professor asks that I had not thought about before. Suddenly, new pathways of thought open up. They could not have opened without the first paper to show me that they were even there in the first place. So I start down these paths, entering this new world. I take with me skills I learned from the last paper as well as my thought processes. I go through my writing process all over again, using my skills and what I've learned in the same way that Mario uses his skills to deal with new obstacles at each level and acquires new abilities (e.g., learning how to breathe fireballs) without losing the abilities he had previously learned. (e.g., running and jumping.) I finally reach something I feel proud of and hand it in. Done. It's final. Or is it?

This is not to say that this analogy of Super Mario Brothers is a complete one. It does not answer the question of how one gets to the different levels in the first place, and it does not address the idea that maybe the process of doing so is important in and of itself. Nor does it address the need to extend this analogy to teaching and learning how to write. For instance, while I view writing as a process, and have done so for years, it took me a while to truly view tutoring in this process-oriented way. I could say I believed in "process over product" as much as I wanted, but it is one thing to say it and another to teach, tutor, and write with this attitude.

A Tutoring Anecdote

The difficulty of practicing what one preaches with regard to process versus product was brought home to me through a tutoring experience. One of the women in the class I tutor was having trouble writing her papers. We went through one of them, and I gave her ideas on how to write, looking for themes in her thoughts, going through the draft paragraph by paragraph, writing down the main points, figuring out exactly what she was trying to say. I talked to her about ways to view her paper and ways to view the process we were following as a necessary part of writing. When she came for help on her second paper, I asked how the last one had ended up. "O.K.," she replied. "I felt pretty good about it and got a B- on it." "B-!" I thought to myself, "But we put so much work into it; does she think I did a bad job tutoring her?" Then she added that she was happy with the grade, however, because she felt she had learned a lot in the tutoring session and had written the paper in a much better way than what she was used to doing. The paper may not have been wonderful, but she was content with the knowledge that the way in which she wrote it improved.

This experience taught me that I have to remember my own convictions when I am tutoring and not be a hypocrite: learning to write well is not instantaneous; it is a process that unfolds, often slowly. In the case of this tutee, I was looking for immediate and dramatic results from one tutoring session, even though I knew in a theoretical way that such expectations are unreasonable. What my tutee told me was that through various sessions she was learning how to view the writing process and how to compose papers differently, whether or not her grades were showing it. The new paradigm may state "process over product," but we have to be aware of what that means. It does not only mean viewing writing as a process, but viewing teaching and learning writing as processes as well.

Back to My Process: A Writer's History and an Anecdote

While writers' workshop was extremely important in my development, my learning to write extends farther back and farther forward than my involvement with that approach. In my early schooling, my teachers encouraged me to use my imagination. In addition, I was asked to illustrate the work I did, whether it was a story I invented or a report on sea anemones. The next stage came when I had to learn how to write analytical papers in high school. There I met the five-paragraph form and learned to remove references to myself in papers. I was taught that my authority was not welcomed in a paper except in disguised form. After mastering this technique of hiding myself, I went on to write lengthier but still highly circumscribed analytic essays with the thesis in a fixed location, three examples for proof and a conclusion in which I restated my thesis and was prohibited from adding any new information. During my senior year in high school, we tried different forms of essays: cause and effect, comparison/contrast, deductive order, and inductive order. We also learned how to incorporate other critical writers into an essay.

The most important lesson I learned, however, had to do with the emergence of my voice and authority; it was a lesson that was hard-won and learned by chance after a long struggle with writer's block. I was struggling with an essay on Thornton Wilder's play, *The Skin of Our Teeth*, trying to fulfill the teacher's assignment, which was to provide an answer to the very perplexing question of why the characters in the play kept plugging away through all sorts of disasters. I dutifully made an outline and found quotes to support an argument, but as I sat at the computer, I got hopelessly stuck. I realized that I did not believe what I was writing—there was an inherent contradiction in my argument. I kept trying to compose the piece, but I could not advance an argument that I did not believe in and about which I felt that everyone else in the class was going to say pretty much the same thing. Around one a.m. the night before the assignment was due, with the aid of some tutoring from my father, I finally hit on an idea for the essay. However, I didn't know if I would be permitted to write about the idea, for it involved the use of the forbidden pronoun, "I."

The next morning, petrified, I found my teacher and explained my plight. To my amazement, she readily gave her permission and encouraged me to follow my plan. That evening I went home and wrote an essay about what makes people strive against adversity, about what makes them start over again and again. I included information from a report I heard on National Public Radio about a woman in Sarajevo who, before the Balkan war, had trained to be a concert pianist. Her dream of being a pianist sustained her throughout the war, and, as often as possible, amidst the bombs and the hunger and the bitter cold, she made her way to a piano in an abandoned music school. She played this piano even when the sounds were distorted and she could no longer feel her fingers—keeping the pieces, her work, and herself alive every time she played. The dissonance of her notes struck me, transmitted through the radio from a country far away from my home in Connecticut, and I incorporated elements of her story in my essay on Wilder's play. In retrospect, I recognize that that essay was the first piece in which I used a voice I had reserved for my poetry and melded it with my analytic voice. "I" was allowed into the essay because there was no impersonal way to communicate how I experienced the subject of the paper. I had not only overcome my writer's block but created an analytical piece that I felt was beautiful. Yet I have wondered why no one really taught me that in some cases it would be acceptable to use "I" and to assert my authority as the writer of a piece. I had to follow an unusually stressful writing process to learn that lesson.

Then what?

I said in the beginning that to emphasize the complex nature of revision and the writing process, I wanted the seams to show through in this essay. One technique I have employed to highlight the "seamy" nature of this piece is subheadings, a device I have never before used in a paper. What cannot be seen in this "final" revision, however, what remains hidden, is the behind-the-scenes shifting. I cut and pasted a great deal in revising this paper, doing such things as moving the Nintendo analogy from the second page of the essay to its current location about five pages into the piece. I felt such changes would help the paper to say what I wanted it to say.

And finally, I am happy with it. As I make the final changes to it, adding a comma here and taking one away there, I watch the snow falling outside my window. Soon I will put on warm clothing, bike to the library to print out this paper, and then hand it in. Yet, as I sit here thinking about joining my family for the winter holidays, I realize I already have more ideas to add. So, once again, I press the pause button on this conversation. I don't know when I will reenter it, but I do know that it is not really over yet.

Section Three

Facilitating and Responding to Student Writing

Form and Content Grade: A (the usual)
Grammar Grade: A (great deterioration in comparison with the grammar of recent papers. Underlining of *Bible* is required by formal rules despite common use of not underlining. […])
E. P. P. ["errors per page"]: 1.0 (back to the whole numbers)
When will I see a grammatically perfect paper?   Paper Grade: A

—English teacher's end comment on a student paper

Writing associates and teaching assistants who work closely with students in writing classrooms are most effective when they create a spirit—and establish a regimen—of collaboration. Along with encouraging collaboration, contemporary composition pedagogy attempts to foster *agency* within the student writer. Indeed, both collaboration and agency fit together in this overall strategy as part of the effort to treat students as *writers*—that is, to duplicate for them the features of practicing writers' situations within the confines of organized education.

The English teacher's comment cited above came to our attention when a tutor trainee brought it to class to illustrate what she considered a counterproductive approach to responding to student writing—an approach she found typical of the comments she had received on papers over the years, and which made her feel like anything but an authoritative writer. Her three-page essay itself was well developed and even poignant in its analysis of the nature of "emotional scars," so the grade of A was appropriate. However, she explained that the intense fault-finding attitude that ran through the comments, which were focused on minuscule points of form and mechanics, had the effect of dispiriting her. The comments made her feel as though she had very little agency, for despite the excellence of her thinking and writing, it was clear from the nature of the comments and their indignant tone that she

could be scolded and chastised with great fervor for the most trivial of surface errors. She allegedly committed three errors (hence an "E.P.P." of 1.0 in
a three-page paper): Twice she failed to underline (or italicize) "Bible," and
once she wrote "asked for," which the teacher changed to "requested." But
looking at the paper, we think "asked for" was a better usage: "[The attitude
that emotional scars are a badge of honor] encourages people to take risks for
others rather than to exalt themselves, and it reveals the true worth of those
such as nameless victims of the Holocaust—silent sufferers who asked for
[corrected to 'requested'] no glory." Readers may judge for themselves.

In any case, the long tradition of teaching English by concentrating on
errors in form and mechanics is, despite recent inroads, alive and well. And
where it is challenged by newer approaches, those newer approaches are
often held up for ridicule by traditionalists who cite their "permissiveness" as
a cause of poor student writing. The articles in this section make many
suggestions for teaching and tutoring in ways that depart markedly from the
authoritarian approach we have been discussing. In place of such authoritari-
anism, they recommend teacher-student dynamics that endow students with
something like the agency of practicing writers—who, despite being open to
suggestions and subject to criticism from editors and readers, generally
receive the benefit of the doubt as possessing a degree of competence and
authority to speak about their subject matter.

To convey their ideas with authority is, after all, a major motivation for
most writers. However, in a climate where one's readers (for example, the
teacher of an English class) project a desire for absolute control over what
should be said and how it should be said, there is a danger that writers may
lose their sense of authority and agency—and with it their motivation to
make themselves heard. Unfortunately, the authoritarian enforcement of
"correctness" in grammar, usage, and mechanics is a common technique that
undermines the agency of student writers. Student writers are typically much
less familiar than their English teachers with the technical aspects of written
communication, even when (like the tutor who wrote the "emotional scars"
paper) they do have a sound practical command of correctness. As studies
have revealed, teachers looking for surface errors in students' writing will
certainly find them—usually in abundance—and they may even find some
errors that the average reader would say aren't even there (such as writing
"asked for" instead of "requested"). Rejecting such an error-hunting mentality, the four articles in this section emphasize the need to facilitate, respond
to, and evaluate student writing within a framework that establishes student
writers as having agency and authority over their work.

The Articles

The first article (Chapter 8) is "'Like, it was, you know what I mean?': Conversational vs. Presentational Speech in Student Academic Discourse" by Emily Fawcett, a writing associate in a poetry course in which she was sometimes asked to act as a teaching assistant. Drawing on her experience of leading a striking class discussion (which actually began as a painful "non-discussion"), Fawcett focuses on students' use of oral discourse to suggest ways of improving their participation in academic writing. Fundamentally, she is concerned with how to restore agency to students as participants in the "ongoing conversation" that characterizes disciplinary discourse in the academy. She is not here concerned with challenging authority figures who use "correctness" to undermine student agency, but rather she questions the practices of those who set up class discussions in which the leader dictates the "right answers" and in which "each student's comment is fielded in isolation by the discussion leader." Fawcett explores how a tutor can help students attend to the voices that she, as a writing associate, has heard students use in discussions when they are not intimidated or dominated by the discussion leader: "the flexible voice that's not afraid to take risks, that's interested in what everyone else is saying, and interested in rethinking and modifying what it has to say to address others' concerns." In essence, Fawcett pursues the thread established in Koundakjian's "Speaking the Written Voice" (Chapter 3); appropriately, she cites that article as well as other scholarly pieces that focus on ways in which student writers negotiate their authority as members of academic discourse communities. When students succeed in tapping their "conversational" voices as opposed to the conventional "presentational" voices they are usually expected to use, they invoke "a whole set of assumptions about the equality of speaker and listener that helps to undermine the vicious circle of authority based on fear that normally dominates classrooms." The happy result, Fawcett believes, is a liberation of the student from "an underlying cycle of fear and performance that sometimes supplants learning as the primary goal in the classroom."

Chapter 9 is a previously published article by JoAnne Podis and Leonard Podis, "Improving Our Responses to Student Writing: A Process-Oriented Approach." The essay, which appeared in *Rhetoric Review* 5 (1986): 90–98, looks at several ways in which teachers and tutors can respond to student drafts in a spirit that encourages student agency. Specifically, Podis and Podis are concerned to show that many of the "deficiencies" academic readers traditionally criticize in student papers can be read as byproducts or residues of sound composing processes. Once this recognition is made, the responder can offer encouragement and direction for productive revisions rather than severe criticism of supposedly finished products. For example, they discuss how plot summary in a paper about literature—typically seen by English professors as indicating the student's failure to be analytical—may reveal that the writer is still working towards a clearer understanding of the literary work. As the newer approaches to pedagogy teach us, writing is a tool for discovery, and students struggling with interpreting a work of literature may be groping toward a better understanding by summarizing parts of the work on paper. The key to crafting useful responses in such situations, Podis and Podis believe, is to recognize the process for what it is—a promising and still-unfolding activity—not to cut it off prematurely by scolding the writer for failing to produce a successful finished product.

In Chapter 10, "The Comments They Made: An Exploration of Helpful and Unhelpful Commentary," Naomi Strand takes a retrospective look at the types of comments she has received on papers during her college career. Since she works as a writing associate at the writing center, one might expect that she has received mainly positive comments on her papers, but this is far from the truth. In this essay, she considers the effects of written commentary on the writer. She bases her analysis on a close inspection of the types of responses—both salutary and detrimental—that her professors made to a range of her own college papers. Strand categorizes the comments into four types, three that are unhelpful and one that is useful for the writer. In her view, "the key purpose of written comments is to provide a guideline of what the writer might do to improve the paper through revision. [...]"

The final selection (Chapter 11) is Noelle Howey's "The Dilemmas of Grading." Focusing on her encounters with the grading system, Howey creates a vivid scenario that speaks to the experiences of many students who have been conditioned to worship grades, but who find that the system may serve to stifle learning more than to encourage it or to chart its progress accurately. As she puts it, "Like many other students, I simply bought into the grading system to such a degree that I was willing to deprioritize learning." For Howey, grading is the ultimate symbol of the "old paradigm" in that (at least in her experience), grading is all about product, not at all about process: "The learning process is self-specific; unlike grading, it is not dependent upon a finished product; unlike grading, it is not dependent on competition. Rather, the process is self-defined, self-motivated, and self-rewarding." Seeing grading as a form of indoctrination "into a world where everything is categorized and pigeonholed," Howey concedes the seductive hold of grades despite her aversion to them. She does not call for an end to grades but does urge readers to be aware of their potentially destructive qualities and to seek "possible alternatives."

Chapter 8

"Like, it was, you know what I mean?" Conversational vs. Presentational Speech in Student Academic Discourse

Emily Fawcett

As a writing associate for a writing-intensive introduction to poetry class this semester, I was asked by the professor to lead class discussion on a day when the professor was going to be out of town. I was a little scared to attempt this, as I wasn't sure it was part of my "job description," but I agreed to do it anyway, partially because I had, in the past, been frustrated by the low level of energy and interest in discussion. I thought maybe I could do something to make it more interesting. The class was reading two poems by Keats. I discussed them with the professor beforehand and prepared a set of questions on "La Belle Dame sans Merci." I was worried about the whole thing because I obviously did not have the professor's expertise—I had never even taken a course in Romantic literature.

At the start of the class I chose not to sit at the professor's desk, but rather in a more inconspicuous location in a corner of the room. I did this partly to avoid giving the impression that I was a highly knowledgeable authority figure and partly to avoid making myself the center of a discussion in which the other students were to be the main participants. Everything turned out to be more difficult than I had thought it would be: I forgot my watch, couldn't see the clock, and didn't even know when to start class. Even worse, once we began, the discussion was painful. There was a long silence after each question I asked on "La Belle Dame sans Merci." When I did manage to get any response, the person talking did not appear to address her classmates but instead would look at me expectantly as if she were speaking only to me and thought that I should be the one to respond directly to her comments. The few remarks that the students did make would be followed by dead silence, so I found it very difficult not to leap in with a response of my own or with another question. This kind of discussion, or non-discussion, in which each student's comment is fielded in isolation by the discussion leader, was exactly what I had been hoping to avoid. I began to understand how hard it is to get people in a class to talk to each other.

After only ten or fifteen minutes of the hour-long class, I came to the end of my prepared questions without having really gotten the class to talk about the aspects of the poem I had meant to probe. It seemed as if I just hadn't been able to think quickly enough on the spot to respond to what others had said in a way that would further discussion. I was frustrated that the other students weren't taking more responsibility for the discussion, and I felt completely at a loss since I had nothing else prepared to do. In the end I just told them that I had no more questions left. They laughed, and then there was a long, nearly unbearable silence.

Finally, someone began to give an opinion about the poem while looking at some of the others in the room who had spoken earlier. Soon a discussion started in which the other students were no longer looking at me or raising their hands for me to call on them but were formulating their comments in direct response to previous comments, referring to the text of the poem and even talking over each other. Two camps emerged with conflicting interpretations about the relationship between the two main figures in the poem, the knight and the fairy woman. One of the most outspoken people in the class (who saw the knight as a complete victim of the fairy woman's seduction) modified his opinion during the course of the discussion in response to what others were saying, while not abandoning his position completely (he came to think that maybe the knight was allowing himself to be seduced). Basically, the class had a good conversation about the poem that lasted fifteen or twenty minutes and touched in some way on most of the material I had discussed in my conference with the professor. The students even briefly raised a point that the professor had mentioned to me about the connection between the fairy woman and the knight's imagination; however, I fortunately had the discipline not to barge in and appropriate the discussion by suggesting to them that the woman might be a symbol of the knight's imagination, since that didn't appear to be what they wanted to talk about. Soon we turned to "Ode on a Grecian Urn."

I don't think I recognized at the time what I'd done right because when we began the discussion of the second poem, I started asking my prepared questions, and I got the same sort of reluctant responses that I'd received earlier in the period. The class ended approximately the way it had begun, but for a few minutes during the discussion of "La Belle Dame sans Merci," something exciting had happened. The successful exchange that had occurred was definitely not the result of good discussion leading on my part: I don't think I said one thing during the whole time that things were working well, although the questions I asked at first might have sparked some ideas that came out later during the more fruitful part of the class. The only significant thing I did was to remove my own authority from the discussion.

I would like to use the rest of this paper to analyze what was going on in this class because I think that issues of authority are central to the problems that course tutors face. I also think that what happens orally in a writing-intensive course—whether in class discussion where methods of analysis are introduced by the professor or in conferences with writing associates about papers—has a lot of influence on how students write their papers. (I believe that speech affects writing in general: when I write papers, at least, I write the speaking voice I hear in my head, a voice that tries out different phrasings as I type, a voice molded by the way I've learned to speak in the classroom as well as by what I've read and had to write in the past.) I want to ask how a tutor can help students listen more closely to voices such as those the introductory poetry students were using during the brief period when no authority figure intruded on their discussion: the flexible voice that's not afraid to take risks, that's interested in what everyone else is saying, and interested in rethinking and modifying what it has to say to address others' concerns. I believe this voice can be termed "conversational," and I would like to begin by exploring how it differs from the voice used in the kind of desultory discussion between students and professors that often characterizes English classrooms, and that even finds its way into students' individual conferences with professors, teaching assistants, and writing associates.

I use the term "conversational" for the discussion that took place during the absence of the professor (and during my retreat from the role of leader) for at least a couple of reasons. First, the students seemed to become interested enough in the topic (and to lose enough of their self-consciousness) that they were willing to take risks and use their comments about the poem to *explore* rather than to *present* a meaning. They seemed to be sharing their own responses to the poem because they wanted to understand it better, not because they needed to show the professor that they understood it.

Second, the discussion was also "conversational" in that students in the class defined their own positions in response to the arguments of others around them. They were willing to listen to what others had to say and even to change their own views in response. There was, in other words, meaningful give and take. This stance, in which individual students saw themselves as positioned within a larger discourse about a subject, created a much livelier and far more productive discussion.

I think such discussions also lead to more interesting papers. I have tutored students from the same English class on papers both before and since who either made too many broad, safe generalizations and never really took up a challenging thesis or, on the other hand, tried to argue a potentially promising point of view but never addressed opposing interpretations fully enough to show why they considered their own to be superior. In "Reading and Writing Without Authority," Penrose and Geisler report the results of a study focusing on the experiences of two very different students writing a philosophy paper on the same topic, paternalism. They contrast Janet, a less experienced undergraduate who sees the various source materials collected in one notebook as a single, definitive source and who tries to write a straight-forward guide to moral problems encountered in life, with Roger, a graduate student in philosophy, who was found to be "making distinctions, embracing or rejecting claims tentatively, and flatly changing his mind, all in ways consistent with his view of truth as multivalent." (Penrose and Geisler, 510) They report that when Janet noticed that the authors' claims did conflict, but couldn't figure out which claim was correct, she left the whole topic out of the paper, or she only reported the side of the argument she agreed with. (511) Interestingly, Penrose and Geisler report that Janet ended up writing a kind of how-to paper that simply laid out ways to determine whether or not an act was paternalistic. (508) Janet's approach can be viewed either as a failure to enter a conversation with the authors who made conflicting claims, or as a different (but equally valid) kind of project altogether, one that aims at practical application rather than academic theorizing. In any case, however, it's true that by failing to enter a scholarly conversation about paternalism, Janet was not engaging in the sort of discourse most valued in academia.

Of course, there are limits to the analogy between good written academic discourse, or the academic discussion that went on in the English classroom, and a conversation. The conversation in the classroom had to do directly with a poem, and it was conducted for the academic purpose of figuring that poem out. However, the sharing of points of view and reading experiences that occurred in the poetry class did resemble the kind of conversation that might transpire between two students in the mailroom. In written discourse, the situation is a bit different: No on-the-spot give and take can occur between the writers and readers of either scholarly journal articles or student essays, so writers must anticipate opposing arguments if they have not already been advanced in other works and respond to them on their own initiative. However, if a kind of conversational give and take is not already established in the classroom—if the professor tends to dominate discussions, fielding all student comments and spending a large proportion of the class period developing her own opinions—then it's hard to imagine how students who don't already know how to write by positioning themselves for and against different views will automatically learn. It seems all the more important, then, for the writing associate within the space of the writing conference to try to engage in a conversation about the subject matter that sets up different or diverse viewpoints. In "Speaking the Written Voice," Alicia Koundakjian writes of the importance of conversation in the tutoring session:

> We would often begin with a reading of their draft or rough outline and then lead into a discussion of their concepts or arguments. It is these discussions that I found to be a basic element in the process approach to writing. By giving my tutees the time and space to play with their knowledge, I was generally able to increase their confidence to the point that they felt compelled to explain their arguments on paper.
>
> (Koundakjian, 36)

In calling the kind of discussion that took place in the poetry classroom "conversational," I have to admit some other major differences with casual conversational style. Oral conversations often depend on the context in which they are taking place (the location or the occasion, for example), and on shared, unspoken knowledge or experience of the participants. People say "You know what I mean" when referring to something that those to whom they are talking will automatically understand. Of course, as well as excluding most people from their immediate discourse, such an approach also leaves room for ambiguities, misunderstandings, and poorly defined meanings, all of which are antithetical to the goals of the academic discourse that students are expected to attempt for their course papers. The discussion that unfolded in the poetry classroom was actually *non-conversational* in the sense that its aim was to define and explicate as precisely as possible the experience of characters in the poem, not just to share reading experiences.

At first glance, this emphasis on explaining rather than sharing seems to be one of the most important characteristics that divides casual conversation from what's expected of students in academic papers. In oral conversations, people often describe rather than explain or analyze experiences. People say: "It was like. . . ." In "Reflections on Academic Discourse: How It Relates to Freshmen and Colleagues," Peter Elbow calls the kind of writing that evokes experiences "rendering," and he argues that it should be taught more extensively in the classroom along with the kind of academic discourse that teachers traditionally want from students, discourse with an emphasis on "labeling and defining." (Elbow, 135) He even goes so far as to say that "rendering" doesn't just evoke a feeling but can be used to illustrate or make a point. I think that there's a certain kind of particularly straightforward "rendering" that does not have a place in academic discourse. I began this paper with the rendering of an experience, but notice that I have been making an effort to analyze it, defining and labeling parts of a poetry class discussion as "conversational" or "non-conversational." I have certainly read academic essays, especially in the field of composition studies, that begin with or include anecdotes about the authors' experience, usually experiences related to the teaching of writing. The kind of academic discourse that students are expected to write differs from the rendering aspect of some conversations only because it requires the author to use any experience described as data subject to an analysis that becomes the more important part of the paper. So I don't think that a writing associate's role should be to advise students to exclude the rendering of personal experiences from their papers in the belief that this kind of material is not what the professor is looking for. Rather, I think it's the tutor's job, in such a situation, to encourage tutees to talk about the ways in which their experiences illuminate the topic at hand, with the goal of getting the tutees to use their speaking voices to explore those connections so that they can ultimately be made more explicit in the paper.

Along these lines of encouraging students' conversational voices, I think that during the briefly successful poetry class discussion when I stopped asking questions, students became more willing to explore new ideas that they had not completely thought out or tested, using a very different voice from the one with which they had been making safe, uninteresting observations directly to me (as discussion leader) at the beginning of the class, and normally to the professor. Koundakjian sets up a dichotomy between an "academic" and a "social" speaking voice, and she talks about the way the boundary between the two is blurred to good effect by writing associates. (38) In "Talking in the Middle: Why Writers Need Writing Tutors," Muriel Harris refers to "presentational" talk, a term she borrows from Douglas Barnes to describe the speech that students use when they are under evaluation and want to give a correct answer rather than risk exploring new ideas. (Harris, 31) The desire to stick to what is safe is very understandable because often the attempt to explain something new comes out in a way that isn't clear to others. When I try to explain something I'm not sure I understand, when I'm trying to figure it out in words, the idea often emerges in the form of incomplete sentences that switch directions halfway through or tentative questions that are not themselves at all clear but sound too general or unrooted in the literary text I'm trying to interpret because I haven't yet made the connection between the text and my feelings explicit in my own mind.

In this mode of thinking things through, I tend to use lots of "like's" and "You know what I mean's." Talking this way may not be a viable option for students who feel that they are being evaluated on what they say in class. Moreover, it may be intimidating, even without the threat of being graded, for students to make observations on a subject they know little about with someone who has studied it for years and may even be a renowned expert in the field. The job of the tutor in a conference, or, in an ideal world, the students in class discussion, might be to ask the speaker to refine and clarify her argument through exploratory talk. Exploratory talk may be a valuable end in itself as well as something that can help students write better conventional papers—a process that can open up academic discourse, bypassing the traditional, constraining emphasis on bringing an argument to a definite, non-negotiable conclusion. Lillian Bridwell-Bowles, in "Discourse and Diversity: Experimental Writing within the Academy," describes characteristics she has sought in her own writing: "a more personal voice, an expanded use of metaphor, a less rigid methodological framework, a writing process that allows me to combine hypothesizing with reporting data, to use patterns of writing that allow for multiple truths [...] rather than a single thesis, and so on." (350) Interestingly, at least three of these elements—use of a more personal voice, emphasis on metaphor or description, and acknowledgment of many possible truths—are closely associated with oral conversation.

Now I want to address more closely some of the reasons that students tend to use presentational instead of conversational speech in the classroom and in papers. Understanding these reasons should enable us to clarify how the writing associate or teaching assistant can counteract the tendency toward this kind of expression. In "Pedagogy of the Distressed," Jane Tompkins writes about what she calls the "performance" model of teacher-student interaction from the teacher's point of view. She discusses a time in her career as a faculty member when:

> I had finally realized that what I was actually concerned with and focused on most of the time were three things: a) to show the students how smart I was, b) to show them how knowledgeable I was, and c) to show them how well-prepared I was for class. I had been putting on a performance whose true goal was not to help the students learn but to perform before them in such a way that they would have a good opinion of me. (Tompkins, 654)

Tompkins claims that it is not only the students who feel they must respond to the professor with presentational talk but the professors themselves (at least some of them) who feel as if they must concentrate on giving polished performances in class to prove their merit. I would be surprised if this was not especially true for women, who generally feel even more than men that they must prove their right to hold positions within the academy.

Tompkins goes on to speculate on the driving forces behind this phenomenon and advances one possibility:

> Fear is the driving force behind the performance model. Fear of being shown up for what you are: a fraud, stupid, ignorant, a clod, a dolt, a sap, a weakling, someone who can't cut the mustard. In graduate school, especially, fear is prevalent. Thinking about these things, I became aware recently that my own fear of being shown up for what I really am must transmit itself to my students, and insofar as I was afraid to be exposed, they too would be afraid. (654)

Tompkins, then, portrays the phenomenon of performance and "presentation" in the classroom as a vicious circle. The professor, fearing to be shown up as ignorant in some way, presents all she knows to the students in the most authoritative way possible. The students respond to the professor's show of authority with the fear that they will themselves look stupid. Those students who go on to be professors themselves carry this fear with them, and it makes them, in their turn, most anxious to assert their authority.

The day I led the English class I got nervous, I think, because I felt this same pressure to assert authority—an authority I didn't genuinely feel I had—even down to the authority to decide when to start the class. In my case, the feeling that, as a writing associate, I didn't have the expertise to back it up was, of course, completely justified. I was at least as worried that my questions sound semi-intelligent (so I wouldn't expose myself as dumb or boring, resulting in no one's wanting to come to me for tutoring) as I was that the discussion should go well and that the students be the ones to figure everything out for themselves. Perhaps that was one reason my questions weren't very effective. Like Tompkins, Peter Elbow discusses the effect of the legacy of graduate training on professors. He examines the elements of *display* sometimes evident in academic discourse when he writes that "full-fledged academics are sometimes so enmeshed in the rhetorical context of school discourse that they keep on writing as though they are performing for teachers with authority over them." (Elbow, 147) He observes that when we're nervous, we "tend to 'cover' ourselves by speaking with more passives, more formal language, more technical vocabulary" (147) and notes "the subtle difference between the discourse of people who are established in the discipline and those who are not—particularly those without tenure. Certain liberties, risks, tones, and stances are taken by established insiders that are not usually taken by the unannealed. Discourse is power." (139) Similarly, in "Refusing to Play the Confidence Game: The Illusion of Mastery in the Reading/Writing of Texts," Sheree L. Meyer states that "Being 'in control' [...] exacts a heavy price and strangely enough, exacerbates rather than relieves anxieties about inadequacy." (7) Meyer writes this in regard to the work of bright students on papers, but it seems to me that it applies equally well to at least some faculty members who have secret fears that they aren't equal to the task of teaching a class. In sum, the authority relationships we see in a typical English literature classroom not only instill fear in students and cause them to use more presentational, less interesting, speech both in class and on paper, but also cause English professors to present material in an authoritative way that only perpetuates the myths that one answer is more correct than all others, that personal experiences don't have a place in the classroom, and that exploratory talk is inferior and undesirable.

Tompkins argues that it's important for professors to counteract the cycle of fear perpetuated in the classroom because "what really matters as far as our own beliefs and projects for change are concerned is not so much what we talk about in class as what we do." (656) What professors do is what students really learn. She goes on to say that "teaching and learning are not a preparation for anything but are the thing itself." (656) This sounds like the more recent versions of the "New Paradigm" idea that the writing process is not just aimed at producing an essay but is an important end in itself. Some writing associates do find themselves in writing-intensive classes where professors make significant attempts to counteract traditional authority relationships by letting students control discussion, asking them to take charge of presentations, and encouraging everyone to learn from each other (techniques suggested in Tompkins, 657–659). But if a tutor or teaching assistant finds herself in a class in which the practices of the professor run counter to everything she believes about the importance of student control in discussion and the value of the writing process as an end in itself (if the professor tightly runs discussion and devalues drafts containing half-formed, tentative conceptualizations, for example), then even if the faculty member *purports* to be teaching students to think for themselves or to explore writing as a process, the tutor or teaching assistant will have a much harder job to do.

One of the most important parts of tutoring, I believe, is giving students the self-confidence they need to be able to begin writing in a voice that is closer to their own conversational speech. Meyer argues that although some students can write the way they are expected to and can assume the authority they need to write "up" to an audience who knows more than they do about their subject, "they may still have a great deal of difficulty overcoming their feelings that they (and therefore their essays) are frauds." (7) I can attest to this exact feeling. I seldom, if ever, feel that I deserve as good a grade as I get on a paper. And if even strong student writers feel this way, then it's no wonder that most students hesitate to use their speech or writing to explore their subjects, preferring the safer course of clinging to a fixed and unimaginative thesis in their essays. No wonder that students who don't come into introductory English classes with a confident grasp of paper writing often end up making general, abstract, and uninspired points: They are playing it safe and understandably so. Muriel Harris devotes a whole section of her essay to the tutor's role in dealing with "affective" concerns. She writes that "When a tutor helps the writer set up criteria to use for her own assessment, the writer gains confidence in deciding whether the paper is ready to be turned in," and that it's simply "stressful for them to talk about their writing with someone whom they perceive as having some institutional authority over them." (35) Obviously, with a professor who is going to give a grade, this authority is not only a perception but a reality.

Most students have more confidence in their ability to express themselves in conversational voices to their friends outside of class than in their ability to communicate effectively with their professors in class. I believe greater strategic pedagogical use of this conversational voice can give students more confidence in discussing academic subjects—witness what happened in the poetry classroom when the professor was absent and I, as writing associate, removed myself from the discussion. I think that in classes where students do manage to tap these voices in the presence of a faculty member (our teaching and tutoring class, for example), they bring with them a whole set of assumptions about the equality of speaker and listener that helps to undermine the vicious circle of authority based on fear that normally dominates classrooms. So I think that writing associates, by establishing the use of conversational speech in the academic context of the writing conference—whether or not the speech ultimately takes on the outward trappings of academic discourse (i.e., formal tone, discipline-specific language, conventional structure)—can help students learn to take risks, explore new ideas, incorporate their own experience into the discussion, and see their own ideas positioned within a larger field of discourse that they can enter. This voice may help liberate them from an underlying cycle of fear and performance that sometimes supplants learning as the primary goal in the classroom.

WORKS CITED

Bridwell-Bowles, Lillian. "Discourse and Diversity: Experimental Writing within the Academy." *College Composition and Communication* 43 (1992): 349–368.

Elbow, Peter. "Reflections on Academic Discourse: How It Relates to Freshmen and Colleagues." *College English* 53 (1991): 135–155.

Harris, Muriel. "Talking in the Middle: Why Writers Need Writing Tutors." *College English* 57 (1995): 27–42.

Koundakjian, Alicia. "Speaking the Written Voice." *Working with Student Writers: Essays on Tutoring and Teaching*. Ed. Leonard A. Podis and JoAnne M. Podis. New York: Peter Lang, 1999: 33–37.

Meyer, Sheree L. "Refusing to Play the Confidence Game: The Illusion of Mastery in the Reading/Writing of Texts." *College English* 55 (1993): 46–63.

Penrose, Ann, and Cheryl Geisler. "Reading and Writing Without Authority." *College Composition and Communication* 45 (1994): 505–520.

Tompkins, Jane. "Pedagogy of the Distressed." *College English* 52 (1990): 652– 660.

Chapter 9

Improving Our Responses to Student Writing: A Process-Oriented Approach

JoAnne M. Podis

Leonard A. Podis

"Awk!" "Frag." "Unity?" "Coh." Such are the response symbols on which composition instructors have traditionally been reared. Of course many writing teachers have come to reject such responses and the evaluative approach to commentary they bespeak, viewing them as useless (Knoblauch and Brannon, "Teacher Commentary," 285–288), if not downright harmful. (Hartwell, 9) In recent years, a significant number of instructors have adopted more thoughtful, enlightened attitudes in commenting on student writing, in some cases not merely eschewing the strictly evaluative response, but going so far as to "deconstruct" drafts in order to perceive student intentions so that these may be "mapped onto later drafts." (Comprone) It is just such a "deconstructionist" approach that we would like to set forth in this essay, although our method, rather than consciously drawing on postmodernist literary theory, emphasizes the attitude of the error analyst in responding to writing. (Shaughnessy; Kroll and Schafer; Bartholomae) We hope this essay will also constitute a step toward taxonomizing some of the more process-oriented responses to student writing.

A brief survey of recent literature on responding to student writing indicates that the dominant model for instructors' comments is still the traditional evaluative response. In their first of several statements on the subject, for example, Knoblauch and Brannon reported that product-centered, judgmental responses have overwhelmingly remained the norm: "Our assumption has been that evaluating the product of composing is equivalent to intervening in the process." ("Teacher Commentary," 288) Even less flattering to our profession was Nancy Sommers' "Responding to Student Writing." In the responses of the instructors whose work she studied, Sommers found "hostility and mean-spiritedness." (149) Moreover, she judged most comments to be confusing to students because they failed to differentiate between low-level and high-level textual problems. In a follow-up to their earlier article, Brannon and Knoblauch concluded that instructors tended in their responses to appropriate students' texts, devaluing them in relation to some "Ideal Text" the instructor had in mind. ("On Students' Rights," 158–159). Knoblauch and Brannon's most recent treatment of the subject discusses at length the type of "facilitative commentary" that might profitably replace the traditional evaluative response. (*Rhetorical Traditions*, 126–130) They appear to endorse Sommers' belief that "We need to develop an appropriate level of response for commenting on a first draft. [...]" (155)

In our approach, instructors encourage student potential by identifying draft weaknesses and interpreting them in the light of recent findings about the composing process. Specifically, we propose that, by analogy to the work of those who practice error analysis, writing instructors routinely undertake close readings of student drafts in order to pinpoint rhetorical or structural problems that might signal legitimate intentions rather than simple failure or inadequacy. Although draft weaknesses are not technically "errors" in the same sense as syntactic or grammatical problems, we believe that the *attitude* involved in error analysis—the desire to comprehend the mental process that underlies some evidence of difficulty in creating a discourse—is appropriate in reading and responding to the writing of learners. We have recognized that many textual weaknesses represent useful stages in the writer's composing process. Such an approach seems particularly valid in light of the work of process advocates and researchers, who tell us that normal composing often includes the production of incomplete or flawed drafts. (Murray; Hairston, 85–86) Our method, then, calls for instructors to approach draft difficulties as potential keys to understanding student writers' intentions and in some cases as keys to helping the writers better define their intentions in their own minds.

We have chosen three examples to illustrate our method and to provide the beginnings of a taxonomy for this kind of response. In addition, in our conclusion we briefly identify several more kinds of draft weaknesses and suggest appropriate responses. Each of the three main examples was selected because we believed it represented some issue that teachers of writing may face while responding to student drafts and because we were successful in guiding revision by first identifying a draft weakness and then interpreting it as resulting from a healthy difficulty in composing. In each case, we explain what the initial problem was, how we interpreted it as signifying a potentially legitimate difficulty in composing, how we responded, and what happened in subsequent revisions.

Our first example begins with a paragraph written in a basic writing course, addressing the topic of "an unreasonable assignment made at school or work." We can see that the student began with the intention of discussing unreasonable math assignments but then moved away from that idea:

> I had a math teacher in junior high named Mr. Douglas that I thought gave a lot of homework. Maybe it was because I didn't like math that much. I feel as you get older you start to realize that you have to have some sort of responsibility. In a way I think homework is a form of responsibility. In my first year of high school I hardly ever did any homework and barely passed. In my junior year I did a little better because I started realizing that homework was important. At the end of my junior year I told myself that I was going to put homework first on my priority list. I never really had an unreasonable assignment made at school. I think I was blessed with some good teachers in my first 12 years of school.

If we evaluate this paragraph according to traditional standards, we must judge it as disorganized and uncertain in focus, particularly in relation to the assignment it was addressing. It is the type of writing that can all too easily lead a composition instructor to resort to the "mean-spirited" marginal comments that Nancy Sommers found so prevalent in her study. However, a closer look at the paragraph's major flaws shows that the rambling organization and uncertain focus, while they make for a weak text, do appear to be leading the student to some kind of understanding about his school career. Starting with sentence three, we can detect a group of sentences that apparently lead the writer toward the realization that his attitude about assignments changed.

Sensing this possibility, the instructor decided not to concentrate on the paragraph's weakness as a sign of failure, but rather as a potential reflection of a healthy difficulty in composing, as the messy residue that can accompany writing as discovery. In so doing, the instructor decided against urging the student to revise in order to create her own "Ideal Text"—one that would discuss "an unreasonable assignment made at school." Instead, she responded by noting that the paragraph suggested the student had learned something important about assignments while in school and that the writing seemed to be helping him to discover what it was he had learned.

The instructor's response, then, was not a negative evaluation of the paragraph but an assurance to the student that the paragraph was indeed a good way to have *begun* his composing, though it was not necessarily a good finished product. Instead of strongly criticizing the paragraph, she conveyed a positive message about it and emphasized the new awareness the student had achieved through the act of writing it. She concluded by asking the student to revise. The following is his second draft:

I guess I never really had an unreasonable assignment made at school, although sometimes they seemed unreasonable to me. In junior high school I did think my ninth-grade math teacher gave an awful lot of homework, but maybe it was because I didn't like math much and didn't understand the importance of school work. Over the years I realized that homework is important and should be put high on the priority list as far as school goes. It's no coincidence that I started getting better grades once I changed my attitude. Now that I'm older I can look back and say none of my assignments was unreasonable. They helped teach me a sense of responsibility.

The second version is better organized and has a clearer focus. It could, of course, be improved further. However, it shows that the student, having been encouraged to view his original paragraph as a promising draft rather than a flawed text, has begun to understand how he can improve both his writing and his awareness of the process that effective writers often follow.

Our second example focuses on another common student text weakness, plot summary in the critical essay on literature. It can perhaps be most usefully understood as a manifestation of what Linda Flower and John Hayes call "writer-based" prose, prose that uses patterns borrowed, in the case of plot summary, "from a structure inherent in the material the writers examined." (459)

The student's initial text was laden with sections in which she retold parts of Faulkner's "The Bear," adding few interpretive remarks and seemingly allowing the story to speak for itself. In this case the instructor's initial response was more traditional. He had disparaged the paper as a poor critical essay that substituted plot summary for interpretation.

Bringing her marked paper with her to her conference, the student expressed her frustration with comments in the margins about the need to avoid summarizing the plot. That advice, she said, is what her English teachers had always given her, but she couldn't understand how it was possible to do what they told her to. How, she asked, could she write any generalizations about the story when she didn't know what they were until she worked through some of the important parts of the plot on paper? Her method had been to choose instinctively the events she felt to be important and to let her discussion of them lead her to an understanding of them. By writing down exactly what happened, in the order it happened, she clarified, even discovered, the meaning of the material. What she had not realized was that her weak "finished papers" might be legitimate discovery drafts. For her, the chief effect of the instructor's plot-summary comment was to make her doubt the value of the *way she was composing* as much as the text she composed.

Reconsidering her paper, the instructor attempted to understand how its chief weakness might reflect some legitimate problem of composing. For this writer, it occurred to him, retelling the plot was apparently a necessary stage in invention. Thus she was perplexed by responses that criticized her own approach and enjoined her to "put generalizations first." She apparently needed a response that initially *valued* her plot-summarizing as a useful drafting technique but then recommended a revision in which the plot summary, having served its heuristic purpose, would be condensed or eliminated to create a more presentable finished paper.

In her revision, she was in fact able to pare down her retelling of the story and to add more interpretive generalizations about the importance of the episodes she did discuss. The problem finally did not rest in her inability to interpret the story or to express herself. It rested in her inability to function well within the traditional single-submission, evaluative-response system, for given only one chance at drafting, she had an inability to distinguish between the written record of an invention technique and an acceptable finished text.

Writer-based prose such as plot summary may be a natural stage in the process of learning to write more effectively, but both students and instructors need to be aware of this before students can improve. Moreover, the nature of the instructor's response is often crucial in determining whether a student such as the one just discussed will come to recognize the distinction between a discovery draft and a completed paper.

Our final extended example is somewhat similar to the first one we discussed in that the student apparently failed to do the assignment requested of her. But the reasons in this instance were much different. In such a case we've found it's important for the instructor to tailor a response by first attempting to determine the writer's intentions. Whether the assignment is completely unsatisfactory because of an honest misunderstanding, because of ineptitude, or because of chicanery, for instance, should make a big difference in the instructor's response to it. In our example the instructor learned that the student's first draft signified her attempt to negotiate a rhetorical situation complicated enough that she could not accomplish her aim without some further guidance.

The following paragraph is the introduction to a four-page draft in which the student apparently failed to respond adequately to the assignment her women's studies instructor had given her. She was to interview an older working woman and then write an essay analyzing the pressures that woman had faced during her career. The opening paragraph reflects the content of the draft:

> Mrs. Thelma Morton Arnold has worked for Oberlin College for thirty years. In December of 1981, she was promoted from the position of dormitory custodian to that of supervisor of dorm custodians on the north end of campus. Last week, Mrs. Arnold talked with me about her life.

Essentially, the paper that followed was a biography of Mrs. Arnold, with no apparent analysis of any pressures she had encountered. Significantly, there were passages that could be construed as bearing on career pressures, but the writer herself didn't seem to recognize their relevance. The instructor noted these points in his initial response.

In conference, the student confided that she in fact knew her draft had evaded the issue. Apparently she had avoided explicitly analyzing the pressures in Mrs. Arnold's career because she had promised to let Mrs. Arnold read the paper that would result from the interview. Mrs. Arnold was such a trusting, pleasant woman that the student couldn't bring herself to do what she regarded as a "cold, clinical analysis" of her life. She was so uncomfortable with this notion, in fact, that she was willing to receive a poor grade in her women's studies course to avoid displeasing Mrs. Arnold and embarrassing herself.

In this case the student had written the paper mainly to one audience— Mrs. Arnold—because she assumed that writing more to her other audience—her women's studies instructor—would ruin the paper for Mrs. Arnold. Her composition instructor attempted to convince her that it was possible for her to juggle the expectations and demands of both audiences, to please both Mrs. Arnold and the women's studies instructor. If she could see herself at some points in the role of the *lab-coated clinician*, but at other points in the role of, say, the *main speaker at a testimonial dinner* for Mrs. Arnold, she might be able to satisfy both audiences. Here is the opening paragraph of her revision:

> Mrs. Thelma Morton Arnold has worked for Oberlin College for thirty years. In December of 1981, she was promoted from the position of dormitory custodian to that of supervisor of dorm custodians on the north end of campus. As a black working woman, she has faced discriminatory pressures in choosing her occupation, as well as in her attempts to earn promotions and equal pay. She has fought to overcome these pressures and gain just treatment for herself and others.

While the first two sentences of this paragraph are the same as in the earlier version, the third sentence of the earlier version—"Last week, Mrs. Arnold talked with me about her life"—has been replaced with two sentences, each of which represents a nod toward one of the two competing audiences. Sentence three of the new version is aimed at the instructor, for it encapsulates the analysis of pressures that is to come in the paper. Sentence four, on the other hand, prefigures the tone of praise that will also characterize the paper to come.

Having conferred with her composition instructor, the student was able to revise in such a way that her dilemma was solved. Her first draft represented her view of a problem that she was unsure of handling. In one sense her attempt reflected a genuine strength: She had chosen a single audience toward which to write, a legitimate intention underlying the weakness in her draft. To make the most helpful response in this instance, the instructor needed to recognize another facet of the composing process, one also stressed by proponents of the new pedagogy: that writing does in fact occur in the context of a rhetorical situation.

We want to suggest some other possible situations in which our approach would help students to revise their work. For example, the student narrative, whether written about historical events for a history class or about personal experiences for a composition class, will often feature an overabundance of short, simple sentences and a lack of subordination and complicating modification. Rather than simply indicating a weak style or even an inability to interpret the material, such writing often stems from the student's respect for reporting the verifiable facts related to a given event. In other words, some students produce flat, deadpan narratives, not because of limited verbal ability or inadequate analytic powers, but because they believe they are doing the right thing in providing what they consider to be a camera-copy of reality. Probably the most helpful response in such a case is to correct the student's view of the purpose of such writing, to clarify what the audience's demands and expectations really are as opposed to what the student supposes them to be.

Similarly, consider the case of the student paper which is written in overblown generalities and which makes use of pompous academese. Typical responses to such writing urge the use of more concrete details and specific examples, which is certainly fine advice. Yet the most effective response may be the one which recognizes that the student's writing has resulted from a belief that his or her audience values overblown generalities, and which then attempts to clarify the student's picture of the audience.

The artificial nature of the classroom setting may also create difficulties in students' composing processes. We have encountered, for instance, reasonably diligent students whose concern to emulate the prescribed *form* of an assignment may override any considerations of what they actually have to say. They then produce writing which employs the required "comparison-contrast" or "descriptive" modes, as the case may be, but which is woefully inadequate in terms of content and style. We have found that by discussing with students their motivations for choosing, say, a particular pattern of development, we can determine whether the students made their selections after following sound invention strategies or whether they selected their organizational schemes on the basis of pressure to turn in a paper that fit the required form. If the latter is true, then an effective revision may result after the student is counseled to follow better heuristics for invention.

Digressions are another common text weakness, the exploration of which may lead to an improved product. In our experience digressions sometimes signal that a writer's thinking has moved in a potentially more interesting or valuable direction. Discussing with students the way in which composing can encourage thinking, and suggesting that perhaps that is why a digression occurred, may lead them to realize that they are just beginning the writing process for a paper they assumed was completed. In short, the digression may represent a fruitful line of inquiry stimulated by the composing process itself. We have seen many cases where students have successfully revised their work by refocusing it on ideas initially thought to be "digressions."

Finally, students who produce drafts with repetitive ideas couched in slightly different language have generally been criticized for authoring texts that are weak in both content and structure. But is their conceptual repetition always the sign of a tenuous grasp of exposition and a paucity of ideas, or might it reflect a more positive attempt to try out different ways of saying something in an effort to achieve greater clarity or effect? Might not a repetitive discourse sometimes reflect a healthy attempt to achieve a fuller command of style and substance?

Certainly for some instructors this method of interpreting draft difficulties in order to understand the mental processes that gave rise to a writer's problems is not completely new. Particularly those instructors who teach process-oriented courses featuring multiple drafts and revisions may already be reading and responding to drafts in ways similar to those we have recommended. Still, the findings of Sommers and Brannon and Knoblauch suggest that our profession as a whole is far from adopting such "facilitative" approaches to commentary. We believe that, with further attempts to identify and codify draft weaknesses matched with the kind of comments we have recommended above, our profession can make successful inroads against the domain of the evaluative response.

WORKS CITED

Bartholomae, David. "The Study of Error." *College Composition and Communication* 31 (1980): 253–269.

Brannon, Lil, and C. H. Knoblauch. "On Students' Rights to Their Own Texts: A Model of Teacher Response." *College Composition and Communication* 33 (1982): 157–166.

Comprone, Joseph J. "Recent Literary and Composition Theory: Readerly and Writerly Texts." Presented at the Conference on College Composition and Communication, Minneapolis, MN, 21 March 1985.

Flower, Linda, and John Hayes. "Problem-Solving Strategies and the Writing Process." *College English* 39 (1977): 449–461.

Hairston, Maxine. "The Winds of Change: Thomas Kuhn and the Revolution in the Teaching of Writing." *College Composition and Communication* 33 (1982): 76–88.

Hartwell, Patrick. "Paradoxes and Problems: The Value of Traditional Textbook Rules." *Pennsylvania Writing Project Newsletter* 3 (1983): 7–9.

Knoblauch, C. H., and Lil Brannon. "Teacher Commentary on Student Writing: The State of the Art." *Rhetoric and Composition: A Sourcebook for Teachers and Writers*. Edited by Richard L. Graves. Second Edition. Upper Montclair, NJ: Boynton/Cook, 1984: 285–291.

_____. *Rhetorical Traditions and the Teaching of Writing*. Upper Montclair, NJ: Boynton/Cook, 1984.

Kroll, Barry. M., and John C. Schafer. "Error Analysis and the Teaching of Composition." *College Composition and Communication* 29 (1978): 243–248.

Murray, Donald C. "Internal Revision: A Process of Discovery." *Research on Composing: Points of Departure*. Edited by Charles R. Cooper and Lee Odell. Urbana, IL: NCTE, 1978.

Shaughnessy, Mina. *Errors and Expectations*. New York: Oxford University Press, 1977.

Sommers, Nancy. "Responding to Student Writing." *College Composition and Communication* 33 (1982): 148–156.

Chapter 10

The Comments They Made: An Exploration of Helpful and Unhelpful Commentary

Naomi Strand

How do the comments we receive on our papers affect our ability to write? How can teachers and tutors effect change in a writer through their comments? I would like to examine the impact of various comments I have received over the past few years of academic work—my senior year in high school and three and a half years in college. Through this overview I hope to theorize what caused the wide range of reactions in me: from being inspired to revise a paper immediately to feeling like I never wanted to write again.

I believe the chief purpose of comments is ultimately to encourage more work on a paper through subsequent revisions, rather than simply to justify a grade. With this criterion in mind, I hope to identify what constitutes constructive criticism and what makes comments useful to writers. Essentially, my analysis shows that the comments I have received can be grouped into four categories. The first three represent comments that were ineffective or detrimental; the final category comprises those comments that helped me to work with my writing to produce better results in successive tries.

First of all, there were those comments that I, as a freshman in college, could not decipher—not because of the professor's illegible handwriting (although that has occasionally posed a problem) but because of the highly academic language used in the comments. For example, I could not for the life of me understand what my women's studies professor was asking me to do when she wrote that I needed to "problematize notions of gender here." This is the type of comment that was totally useless to me at the time. Without the necessary tools of academic analysis in women's studies—and the vocabulary to go with those tools—I was left frustrated, with no idea of how to revise. I now realize that I did not yet have a command of the disciplinary discourse necessary to process those comments. For comments to be meaningful, the writer must be able to process them. Obviously, learning the discourses necessary to comprehend comments on papers is part of the point of attending college, but my experience suggests that perhaps there should initially be some sort of "grace period" for freshmen to allow them to absorb a significant amount of academic lingo before they are expected to understand and use these terms. In any case, teachers and writing associates should recognize that making such comments to students who lack the necessary tools of analysis—including the requisite vocabulary—will likely leave students frustrated and clueless about how to proceed with the paper.

As I slowly learned the tools necessary for academic analysis, writing papers became easier, as did making use of the comments I received. By the end of my third semester I finally began to receive comments that my paper was, for example, "a strong and lively reading of the play," but that in order to improve, I would need to "work more closely with the text and edit more thoroughly." I must stress that although early in my college career the latter part of the comment would have been too vague for me to process, I had learned enough to comprehend the comment and revise my paper accordingly. Thus, although I would have been thrown by such a response when I was new to the discourse, after immersion in the discipline, I was able both to understand the comments made within this type of discipline-specific discourse and to feel confident enough to apply them.

In my experience, confidence is a major issue in the decision to revise a paper. I have always been self-conscious of my writing skills. Even now, I feel unsure about my ability to write this paper because the topic and approach are outside my area of expertise, and I feel completely out of my element. (Ask me to write a ten-page biblical exegesis for a religion class, and I'll happily produce one, but this essay seems foreign to me.) I believe that writing puts one in a very vulnerable position. Therefore, a fundamental goal of comments on papers should be to encourage the writer's confidence. I do *not* mean to suggest that people who make comments on papers should manufacture false praise. Rather, they should encourage the writer by indicating the strong points in every paper to show what the writer has done *effectively* as opposed to concentrating on mistakes.

This brings me to the second category of written comments: those that destroy the sometimes-fragile confidence level of writers through excessively harsh or sarcastic criticism. Comments of this nature are some of the most obviously harmful and destructive forms of feedback (and disturbingly some of the most common). For example, one paper I wrote last year was returned to me littered with such comments as "careless!" and "I don't want to see this again." These comments completely robbed me of any authority over my own work, seeming more like the kind of comments I received in grade school. The most frustrating thing about the professor's response in this case was that I had actually spent a very long time agonizing over the editing process for the paper. Nothing I wrote in that paper was "careless." Instead, there were merely some grammatical mistakes I had overlooked, some of which were not even "mistakes," but made the sentences less clear than they could have been, and a few phrases that apparently irritated her. Although I got a decent grade on the paper overall, I couldn't help feeling utterly helpless in the face of such a harsh reaction to my hard work. Even as I write this essay, I still feel defensiveness toward that professor's severe critique of my writing.

At the time I wrote that women's studies paper, I viewed my professor's comments as evidence in support of my belief that I was unable to write or edit good papers. This mindset made my next paper for that class unbelievably difficult to produce. Not surprisingly, that paper turned out even worse than the first one. Instead of providing comments that helped me to produce a better paper the second time, my professor's response had destroyed any confidence I had in my ability to write and therefore contributed to my producing a weaker paper. Rather than consider a possible connection between the discouraging comments I received on my first paper and the disappointing quality of the second paper, the professor let loose a slew of sarcastic comments on the second paper, and I ended up furious and demoralized. I remember deciding I never wanted to write again, and I almost went so far as to drop the women's studies major.

There are two important things we can learn from my experience with this professor's approach to feedback. First, harshly critical comments are never useful, no matter how much the commentator believes they are "helping" the writer by pointing out the "mistakes." Ironically, I ended up confronting the professor about her comments on my second paper, and she was astonished by my reaction, which included bursting into tears in her office. She told me that she never had any idea that she was being "overly harsh," and that she actually believed I was a good writer. Her criticisms, she felt, were a way to encourage me to "live up to my full potential." Of course, as I have shown, what she in fact accomplished was something completely different. This inability to distinguish between helpful and harsh, demoralizing commentary is a tendency I have noticed too often in professors. It seems that when it comes to responding to student papers, academics have a tendency to disregard the humanity of the writer, forgetting that the writer has feelings.

In reflection, my strong reaction to this professor's responses was based not only on the harshness of the remarks, however. I was also overwhelmed by the sheer *amount* of the commentary. In my experience, sometimes a similar state of demoralization occurs when an over-eager teacher makes only mildly critical comments, but they are so numerous that they cover every inch of white space on the page. In order for me to be able to process all the information I receive through paper comments, they must not be overwhelming in number. Practicing some restraint in the number of comments is something I have learned to do when tutoring. Sometimes it is necessary to hold back on excessive commentary in order to avoid being seen as overly critical, thereby crushing the writer's confidence. Extremely prolific commentary, while usually well intended, can backfire.

Some of the most frustrating comments I have received have not been unkind at all. They fall under the third category, which are brief, positive remarks that have very little substance or elaboration. Usually these are well meaning notes hastily scribbled on a paper that the professor believes is "good." Unfortunately, the professor in such cases neglects to add supporting or clarifying commentary. This lack of commentary on so-called "good" papers, although not destructive, is completely unhelpful. I have received many papers with little more than a few check marks apparently scattered at random in the margins, with a grade at the end. This approach does nothing to help me figure out what worked well in the paper or what possible improvements I might still make. The only possible benefit that comes out of these comments is an increase in confidence from the knowledge that— somehow—I wrote a "good" paper. But this confidence alone does not do much to help me write similarly "good" papers in the future.

Overall, my college writing career has been marked with frequent incidences of receiving either a high grade and no comments informing me of what I did well, or a lower grade and many comments that I have been unable (or unwilling) to use due to their overly critical tone. Just as it is necessary to steer clear of the extremes of overly harsh commentary on the one hand and ineffectual, unsubstantiated praise on the other, commentators should seek to balance the amount of comments they place on papers against the need to avoid overwhelming the writer. My experience has taught me that comments need to be comprehensive yet concise and contain a balance of criticism and praise to be helpful. Moreover, to reiterate what I discussed in the first part of the paper, commentators must take into consideration the level of comprehension of the writer to avoid giving cryptic feedback.

If we understand that the key purpose of written comments is to provide a guideline of what the writer might do to improve the paper through revision, then it is easy to see how many of the comments I have been discussing are ineffective and unhelpful. Likewise, when we assume that the purpose of comments is merely to justify a grade, the comments lose power for effecting any positive change and become less valuable as a teaching tool. When we examine some of these comments from the perspective of justifying a grade, they seem to make a little more sense (i.e., the "good" papers get few comments because they are closer to what the professor wanted, and the "bad" papers are covered with comments because they failed to live up to the professor's expectations). Although sometimes these two purposes can act together, the emphasis on the grade as certifying the final product or on the "good" paper as not worth revising is useless in teaching writers how to produce more coherent, meaningful, and insightful papers in the future.

As we have seen mainly by negative example, a helpful comment is one that allows the writer to feel confident in his or her work while interacting with that work in a constructive way. Specifically, for example, it would be helpful, in the case of a paper that lacks cohesion, for the commentator to repeat what he or she believes the writer's thesis is (e.g., "I believe you are arguing that..."). Many times, for instance, I know what I want to say, but have not been able to successfully express it. Often I don't even realize that my ideas are not apparent on paper but only exist in my head. This is because although the idea is obvious to me, it only became so after I went through the process of writing the paper, or I was simply unaware that I did not express it because *I* knew what I was saying. For these reasons I believe that a successful comment must include some sort of attempt at understanding the underlying meaning of the piece, even if it is not clearly communicated.

The most constructive comments I have received have been those that attempt to understand my intention even when I have not articulated it well and recapitulate my main points in ways that allow me to comprehend what I have effectively communicated as well as what is lacking in my argument. This approach to commentary is outlined in "Improving Our Responses to Student Writing: A Process-Oriented Approach," by JoAnne and Leonard Podis. I believe the type of comments that are most valuable are best described in the following passage from their article:

> Our method, then, calls for instructors to approach draft difficulties as potential keys to understanding student writers' intentions, and in some cases as keys to helping the writers better define their intentions in their own minds. (Podis and Podis, "Improving," 96)

The authors effectively explain one of the keys to helpful comments: making an effort to understand the writer's intentions, even if they are still murky.

For example, in high school and for the first few years in college I believed that my inability to translate my ideas successfully into a paper that met my teachers' expectations meant that I simply did not know how to write. Instead, a more productive approach on the part of my teachers and professors would have been to give me feedback that demonstrated how the work I submitted was *a good step* in the process of writing a solid paper. I can now see that my tendencies to write run-on sentences and to over-generalize were ways I was using to get ideas out of my head and onto paper. My papers tended to be unstructured and vague because what I had mistaken for final drafts were really only the beginning stages of good papers. If only my teachers had told me that I had successfully completed an important step in the writing process (i.e., getting words on to the page) but I still had to work further to clarify my points, I would have rejoiced at the chance to improve my writing.

Ultimately the most important element in crafting effective commentary is the creation of dialogue. I have discovered that when a criticism is phrased within a dialogue regarding my paper, I am more willing and able to get the most out of the comment. In "The Rhetoric of Reproof," Podis and Podis give a remarkable example of the effect of dialogue-based commentary. The article discusses the academic tendency to be overly critical or to "get nega-tive." The authors recount how an early reviewer of their manuscript who was initially very caustic in evaluating their piece proceeded to alter and clarify his or her response to the piece after he or she began to understand what they were arguing:

> A specialist in ethics, this reviewer stopped and said, "okay, so I've 'gotten nega-tive.' I think that's okay since. [...]" From this point, the reviewer changed tactics and moved gradually toward trying to *understand why* we had we had written what we had. [...] While not necessarily agreeing with or accepting our views—indeed, while critiquing them—he or she was suddenly more willing to "share the podium." (Podis and Podis, "Reproof," 227)

This is a prime example of the type of helpful dialogue that can be created when a commentator attempts to understand the intention behind what the author has written, rather than dismissing it as simply inept.

I have always made an effort to consider the comments I received to ascertain whether or not I agreed with my professor's response. I still love receiving lots of comments, but the best and most useful ones are those that interact with what I am saying in the paper before criticizing the way I say it. Helpful commentary, I believe, is also rooted at least partially in understand-ing the intent of the professors who apparently make unhelpful comments. In such cases, a student writer can help the professor to discover how to express the critique more constructively. For instance, I once received an exceed-ingly harsh response on one of my religion papers. The professor scrawled,

"Who cares?" in the margins. When I confronted her about the true intent of her comment, she amended it to "Would this necessarily be inconceivable to your intended audience?"—a comment I found much more useful.

Part of the problem, as I have stated before, is the tendency for professors to either "forget" that the writers are human beings as well as attack them (which, as we have seen, does not produce good results), or to assume that there is nothing more to be done once the paper has been submitted (which does not produce any results). Instead of motivating the writer to revise, the commentator freezes communication on the subject, and the writer is left on his or her own with little or no guidance. Commentators should, rather, seek to understand writers' purposes and thereby engage in a critical dialogue with them. In my experience, this is the only form of commentary that is useful in persuading writers to make positive changes, thereby promoting the improvement of their writing skills.

WORKS CITED

Podis, JoAnne M., and Leonard A. Podis. "Improving Our Responses to Student Writing: A Process-Oriented Approach." *Rhetoric Review* 5 (1986): 90–98.

Podis, Leonard A., and JoAnne M. Podis. "The Rhetoric of Reproof." *College English* 63 (2000): 214–228.

Chapter 11

The Dilemmas of Grading

Noelle Howey

In high school, I learned that Hester Prynne had it coming, that Nixon was framed, and that grades were all-important. While I effectively disposed of the first two myths, it is almost embarrassing how persistently I have clung to the third. While publicly disdaining grades, I privately agonize over them. While telling my friends that B's are nothing to be disturbed about, I flagellate myself over an A minus. Rationally, I have come to learn that grades are neither an indicator of "intelligence" nor a necessary rung on the ladder to the ubiquitous American Dream. Yet I still struggle daily between pleasing myself and pleasing the professor, between focusing on the learning process and focusing on the product. In short, despite several years of college, I remain caught between two paradigms.

During high school, the Old Paradigm notions of grading were firmly fixed in my head. As my ninth grade honors math teacher explained to me one day, "anything but an A might as well be an F." Since I was barely pulling a C, I dropped the course. Like my teacher, I equated not getting A's with not learning.

Junior year, when college searching became an obsession for all, charts were posted in the school office every six weeks ranking each student by grade point average. I remember when I slipped to number twelve. I shut myself inside a bathroom stall for forty minutes. "Stupid," I told myself.

Thus, my senior year in high school was wholly dedicated to the care and upkeep of the oldest of the Old Paradigm clichés: grades are equivalent to a student's intelligence, intrinsic worth, and future bliss. Thus, I didn't write my *Othello* paper in iambic pentameter: too risky, the teacher might not like it. Thus, I didn't write my senior essay on transsexualism: too controversial, the teacher might not like it. I consciously altered the depth and range of my writing to appease my conservative teachers and to obtain the necessary grades.

While I do not operate under the same fear of grades in college, more than a vestige of "grades anxiety" still factors into nearly every assignment I encounter. I am still reluctant to question the assumptions of a professor. I still fear injecting controversy into a classroom setting (though I am now more apt to do it). And, most unfortunately, I do not think I am entirely unique in this regard.

Many students harbor considerable fear about grades, not because of some personality deficiency or deep-seated superficiality but rather out of insecurity. For example, I told myself that if I did not receive all A's, then I must not be intelligent enough to become a contributing member of society. I viewed grades not as a subjective, isolated reflection upon work done, but rather as a broad summation of my potential as a person. I believed that if I was an A student, then I was also an A person.

Like many other students, I simply bought into the grading system to such a degree that I was willing to deprioritize learning. Our culture puts the emphasis not on learning but on achieving, as if the two were mutually exclusive. Students are not rewarded (or even recognized) for mastering the arduous process of learning. They are rewarded for achieving the grade that is supposedly, but not necessarily, the simplified result of that process. Thus, parents do not ask "What did you learn in school today?" but instead, "How did you do in school today?" Thus, students, like myself, do not focus on the learning but on the brass ring: the A.

In many schools, A's are not hard to come by. In high school, I discovered myriad ways of circumventing the learning process, even when writing papers. A polysyllabic vocabulary, a plethora of quotations from somewhat obscure sources, and a few "perhapses" thrown in could earn me a decent grade alone. My teachers may have recognized that the papers were essentially void of substance, but they honored me for appropriating the language of academic discourse so well. Or they may just have given me that infamous "A for effort."

The message I received in this not-so-unusual scenario: If you can *sound* "educated," you *are* "educated"; if you can mimic thought, then you are thinking. Such faulty logic only propagates the Old Paradigm notion that there are hierarchical patterns of knowing.

For example, I used to believe that with each successive "A" I would be that much closer to achieving Truth and Meaning. I did not realize that Truth is not something to be achieved but is rather something to be sought (often in vain) through the learning process. This learning process is self-specific; unlike grading, it is not dependent upon a finished product; unlike grading, it is not dependent on competition. Rather, the process is self-defined, self-motivated, and self-rewarding. The product is the sense of joy inherent in any process of discovery; this product is certainly much more valuable than any gold star, blue ribbon, or straight-A average.

The learning process, or at least the writing process, is the most intimate sort of self-discovery. Through writing, I have learned what my voice is and how to express it on paper. My identity is now inextricably linked with my writing voice; yet through the pressure to conform to a more traditionally stoic voice for a grade (such as in my twelfth grade *Othello* paper), I left high school with the misconception that there was only "one way": one way to write, to view the world, and to succeed.

These three phrases (to write, to view the world, to succeed) are linked in the Old Paradigm model, because "to succeed" you must first situate your seeing and writing within the "one way" or "the standard." My eleventh-grade teacher often used to say, "Well, we must have standards, mustn't we?" Yet what is this standard, and who is making these judgments?

Usually the standard by which grades are determined is simply that of the status quo, of the mainstream, of the benignly negligent patriarchy. In my school, writing "up to standard" meant using no generic feminine pronouns, no anecdotes, no "I." Thus personal experience or even alternative readings of texts were not permitted to enter my papers if I wanted a respectable grade. Such features were not sufficiently "academic" according to the fastidious standards of my conservative high school. They were merely my personal views and observations.

Divorcing the personal self and the academic self is dangerous for all students, but particularly for females and members of minority groups. Too often we are told to subvert our selves in order to appropriate the dominant discourse that is necessary to succeed. When we comply, our work becomes distilled for the mainstream palate. For example, a tutee once told me that she deleted all the "Afrocentric" references from one of her English literature papers because she feared that the teacher would label her as an ideologue and grade her down. In twelfth grade I feared writing about my father's transsexualism because I thought the teacher would become repulsed and grade me down. Each idea we drop or conscious omission we make for the sole purpose of pleasing the teacher may be a sacrifice of autonomy, identity, and most of all, genuine learning. After all, while the grading system may often reward those who conform the most, the learning process reveals itself only to those who stubbornly attempt to remain themselves.

Yet all of this sounds rather ominous. Is the grading system really so counterproductive in our society? After all, despite myriad drawbacks, it remains firmly ensconced. Whether we conclude that its stability is due to our need for approval, our laxity, or our weak "family values," the fact is that grades govern the educational world. So, we are tempted to ask, is there any silver lining? Are grades doing anything positive at all?

The grading system, like most of our social institutions, is not inherently "evil," even if it could stand improvement; at its root, there is a solid goal and purpose: to provide incentive and feedback to students. Grades can motivate a student to work more diligently in a subject in which the student feels lost or ill at ease. For example, a friend of mine was coerced by a college distribution requirement into taking a physics class. As it happened, she needed to maintain a high G.P.A. in order to keep her financial aid; thus, she studied extremely hard in the course, sparked her own interest, and became a physics major. (This case may be exceptional, but I can recall many less-than-thrilling classes that I learned from *only* because I was forced to study hard to get a decent grade.) Grades can also give a student some indication of how well she is grasping the material. After all, a student may think she is making progress in a class merely because she "did well" in a similar class. A grade may be a quick, simple way of telling her that such an assumption may not be serving her well.

However, the primary function of grades is to prepare students. Grades serve to indoctrinate the student into a world where everything is categorized and pigeonholed. In fact, I would venture that "the trouble with grading" lies, in part, in our cultural context. Our educational system is constantly under pressure to become more efficient and competitive (even for-profit) in our capitalist society.

Education, if anything, has become so specialized that we pigeonhole students from day one. We want bilingual fetuses. We want prodigious preschoolers. We want fourth graders who know their math tables, periodic charts, taxonomic divisions, and clause options.

We test preschoolers on their "aptitude"; fifth graders on their "potential"; high-schoolers on their "cognitive ability." We do not claim that these tests are fair in terms of race, ethnicity, or gender. We do not claim that these tests are comprehensive, by any means. Primarily we claim them to be "a necessary evil." Like grades, they fill our need to monitor the growth of the student commodity. In our culture, this task is of the utmost practicality; we are, after all, a culture of conscious consumers.

Since the grading system has proved its practical worth, it is unlikely to become obsolete or outmoded anytime soon. Despite the headway that the New Paradigm has made in restructuring student-teacher hierarchy in the composition classroom, it has yet to effect a major change in methods of evaluation. Therefore I would like to explore possible alternatives to, and reforms of, the system—alternatives and reforms that might have assisted me during high school.

One such alternative might be the increased use of written evaluations. Written evaluations illuminate the basis for the teacher's grades, as well as provide reflection on the student's work. Ideally, the written evaluation is less a stamp of (dis)approval than a means of communicating expectations between teacher and student; this method more nearly establishes teacher and student as equals in the evaluative process. I believe I would have been more willing to take chances on paper topics if the opportunity to receive thoughtful, less-judgmental criticism had been forthcoming.

Needless to say, there are also some drawbacks to the use of written evaluations. One obvious problem is the time required for such an approach. If the teacher has five hundred students in a survey course, written evaluations are nothing short of impossible. Even in a small course, the demands of a written evaluation far outweigh those of simple grading. While we may theoretically applaud spending more time on the evaluative process, it may simply not be possible to fit written commentary into the already-hectic life of most teachers.

Another method, perhaps somewhat less time-consuming, would be oral evaluative conferences. Open discussion would allow for even more honest communication to occur, and it would help to break down the barriers inherent in classroom power dynamics. Of course, this method also requires additional time as well as good articulation and interpersonal skills. While a grade is allowed to be abstract (as in "A for excellent," "B for good"), dialogue between teacher and student must be concrete to be effective.

If the grading system continues at all, it needs to aspire to the concrete. Teachers must deconstruct those vague words they use with regard to grading. "Adequate," "good," and "fair" are useless terms in a dialogue about grading; they only create a smoke screen around the teacher's real expectations. In addition, teachers might be more willing to discuss their approaches to grading, to be more open about their procedures. I have often viewed grading, particularly the grading of papers, as some mystical activity informed by neither reason nor consistency. If teachers were to openly consult with students on how they grade writing, students' "grades anxiety" might be somewhat allayed.

For example, one of my high school teachers held individual conferences with students each semester just to discuss her grading practices. I recall her asking me how much I had worked in the class; I felt such overwhelming relief when I was permitted to *tell* her how diligently I had applied myself. In addition, when the grade came out, I felt I had contributed to the decision. It was not a judgment handed down to me from "on high," but rather a sign or gesture of the teacher's cooperative approach, which had the effect of empowering me.

In the end, however, the most important thing that needs to be communicated about the grading system (or any similar mechanism of our society that judges and categorizes) is its insignificance. A grade is not a person; it cannot breathe and express itself or sing and dance. We may be evaluated inside and out during the course of our lives, yet our value comes not from our quality sticker, but from our basic essence as human beings.

Section Four

Writing in the Classroom: Approaches and Methods

While tutoring and teaching writing are distinct activities, they have much in common. The goal of both is, after all, to help students become better writers. The overlap between teaching and tutoring is often most striking when teaching is conducted in the spirit of the collaborative ideals that inform tutoring at its best and when tutoring is likewise influenced by the newer developments in writing pedagogy. To be most effective, writing associates, like teachers, must operate from an enlightened understanding of composing processes and the nature of discourse communities, while also being aware of how personal, social, and contextual factors are likely to affect their tutees. By the same token, to be most effective, writing teachers should periodically function like associates. They should, for instance, hold individual conferences with their students to provide guidance on composing and revising works in progress. Additionally, they should, for the most part, conceive of themselves as *enabling* the authority of student writers rather than *constraining* that authority. Many of the practical techniques used in tutoring are thus also essential in the teaching of composition. For example, many of the ways of facilitating and responding to student writing discussed in Section Three are relevant for teaching as well as tutoring. While the articles collected in this section are aimed mainly at writing teachers, they have much to offer writing associates and teaching assistants as well.

The Articles

An important idea underlying the pedagogical vision in these pieces on teaching writing is that of student *agency*, a theme that has been sounded in many of the earlier pieces on tutoring. Just as tutoring is more effective when tutees can claim some ownership of their writing, so too is classroom instruction more effective when instructors create and sustain learning environments in which students have some authority over their own emerging texts.

One way in which teachers can support student agency is to set up class-rooms in which students are treated as *writers*—with all the freedoms and responsibilities that term implies—rather than as *pseudo-writers* who must be monitored and controlled at every step by instructors who presumably know exactly what should be written and even exactly how it should be said.[1]

Chapter 12, "Perspectives on the Writing Classroom" by Leonard A. Podis, was originally presented at a conference of high school teachers held at the Germantown Friends School in Philadelphia. A veteran composition instructor, Podis was asked to address the conference on how high school English teachers might best prepare their students for the demands of college writing. To supplement his views, Podis sought advice from the tutors who were enrolled in his training course at the time as well as from some first-year students. Significantly, the advice the students said they wanted to give high school teachers coincided with the advice Podis himself offered after many years of teaching writing to students newly arrived from high school, and he distilled those observations into the following five injunctions:

> (1) to make classroom writing more engaging and enjoyable; (2) to emphasize rhe-torical flexibility rather than constraining cure-all formulas; (3) to teach the process of drafting and revising more actively; (4) to respond to students' ideas and not just their grammar, form, and usage; and (5) to stay in touch with the process of writing by being active as writers themselves.

In Podis's view, these goals and precepts support the premise that English composition must not be conceived of narrowly as a "service course, a course that grimly, dutifully, and specifically readies students for some other, presumably more important, educational activity down the road." Rather, he believes that high school courses best prepare students for "higher levels" of writing by exposing them to the challenges of writing for their immediate situations, not by haranguing them to keep a nervous eye on some shadowy conception of a future in which anonymous "college readers" will suppos-edly be looking for certain qualities in their work. The process of meeting the expectations of diverse college readers will best be learned in college itself.

Complementing Podis's warnings against prescriptivism in the class-room is Chapter 13, Noelle Howey's "No Answers: Interrogating 'Truth' in Writing." Howey, who also wrote Chapter 11 ("The Dilemmas of Grading"), here examines her experiences as a student in two different writing courses, one taught by "Ms. A" and the other by "Mr. B." She concludes that instruc-tors' attempts to force students to write according to a rigid set of prescrip-tions are misguided. In comparing the styles of instructors A and B, Howey notes that "Ms. A is a firm believer in the old paradigm hierarchy in which a teacher is the Authority and the students are empty vessels waiting to be filled top-full with Knowledge." Mr. B, by contrast, "established a dialogue in which he facilitated our searches for our own conceptions of what writing should be. He [...] did not coerce us into accepting his theories."

Like Podis, Howey rejects professorial heavy-handedness not merely because it sets up tense and unpleasant dynamics in the classroom, but because it is fundamentally wrong in misrepresenting writing as narrowly adhering to a limited set of rules, rules that most often fail to hold true in real writing situations and which gain their force artificially through the power and institutional authority wielded by the instructor. While Mr. B's open-minded approach was not without its difficulties (being subject to abuse by some students who mistook it as giving them complete license to do whatever they wanted because everything is relative), Howey believes that she learned much more from it. Howey's essay is also valuable in its implicit view that techniques pertaining to the teaching of creative writing are applicable to the teaching and tutoring of expository writing. Indeed, while no one would deny the existence of salient differences between creative and expository writing, the thrust in the wake of postmodernism has been to look back in the other direction to see what diverse types of discourse previously viewed as oppositional may have in common. In recognizing that her experiences in creative writing are connected to issues in teaching and tutoring composition, Howey illuminates a promising path.

Chapter 14, new to this edition of *Working with Student Writers*, is Kate Daloz's "Glazed Looks and Panic Attacks: Teaching Grammar to Basic Writers." Daloz, a writing associate who volunteered to teach a continuing education class at the local joint vocational school (JVS), discusses her efforts to teach English to a group of non-traditional students working toward a G.E.D. She explores the challenges and rewards of teaching writing to such students, documenting her largely unsuccessful efforts to inculcate the rules of grammar in her pupils. For a variety of reasons, including the panic and confusion her students experienced when she asked them to master basic concepts including parts of speech and punctuation, she more or less abandoned her direct approach to teaching grammar and gravitated toward assigning short compositions to her students, hoping to draw on the strengths her students displayed in class conversations. This method proved more effective because, she conjectures, her students "have information they know about, want to convey, and have been conveying in conversation." Happily, she discovered that, when working with subjects about which they were authorities, her students displayed a surprising command over the mechanics and conventions of writing. Based on her JVS teaching, Daloz recommends "tackling grammar through the context of students' own written work" rather than relying on "traditional grammar instruction."

NOTES

[1] In the words of a recent article, writing courses that fail to support student agency often "include the assignment of student writing in the context of childlike practicing, with authoritarian control of the writing situation and the written product [...] with topics that play to the authority of the [teacher] and penalties for those who violate the rules. [...]" (Podis and Podis, 123).

WORKS CITED

Podis, JoAnne, and Leonard Podis. "Pedagogical *In Loco Parentis*: Reflecting on Power and Parental Authority in the Writing Classroom." *College English* 70 (2007): 121–143.

Chapter 12

Perspectives on the Writing Classroom

Leonard A. Podis

Before I start pontificating about what you, as teachers of high school English, ought to be doing to prepare your students for college writing, I feel compelled to point out that I have never taught a day of high school English in my life. It's not that the possibility never crossed my mind. In fact, at one time I thought about it a lot, and, as an undergraduate, I even took most of the courses needed for teacher certification in Ohio. But, as my senior year in college drew near, I lost my nerve. It's clear to me now that one of the main reasons I went on to graduate school—and ultimately to teach in college—is that I was afraid of teaching in high school. Nor was I alone in this mindset. The first classmate I met on the first day of graduate school (who, coincidentally, became my wife) had only recently bailed out of teaching high school English *after* completing her student teaching. I don't, however, want to belabor this issue of the fear of teaching, but merely to point out that in my case, it had to do with insecurity about my ability to motivate people who were *required* to be learners. Suffice it to say that I feel slightly sheepish about telling you all what to do without ever having done it myself. But only slightly sheepish—not sufficiently sheepish to have turned down this great opportunity to work with a committed group of teachers like yourselves.

Now that I've expressed my reservations about advising you on what you should be doing, will I go ahead and advise you anyway? Of course. But I'm not going to do so simply on my own authority. It occurred to me that while *I* am most familiar with college English and *you* are most familiar with high school English, I do have access to a group of people who are relatively familiar with both: the students who are currently taking English classes at Oberlin College, and who, not so long ago, were taking high school English classes. And while Oberlin students are too varied and diverse a group to give any single, definitive response about the teaching of writing, I knew I could count on them as individuals to have strong opinions. So several weeks back I explained to some of my students that I would be conducting this workshop today, and I asked them if, now that they were in college, they might have advice to offer high school English teachers about how best to prepare students for college writing. I also asked several of my colleagues if they would ask their students to respond informally in writing to the same question. I want to begin, then, by transmitting the students' advice to you.

Of course some students were bitter or resentful. Here, after all, was a chance to fire back at the system that for years had held them in thrall. But really, there were not many bitter responses. Most students showed an appreciation for what they *had* been given, and they seemed to comprehend the difficult challenge facing high school English curricula, which, as one student put it, must often "kill five birds with one stone": i.e., literature, composition, grammar, discussion skills, and so on. The points that the Oberlin students raised are really the same points that I intend to stress in this workshop. In their responses, the students repeatedly appealed to their imagined high school English teacher audience to do the following: (1) to make classroom writing more engaging and enjoyable; (2) to emphasize rhetorical flexibility rather than constraining cure-all formulas; (3) to teach the process of drafting and revising more actively; (4) to respond to students' ideas and not just their grammar, form, and usage; and (5) to stay in touch with the process of writing by being active as writers themselves. Here are excerpts from the students' responses:

My high school teachers definitely seemed to emphasize a set formula for writing a well organized paper—i.e., introduction (highlighting subject & three points to be covered), point A, point B, point C, and conclusion (usually a recapitulation of subject & points discussed). Although I think that *suggesting* such a way of organizing a paper is a good thing for beginning writers, it is definitely not enough to bridge the gap between high school & college. My ventures in high school off of this hackneyed formula were often penalized, only to be rewarded and encouraged in college. [...] I would [...] emphasize the need to promote even a little paper writing experimentation & risk taking in the junior & senior years of high school—"mistakes" are okay!

I was fortunate enough to have many excellent English teachers in high school. Perhaps the most beneficial contribution they made to my writing was consistently to support my endeavors. We forget, too often, that writing *anything* is frightening, sometimes even for the advanced high school writer. It is vital that the student feels they can write a paper that is not letter-perfect—teacher expectations need to be reasonable.

I wish there was more encouragement for us to *enjoy* writing. (In high school, writing English papers seemed to be such a burden.)

What I missed in my high school was a process-based [approach]. Revision meant only spell-check, pre-writing meant the introduction. The five-paragraph structure is a good tool as far as it forces students to break down their ideas. But too many teachers treat this structure as the *only* way to write. Thus, students begin to use it as a crutch rather than learning to make their own structures. Teachers need to emphasize *discovery* in writing; for if students are not able to discover, they will never willingly write. The joy from writing is discovering. If I could tell my old English teachers anything, it would be: find out how *you* write & why it brings you fulfillment.

I had a very good English department [in high school], but there is always room for improvement. I never really experienced the multi-draft writing *process* [...] which is of course useful. I learned OK by the product-oriented method but a *bit more* process [would be desirable] ([we did] only *one* paper revision that I can recall *ever*—and that as an emergency measure [because the teacher said] "this paper is very disappointing"). [We did not revise] as a normal and usual part of the syllabus.

I feel very strongly that the structures I was given or told to write with in high school limited my performance of college writing. When I was in high school, I was expected to write essays that followed a strict format. The goal was to follow this format as closely as possible. I was always able to follow it exactly, but this didn't help me with the problem-solving approach I was forced to follow in college. Instead of giving students a format to follow, maybe students and teachers could discuss what formats would work best for any given paper topic and why. Also, if students could at least be exposed to process-oriented writing in high school I think it would increase their chances of being multi-draft writers in college.

I know that my high school English teachers worked with us extensively on the development of a thesis of our own—I think this helped lots, though I began to be under the impression that I needed a highly developed thesis before I began writing. Let your students know that writing is a difficult thing; it can also be one of the most effective means of communication. But have fun with writing, too, to keep students interested. Challenge them. I remember one teacher who structured an assignment so rigidly—giving us a topic to write about and a model paper to follow—that we all lost interest in the writing process.

I liked it when we exchanged papers among ourselves in my high school English classes (I still like it.). In conversation over the papers, ideas evolved in an easy, comfortable rhythm. The exchange relocated the ability/authority to judge [our writing] from teacher to peer & so, by association, to writer. As a result, we students felt *worthy* of our endeavors & [...] *excited* about them. I find that writer & writing suffer most when writing is not *talked* about. [...] High school teachers need to *make a big deal* about student writing: Discuss it; ask questions about it; encourage students to talk about it; examine it; get excited about it!

[In high school] they never taught us how to write. They taught grammar, but beyond its essence, grammar is useless. They just made us write, mostly expository or critical stuff on books. Rarely creative. Then they graded it & it was put away.

Never re-writes, never second chances for better grades. We did not learn any style or enthusiasm. It was all just assignments for grades & nothing else.

[My advice would be] respond to ideas, don't respond to [the mechanics of] writing. [...] There was nothing I was less interested in during high school than what teachers had to say about the mechanics of my writing. Not that technical problems are not an issue for high school writers, but they should be made secondary. By first showing the student the strength of his/her ideas, you have established the ground to go on and illustrate the weaknesses of his/her presentation. If you attack presentation first and foremost, you are shooting yourself in the foot. Remember that good writing comes out of self-confidence. The teachers who have really sparked me are those who go one step further, [who] respond outside of the text of my essay, and show me how my ideas fit with the ideas of other thinkers. I had one teacher who would write a page of his own creative [thoughts], expressing ideas sparked in him by my essay [...] what a way to build confidence and demand that I take my own thinking further. [...]

Well, I honestly feel that the students I've just quoted are a tough act to follow, and in many ways I don't think anyone can improve on the kinds of advice they've offered. But perhaps I can build on it, elaborate on it, translate it into more specific plans for action in the classroom.

I want to proceed by going back to reconsider for a moment the assignment I took on when I originally agreed to do this workshop. Anne Gerbner of Germantown Friends School, who was kind enough to invite me here today, suggested that one of the most useful things I could do would be to help you all to think further about how you might best prepare your students for the writing tasks they would encounter in college. And I think that the student opinions we've just heard are intended to do exactly that: suggest how high school English teachers can better prepare their students for what is to come in college. But I want to emphasize something about the very nature of preparing people for the next stage in their careers as writers. Thinking about what the students have said and also reflecting on my own observations of the attitudes towards writing that first-year students bring with them to Oberlin, I have concluded that, in a very real sense, the best way to prepare students for what is to come at the *next* level is to engage them fully in pursuing and enjoying writing at their *present* level.

Several years ago, Joe Williams, the well-known professor of rhetoric and linguistics at the University of Chicago, led a workshop on the teaching of writing at Oberlin, and something he said about the issue of preparation has stuck with me. He said that in his years of experience in consulting with teachers of writing at all levels of the curriculum, he was struck by the fact that teachers universally complained that the teachers who had their students before they did had failed in their obligation to prepare them properly. He said that this was true of the high school teachers he had worked with: they complained that the primary school teachers hadn't properly prepared their students for high school writing. He said that it was true of college professors, as well; his colleagues at the University of Chicago, for example, were routinely bitter about the supposed failures of high school teachers in this regard. He said that it was true of graduate and professional school faculty, as well, who, for example, were routinely bitter about the apparent failure of his colleagues at the University of Chicago to prepare their students for the challenges of, say, legal writing in law school. But it didn't stop there. Having served often as a consultant on legal writing to law firms, Williams was able to observe that practicing lawyers were also routinely bitter about the failure of law school professors to prepare their students for the rigors of the legal writing they would actually need to do on the job. And beyond the legal profession there is of course the judiciary, many of whose members start out as lawyers. Professor Williams was also privileged to have consulted with the faculty of the national State Supreme Court Justices academy (yes, there apparently is a school for State Supreme Court Justices in Nevada). The faculty members in charge of teaching the novice State Supreme Court judges how to write judicial opinions were, not surprisingly, quite vocal about the deplorable instruction in judicial writing that these judges had received on the job.

Professor Williams' conclusion, quite sensibly, I think, was that any person entering a new arena of writing may properly be considered a novice in that arena and should therefore not be expected to know how to perform well in the new setting without a good deal of direct instruction at the new level. For whatever reason, the people entrusted with giving that instruction have traditionally not seen the matter in this way. Rather they have often felt that students coming to them should already have been taught how to perform the writing tasks needed at the new level. But in fact, the weight of current research and scholarship on writing supports Joe Williams' view that one generally needs to have entered a certain writing community before one can learn to function properly within it.

Since I strongly agree with Professor Williams' view, I accept that it is the responsibility of the college writing teacher to teach college writing. Indeed, most Oberlin students arrive for their first year with a good command of writing skills. It seems to me that any deficiencies that might appear to exist in their preparation are, ironically, not due to any lack of preparation, but rather are the result of the very efforts that are so well-intended to prepare them for college writing. In some cases students' conception of college writing appears to be a narrow, constraining, authoritarian one. Many of the incoming students I work with, despite their obvious intellect and verbal facility, come to college terrified of writing. They appear to have developed the view that writing is a dangerous and uncomfortable activity, akin perhaps to tightrope-walking, certainly not an exercise in learning, discovery, self-expression, communication, and problem-solving. It is something they are compelled to do by and for someone else, not something they do by their own initiative or to fulfill their own needs. It is not a vehicle through which they might inform or persuade others but rather a means whereby the world of school acts upon them and keeps them in line.

Lest I seem to be hypocritically joining Joe Williams' many groups of teachers who complain about what the teachers before them have failed to do, I want to reiterate that I don't believe the high school teachers of students who have gone on to attend Oberlin have failed to prepare them. If there is any problem, I would say that it is just the reverse. Students seem sometimes to have suffered from a kind of narrowly conceived overpreparation that has left them fearful of, suspicious of, even hostile toward school writing situations. In many cases students arrive at college having absolutely no desire to write, despite having rather clear scholarly orientations in other respects.

Here are some specific concerns distilled from my experiences with first year students. Again, I don't offer them as indictments of anyone in particular but rather as factual observations. In my own teaching, I anticipate these problems and try to deal with them.

I've observed over the years that nearly all of my first year composition students report that they have been forbidden ever to use "I" in a paper. Many also say that they have been discouraged from including anything resembling an opinion in a paper because they have been told repeatedly that they don't yet have the authority to do so. A sizable proportion of students have been given a whole list of words with which they are not permitted to begin sentences. Most are confused about essay structure, alternately clinging to the five-paragraph theme model and expressing contempt for it. No matter what the writing situation, whether the topic is serious or humorous, scholarly or journalistic, scientific or autobiographical, they appear to believe that there is one correct way to write a paper and seem confused by the possibility that it might be all right to write one paper, say, with a thesis in the opening paragraph and another paper with a thesis in the conclusion or without an explicit thesis at all. Above all, they are certain that they are not very good at writing. Teachers have repeatedly torn their papers apart, often using the justification that that is what college professors would do to them. And in fact many college professors do tear their papers apart, sometimes because the papers are in fact weak, and other times because they want to prepare college students by showing them what they are sure graduate school professors or supervisors on the job will do to their writing.

So how might one teach *against* such tendencies? Again, I believe it's important *not* to simply view oneself as the teacher of a service course, a course that grimly, dutifully, and specifically readies students for some other, presumably more important, educational activity down the road. That is, writing teachers can best serve their students by treating writing as a primary intellectual and social activity, as a means whereby students can concentrate on their immediate needs, interests, and concerns. Successful writing courses at whatever level are those that focus on providing students with the motivation and opportunity to engage in discovery, social interaction, and real communication and problem solving. Such courses aim to get students to enjoy writing, or at least to appreciate its rewards and challenges, not merely its frustrations. Students in high school should, I believe, learn to develop not only skill in written expression but *confidence* in their own ability to write. They need to feel the rewards of using writing to express themselves. They need to experience what writing can do for them and for their audiences. They should come to understand how they can learn from or be entertained by the writing of their peers, and how their peers and their teachers can likewise learn from or be entertained by their writing. Of course they should also try their hand at more scholarly forms of writing, such as critiques and literary criticism. But it is imperative that they develop rhetorical flexibility.

Scholarly writing has an important place, but we should not base all our teaching on it. As Peter Elbow has said, "life is long and college is short." (136) By the same token, we should not base all our teaching on the personal essay. When we do teach scholarly writing, we should shy away from giving the impression that there is a single "correct" way to do it. In college, a philosophy paper will be very different from a literature paper, and literature papers, too, will vary greatly depending upon the situation and audience. But students will, if all goes well, learn the specifics of writing for different disciplines when they take college courses in those disciplines. What they need to begin to appreciate in high school is the great diversity of approaches that one can take to writing. What they need to do is to think of themselves as *writers*, writers who are immersed in the world of the readers and writers who immediately surround them, not writers who are in danger of drowning amid the expectations of some hazily defined and intimidating world of readers and writers that may or may not figure in their futures.

What sorts of teaching and learning strategies might enable high school students to develop not only ability as writers but also confidence and pride in that ability? Again, as members of those high school writing communities, you probably know better than I. The Oberlin students' advice cited earlier is, I think, an excellent place to start. In concluding this part of our workshop this afternoon, I'll briefly sum up three of the main teaching strategies we've touched on so far:

1. Teach writing as a vehicle for discovery. This may mean downplaying the traditional emphasis on formulating either a precise, carved-in-stone thesis statement or a perfectly predictive outline before the writing of a paper. It will almost certainly mean incorporating multiple drafts and revisions into paper assignments and deadline schemes, in order to allow students to experience the process of retailoring a paper to accommodate discoveries, sudden insights, or changes in course that have occurred since the process of writing the paper was begun.

2. Teach writing as a form of social interaction. Many recent thinkers on language stress that knowledge in general tends to be socially constructed in a process of give and take among speakers, listeners, writers, and readers. Teaching toward this idea will usually mean that students should collaborate on their papers in progress, whether it takes the form of pairing off in class to exchange and comment on developing drafts or forming into larger peer response groups to give feedback to writers. Of course students should be encouraged to revise their work in light of any useful feedback they receive.

3. Teach writing as a form of genuine communication. Writers tend to feel much better about what they're doing if they believe that their readers are looking forward to learning something from what they have to say. They tend to respond most poorly when they feel as though they are simply going through the motions of telling readers what they already know: there's no urgency, no spark of life. In the classroom, using this teaching strategy will affect the kinds of assignments you give as well as the types of audience-reader situations you set up. In other words, you should attempt to give assignments that will enable or allow students to inform, enlighten, persuade, or entertain their readers, yourself included. Be wary of assignments that put students in the position of trying to figure out some right answer that you already know. Likewise be wary of assignments with rigidly set tasks that exist mainly to allow you to evaluate students' performance against that of their peers, rather than allowing them to use writing to explore a subject of interest or to inform a curious audience. Such fixed types of assignments may offer students external motivation, such as the opportunity to earn the praise or avoid the wrath or contempt of an authority figure, but they offer students very little *intrinsic* incentive to write. As an alternative to those kinds of assignments, consider giving assignments that will result in your being able to learn something from reading the writer's work. In order to embolden students further to attempt real communication with others in their writing, you will want to have students read their work to each other in pairs, groups, and full class sessions. But it is crucial that such sessions play out as supportive draft-reading-and-response workshops rather than as typical "tear-the-writer's-grammar-apart-to-show-off-for-the-teacher" exercises.

Before we break into small groups for the next phase of our workshop, let me stress the importance of encouraging and allowing your students themselves to take the lead in soliciting responses to their writing (from both yourself and their peers). In my experience, the best way to achieve such a situation is by asking them to develop a set of questions to submit with each paper, questions that they themselves would like their readers to address. Such questions should be specific, if possible (e.g., a question like "Did you understand the reasons for my unhappiness with my former history teacher on page 2?" would be preferable to "Was my paper clear?"). They should also be genuinely motivated by writers' curiosity about their handling of their topics, as opposed to being stock questions about form or style (e.g., a question like "Did the ending seem like just a forced 'happy ending'?" would be preferable to "Does it flow okay at the end?"). When students themselves want to ask the questions about their own work, something very productive usually starts to happen in the classroom. You may find that you need to be patient in teaching your students exactly how to ask good questions, since it is probably not something they have much practice in, but I think that the rewards for succeeding in that respect can be great. Indeed, the kind of preparation that begins to put high school writers in charge of their own work in this way will be useful not only in readying them for college writing but for writing in all spheres.

WORKS CITED

Elbow, Peter. "Reflections on Academic Discourse: How It Relates to Freshmen and Colleagues." *College English* 53 (1991): 135–155.

Chapter 13

No Answers: Interrogating "Truth" in Writing

Noelle Howey

There are those who would say that creative writing—or any writing—cannot be taught. To some degree, the naysayers are correct. Creativity in whatever form it takes cannot be learned from a review sheet in the way that one learns Spanish vocabulary words. There are few absolutes in art or writing. And for every rule set up in creative writing, one can find an exception that worked (e.g., the experimentation of Gertrude Stein). Thus, those professors who establish themselves in writing workshops as the ultimate disseminators of Truth rarely illuminate the writing process and are actually more likely to inhibit it. Yet, fortunately, there also exist professors who see themselves as facilitators of writing—they seek not to proselytize students to their theories or subjugate them to their wills, but to assist students in developing their own theories and approaches. In my studies in creative writing, I encountered two professors, Ms. A and Mr. B, whose teaching techniques, respectively, exemplify prescriptive and facilitative approaches.

Ms. A is a firm believer in the old paradigm hierarchy in which a teacher is the Authority and the students are empty vessels waiting to be filled top-full with Knowledge. This hierarchy is presumptuous in two ways: one, it assumes that there is an ultimate truth behind writing, and two, it assumes that the teacher, by virtue of an M.F.A. or similar credential, is the only qualified vehicle for receiving and preaching this truth. For example, Ms. A once said that all "good" literature must move in a circular fashion: "Linearity is death," she proclaimed. By making such an absolute statement, she was attempting to force us to adopt her theory without first filtering it through our own minds or considering it in the light of our own experiences as writers and readers.

However, various members of the class did not meekly submit to her coercive version of truth. In an effort to broaden her rigid conception of good writing, we suggested names of various writers, from Charles Dickens to

Zora Neale Hurston, who had written linearly. But, rather than responding directly to our challenge, Ms. A. dodged the issue and relied on her authority as leader of the class. Unfazed, she quickly reiterated her point that all good literature was written in circular fashion and changed the subject. Her assertions led us to draw the immediate conclusion that either (a) the writers we had adduced as evidence to refute her contention only *appeared* to have written linearly but had actually written circularly, or (b) these renowned writers were mere incompetents rather than creators of "good" literature. The ongoing effect of this type of exchange was even more detrimental. It was part of a process through which Ms. A felt she had to undermine our search for understanding in order to assert and validate her own views.

Mr. B, on the other hand, established a dialogue through which he facilitated our searches for our own conceptions of what writing should be. He commenced the first class by asking us what we felt our own aesthetics of writing were and what assumptions we brought to our writing processes. This exercise established the structure of the class as being based on a free exchange of ideas among equals. As we went around the room, each of us attempted to define what we considered "good writing." Mr. B did not pass judgment on any of our definitions; he did not seek to coerce us into accepting his theories. In short, he portrayed himself as more of a resource than a transcendent Authority.

The open workshop atmosphere cultivated by Mr. B yielded many rewards. At the beginning of the course, we all seemed to have fairly rigid judgments about what constituted good literature (e.g., "I mainly like poems that are really rough and violent"; "I like archaic poems"; "I like metered verse."). Early on, our class discussions rarely rose to a substantive level because we were so preoccupied with being judgmental about literary merit. Yet, by the end of the course, after having been exposed to so many different types of "good" writing, we often praised the kind of works we had initially denounced. By allowing each of us to expand our frames of reference, Mr. B helped us to become less evaluative and more constructive in our comments. We felt freer to express our ideas because we knew we did not risk censure by the professor or our classmates.

In Ms. A's class, however, censure became a tool whereby we examined each other's work. Class format was generally structured as follows: One student would begin to read her writing aloud; then, Ms. A would stop her after every second or third sentence. Each time, she would expound for ten minutes on why the student's work violated Ms. A's rules of literature, or, even worse, she would enlist the aid of other students in this destructive process by exclaiming something like "What's wrong with Raquel's sentence, Craig?" Thus, Ms. A forced us to tailor our comments—and our writing—to suit her rigid conceptions of literature.

Often the "sacred rule broken" would be merely a word choice Ms. A did not like or a small (though hardly insurmountable) leap in logic. In the case of the sample scenario given above, for instance, if, when Craig was called on by Ms. A to censure Raquel's wording, he could not guess what Ms. A was getting at, Craig would then be castigated for his "ignorance." Thus, out of fear, we generally tried our hardest to slip into her mindset, to comply with her dogmatic theories. Some of us even adopted her pugilistic and intimidating demeanor, perhaps in an effort to feel more comfortable in such a constraining atmosphere. As might be expected, such blind obedience and deferential compliance did not generate much real thought about what *we* believed writing was or should be. In fact, in Ms. A's class it seemed that independent thinking about writing was tantamount to subversion, a behavior certainly not to be exhibited lightly in a college writing workshop. Fortunately, a few of us were subversive by nature.

The subversiveness of a few students notwithstanding, Ms. A's fixation on her theories of writing had tangible effects on our writing for class assignments. Speaking only for myself, I realize that I unconsciously began trying to please her rather than myself or my peers. Though I railed against her theories and condemned her easy value judgments, I found her stylistic rules creeping into my discourse. My sentences became more clipped, my tone more distant, my fictional settings more obscure—all tendencies that she advocated. I also began to see similar affectations of style and structure infiltrating the works of my peers. For example, after Ms. A decreed that "southern accents make your work sound deeper," several Mississippi Delta stories (including my own) began appearing

Yet students typically pick up influences from a teacher; what made this situation an "infiltration" rather than a "learning process"? The difference, I think, lay in our intentions as writers. I would guess that many students, like myself, were not emulating her style or adopting her theories because we had interrogated them—alongside our own conceptions—and had found her views valuable in forming our own interpretations. Instead, I believe that some of us adapted our writing (in differing degrees) precisely because we did not have the confidence to challenge her on paper. Confidence, after all, requires a modicum of experience, and few of us would say that, after nineteen or twenty years of living, we have solid conceptions of what we think writing is or should be. Ms. A, rather than recognizing this conformist tendency and seeking to challenge it by questioning our motivations for accepting her theories, only questioned us when we diverged from those theories.

Mr. B, on the other hand, encouraged experimentation in both our writings and our aesthetic conceptions. His goal was not to form little Mr. B's out of us nor to force us to come to his conclusions about writing in general. His only request seemed to be: "Have enough of an open mind so that you will be able to accept the influence/advice which you feel is applicable." For example, often students (such as myself) would ask him whether he thought a piece was "good" or whether he thought a certain writing process was "correct." He always shied away from giving us easy answers. He was not evasive, certainly, but he urged us to draw our own conclusions and only *then* to filter in his perspective. Since he valued our opinions, we valued his more strongly. He taught his own theories by allowing us to come to them freely, out of curiosity rather than intimidation.

Indeed, the writing for that workshop was never monolithic, never altered to please the professor or fit into his framework. Many students, like myself, experimented a great deal with different topics, themes, and voices. Mr. B always provided support for our endeavors, even when they needed a bit more work. Thus, we felt we could go out on a limb in our writing, and if we fell, there would be a cushion. Through this supportive workshop setting, I discovered myriad surprises about my writing. I learned that I could write love poems, political poems, metaphoric poems. My writing process was allowed to branch out into true discovery because I was given some freedom.

However, it is important to note that there were aspects of Mr. B's workshop that sometimes obscured the learning process. Certain students abused the privilege of independent work by refusing to accept criticism, basing their resistance on the excuse that there were no absolutes in writing. For example, in response to the class's observation that her poem seemed perhaps overly obscure, one student writer asserted, "Well, I understand what happens in my poem, and I don't think it needs any work." She remained defensive and closed to criticism throughout the semester. To his credit, Mr. B recognized that this type of abuse was occurring, and he attempted to make such students understand that they didn't have to accept *all* the criticism they received but needed to be open to others' suggestions. In short, Mr. B was aware that his teaching method was not foolproof, but at least he attempted to remedy the problems.

Mr. B was aware that neither writing nor the teaching of writing has absolute "rights" or "wrongs." He realized that often when students ask teachers questions about how to write, they do not *really* want definitive answers. Any attempt to offer the final word about a process as open-ended, mystifying, and thrilling as writing would be inadequate and incomplete.

Of course, this is not to say that a professor cannot set any guidelines or indicate what works in a piece of writing and what does not. However, Ms. A needed to realize that her opinion was only one in a huge canon of thought and criticism. She did not have to change her own theories, but she should have allowed her students to develop their own. For example, one teaching technique she frequently used was to read aloud stories that illustrated her theories. To facilitate our learning, she could have asked each of us to read aloud a story that we thought fit in with our aesthetic.

To encourage us to challenge her mind set, she might have permitted a question-and-answer period after each point or theory she presented to us. She also could have asked us to write down three questions regarding her philosophy of writing for each class discussion period. The result of Ms. A's using such teaching techniques, I believe, would have been to allow her to maintain her own ideas while assisting us in our own thought processes. Importantly, by employing such techniques, she could have emphasized to every one of us that our opinions about writing were also valid.

Even if one maintains that creative writing cannot be truly *taught*, it is still important that professors approach writing with an open mind, for students will emulate them. If professors would interrogate their assumptions about writing and openly encourage students to follow suit, the resulting improvement in students' confidence about their identity as writers would be well worth the time and effort.

Chapter 14

Glazed Looks and Panic Attacks: Teaching Grammar to Basic Writers

Kate Daloz

I will never forget the day I tried to explain quotation marks to the Adult Basic Education class I teach at the Lorain County Joint Vocational School (JVS). It was early in the semester, and I had recently looked at the exam my students would eventually have to take, had a quick panic attack at seeing the distance between where they were in terms of grammar and where they would have to be in order to pass the test, and decided to start out at a steady pace through grammar until they had learned all the necessary rules. We covered capitals at the beginnings of sentences and punctuation at the ends without a problem. I faltered at commas and decided to move straight to quotation marks, which seemed innocent enough.

Not so. I had never thought about what quotation marks actually denoted, but I recognized quickly that they involved a more complex concept than I had realized. There are actually two layers of text with quotations: what the writer says, and what the writer says someone else says, as in the following example:

> Rita was always struggling to overcome her boredom. "I am going to the zoo," she announced one day. "I want to see the elephants."

The more I tried to explain how quotation marks are used, standing at the chalkboard, the deeper I dug myself into a hole as my students drifted farther and farther from understanding, their confidence plummeting.

It was their falling confidence that was the biggest blow. I consider my most important responsibility as a teacher of basic education students to be the task of undoing some of the damage done by the last round of schooling they went through. Since all my students are nontraditional and have in some way been failed by schools or schooling and have been led to drop out for some reason or other, they tend to have negative attitudes about schooling and about their own ability to learn, especially the older ones, who may have spent up to forty years at a level of functional illiteracy. At the same time, they have made a choice to come back to school (except for those forced to return as part of a parole agreement), and are therefore willing to make an effort toward their education in a way they were not the first time through the school system. In spite of their commitment, however, for most students it takes a huge effort to make it to class for three hours twice a week. Many of them come off long shifts doing physical work, and they are exhausted before they even get to the classroom. They need to feel like the time they are sacrificing is worth their effort.

It has become very clear to me that you can't teach anything to people who think they are dumb or incapable of learning. Students who feel smart and who can see the improvements they are making will improve faster than those who do not. So it's for an entirely pedagogical reason that my first duty as a teacher is to help my students feel smart and capable. I start my classes with math as the students trickle in, and their confidence rises as they move steadily through long division to fractions and decimals, one page of problems at a time. With math, they improve every day, learning something solid and concrete. After math, I have them write for fifteen minutes. While this was initially a chore, almost everyone looks forward to it now, and as their compositions grow longer, their confidence increases as well.

The class gets along well together, and we'll often be laughing and joking, relaxed about the schoolwork—until we get to grammar. Anyone who's ever tried teaching knows the sinking feeling that comes with watching a learner's eyes glaze over as the explanation of the subject goes nowhere. As I try to explain the rules of grammar, my class goes quiet—they are suddenly back in *school* school, the one that failed them, the place they used to be stupid. And I am, too, for that matter, as my confidence drops along with theirs, seeing them lose interest and the confidence I worked so hard to build up. Their insecurity feeds off mine, and vice-versa, and the cycle continues. Inasmuch as building confidence is my first priority, those moments of decline are, from a pedagogical standpoint, too big a sacrifice to make.

At the same time, my students are basic writers who need to learn to compose functional sentences using correct grammar to eventually pass the G.E.D. exam. I had thought, at first, that presenting grammar in terms of rules would work best—it worked for math, after all, and my students were cruising through fractions at a pace that satisfied them and me, their confidence bolstered by the idea that they only had to learn a few rules that they could apply to any problem I gave them. Unfortunately it didn't work the same way for grammar. Every time I presented a rule and then asked them for examples to illustrate it, they offered up an exception I had forgotten to mention. For example, one day I told the students, "If a sentence is complete, you should be able to find a subject and a verb." One student asked, "How about, 'Go away!'" Of course in this case the sentence is "imperative" and the subject is understood as "You," but my tortured explanation of this did not do much for anyone's confidence, causing the students to doubt the soundness of what I was trying to tell them.

While I'll be the first to admit that one of the reasons I resist teaching grammar in terms of formal rules is that it scares me, my gut reaction that it is not the most effective method—and might even be detrimental—has been backed up by scholars of composition studies. One scholar, for example, cites a study which found that "the formal study of grammar, whether trans-formational or traditional, improved neither writing nor control over surface corrections," and adds that "the small differences [that] appeared in some minor conventions favoring the [transformational group] [...] were more than offset by the less positive attitudes they showed towards their English studies." (Hartwell, 107) In the case of at-risk students such as those in my JVS class, the implications of this study are chilling. These basic education students, more than most others, cannot afford the "less positive attitudes" toward their studies. If they are made to feel stupid in a classroom again, they may well never return.

One reason that grammar carries such a risk of making people feel inadequate is that so many concepts are necessary for even basic punctua-tion. The day I finally decided to try my hand at explaining commas, I duti-fully took out the list of rules for comma placement and began. "You put commas around any phrase that modifies a noun," I read off the sheet. "What's a noun?" asked Philip.[1] And we started again. As Hartwell points out, "In order to get to the advice, 'as a rule, do not write a sentence frag-ment,' the student must master the following learning tasks: recognizing verbs, recognizing subjects and verbs, recognizing all parts of speech, recog-nizing phrases and subordinate clauses, recognizing main clauses and types of sentences." (120) While these are certainly important components of understanding sentences, my feeling is that not all of these tasks need to be made explicit. English speakers use all kinds of complex constructions when they speak; requiring students to think in terms of "subject," "predicate," "subordinate clause," and "indirect object" masks the fact that they have a daily control over those elements and represents them as yet more daunting skills to be mastered.

Another major part of my hesitation to teach grammar in terms of rules is that I myself almost never call upon classroom-learned rules in my own daily writing. This is one reason that I balked at teaching commas—while I feel like I am a perfectly functional comma user, I could not for the life of me recite a complete list of official rules for comma usage, and neither could any other writer I know. In my understanding, commas are one of the more subjective aspects of writing (consider the optional comma following the opening phrase of this sentence). Consequently, I sometimes temper the comma suggestions I offer as a tutor at the Writing Center with a disclaimer that I'm only offering my opinion. I feel more comfortable explaining the rules for semi-colons and colons, but I never used a semi-colon in a piece of writing until I read John Irving, who uses them liberally; colons came with a group of essays I read for a creative writing class last semester. But I suppose the point here is that I use these elements confidently without having been taught "the rules" for them. Most striking was the moment when I took a second look at the grammar section of the G.E.D. test and realized that I had answered all the questions by ear, without applying a single rule. I know how to punctuate because I learned from reading and from being corrected by knowledgeable writers. Why should I expect differently of my students?

I started to think about the difference between my JVS students' composition writing, which boosted their confidence, and the grammar lessons that undermined it. I had begun having my students write as a way of making them feel comfortable with sentences and expressing themselves through the written word. As part of my confidence-boosting tactic, for the first few months I never corrected any of their compositions. I made sure they understood that there would be no grade, no corrections and that they were to pay attention to content rather than the prose itself. While occasionally I had to have the writer read the piece aloud because I couldn't decipher the spellings, as people felt more comfortable writing and began to realize they would not be judged on the quality of their compositions, many mistakes began to fall away by themselves. Around this time, I came to the realization I mentioned above, that the drawbacks of teaching grammar rules outweighed the benefits. I also realized that as people became more invested in what they wrote, it was important to make them feel that their compositions were real, legitimate pieces of writing and not merely a classroom exercise. They knew they had made spelling and punctuation mistakes; it wasn't fair to them as writers to let their pieces stand uncorrected. I decided to use the compositions as starting points for grammar lessons.

The best compositions, I found, were those that came out of conversations we started in class: What would you do if you won the lottery? Will the Indians win the World Series? One evening, Greg told me about the graffiti mural he had spent four hours on over the weekend, so I made him write about it instead of telling me. Bobby writes every composition about his four-wheelers, the races he enters and the amount of money he needs to earn in order to buy a car. All these things—opinions, desires, hobbies—are subjects that the students are absolute authorities on. Speaking, they know this. My class could easily spend the entire period in conversation. Beginning a subject in a medium in which they already have confidence—speaking— makes the shift to writing, where they generally don't feel they have the confidence, much easier. They have information they know well, want to convey, and have been conveying in conversation. I just ask them to convey the same thing another way: through writing.

Because people felt more invested in the subject matter, they tended to be more open to correction without having the idea of "mistakes" undermine their self-confidence. In fact, I was shocked more than once at the grammar skills that my students displayed when working within the context of their pieces. Once I was sitting with Andrew, helping him punctuate a story so that it conveyed the effects he wanted it to. In a piece of dialogue, the character's sentence trailed off. I was about to suggest an ellipsis when he said, "Couldn't I put those little dot thingies?" If I had stood in front of the class and presented an ellipsis as an abstract concept, I doubt that Andrew would have thought to apply it to his story, but he remembered the necessary punctuation for his desired effect, drawing, no doubt, from something he had read. Ever since Bobby started to get interested in what he writes, he has begun asking me how to spell things on the blackboard. We went over run-on sentences and sentence fragments, again in the context of individual papers, and while I won't claim dramatic improvement, the length and natural flow of my students' prose have been improving. I would credit simple writing practice more than specific grammar instruction for these changes.

One of the techniques recommended to writing associates in the Teaching and Tutoring Writing course has actually come in handier in my JVS classroom than it has at the Writing Center: getting the students to read their compositions aloud. It helps me, especially when the spelling or handwriting is hard to decipher, but it is also one of the best ways to point out mistakes. Often people will naturally correct a verb tense they had written wrong as they are speaking, and my job as teacher is not to correct them from a place of authority but to point out their almost typographical error—they still know what is correct, they simply wrote down the wrong thing.

Emphasizing the similarities between speaking and writing seemed like a good way to make people relax about their command over the English language. My students are all native English speakers, and I kept telling them, "If you speak English, you can write it." I still think this is mainly true, but it's important to remember that some people's English is farther from "standard written English" than others' is. The English I speak, for example, with an accent and vocabulary more or less like that of news anchors, is probably what most people refer to as "standard English." For me, and others like me who speak as I do, the distance from speaking to writing in culturally accepted terms is not very great. In fact, my family is probably an excessive case: on top of being reprimanded when I came home saying "ain't" after playing with the kids on the farm down the road, my family corrected even such minor details in speech as "lie" and "lay," "who" and "whom," and "to she and I." I now regard those "corrections" as antiquated forms of elitism, but it means that even the minor details of grammar were of concern in my household. Clearly for many of my students, the distance between the way they speak and what is acceptable in writing is often greater than it is for me.

One of the most striking places where I notice this is in Bobby's compositions. Bobby is a local boy of sixteen who likes to race four-wheelers and dirt bikes. His compositions, while showing major improvement over his first attempts, are still full of what any composition teacher would regard as major grammatical and spelling mistakes. I noticed, however, as I had him read an essay aloud to me, that his attempts at spelling were actually quite calculated. Here is an excerpt from one of his latest pieces:

> I mest up 1 axal on my wheres [wheels]. We tock them to the shop to get fix it is gone coss my cousin 250.00 to get it fix. It is gone coss me 375.00 to get my fix.

When the piece is read silently, it looks as though Bobby simply has hopeless spelling and grammatical problems. When it is read out loud, however, the similarity between the way Bobby speaks and the way he chose to spell major words becomes very clear. In Bobby's speech, the "t" in "cost" is almost silent, and thus it makes perfect sense for him to spell it "coss." "Gone" and "fix" are not verb tense mistakes but misspellings of "going" and "fixed," also both based on Bobby's pronunciation, as are "mest" (for "messed") and "my" (for "mine"). Bobby is anything but stupid, and he is not lazy. His spelling, while not following standard, accepted conventions, nonetheless follows an unwritten rule: write the word like you say the word.

While I wouldn't propose total relativity in terms of spelling and grammatical rules, I think this is an important place to bring up the issues raised by Dennis Baron in "Why Do Academics Continue to Insist on 'Proper' English?" Baron writes, "Even as we celebrate cultural difference in American history, society, and literature, we fear and reject diversity in the American language where 'correctness' and standardization remain the academic goals." (B1) Referring to "Standard" spelling and grammar actually implies the spelling and grammar closest to the spoken "standard English"—that English used by the people in power. Excessive clinging to rules of a grammar that is not in use by every sector of a population can be viewed—as in the example of my family—as an elitist attempt to hold on to that power.

All this is interesting to explore, but it doesn't finally have too much practical application to my students. Most of them are not primarily interested in the injustice of their subaltern status as English speakers. They want to pass the G.E.D. exam, get their high school diploma, and reap the benefits that education provides in our society. Recognition of the social factors (certainly classist, if not also at times racist) that go into questions of grammatical "error," even if not made political, at least helps the teacher figure out how best to help the students.

Even beyond the requirements of the exam, writers need to use some sorts of conventions to convey what they intend. For example, in the first draft of a story, Andrew appeared to go far outside of narrative convention in a way I found creative. However, going over the story with him, I realized that I had simply misinterpreted his intentions. For example, at one point in the dialogue, Andrew wrote:

> Who are you im Zeke, I own an old shake just yonder on the other side of that dere hill. That's ok. DAD well how much 20.00 a day

I had initially interpreted the "DAD" in all capital letters to be almost like the dialogue markers that playwrights use to indicate a change in speakers (as in "DAD: Well, how much?") This would have been an interesting use of narrative technique. What he had intended, however, was a piece of dialogue that should have been punctuated, "DAD!" as spoken by one of the other characters. All of this is a circuitous way of saying that even as beginning writers should be given credit for the inherent intelligence of what they write, they, like any other writers, still need conventional notation to accurately convey their ideas.

Having begun with a rejection of traditional methods of grammar instruction, I should attempt to propose concrete alternatives. My initial reaction was to reject chalkboard-lecture methods altogether and to recommend helping people learn through increased exposure to reading as the fundamental way to help broaden their choices of discourse, syntax, and proper punctuation. I still think that reading a variety of texts and styles is the most valuable background for any writer at any level. However, my experience as a writing associate has shown me the importance of at least some work with the conventions of grammar and usage. For example, I recently tutored a student at the writing center, helping her with a paper that was full of grammatical mistakes, misspellings, sentence fragments, and run-on sentences. She is a native English speaker enrolled in college classes that require a heavy reading load that she apparently has no trouble handling. She said she had attended an alternative school where the students were not taught grammar and that she and her friends from the school have never developed the writing skills necessary for college-level classes. Based on her example, it would seem that simply reading without learning at least some guidelines of sentence construction is not enough. Additionally, the problem presented to non-traditional students like my JVS pupils is that they simply do not have time to read. I kept telling Philip, a sixty-five-year-old man struggling with his reading, that nothing would help him more than sheer practice. He finally told me, "You know, I work all day, I come home, I want to relax. Reading is not relaxing for me." He probably speaks for many.

With these cautions in mind, I do believe that tackling grammar through the context of students' own written work is the best alternative, as it keeps the concepts of grammar relevant and not fully outside of something they already know. By helping students to become invested in their writings, we stand the best chance of encouraging them to embrace the need for correct grammar as a necessary tool for conveying ideas to readers. The rules and conventions still apply, but by not making them into overly abstract concepts, teachers and students can all come closer to avoiding the glazed looks and panic attacks that seem to go hand-in-hand, at least in my JVS classroom, with traditional grammar instruction.

NOTES

[1] Names have been changed.

WORKS CITED

Baron, Dennis. "Why Do Academics Continue to Insist on 'Proper' English?" *Chronicle of Higher Education,* 1 July, 1992, B1–2.

Hartwell, Patrick. "Grammar, Grammars, and the Teaching of Grammar." *College English* 47 (1985): 105–127.

Section Five

Writer's Block

In working with student writers, teachers and tutors inevitably encounter those who are unable to proceed with their writing or who compose with only the greatest difficulty and anxiety. Authorities on writer's block have sometimes drawn a distinction between merely *anxious* writers and genuinely *blocking* writers, and this distinction may be important in considering what approach to take with particular tutees. However, in our experience, it is also useful to think of writer's block not as an absolute category, but as existing in degrees, such that students who are finally successful in overcoming their anxieties in order to write may still be considered as having "writer's block."

Another point to consider in working with blocking writers is that practically anyone who has ever faced the blank page or screen has at some time or other experienced writer's block. Thus, while writer's block nearly always presents itself as a serious problem, it is a problem of a different order of magnitude for someone who encounters it routinely than for someone who only occasionally runs into a dead end while writing. Tutees who are in the throes of writer's block may be upset or even panic-stricken, and one way that tutors and teachers can offer assurance is by being frank about their own experiences with writer's block. In the case of perennial blockers, however, this technique may not be as effective as it is with occasional blockers.

It has become common to define writer's block as a condition that mainly applies to students who are stymied for reasons other than a lack of compositional skill or commitment to a task. (Rose, *Cognitive*, 3) In other words, students thwarted due to a lack of skill or commitment have generally not been classified as true blockers; rather, they have been deemed to lack the basic qualifications for writing in the first place. However, increasing attention to the *contexts* in which writing takes place has tended to blur such distinctions. For instance, students may reasonably be diagnosed as having writer's block when they lack the writing skill or the commitment needed to satisfy certain kinds of demands made by their academic audiences. A writer who functions most naturally and effectively in, say, an autobiographical mode—perhaps because he or she subscribes to the credo that "the personal is political"—may lack either the skill or the commitment to write a typically impersonal "objective" analysis in which the professor has forbidden personal material and perhaps the use of the "I" as well. When such a writer is unable to proceed with the task, we believe it is fair to characterize the problem as writer's block.

In cases such as that just described, writer's block may be seen not as a problem that exists in isolation but as a manifestation of *authority relations* in the classroom. Such students may be able to function quite well when they can write with authority (e.g., choosing their own material, deciding how to render it, controlling style and format, etc.), but they may encounter serious obstacles when they are denied the authority that practicing writers usually have. That said, in many other cases, of course, students may encounter writer's block due to the approach they take to the process of writing rather than to the authority dynamics of their rhetorical situations, as Rose pointed out in examining the problem of students whose "rigid rules" and "inflexible plans" for writing sometimes induced writer's block. ("Rigid," 389–400)

The Articles

In Chapter 15, "Learning from Writer's Block," Jenny Love uses as her point of departure Mike Rose's 1984 study, *Writer's Block: The Cognitive Dimension*, querying her peer tutor classmates to determine whether they can offer further insights into the "small or terrible nightmare" of writer's block. Her study is far from being empirical, yet the highly informal responses she received enable her to enhance her understanding of writer's block and to offer suggestions that may be helpful to all writers as well as most writing associates and teachers of writing.

Through conducting her survey, for example, Love can identify some of the causes to which her fellow tutors attributed their blocking as well as some of the techniques they had developed in order to cope. Their strategies ranged from introspection to discussing their ideas with friends to "giving it a rest." One of the most striking techniques is what one tutor called "normalizing"—that is, simply to be prepared for blocking to occur and to accept it as a regular part of the writing process. This act of recognizing writer's block as "part of the territory" is one of the techniques that Love sees as having potential to help student writers. She concludes her piece with a discussion of the ways in which the respondents to her questionnaire have tried to assist tutees in overcoming writer's block.

In Chapter 16, "Consciousness, Frustration, and Power: The Making of Contextual Writer's Block," Miriam Axel-Lute continues the ongoing conversation on writer's block, noting her indebtedness to both Mike Rose and Jenny Love, whose essay had been written for the same course several years earlier. Axel-Lute's article extends the conversation in an innovative way by examining the previously unexplored role of *context* in the occurrence of writer's block—an element she considers critical to both the development and the potential alleviation of blocking. Like Love, Axel-Lute decides to query her fellow students, but unlike her predecessor, she focuses her questions on blockages that are context-specific, such as those caused by conflicts with the professor or by dissatisfaction with the construction of a writing assignment. She finds no shortage of students who can provide examples of this type of writer's block. On the basis of their experiences and her own as well, Axel-Lute attempts to theorize about the source of such blocks, concluding that the problem is a "hegemonic academic paradigm" that results in writers' feeling counterproductively restricted as to what they may say and how they are permitted to say it.

Axel-Lute goes on to discuss how the unequal power relationships between professors and students may further exacerbate writer's block, and she sees in liberatory or critical pedagogy a possible solution for the future. Her essay ends, however, grounded in the here and now, with several concrete strategies that tutors might use to help student writers who are confronting the sort of contextual blocks that Axel-Lute has identified and analyzed.

WORKS CITED

Rose, Mike. "Rigid Rules, Inflexible Plans, and the Stifling of Language: A Cognitivist Analysis of Writer's Block." *College Composition and Communication* 31 (1980): 389–401.

_____. *Writer's Block: The Cognitive Dimension.* Carbondale, IL: Southern Illinois University Press, 1984.

Chapter 15

Learning from Writer's Block

Jenny Love

I went about thinking and forgetting—sitting down before the blank page to find that I could not put one sentence together. [...]

Joseph Conrad here speaks for many writers when he describes the frustration, anguish, and misery that the act of writing—and being unable to write—causes him to feel. Expressing oneself on paper is for most people, as for Conrad, difficult, agonizing, frightening: a shattering, tumultuous ordeal; a small or terrible nightmare. We often do not write when we should write, or even when we think that we may, in some remote corner of our consciousnesses, *want* to write: We instead brew a cup of coffee or tea ("Tea cures everything," I tell myself vaguely), or make a phone call, or clean our room, or do other homework. Most of us find hundreds of little chores to go about when we should be putting words and thoughts on a page or a screen— activities that don't make us feel angry or afraid or inadequate, or hurt our bottoms and our heads, or tense our muscles, or fray our nerves. And there is, unfortunately, little evidence that writing gets easier with practice: In fact, that a person's writing often improves with many endeavors and achievements seems almost to be canceled out by what is for many the increasing difficulty and slowness of composing. (I bite my nails down to bloody stumps now when I write anything that I must think and think about and want to be proud of. But during my first year of college my nails were sort of long.) Writer's block, which Mike Rose defines as "an inability to continue writing for reasons other than a lack of basic skill or commitment" (*Writer's Block*, 3), is for many people who write, even—as Conrad's confession suggests—for experienced writers, a relatively common occurrence. Everyone who writes often has probably suffered writer's block in some degree; writers whom Rose calls "non-blockers" may not often find themselves unable to begin or continue writing—but it is likely that they sometimes do.

In his book *Writer's Block: The Cognitive Dimension*, Rose, who directs the Freshman Writing Program at UCLA, explains:

> We spend a great deal of energy diagnosing our students' writing skills. The present study suggests that we should also spend time exploring their writing processes. We simply can't tell enough from finished essays alone. (85)

Rose's study, which must have originated in his very awareness that it is not beneficial to look at "finished essays alone," was participated in by ten UCLA students, four identified by their answers to a questionnaire as low-blockers and six as high-blockers. Their majors, years in school, and writing experiences were various. The students had an hour to answer an essay question (the same question for everyone) and were videotaped while writing, as were their pads of paper (which were fixed to their desks). Immediately afterward, each student watched the tape of herself or himself involved in the writing process and at the same time was audiorecorded while answering a helper's questions about what had been going on in the writer's mind: "What were you thinking here?" and so on.

One of Rose's main findings in looking closely at the writing processes of the students, and in talking with them about how they wrote and write, was one he had introduced in an article ("Rigid Rules") a few years previously—namely, that writers who use stiff rules are the ones who most often experience writer's block. For example, one of the students he worked with in an earlier study operated by the rule, told to her in high school, that at the start of an essay one must always "grab one's audience." As Rose points out, although this is not a "wrong" notion or a "bad" idea, it can be confining and crippling to the writer if conceived algorithmically rather than heuristically—as a commandment to be adhered to completely and infallibly rather than as a good-humored, light-handed piece of advice. Ruth believed that she had to "grab" her reader at the outset; as a result, she agonized for hours over her first paragraph, often finishing it only to scratch it out again, fearing that she would "bore them to death." ("Rigid Rules," 389) Rose finds that, on the other hand, the students in his later study who did not block and were normally low-blockers, made use of functional, multi-optional rules when they wrote, such as "When stuck, write a few words." (*Writer's Block*, 79) Rose also concludes that his data "do not support popular notions that writer's block is primarily a manifestation of low opinion of one's work and fear of evaluation." (76)

After reading about Mike Rose's studies and nodding in agreement over his conclusions, I found it interesting and helpful to read the responses that people in our teaching and tutoring class gave when asked about their own experience—and that of the people they have tutored—with writer's block. I don't claim these findings to be necessarily more truthful or "generally the case" than are Rose's. His study has many advantages—for one, most of the students he worked with were majoring in areas other than English, and some indicated that they rarely enjoyed writing. Our teaching and tutoring class, by comparison, is made up of fairly experienced writers (by no means necessarily English majors, though many are) who often do enjoy writing, despite the feelings of frustration that may accompany it. The people in Rose's study, then, represent a broader range of interest and experience in writing. Also, Mike Rose was able, having had the benefits of advanced technology and helper-outers and plenty of time, to view writers while they were writing, to see what sorts of things they jotted in the margins and crossed out, and to find out more or less what they were thinking at a given moment in the writing process. Yet, the same measures taken by Rose to ensure that he would learn as much as possible about writers' habits and the reasons for writer's block—video cameras, timed exams, bolted-down tablets—can also be seen as artificial and distracting, and unlike the conditions under which students, and all writers, do most of their writing. Therefore, while simply asking the people in one's class to write about writer's block as they and others have experienced it doesn't have the immediacy of watching and asking questions of writers who are (or have just been) in the throes of writer's block (as did happen with some of Rose's writers), I nonetheless see the discussions of people in the present "study" as being relevant for many, and perhaps most, writers at the college level and beyond.

Many patterns came to light when people in our class responded to the question, "What do you think often causes you to block while you are writing?" Contrary to what Rose found, writer's block for some of the members of our class seemed to come from anxiety or fear about how "good" one's work is or how well it will be received. As Liz notes, "How can you sound knowledgeable if you're not sure you are?" Len writes that an important factor in his blocking "is lack of knowledge about what I think I'm supposed to be writing." He describes his worst blocking experience, which happened when it came time to write his master's thesis: "I was under the impression that as a graduate student I had to come up with something completely original." He continues:

> In retrospect, I think fear as well as lack of knowledge played a role in my blocking. I was practically frozen into nonproductiveness by the awful specter of being exposed as inadequate, so I kept telling myself that whatever I thought of doing was going to be inadequate.

Along the same lines, Rich writes that he often feels inadequate due to a lack of knowledge—although he's usually able to calm himself down and "start writing anyway." As an example of his problem, he talked about the experience of writing his honors thesis, noting that "the material I was working with was too big for me, or I was too unfamiliar with it." And Jennifer writes that her own high expectations, and the image of "the perfect paper" in her head, seem to cause her to block:

> [...] Sometimes I build on this [paper in my head], and it becomes an expectation, and unless the first word fits within this absolute [image]—as it exists in my head (which it *never* does)—I feel like a failure [...] all of my insecurities come rushing in—I panic and go *blank*.

Clearly, writer's block *can* come from the feeling that we are inadequate, unknowledgeable, and will be exposed (to ourselves or our readers) as "failures." Help for such people (myself included) might be found in the words of the poet William Stafford, who, although notoriously prolific, also knows a little about writing and about human nature: "People might think that their product is not worthy of the person they assume they are. But it is." (117)

Jennifer's response also shows another cause of blocking mentioned by many in our class—a problem that might almost be taken as a given in writing: that of getting one's thoughts onto paper. Liz calls it "the pressure of trying to correctly elucidate my feelings." Perhaps part of the difficulty of writing is, as Liz seems to suggest, that many of our thoughts are less *words* than *feelings*. Jennifer writes that before writing a paper she forms a sense of what she wants to say, "amorphous though it is," and that

> the block happens in that moment before I take the doorknob in my hand and open the door—the door behind which I have been storing all of this information.

As Jeff writes with some understatement, "It sometimes can be difficult to translate ideas into words." And as Rich writes with candor, "I knew what I wanted to say, but I couldn't write anything." The "perfect paper" seems to tease and plague and daunt many of us.

Mike Rose writes that, in a more natural environment than the one in which his ten subjects wrote their essays, a paper's deadline could very well help blocked writers to get started (as it would seem, from their questionnaires, to have done for three of the UCLA students who were high-blockers). Rose suggests that, as a result of the deadline, thinking is channeled, "the weighing of alternatives" is cut short, and the writer's anxiety is raised enough to "spark fluency." (*Writer's Block*, 101) But Liz and Stephanie in our class write that one cause of their blocking is this same approaching due date. Stephanie explains:

Knowing that there is a time limit, or if I'm pressed for time, I can't be creative. Nothing will come to me. It becomes a vicious circle because then I start to panic and then I really block.

Stephanie writes that her procrastination in waiting so long to start a paper can be seen as the cause of her blocking. So does Liz:

Time is a factor, as sometimes you might procrastinate and then wait until the last minute when you can't do anything *but* write, leaving yourself to the mercies of the spell check. [...] This happens often, and I realize that my paper looks pretty bad. Why did I make this mistake? Because I was too afraid to start any sooner, or I was not assertive enough with my topics and ideas.

Fear, then, may be at the root of procrastination—perhaps the same fear of being inadequate vividly described by Len and Jennifer. Liz is obviously acquainted with many of the causes of writer's block.

Patterns emerged, too, in the responses people in our class gave when asked to describe some strategies they use when stuck on a paper. Jennifer has finally learned, after having cried with every essay she wrote during her first two years at college, to accept her blocking "as part of the process":

I sort of expect it now in some way. To some extent I have incorporated it as part of my writing process. [...] [O]nly through normalizing this experience has it become manageable.

And Liz writes, although perhaps not including herself in this group, that "serious blockers should realize that they *do* have this problem." As I mentioned earlier in this paper, and as Rose suggests (*Writer's Block*, 104), a tendency toward blocking very likely increases with the amount of writing one does: blocking may "in some cases [...] be an inevitable part of compositional growth." This has been a hunch of mine lately, and it surprised me that more people in our class don't find it helpful (or at least didn't write that they find it helpful) to consciously *normalize* the experience of blocking, as Jennifer does. Extremely serious blocking of the kind that Anthony [another student in the teaching and tutoring class] described in talking about his friend who was medicated for the problem is one matter, but lighter blocking may be helpfully seen as less an insurmountable brick wall than a series of hurdles to be taken in resigned stride. On the other hand, that everyone in our class was able to name many ways to surmount writer's block—strategies that have helped them in the past—implies that, whether or not we think of blocking as normal, most of us at least have learned to deal with it and have come, with gritted teeth, to accept it.

A method for overcoming blocks that must, judging simply from its many proponents, often work wonders, is to talk about one's topic or paper with a friend, a professor, one's classmates or tutees, or a relation. Jeff, Stephanie, Liz, and Len all mention this as a steadily helpful means of coming to a clearer understanding of what one wants to write, and why. Liz does note dryly that she hasn't used this method in a while, "as everyone else is always busy doing *their* papers."

Other successful strategies described by our class members include reflecting on one's purpose (perhaps the lonely writer's equivalent of talking with a friend). Liz and Rich both do this. Rich writes:

> When this sort of thing occurs in a less severe way [...] the most helpful tactic I have found is a reflection on my purpose at that particular point in my paper; either why I'm saying what I'm saying, or just articulating to myself out loud what it is that I'm trying to say. I try to pull back and summarize my thoughts to myself; and then write down what I just thought, as this is often pretty close to what I want to write in the first place.

Liz also speaks of pausing and asking herself questions like, "What is the message I want to convey? Who is my audience? Am I readable to them?"

Although Stephanie dislikes her tendency to procrastinate, she also admits that "a little time away from it, time to work on the paper subconsciously and then consciously begin to formulate ideas is helpful." Rich goes for long walks. Jennifer writes that there are times when it is best to realize that she is just "not in the mood." Len speaks of the value of having "some incubation time" following reading and thinking about a topic, and he implies that the deadline is no more a spur to creativity or productivity for him than it is for Stephanie and Liz:

> [I] take the pressure off by reminding myself that the way one gets to good ideas eventually is by first starting with not-necessarily-so-great ideas and pushing them forward on paper. So I almost always start projects early now.

As Jeff notes, "once there's one word on the screen or page, you've begun." Such ideas resemble the functional rules of many of the low-blocking students in Rose's study, heuristics such as "When stuck, write a few words." Stafford thinks "there are never mornings that anybody 'can't write.' I think that anybody could write if he would have standards as low as mine." (104)

Finally, members of our class wrote about how they were able to help tutees they had worked with who were blocked. Almost universally, people wrote that tutees they had spoken with had benefited greatly from talking about their papers. Jennifer and Liz both emphasize the necessity of asking the blocked writer questions—"Listening is very important," writes Liz. Len has found that if a student's blocking is deeply rooted, he is not always able to help—yet often he is able to be of use, "if I can restore some control of the writing situation to them [...] by having them tell me something they know that they think I ought to know." It is important to show that we, as tutors, have learned and benefited from what our tutees have written or told us. I think many of us in the tutoring class have learned that these writers are most likely to gain insight and fulfillment from a help session if they are able to speak at length about their ideas—if they themselves are the helpers, clarifying for the tutor what they have written or hope to write and at the same time making it clear to themselves. Ensuring that writers feel a sense of authority over their papers is essential—they, after all, are the authors—and is an important means of helping them to overcome their blocking, blocking that comes, for many writers, including experienced ones, from feelings of inadequacy and fear.

Epilogue: Writer's Block and Henry's Experience

For most of the eighteen years that have passed since I wrote "Learning from Writer's Block," I have been teaching college-level writing. Have I learned more about writer's block during this time? The question is difficult to answer. I teach at a community college. The students in my classes often need a great deal of encouragement to succeed in their college work. I have taught myself to be consciously enthusiastic in my classroom, creating a positive environment that students can thrive in. Because of this commitment to generating positive energy surrounding the task of writing, I hesitate to mention the phrase "writer's block" in my classes because the act of doing so might create a situation where students fixate on the blocking instead of just assuming (as I encourage them to do) that they always can write.

So I don't often talk with my students about writer's block. But that doesn't mean that it doesn't exist in my classes. Recently, I came across an example of what Miriam Axel-Lute, in her wonderful essay in this volume [See Chapter 16] calls contextual writer's block. This spring in my Writing 227 (Technical Writing) class, a student I'll call Henry wrote a first draft of a resume and cover letter in response to an assignment I'd given. Henry's documents were underdeveloped and needed active revising for the required second draft. Despite the fact that in my written response to his documents, I'd offered Henry a great deal of encouragement and many suggestions, he did not turn in his final copy of the assignment. Until this point in the term, Henry had seemed to me a relatively conscientious student, and I was surprised that he didn't turn in his revised papers.

Later, however, in a private meeting with me, Henry described his experience of what I now realize was a contextual block. He told me that he had had only one job in his life, and that the organization he worked for (a computer company) had a poor reputation. Henry felt that he simply could not write a resume and cover letter with such limited experience and could not comfortably name in his resume the company where he had worked. As Miriam Axel-Lute's essay helps me to realize, Henry had had a contextual block—a philosophical difference with the assignment—and, by extension, with my teaching, despite my zeal to be student-centered and progressive. Understandably, Henry could not "normalize" the conflicted experience he was having, and he ended up not doing the assignment.

From this recent experience with a student who blocked, I recognize that the phenomenon of blocking, and specifically contextual blocking, is alive and well in my students. As an instructor who strives to "teach to transgress" in bell hooks's words (stirringly invoked by Miriam Axel-Lute), I need to make time to learn about students' experiences of writer's block, and to help students work through these difficulties especially when their blocking is, as Henry's was, initially unspoken.

WORKS CITED

hooks, bell. *Teaching to Transgress: Education as the Practice of Freedom.* New York: Routledge, 1994.

Rose, Mike. "Rigid Rules, Inflexible Plans, and the Stifling of Language: A Cognitivist Analysis of Writer's Block." *College Composition and Communication* 31 (1980): 389–401.

_____. *Writer's Block: The Cognitive Dimension.* Carbondale, IL: Southern Illinois University Press, 1984.

Stafford, William. *Writing the Australian Crawl: Views on the Writer's Vocation.* Ann Arbor: University of Michigan Press, 1978.

I also wish to acknowledge the wonderful responses of the people in our class: Rich, Jeff, Liz, Stephanie, Len, and Jennifer.

Chapter 16

Consciousness, Frustration, and Power: The Making of Contextual Writer's Block

Miriam Axel-Lute

Mike Rose, author of *Writer's Block: The Cognitive Dimension*, defines writer's block as "the inability to continue writing for reasons other than lack of basic skill or commitment." (3) In this book, Rose explores writer's block primarily from the cognitive angle, showing that much of writer's block may come from writing *process* troubles, occurring most often for writers trying to work with rigid, conflicting, or inappropriate rules, premature editing, misleading assumptions, insufficient planning and discourse strategies, and inappropriate evaluation criteria. (4) While Rose divides writers into high-blockers and low-blockers for his research, an Oberlin College peer tutor's essay, "Learning from Writer's Block," by Jenny Love, looks at writer's block as a more universal phenomenon. Her paper focuses on the experiences of several classmates with writer's block, *experiences which are seen to be almost inevitable steps in their writing process* but which are also connected to fear of inadequacy, overly high standards, approaching deadlines, or the elusive problem of putting thoughts onto paper. Love makes several suggestions concerning writer's block, including accepting blocking as a normal part of the process, talking about the paper with someone, and getting some distance from the paper. (143–150)

Both Rose's and Love's conclusions are clearly applicable to many cases of writer's block. And for all the many cases where they apply they are indispensable for illuminating problems, making blocking writers feel that they are not crazy, and providing some possible steps towards remedies. However, these process-based types of writer's block don't cover the complete range of the phenomenon. Both Love and Rose assume in their approaches that writer's blocks are entirely unrelated to the subject or circumstances of the particular writing task. Love clearly shows this by identifying neither the class nor discipline the students in her paper were writing for when they experienced their blocks, not to mention the subjects of their papers. In the context of her paper, writer's block is something that happens only because of the writer and the writer's relationship to writing. It is seen as usually a normal part of the writing process, to be accepted while being worked through. (Love, 147–148) Rose does acknowledge that "[…] there could be a sociological/political dimension to the writing situations […]" but it was not within the scope of his study. (2)

Could writer's block ever occur for reasons external to writers and their processes? I would like to define a subset of writer's block that takes into account a different set of sources and to explore along the way how several Oberlin College students describe and respond to these blocks. I will, however, start by examining the process by which I identified and defined this subset of writer's block for myself, because I feel the process illustrates something of the power of the causes and the blocks themselves.

Chronology of Discovery

My search to examine this different sort of writer's block starts with a personal experience. The spring of my sophomore year at Oberlin, I took a special topics expository writing class in which I learned about New Paradigm process-oriented writing. The class was incredibly inspiring, especially because I actually enjoyed every step of writing papers for it and was able to bring my new ideas about writing processes into my other classes.

The following fall, however, I found myself in a class where I was struggling and agonizing over papers more than I ever had before. My experience with the final exam/paper for the class is representative of my experience with the whole class. I understood what was expected of me, I understood the material, and I had many strong ideas and opinions about the reading that was supposed to form a basis for our paper. However, I found the topic to be badly defined and indirectly connected to what we'd covered in class. I knew from past experience that asking the professor to clarify the topic would be unhelpful. On top of it all, or perhaps at the bottom of it all, many aspects of the topic were connected to difficult issues I was involved with outside of class. So when it came to writing this particular final paper, I found myself running up against a strong, emotional writer's block. I didn't *want* to write the paper. Or better yet I wanted *not* to write it, very, very strongly. I had problems with everything I put on paper. I wrote a little and deleted it. This was not a usual reaction for me.

Had process-based expository writing failed me? Or was this a different category of problem that I had not been able to encounter in the expository writing class? This question prompted me the following spring to use the final paper in another expository writing class, "Teaching and Tutoring

Writing Across the Disciplines," to look into how other students dealt with problems like this in their own work.

But first I needed to define what I meant by "problems like this," which has turned out to be a major theme of my work in itself. I started my first free-write for the paper by saying I wanted to investigate the difference between working on papers we want to write as opposed to those we just don't want to deal with. I quickly had to refine that, because there have been plenty of papers I didn't want to write that haven't caused me quite the strong reaction and struggle I was remembering. Next I moved to calling the problem "emotional" blockages, recalling how strongly upset I had felt when trying to deal with papers for that class. I loosely defined these as anything that didn't fall under the categories of time shortage, not having done the reading, or problems with writing process.

"Emotional blockages" was the phrase I used when I first presented the topic in class for discussion and on my first round of questionnaires. However, a friend pointed out to me that while the blocks were emotionally upsetting, using the term "emotional" in the name seemed to place the blame for the block within the writer experiencing the difficulty, which also did not seem to be what I was getting at.[1]

Again, I needed a new way to think about the category of writing blocks I was investigating. For a while it was up in the air. When I handed out questionnaires and conducted interviews, I explained the kind of situation I was interested in only by listing examples of the situations (definition by enumeration). On the questionnaire the potential examples I gave were:

> (1) A personal conflict with the professor; (2) Having your opinions on the topic invalidated or dismissed in class, either by the professor or another student; (3) Having a strong personal connection to the subject matter but being forced to write about it in an impersonal way; or (4) Taking issue with the way the paper topic is constructed or written.

Then I invited the respondents to relate a story that fit into one of those *or* something similar. Invariably, people seemed to know what I was talking about, and many were eager to fill out the questionnaire.[2] Others said they had no experience that fit what I was describing. I was convinced from this response that there must be a particular phenomenon that I was describing and not just a loose set of external factors or a list of times "when you really don't want to write a paper."

I finally began calling my paper topic "contextual blockages," because the blocks seemed to have to do with the specific context (professor, topic, discipline's discourse) of a particular writing task, as opposed to being a generalizable phenomenon. Contextual blocks, because they *are* specific in cause, may manifest differently in different situations and often will exist for one writing task and not another. And yet I want to argue that they are not isolated or unique but connected to something larger than the writer's interaction with the material or their text.

Examples of Contextual Writer's Block

To get stories from people other than myself, I distributed questionnaires in my Teaching and Tutoring class, and I made several announcements about my project in a campus dining cooperative that has a focus on Third World issues, through which I distributed a few more questionnaires. I also solicited one questionnaire from a friend whom I knew had a relevant experience. For further examples, I also drew on Gwynn Crichton's Spring 1994 paper for the Teaching and Tutoring class, "Appropriations and Negotiations of Authority." I was looking for how members of the academic community at Oberlin, particularly students who are experienced writers,[3] both define and respond to these contextual issues in their papers. Since I was still in the process of laying out the defining characteristics of what I was examining, I first looked through my responses to see if there was any pattern in the kind of situations that respondents described. There was a quite clear one, despite the fact that the situations described were incredibly varied in terms of writing task, discipline, and the writer's action.

Cases of Contextual Blocking—Part 1

Ben[4] wrote about a block he had in a social science class in which he disliked the professor. In his questionnaire he writes that he found the professor "pompous and condescending," and "worst of all, he would always talk about how he had this 'feminist, liberatory classroom,' which was complete B.S." Ben felt strongly enough turned off by the classroom setting that he began skipping lectures, which was not a usual practice for him. Ben did not feel personally attacked but primarily disdainful. His block occurred when writing an open-ended paper on the readings for the class because he disliked the professor so much he didn't want to take anything about the class seriously.

Judy, on the other hand, also had a conflict with a professor, but one in which she felt more directly affected. The course was a poetry-writing class, where the material the students were writing was often personal. Judy's writing often contained political content, but she says in this class the professor made it clear that he considered writing on political themes to be of lesser quality. On top of this, according to Judy, two of the men in the class (which had three men and twelve women) dominated discussion on a regular basis, a practice that was encouraged by the professor's actions in the classroom. For example, at one point one of these male students was having two poems workshopped in class, one about drinking with his buddies and one sexual poem, which Judy felt objectified women. She had responses planned to the second poem, but first the professor responded to the drinking poem by saying, "Yeah, I've had a lot of Jack Daniels in my time," and punching the author on the arm. Judy felt silenced by this buddy-buddy camaraderie that openly placed the professor "on the side of" the male student. She and a few other women went to see the professor, and their concerns were dismissed. Judy then developed a writer's block that she said covered pretty much the rest of the class's assignments.

Andrew did not have a conflict with his professor nor with the specific classroom setting for the block he described in his questionnaire. Instead he had a personal stake in his topic and a conflict with what was assumed to be acceptable subjects for academic discourse. Andrew was writing a paper on social deviance when a friend of his who was living far away was raped. Feeling helpless because he was unable to be with his friend, Andrew spent three solid days and nights in the library researching rape. He got an extension on his paper and decided to switch his topic from vandalism to rape. He wanted to *do* something, especially to say something useful about rape prevention. However, he found himself floundering. "I couldn't write with any emotion or interest. Although I was compelled to read everything I could about rape, when a response was required of me, I became mute. I had no voice." His first draft came out "like computer data." He felt it was a regurgitation of the information about rape that had been in his head, all numbers, and that it was completely unsatisfactory.

Debbie identified her block as beginning with the narrow focus of the assigned topic of a final paper, which represented her disagreements with the class focus throughout the semester. She says, "The assignment was to fix the world, but the [real] assignment seemed to *me* to be to take a case study we were given and spit back limited models of policy that we were given in class." She called this a "ridiculous exercise" which left her completely overwhelmed, and unable to start writing until after the paper was due.

Gwynn Crichton, in her paper about certain interdisciplinary discourse communities at Oberlin, mentions situations similar to those of the respondents to my questionnaire. She says some of the major problems facing the students she spoke with were (1) rhetoric that assumed all people to be equally responsible for the environmental crisis, (2) papers that were supposed to be regurgitations of the readings, and (3) the delegitimization of using information from other disciplines to inform these interdisciplinary papers. This led to writer's block for several of the students Crichton surveyed for her paper, including one who also filled out a questionnaire for me.

So What's Going on?

Looking at the cases above, I have finally been able to create a clearer description of the "problems like this" with which I started. They involve three basic components. First, in these cases of writer's block, the set of assumptions that govern either the classroom or the discipline's discourse are hegemonic,[5] controlling, and distinctly *not* self-reflexive. These kinds of educational environments have been identified by many progressive writers in different contexts, and they are often contrasted with "liberatory" or "critical" pedagogy. bell hooks, for example, in *Teaching to Transgress*, says that when she was in college, the majority of professors "didn't have a clue that education was about the practice of freedom," and consequently she often found classrooms to be boring and the sites of "rituals of control." (4–5) In general, the degree of restrictiveness varies from class to class and discipline to discipline, often related to the degree of the self-reflexivity present. Even in classrooms that are progressive in many respects, however, a dominant discourse or specific blind spot of a professor can easily be present and have a similar effect.

The second component is that the students who told me about contextual writing blocks were consciously, explicitly aware of this academic hegemony. Ben and Judy recognized sexism in their professors. Debbie and I and the subjects of Crichton's paper recognized a narrow perspective in certain discourses that wasn't letting us say what we needed to say. Andrew saw the limits of an academic discourse that didn't recognize pragmatic solutions as a legitimate task for a paper or male auto-eroticism as a legitimate topic. In the situations these writers describe, they disagree with the boundaries of the writing process created by this hegemony. The traditional paradigm is in some way not serving their needs as students, writers, human beings. It is important to note that I say that the writers in these situations are *explicitly* conscious of what is happening. They can describe the conflict, and they are aware that the problem does not lie entirely within themselves.

Third, these conflicts and restrictions that the students are aware of, and often even the basic issues involved in the conflict, are generally unacknowledged by those for whom the paper is to be written and sometimes are directly denied. Judy confronted her professor, who dismissed her concern. Ben's professor actively claimed to be doing something Ben felt he wasn't. The issues of why certain things are acceptable in academic papers and not others or the possibilities of autobiographies or of activism through papers had never been discussed in Andrew's classroom. The professor who assigned the paper that Debbie struggled with acknowledged when he handed it out that many would hate him for it but said at the time, "Tough." I had spent a fair amount of time on disciplinary committees trying to explain the blind spots in the discipline in which I later had my block.

So we have an academic tradition that is restrictive to students in some way—and they are conscious of how—but it remains unacknowledged in the classroom setting. The fact that it took me so long to arrive at this definition of the problem shows how strong the ideas of the traditional academy are. As members of the academy, we are taught to see writing as a way to express the ideas that we have and to show the knowledge we have gained. We are taught that if we have a disagreement or a divergent viewpoint, that we should use the tools of the discourse we are in to try to prove that we are right, using the standard essay format and simultaneously showing that we understand the accepted views. If we cannot do this, then our disagreement is not a real, academic one. Even under the New Paradigm of composition studies, writing is seen primarily as an act between the writer and the text, with helpful guidance from sympathetic readers, where writing problems are to be solved using innovative ways of approaching drafts and conferencing.[6] When thinking about writing blocks only within these areas of understanding, I came first to the conclusion that the problem Oberlin students were facing was "papers we don't want to write." It took all the steps I laid out above for me to recognize that external and systemic influences could limit such a personal academic act and that our conflicts with those influences were causing writing blocks.

There is one last factor that combines with the three basic components above to make contextual writer's block a potentially pernicious occurrence. Something about the situations makes the writers unable to easily ignore or avoid the conflict. This is somewhat implicit in the definition of hegemony. That which is hegemonic has predominant influence over others. In this case, the power to judge, evaluate, and grade the paper, as well as to validate, encourage, write recommendations for, and pass the student, lies in the hands of those controlling the academic discourse. Even under the tripartite set of conditions I have described, this last factor will introduce a range of variation in students in terms of whether or not they block and how they deal with their blocks. Many factors can make students more vulnerable to the power dynamics of the classroom. Students who are already often marginalized may feel their position in the classroom and as writers to be more precarious. As bell hooks says, "Individual white male students who were seen as 'exceptional' were often allowed to chart their intellectual journeys, but the rest of us (and particularly those from marginal groups) were always expected to conform. Nonconformity on our part was viewed with suspicion, as empty gestures of defiance." (5) Marginalized students also may face, or be aware of, more personal conflicts with the dominant discourse, rather than merely intellectual disagreements, or they may be less comfortable expressing themselves in the dominant discourse. The ever-present tension of the student-professor power dynamic can be exacerbated by the addition of other power dynamics and when unacknowledged, can lead to a writing block.

To provide a contrast with these "unavoidable" tensions, I would like to describe the situation of Charles. Charles is not a student but a tenured writing professor. He too experienced a similar kind of writing block as the students above, and yet his relative security allowed him to eventually avoid the conflict and do things his own way. A paper Charles had submitted to a prestigious journal was rejected and returned with comments from a reviewer who obviously disagreed with Charles's thesis rather than the quality of his paper. This reader seemed to be offended that Charles should be comparing the two authors that he was, one of whom is seen as a more popular novelist and the other a "serious" writer. Charles says he suspects the reader was a scholar focusing on one of the authors he was writing about and that the subtext of the critique was pretty clearly "Who do you think you are?"

Charles faced his block when it came to revising to address these comments. His first reaction was to put off the revision, and he began trying to plan strategies in his head, rather than his normal practice of just plunging into a revision, even if he's not sure of where he's going. He considered dropping one or the other of the authors from the paper or emphasizing their differences more. However, he was unable to start the revision, saying it was "like a barrier" and "I would have been willing to deal with problems that were really there."

Charles recognized that the criticism was coming because of the perspective of the reader, who he suspects was a "traditionalist," who was personally closed or resistant to the *ideas* that Charles was putting forward. Having recognized this, Charles says he eventually decided that he respected what he was doing enough to take his own advice and leave out addressing the concerns of the reader at all. Having decided that, he was able to do other revisions, shortening the essay, and making it better along lines he liked. "I would say it was liberating," he comments, referring to his choice, which he saw as a choice to maintain integrity. Rather than resubmitting the paper to the first journal, Charles had the choice instead to put the piece into an anthology on postcolonial literature that he was co-editing. Charles acknowledges that it was his relative freedom of choice in this situation that allowed him to go ahead with the piece in the way he wanted. There was no reason he had to engage with that one reader or have his paper published in that journal, prestigious as it was. "If I had needed that one piece to get tenure, I would've been in bad shape," he says. Students in a similar situation usually don't have the choice to submit their papers to a different professor or to suddenly reinvent the discourse.

To have this kind of power imbalance controlling the writing processes of students whose aim, after all, is usually to learn, more than it is simply to pass a course, is a central educational concern. Among those educators and theorists who have recognized the many problems and limitations with the current educational and academic models, such as Peter Elbow, Min-Zhan Lu, Mary Louise Pratt, and many more, there has been much work and writing devoted to new paradigms and liberatory pedagogy. Much good has come out of the move towards these new pedagogies, probably including the consciousnesses of the students responding to my surveys. The foci of much of the writing of these scholars have been: ways to create liberatory classrooms, what students need from those classrooms, and how the students negotiate in them. As such, these scholars' descriptions of student writers tend to picture them either as struggling with, or conforming to, expectations under old paradigms without really knowing why, or as engaging in the contact zones of more "open" classrooms. Wendy Hesford describes student resistance to dominant forms of discourse through autobiography, which is encouraged in her classroom. Min-Zhan Lu uses subconscious rhetorical moves, such as a bilingual student's construction "can able to" to teach rhetorical importance. ("Professing," 450–455)

The experiences of the students I spoke with and surveyed point to another area of inquiry in addition to this exploring of how new liberatory pedagogies can work in the classroom. Hegemony is always being critiqued, has always been, will always be; marginalized writers have been doing it for centuries. But an increasing number of college students are in an interesting position: they have some exposure to liberatory pedagogy or at least the theory of it and are trying to negotiate in other academic settings that remain traditional or restrictive in their approach. *Students, while they are still students, are gaining the language, theory, and consciousness to actively critique their classes, often from other classrooms or educational spaces.* This awareness of discourse and classroom dynamics may come from many places, including new paradigm composition studies, cultural studies, and women's studies classrooms, activist spaces on campus, dialogue with older students, or personal study.[7] In other words, there are increasingly places where it is acceptable, if not expected, that pedagogy will be interrogated, and that the learning space will be self-reflexive.

What students do when they have a taste of liberatory pedagogy and then face the kinds of classrooms that bell hooks describes is a timely question. My study shows that one of the ways conflicts are likely to surface is as troubles with writing. This fits Min-Zhan Lu's idea of writing as struggle. Growing up in Communist China, she faced two ideas of how to write and use language, one from home and one from school, and she had to keep them as separate as possible. The two merged in the first draft of one essay, which was acceptable to her, but she knew it would not be to either those who represented home or school, so she threw it out and started over. The panic from the mixing of those two worlds gave Lu a version of contextual writer's block for a while. "I was no longer able to read or write correctly without [...] painful deliberation [...] writing became a dreadful chore." ("From Silence," 443) Is it possible, then, that writing could also be the location for challenges to non-liberatory practices?

Strategies for Negotiation

The conclusion to my own story led me to wonder if there were strategies, whether conscious or unconscious, that students use to allow themselves to complete writing tasks in these difficult situations, and to wonder if these strategies are different from the ones the same writers use to respond to more apparently neutral incidences of writer's block. What I did to resolve my contextual block seemed at the time just to be a silly and impulsive act, but it had a sort of specificity to the situation that made it unlikely that I would have done it in a different case. A friend had been visiting and listening to me gripe about the paper, and to get a smile out of me he sat at my computer and began typing several lines of nonsense into the beginning of my paper. They read, "Kerala [India] has a coherent progression of environmental studies courses. We should have that. That would fix this paper, which is about fixing the world, so by flawed logic that would fix the world."[8] My friend obviously expected that I would give him a funny look, laugh, and delete the lines when I went back to work. Instead I put them in ten-point font, centered them, and put quotes around the passage and his name under it. In other words, I made it my epigraph.

The quote had marginal reference to the paper, and neither of us actually knew anything about environmental studies per se in Kerala. However, what the quote did do was give me a delightful way to express my frustration with the paper and the situation as a whole. And by using the epigraph, a conventional form that nonetheless has very few rules or guidelines surrounding it, I was able to express this in a relatively safe manner. It was certainly out of the ordinary, but it was also quite safe, in that the professor could not claim that it adversely affected the rest of my paper in any way. While doing this did not suddenly make me overjoyed to be working on this paper, I do remember a feeling of relief in knowing that my frustrations were going to be communicated in some way, and I was able to go on and finish the essay.

The hypothesis that I drew from this experience was that if other channels failed, some student writers might turn to various strategies within their writing itself to allow themselves to express their situation, either within their process or as something that is actually manifest in the final product. Another approach might be that of making the paper as normal and disconnected and safe as possible, which I have also done on occasion. What kind of risk-balancing goes on in these situations? What situations give rise to different responses? Does a single writer always respond the same?

Cases of Contextual Writer's Block—Part 2

Ben, in addition to disliking the teacher and not wanting to take the class seriously, also says he "couldn't think like [the professor] and didn't know what he wanted." Thus, he put off the paper until late the night before (something he does not usually do) and expressed his disdain by hanging out with friends and drinking wine earlier in the evening when he "should" have been starting the paper.

However, when it came down to the paper itself, Ben *was* interested in one of the three books they had read, and he had things he wanted to say about it. So, although he normally writes papers with the professor in mind, in a last-minute strategy he tried to cut "all mental ties to [the] professor" so "I could produce something of integrity." Ben says as he worked he imagined he was writing for an idealized audience, perhaps himself or a good professor, and that he entirely ignored the lecture material in what he wrote, working directly from readings which had not been discussed in class. He says once he was finally going in this manner, the paper wasn't difficult to write, and he "somehow got an A." So after expressing his lack of respect for the class in various ways (putting it off, wine), Ben was able to consciously put aside his issues and overcome his blocking to write a well-received academic paper that even he found thoughtful and that took only small risks (such as ignoring lecture material).

Judy had more trouble. After her visit with her professor, she began to avoid writing anything either political or emotionally vulnerable. "I would write about a radiator," she says, for example. As with Ben, Judy lost respect for the class. She wouldn't turn in her best work because the "professor wasn't worth it." And while she usually wrote at the last minute, for this class she wrote even more so (the night before rather than a day or so). As opposed to Ben's situation, however, there was also obviously an element of self-protection in this writing situation. Judy felt more personally excluded in the classroom, an exclusion that the professor had directly denied existed.

Judy says that was a difficult class to put behind her, and it inevitably affected her later writing. The self-protective measure she adopted to deal with her blocks made her writing generally more convoluted and indirect, as opposed to dealing with issues as directly as she might have before. This was especially true when she was negotiating her identity as a queer woman and even was true for the one assignment for the class in question on which she did not have a writing block. That assignment asked students to write a poem using information from somewhere outside of a classroom. The poem Judy wrote involved strong emotions about a current event in her life, which took information from signs posted in her dorm. She says "I was in emotional shock, and I didn't really care about the professor. I couldn't stop something that strong." Like Ben, she found herself needing to dissociate from an audience different from the one she would like to be writing to. While she found this poem to be one of her best, and notes that other readers agree with this assessment, her professor's one comment was "doesn't fit assignment."

Andrew eventually threw out the first draft of his paper on rape and moved away from reading sociological studies to reading things like personal testimonies. He said he was finally able to write the paper when he realized that, as a man, he felt guilty for his friend's rape, and that he needed to confront that emotion. From this realization he found a more specific topic for his paper: societal constructions of masculinity and how they create rapists. He says, "I could have written a standard research paper [...] but that would have been inaction."

The paper Andrew wrote was different from a standard paper in several ways, which made the paper feel risky to him. Not only was the paper topic growing out of a personal emotional experience, but the paper was also "applying knowledge to myself." The paper took steps to advocate action, which Andrew was not sure belonged in an academic paper. He also felt that in presenting his conclusions, which emphasized prevention by revisioning male sexuality, he was taking a big risk; he was not relying on others' authority about rape prevention, and he was talking about a fairly "taboo" subject. He says that he was afraid to turn the paper in, because he was afraid that the professor was going to react against it or think that he was not taking rape seriously enough.

Andrew was coming smack up against the restrictions of traditional academic discourse. He balanced his risks somewhat, because he did not make direct reference to personal experience in his paper and carefully limited his use of "I" and other no-no's of traditional discourse. However, he pushed the boundaries enough to accomplish what he felt he needed to do through the paper. As with Judy's one poem, the situation was strong enough to necessitate risk taking.

Debbie also took a risk in finally completing the Fix the World paper. She felt so limited by her possibilities that she sat down to write a journal entry about it first, which eventually became her paper, still in journal form. She began "Dear [Professor X]: I do not have the energy to fix the world on your terms," and she went on to explain why the question and the models available were limiting. At the end she actually did some analysis of the models in the way she felt the professor wanted. She gave it one quick edit and turned it in. She says the result was completely different from anything she'd ever done before, being much more conversational and free-flowing in its style. Although she felt awful about it at the time, now she is glad she answered honestly.

Crichton writes of herself, "I find myself oscillating between challenging and regurgitating the discourse. Many of my papers contain the seeds of what I really want to be writing about wedged within what I am supposed to write about." (3) Many students in Crichton's paper seemed to employ both safer and more risky or challenging approaches in their papers, depending on the situation. Some of them seemed to be just trying different responses to see if anything felt satisfactory.

For example, one of the students in Crichton's essay, Olivia, wrote one paper that both she and Crichton see as a successful strategy of resistance. She took a paper topic on sustainable resource management and used it to bring in ideas of her own, as well as critiques whose absence from the classroom frustrated her, especially race, class, and gender analyses. In her paper, Olivia disagreed with the class readings, and yet she generally stayed within the classroom's discourse. According to Crichton, Olivia was able to pull this off primarily because of her position as a women's studies major and as a woman of color, and because the professor had relatively little expertise in the areas with which she was dealing. Therefore, Olivia had a certain amount of authority in the paper. (Crichton, 14)

By contrast, for other papers in the same class, papers on which she had less knowledge and the professor had a tighter control over what was to be discussed, Olivia had different ways of dealing with her writer's block in light of what she saw as his "restrictive pedagogy." She would start as late as possible and simply repeat the reading material as safely and disinterestedly as she could. "I didn't like the product or the process," she writes. "It was one of those things I did to graduate." In these more typical paper-writing situations, Olivia's position as marginalized from the mainstream classroom discourse made her even more cautious than others who shared her critiques.

Patterns?

There are several ways in which the responses to contextual writing blocks seem to be different from responses to other blocks. One of the major strategies suggested in Jenny Love's paper, besides talking about the paper topic with someone, was "normalizing" writer's block. Love describes normalizing as viewing blocking as "a series of hurdles to be taken in resigned stride." (148) Or, as one of the students in her paper suggests, normalizing is accepting and incorporating blocking as part of the normal writing process.

In the case of contextual blocks, however, caused by student writers' awareness of a problem beyond themselves, this normalizing doesn't work. The students know there is something *wrong*, which is putting them in a very difficult position, and therefore to accept this as a normal part of the writing process would be a disturbing and defeating idea. Many of the students expressed a loss of respect for the class in which they noticed these problems and extreme frustration that they weren't being permitted to fulfill their educational potential. Connected to these feelings is a sense that there is a better way, that this is not how things have to be. Rather than accepting these blocks as part of a normal writing process, there is a sense that they represent an imposed restriction on what could be healthy writing processes. Therefore, dealing with contextual blocks does not get easier; every time these blocks come up, they present similar levels of difficulty, although the differences in specific context make response strategies irregular, as seen in the "oscillating" that Crichton describes. No normalization or universalization of the problem means that the strategies of writers will be highly individual.

Still, there was one completely universal response of the students, and perhaps it is not a surprising one: delay, or completing the writing tasks as late as possible. This was true for every respondent, including those who usually work ahead and produce pre-writing and drafts. Those who normally work at the last minute noted an extreme exaggeration of this tendency. The reasons for this last-minute approach seemed to be larger in many cases than the general frantic nature of college students and our tendency to procrastinate. They evidenced in some cases a lack of respect for the class or professor, or a specific desire to spend as little time on the project as possible.

The desire to spend as little time as possible on these sorts of distasteful tasks brings me back to the time when I was calling these blocks "emotional," because for the writer they certainly are. Olivia filled out my questionnaire sparingly, referring me to Crichton's paper and saying, "I really don't want to relive this experience." Debbie says that filling out my questionnaire about her blocking suddenly made her nervous about all the writing she has facing her right now. And both Olivia and Judy said that although they were aware of the issues involved in their blocks at the time, their writing and confidence in their writing were still altered for the negative.

Suggestions for Writing Instructors and Writing Associates

The professor assigning a paper on which a student is having a contextual block may not be the best person to recognize and deal with the problem (as is somewhat implicit in the definition of a contextual block) unless the block is arising from an issue with the discourse and not the professor. Writing associates and professors who have the chance to work one-on-one with students on papers that are not for their own classes, on the other hand, are in a position to recognize cases of contextual writer's block and possibly help the student writer negotiate them.

This position is clearly a tricky one. As writing instructors or tutors, our job is to help students develop as writers, and if hegemonic practices in some part of the academy are preventing that, then besides advocating for liberatory pedagogy in the future, we should also be addressing the needs of students now. On the other hand, we do not want to create problems where they do not exist by criticizing professors and disciplines or expounding on the limitations of academic discourse to a student who is really "only" having trouble thinking of a topic or getting past the five-paragraph essay model.

However, if done carefully, this third-party position also has powerful possibilities for helping a student writer negotiate this difficult territory. While working with students, keeping the following ideas in mind may help to address the phenomenon of contextual writer's block:

1. Be alert and aware of the possibility of this kind of conflict. Listen for expressions of frustration with the class or professor, or expressions that the student knows what he or she wants to write but can't for some reason. If a student seems to be having a tough time with the paper for no reason you have discovered, perhaps ask how the writer feels about the class in general.

2. Validate the writer's frustrations as best you can (if indeed you feel they are valid). Try not to create new feelings of anger, but provide evidence, explanation, clarification, or authority, to what the student is experiencing. Acknowledge that they are between a rock and a hard place.

3. Determine if the writer seems to be in a position to take a risk with the writing. This would have to do with mundane things like grades, credits, graduation, and also more personal things, such as whether the student may feel directly attacked or vulnerable and how flexible the professor is.

4. Explore ways of negotiating the space that will allow the student to complete the writing task somehow. Depending on the results of #3, this may include challenging the dominant discourse/power structure within the essay by making the writer's frustrations explicit, inserting them implicitly at certain points, or by using unconventional forms, styles, or topics. Or it may include speaking with the professor or writing a separate letter or section of the paper expressing frustration, which may or may not be given to the professor, or may be delivered at a later time. It may involve deciding to conform now and approach the assignment again on the student's own terms at a later date for submission to a campus journal or other independent publication. Or it may mean simply recognizing that this time it is strategically necessary to conform, and that while this may make the writer feel uncomfortable with the process and the product, it is a conscious or strategic choice.

It will involve some readjustment and creativity, but recognizing contextual blocks and their origins can be a step toward more effective strategies for empowering student writers and helping them through their writing blocks. And the reasons for doing so go beyond the commendable goal of helping individual students. Given the challenges inherent in learning to write well and given the often contentious nature of higher education's ideological landscape, contextual blocks are likely to affect some kinds of students more than others—specifically students who are already at the margins in the classroom, either by identity, perspective, or both.[9] Since apprehensiveness about writing can lead students to avoid "classes, majors, and even occupations that require writing" (Rose, 14), the contextual writer's block could be acting as another hurdle, after college admissions and financial aid, that limits the diversity of voices represented in academic and other writing-heavy professions. Strategies for handling it could be valuable, possibly essential, additions to the range of liberatory academic tools.

Epilogue

In the decade or so since I wrote this paper, I have worked as an editor, journalist, and freelance writer and researcher. Over the years, especially during my stint at a newspaper, I have developed a relatively strong ability to "just churn out copy" on deadline. I do, however, continue to face contextual writer's block from time to time—when a client's understanding of what should be covered or how it should be written about differs from mine, for example, or when limited space for an article prevents me from explaining a subject in what I consider sufficient detail for it to be properly understood. In these cases, my first drafts are often littered with snarky comments and paragraphs I know I will have to remove later. Sometimes the risk-taking of changing format or venting on the subject in some other form suffices. In one article I struggled with mightily, I ended up including an unusual disclaimer paragraph that broke with the "objective reporter" voice:

> This is not an article about Israel and Palestine, exactly. It is not an article that attempts to address or assess the differing positions and proposals about how to end the violence there, who's to blame, or how to construct a solution that is peaceful and just. This is only an article that tries to look at how the existence of the issue itself—in all its thorny, complex, and emotional third-railness—is affecting the anti-war movement. It is an article that because of its subject matter, needs the disclaimer I just wrote, because even the base assumptions of people working in good faith to find a balanced middle ground will be disputed by others working in similar good faith. This is part of the problem. (Axel-Lute)

As an editor, I have witnessed young writers struggling with the expectations of their editors and with the broader limitations on how it is considered acceptable to speak on various subjects in manners very similar to what I observed among my fellow Oberlin students over a decade ago.

Contextual writer's block is alive and well. Here's hoping that a generation of new, strong writers will continue to find creative ways to nonetheless say what needs to be said. As editors, teachers, and writing associates, it may be both our privilege and our duty to help them achieve that goal.

NOTES

[1] Another reason for changing the name was that blocks in writing due primarily to time shortages or trouble with writing process can be emotional, too.

[2] Since this paper was initially completed, all the people who have read and responded to various versions of it have consistently contributed an example or two from their own paper-writing experiences, thus strengthening my conviction that contextual writer's block is a useful and viable category.

[3] By "experienced" I mean that they have written a number of at least modestly successful papers in various college situations, not that they necessarily consider themselves to be "good writers."

[4] Names have been changed and academic departments concealed where possible.

[5] Meaning in this case that they not only are resistant to challenges, but that they don't acknowledge the existence of positions outside of their sphere.

[6] I don't want to belittle this: It is a revolutionary and indispensable move that has informed my own writing process greatly. But it alone doesn't completely address the problem of contextual writer's block.

[7] Which is *not* to say that these spaces are necessarily free of hegemonic discourse. They do, however, tend to be more self-reflexive, and they often teach the skills and theories that allow people to actively critique other spaces.

[8] The paper was about possible strategies for moving the United States toward some of the sustainability measures taken in the Indian state of Kerala. The first line of the actual assignment was "Fix the world."

[9] This is a speculation based on my definitions. My sample was too small to yield valid data, but it could be something for someone else to explore.

WORKS CITED

Axel-Lute, Miriam. "Don't Touch This." *Metroland.* 22 September 2005.

Crichton, Gwynn. "Appropriations and Negotiations of Authority." Course Essay for "Teaching and Tutoring Writing Across the Disciplines." Oberlin College, 1994. Unpublished.

Hesford, Wendy S. "Writing Identities: The Essence of Difference in Multi-Cultural Classrooms." *Writing in Multicultural Settings.* Edited by Carol Severino, Juan C. Guerra, and Johnnella E. Butler. New York: Modern Language Association, 1997: 133–149.

hooks, bell. *Teaching to Transgress: Education as the Practice of Freedom.* New York: Routledge, 1994.

Love, Jenny. "Learning from Writer's Block." *Working with Student Writers: Essays on Tutoring and Teaching.* Edited by Leonard A. Podis and JoAnne M. Podis. New York: Peter Lang, 1999: 143–150.

Lu, Min-Zhan. "From Silence to Words: Writing as Struggle." *College English* 49 (1987): 437–448.

_____. "Professing Multiculturalism: The Politics of Style in the Contact Zone." *College Composition and Communication* 45 (1994): 442–458.

Rose, Mike. *Writer's Block: The Cognitive Dimension.* Carbondale: IL: Southern Illinois University Press, 1984.

Section Six

Challenging Traditional Approaches

As an educational movement, peer tutoring in writing has flourished and spread throughout American higher education. At its core, the movement itself constitutes a challenge to traditional approaches to the teaching of writing. Believing that appropriately trained students are capable of helping their peers to become better writers, proponents of peer tutoring call into question long-established hierarchies according to which only authoritative professionals are assumed to be able to provide effective instruction to student writers. Replacing the traditional "transmission of knowledge" model with a model of collaboration, peer writing associates have proven to be successful learning catalysts who can help fellow writers to bring out the best in their work. This challenge to traditional educational hierarchy comes at a time when scholars, researchers, teachers, and students have also mounted challenges to various conventions of academic discourse, conventions often seen as overly formalistic or constraining. Such conventions include the use of strictly objective tone and point of view, the prohibition of the first-person pronoun ("I"), the exclusion of autobiographical material as evidence, the valorization of explicitly analytic and evaluative prose, and the rejection of narration as a mode of intellectual inquiry. The four articles collected in this section all stress the need for, and the value of, strategic resistance to the pressures of traditional discursive modes and forms. The desired result of such resistance, in all cases, is greater inclusiveness in discourse.

The Articles

Chapter 17, "The Hero with a Thousand Voices: The Relationship Between the Narrative and Academic Styles," by Aaron Rester, calls into question the sharp division traditionally drawn between academic discourse and narrative writing. Rester, a religion major and a writing associate for a religion course, narrates the path he followed in writing his honors thesis and, in the process, makes an eloquent argument in support of the value of narrative as a vehicle for serious academic thought. Academic discourse, he argues, actually embodies important elements of narrative—and narrative, he maintains, should be viewed as the equal of analysis in its power to convey concepts and themes.

In addition, Rester puts forth the notion that the writing process itself, including the process of writing academic discourse, is a form of narrative. He notes, "In our narrative system of thought, nothing is ever finished; we continually re-engage past thoughts and build upon them to construct new stories, just as we re-engage our earlier [academic] drafts in the creation of new ones." As Rester sees it, his argument about the value of narrative has major implications for the teaching and tutoring of writing:

> If students and teachers recognize the narrative properties of the act of writing—that the "perfect final product" many students feel is expected of them is simply one version of a story they will continue to refine and retell in their minds long after the paper has been handed in—then perhaps some of the anxieties that attach themselves to the teaching of writing [...] can be diminished.

In other words, Rester believes that storytelling should not be limited to student papers but employed by writing teachers as well. Narrative is, he insists, "a powerful pedagogical tool."

In Chapter 18, "On the Use of 'I' in Academic Writing," Samantha Sansevere challenges another aspect of traditional writing instruction: that of the "objective voice" that students are typically urged to adopt in academic discourse. Sansevere rejects the standard advice to eschew the personal pronoun "I" in academic writing, arguing that "Using the personal is about self-identity and individuality. [...] The decision to exclude the personal is one that, I believe, will adversely affect the writer's growth as an individual, a student, and a writer."

A philosophy major, Sansevere begins with a discussion of the terms *objectivity* and *subjectivity*, questioning whether writing "objectively," i.e., "telling it like it really is," is even possible. As she observes, "Any writing is a form of expression, and essentially a re-telling. [...]" Sansevere argues further that voice is an inescapable part of the text, and that to deny subjectivity is, in effect, to deny voice, resulting in texts that are unstable and lacking in personality and vigor. She links the use of "I" specifically to the creation of "voice" when she states "[...] using the personal [pronoun] is a good way to make writing belong to *somebody*, some *person* behind the words. [...]" Sansevere concludes by commenting on the benefits of using "I" that are specific to students writing in academic contexts. Using "I," she notes, may be an important, even an essential, step on the path to gaining a stable identity as a writer and a sense of authority and accomplishment in writing. It may increase the credibility of the student writer and thereby enable readers to feel more connected to writer and text. Otherwise, Sansevere asserts, "It is easy for students to let go and let the discourse swallow [them] whole."

In Chapter 19, "Why Do We Write?" Dinah Shepherd, a writing associate working at the college writing center, chronicles her memorable session with a student, Jamal, who brought her a draft that he feared was "all over the place." As it happens, Shepherd finds herself irresistibly drawn into the draft, with its poignant narrative and powerful voice. As such, she is saddened at the realization that Jamal, a graduating senior, has been led to doubt the value of his honest approach to discussing the details of his life, his values, and his family history. In this respect, Shepherd echoes a theme voiced by Samantha Sansevere, that the academy exerts strong pressure on students to conform to an objective approach that employs a detached and impersonal voice—a discourse that threatens to "swallow [them] whole."

At the same time, Shepherd makes a strong appeal to her readers to tell their own stories in their writing. Her essay is unusual in that it incorporates brief sections of poetic verse that comment on the value and function of writing, cautioning against producing lifeless prose that is disengaged and far removed from the writer's life stories:

Writing.
What is writing
And why do we do it?
To find a voice
To say
I am here
Listen to me.

Fittingly, in the process of recounting and exploring her experience of working with Jamal's exceptional paper, Shepherd practices what she preaches—she creates a lively personal narrative that reveals her own values and beliefs and shares aspects of her personality with her readers.

Section Six concludes with Chapter 20, "Demystifying the Discourse," by Melissa Hoskins. Based on interviews with two peers as well as her own experiences (all three non-traditional students) Hoskins, a writing associate majoring in Women's Studies, looks at both the capabilities and the limitations of disciplinary discourses. She and her peers reveal how academic discourse has in some ways empowered them, but they also examine what it has cost them. They acknowledge that the use of academic discourse confers credibility and legitimacy in the eyes of the academy and mainstream society. However they lament the elitist nature of such specialized language, especially its tendency to exclude all but a relatively select group of highly educated people.

Hoskins and her respondents do have a more positive view of "resistant" academic discourses—such as that of feminism—for they believe that such discourses are critical of mainstream academic discourse and have the capability to be self-critiquing as well. However, they feel that even those discourses can alienate their users from people outside the academy—a point underscored by one of Hoskins' respondents whose family and friends back home viewed her as "a pompous snot." Additionally, Hoskins and her respondents point out that academic discourse has some major blind spots, areas in which its vaunted capabilities are notably lacking. In particular, Hoskins cites "a perceived inability of academic discourse to address emotion, spirituality, and even everyday reality." Academic discourse, she observes, is indeed a powerful medium, but it is "only one way of talking. It cannot lay sole claim to sound and supported argument, and it cannot address the entirety of human experience."

Chapter 17

The Hero with a Thousand Voices: The Relationship Between the Narrative and Academic Styles

Aaron Rester

As one whose passion in life is the study of mythic narrative, I tend to view the world in terms of stories. Nor am I alone in this. Our worlds are defined, shaped, and maintained by narrative, whether the religious narrative of sacred history or the patriotic narrative of nationhood, the personal narrative of memory or the second-hand narrative of the television news anchor. Even the scientific disciplines are beginning to recognize the importance to their fields of a phenomenon that has long been considered to belong exclusively to the domain of the humanities. For example, Roger Schank, a cognitive scientist at Northwestern University, has claimed that "virtually all human knowledge" is based on stories. "When you remember the past," he asserts, "you remember it as a set of stories, and when you communicate information you also deliver it in the form of stories."[1]

Yet despite the growing awareness of the close relationship between human thought and narrative, academic writing continues to be perceived by many of its teachers and students to be fundamentally different from story-telling. Even at Oberlin, a supposed bastion of progressivism and liberalism, we have two separate writing programs: one for "expository" (read: academic) writing, and another for "creative" writing (poetry, short stories, plays, and other narratives).[2]

Certainly, these two forms of discourse have different conventions and meet different needs. But the idea that such distinctions are set in stone can lead to a crippling lack of confidence among excellent "creative" writers who feel inadequate to meet the demands of academic writing (and, as my writing professor pointed out to me, vice-versa). Yet academic writing clearly evolved from narrative—it did not spring, like Athena, full-grown and armed with buzz-words like *paradigm* and *hegemony* from the skull of the academy—and its roots are still entwined in narrative tradition. In this paper, I will examine some of the connections between narrative and academic writing—in the academic paper itself, in the writing process, and in teaching and tutoring writing—in the hopes that a better understanding of such connections will narrow the perceived gap that exists between the two styles.

Narrative and the Academic Paper

In his article, "A Place for Stories: Nature, History, and Narrative," environmental historian William Cronon examines the role of narrative in his discipline. According to Cronon, environmental historians (and other scholars as well, I would argue) configure their evidence into

> causal sequences—stories—that order and simplify those events to give them new meanings. We do so because narrative is the chief literary form that tries to find meaning in an overwhelmingly crowded and disordered chronological reality. (1349)

Narrative, then, is a fundamental part of any writing that attempts to package a messy world into neat, comprehensible compartments—which, it seems to me, is the essence of academic writing.

If narrative and academic writing do indeed grow from the same linguistic soil—if, as Cronon seems to argue, academic writing is a subset of narrative—why do we, in the academy, believe so strongly in their essential differences? Joseph Trimmer offers a possible answer in the introduction to his edited volume, *Narration as Knowledge: Tales of the Teaching Life*. In the following, Trimmer, an English teacher, describes to his colleagues how he thinks they may have strayed from what is most basic to their profession:

> We became English teachers because we loved stories. We loved reading them, writing them, and talking about them. We loved the way they intensified our lives and helped us understand other lives. But as we worked our way into our professional lives, we slowly, almost imperceptibly, changed our attitudes toward stories. We lived in a world that did not trust them. Stories were not true. Stories were not reliable. If we wanted to keep stories in our lives, we had to convert them into something else. Something more serious. Something more scientific. (x)

Trimmer's description of an academic career mirrors not only my own experience as a student of myth, but also the relationship between story and the learned elite in Western culture that has been evolving for the last several hundred years. For much of that time, science has been seen as the clearest window to "objective" truth, a truth that can be best described through numbers. In the years following the Industrial Revolution, the academy had been "reconceived on a scientific model." (Chang, 334) Stories, once the vessels of sacred history, and thus truth, became largely obsolete, bowing to the weighty credibility carried by diagrams, graphs, and tables of statistics. If stories, and their tellers, were to survive in such an environment, they would have to conform to certain conventions that modeled themselves on the scientific method: hypothesis, evidence, and analysis. Anything that did not conform to these conventions would be considered non-academic, and, thus, it is implied, inferior.[3] Whether or not scholars still consider disciplines like literature, religion, or history to be "scientific" is beside the point; the fact remains that the modern academy was, for better or worse, molded by these principles and continues to be influenced by them even today.

Yet, if we look beneath the surface of what we have been conditioned to believe regarding the narrative and academic voices, we find that a number of similarities emerge. Narrative, for example, is supposed to be descriptive, academic writing analytic; but anyone who has studied folklore (or any sort of literature, for that matter) can tell you that all narratives contain an implicit analysis of the world in which they were produced. It is impossible to tell a story without commenting on the context in which the story is told.

Both styles of writing are tools to facilitate (or hinder) communication of these analyses between the author and audience; neither is always successful. Both voices can build (or burn) bridges between people, can transmit (or obscure) ideas. In both cases, the success or failure of this communication is the product of numerous factors. Some of these factors include: the degree to which the writer/teller and the reader/listener hold a common understanding of the conventions of the genre (e.g., do both the writer and reader have the same conception of "discourse," or do both the teller and the listener take what is told in a tale to be literal truth?); the physical environment (I, for one, find it much harder to concentrate in an overly warm room); and the mental state of the participants (is the reader or hearer distracted, bored, or angry?).

As well as similar purposes and pitfalls, academic writing and narrative often share a surprisingly similar structure. Both tend to have rather formulaic beginnings and endings, which first introduce and later remove the audience from the frame of the work: the catchy first sentence that is intended to draw one's reader in is the academic equivalent of "Once upon a time" or "That reminds me of the time when." The academic conclusion, with its usual call to action ("my research has shown that such-and-such must be done") reminds me of the moral in one of Aesop's fables. In between, the hero (the-author-as-presented-by-the-text), is given a task to complete (the proving of a thesis), meets fantastic and unusual creatures (other authors) who provide him or her with magical items that will aid in the quest (textual evidence), and, if all goes well, succeeds in vanquishing the dragon of ignorance or misunderstanding—at least in the scholar's own mind.

Narrative and the Writing Process

Clearly, the academic paper bears distinct similarities to narrative, in both its structures and its purposes. Its writer is the storyteller, its reader the audience. Yet the writer is not just a raconteur; like Odysseus, or Valmiki in some tellings of the *Ramayana*, the writer is both the teller of a story and a character in a larger story—the story of the creation of the paper itself.

To illustrate, I will tell such a story—not as grand an epic as that of Moses or Gilgamesh but one that spans years and continents nonetheless. Its main character is the honors project that I completed in my final semester of college, a fifty-page paper entitled "Women, Cattle, and Divine Liquid: The Interdependency of Fertility and the Social Order in Three Mythic Contexts." The idea that would become that paper had been born almost four years previously, in a suitably poetic place—a small hotel in Athens, after a bus trip to Delphi, thought by the ancient Greeks to be the center of the world. It was then that I noticed a number of parallels between several mythic figures from different cultures, and started thinking about how I might someday do a comparative study of them.

At that point, having written only a few "real" papers in high school, academic writing was new to me, and its power to communicate complex ideas was exciting and mysterious. That fall, when I entered Oberlin, I started honing my analytical and expository writing skills—and every paper I could, I tied to the idea I'd had in Greece, hoping that someday I would get the chance to tie them together. That wish was granted when I began writing my thesis; by the time I handed in my final draft, I had cannibalized the bodies of at least three previously written papers, all written for different classes, and all (I realize now) written with a different process.

When I started at Oberlin, armed with a new computer with which I was not yet completely comfortable (on which I wrote some or all of the afore-mentioned papers, and on which I am writing this paper as well), I continued to write as I had in my typewriter days: the first draft by hand, then editing and rearranging the text as I typed.[4] As I grew more comfortable with the computer (and as the demands on my time seemed to grow by leaps and bounds), I began writing entire papers at the computer, a process that in-volved a great deal of revision but no independently recognizable "drafts." Finally, while writing the honors paper itself, I was held not only to the structure of producing three separate drafts but also to the comments, suggestions, and questions of my advisors and other readers—a resource I had rarely, if ever, made use of before.

I recount this anecdote to illustrate that *the writing process is itself a narrative*. The story I wound up telling in that paper was far different from the one I had initially imagined: rather than telling a story of psychological commonplaces that unite humanity, as I had originally imagined, I found myself telling a story of three related cultures for whom these stories may have sometimes served to legitimize political and sexual hierarchies. The final draft of my paper had been influenced by any number of readings, conversations, and daydreams that occurred during its year-long gestation.

If the writing process is indeed a narrative, and if narrative is an essential component of how we think, then the writing process itself must be intricately linked to our most basic ways of thinking. For students of writing to realize this is to further dismantle the idea of writing as a product rather than a process. In our narrative system of thought, nothing is ever finished; we continually re-engage past thoughts and build upon them to construct new stories, just as we re-engage our earlier drafts in the creation of new ones. If students and teachers recognize the narrative properties of the act of writing—that the "perfect final product" many students feel is expected of them is simply one version of a story they will continue to refine and retell in their minds long after the paper has been handed in—then perhaps some of the anxieties that attach themselves to the teaching of writing as product can be diminished.

Narrative in Teaching Writing

If, as we have seen, narrative is closely related to the academic paper and the writing process itself, it should come as no surprise that, like so many other means of communication, the act of teaching writing depends greatly on the use of the narrative form.

In the class that I tutored this semester—which focused, appropriately enough, on religious narratives—I have been a witness to how effectively narrative can be used to teach. The students' first paper topic dealt with a storyteller. He is addressed as Swamiji, and he is a *sadhu*, an ascetic wiseman who is the central character of Kirin Narayan's anthropological study of the role of narrative in religious teaching. In the students' papers, the picture that emerged of Swamiji was a virtual portrait of the perfect New Paradigm writing teacher: he is compassionate, does not condemn his students for not understanding, sees himself as a resource for learning rather than as a dispenser of truth, encourages his pupils to question authority (even his own), and uses his talent as a storyteller to help others come to their own conclusions about the world.

Some may think it strange that I am comparing a religious teacher with those who teach writing. However obsessed some writers may be with their craft, and despite the many rituals that accompany the act of writing (I picture the solemn silence during the worship at the altar of the word processor, broken only by the hymns of fingers tapping keys), it would not be accurate to call writing a religion. Yet, there are some similarities worthy of notice. Both the writing teacher and the religious teacher are attempting to articulate the way in which they see the world—and implicit in this is that they think their students should see the world in this manner as well.[5] Furthermore, many teachers, whether they be writers or holy men, are viewed by their pupils in similar ways, even if the teachers attempt to knock down the walls of authority that traditionally surround their positions:

> As soon as the discussion of student poems begins, the poet-teacher is out in the open. Slouched in his seat in the circle, he may try to be just the facilitator; but everyone knows that he's the designated expert and waits for his opinion or judgment or whatever it is the guru of such a gathering is expected to dispense—wisdom, I suppose. (Bowers, 109)

Both this poetry teacher and Swamiji find themselves in similar circumstances: considered the first among equals, looked up to by, and responsible for the well being of, the rest of the group.

So perhaps the writing teacher and the religious guru are not so different after all. But what do we learn from the likes of Swamiji? The answer is something that most of us already know: that storytelling is a powerful pedagogical tool. We have discussed in tutoring class how one can put a tutee at ease or get him or her to try something new by telling him or her a story about a similar situation that we have ourselves experienced: "When I was blocked one time, what I found helpful was..." or "Once, I had to write a paper like this, and here's what I did."

The professor of the religion class that I tutored took this technique one step further and after reading the first papers, wrote each student a comment sheet that described what she perceived them to be communicating as she read their papers: "At first, I thought that you were going to argue this, but this paragraph made me think that..." and so on. In effect, she created a narrative of her own thought processes as she read.

In the rough draft groups we held for the second papers, each student duplicated the professor's process in responding to their peers' papers. There was no "this is wrong, it's supposed to be this way"; only "when I was reading your paper, I got confused by this." It is no coincidence that after digesting so many narratives of what occurred to their readers as they read, the students gained a much better understanding of how to clearly communicate something. Accordingly, many of them wound up writing much better papers, papers that more effectively conveyed their ideas.

Conclusions?

The story of this paper is nearing its finish. I started off into the woods armed only with a sense of curiosity about my subject; I met books that spoke and even an ascetic holy man who helped me find a path through the dark forest. At this point, I am hopeful that the reader believes I have accomplished my quest, and slain the dragon of misperception that maintained a reign of fear over the realm of composition studies. As every child knows, dragons guard treasure; and in the academic narrative, the writer's conclusions must substitute for gold.

In place of a traditional conclusion, however, I would like to tell another story. This story, an adaptation of one of the Grimms' tales by Kay Stone, demonstrates the power of the narrative voice to free its user from the constraints of how we are "supposed" to think or act in a certain context.

> Once there was a girl who was stubborn and curious, and always disobedient to her parents. [One day, she set off into the woods, against the wishes of her parents, to see the witch Frau Trude. Frau Trude, discovering her, turned the girl into a bird and said] "You will remain a bird forever and my servant to all eternity—unless you can fulfill my bargain: If you can tell me one story that I've never heard before, I'll let you go. If you cannot, you'll be in my power forever."
>
> [The girl flew away, and spoke to all of the trees and creatures she met, learning stories from all of them. Many years later, she returned to Frau Trude's house.]
>
> And so she told Frau Trude all the stories she'd learned from all of creation. Some were short and some long, some were plain and others fancy, but they all carried the truth in them.
>
> When she finished, Frau Trude gazed at her warmly and exclaimed "Excellent stories, and well told too [...] But I knew every one of them long before you were born!"
>
> The woman who was a bird stood speechless. She had no more stories. None at all. But when she opened her mouth to cry out, words came out on their own, first one at a time and then running together like a small river:
>
> "Once there was a girl who was stubborn and curious, and always disobedient to her parents..." (Stone, 293–96)

I see in this story an allegory for the academic experience. It could, in fact, be a retelling of Nancy Sommers' "Between the Drafts." The girl leaves the comfort of home (the way she is used to interacting with the world), and meets Frau Trude (the authoritarian voice of the academy), who transforms her into something she is not with the demand that she speak in a certain way, that she speak the words of other people. The girl's quest fails, until she finally gains her freedom by speaking in her own voice, by telling her own story. Or, as Sommers puts it:

> Against all the voices I embody—the voices heard, read, whispered to me from off-stage—I must bring a voice of my own. I must enter the dialogue on my own authority, knowing that other voices have enabled mine, but no longer can I subordinate mine to theirs. (29)

Only by telling our own stories, these narratives tell us, can we step out of the boundaries that have been set for us and create something truly original.

At first glance, this idea appears to be that which David Bartholomae calls "the frontier classroom," (64) the idealistic notion that one can discover "one's own voice," a voice that is entirely new and has never before been heard. Yet both Stone and Sommers speak of drawing from other voices, of, as Bartholomae would say, "writing with teachers." Stone's nameless girl would have a very different story if she had not engaged all the other texts she met in her travels; Sommers allows other voices to "enable" her own. These stories tell us that we cannot possess a voice that is purely our own— just as every storyteller learned how to tell a story from others, those I have read and those who have taught me all contribute their voices to the choir that I call "my" voice—but we can use that composite voice we have constructed to create stories that truly have not been heard before.

With this in mind, I have another story to tell. Early medieval Irish monks found themselves in a position much like that of many beginning college writers: they were trying to enter into a privileged discourse (in their case, that of Judeo-Christian tradition) that not only had its own language (Latin), but also valued written language far more than the oral tradition that the Irish had always regarded so highly. Dutifully, they learned the language of the new discourse and all the conventions of the written word. Yet, once they gained access to this discourse, they found that it made no mention of themselves or their language! The Bible and other Christian texts recounted the origins of the Israelites and many other peoples of the world, but the Irish were nowhere to be found in these stories. Accordingly, they took matters into their own hands, and created new stories that combined their old oral histories with the sacred history of their adopted religion, stories that created a place for them in Judeo-Christian discourse.

One such story was that of Gáedel Glas, supposed to have been a grandson of the Biblical Pharoah. After the destruction of the Tower of Babel, when the single language of humanity was splintered into seventy-two by a wrathful God, it was Gáedel Glas who learned all of the infant languages. From what was best of all of them, he created the Gaelic (Irish) language, to which he gave his name.[6]

So perhaps rather than resigning ourselves to the conventions of academic discourse or rebelling in order to find our "own" voices, we can, like those Irish monks and Gáedel Glas, draw on what is best in each of the traditions available to us. In this way, we may create something that is both new and old, something that recognizes tradition while encouraging innovation, something that will not be just mine or yours, but ours. If we can do so, then perhaps the academic and narrative voices will be able to live, side by side, happily ever after.

NOTES

[1] Roger Schank quoted in Bringsjord, 27.

[2] Of course, it can be argued that not all poetry contains narrative; such an argument, however, is beyond the scope of my paper and not really relevant to my argument.

[3] While recent events (such as the rise of the New Paradigm) have caused a re-evaluation of such attitudes, these views are far from dead; witness, for example, the furor caused by the recent biography of Ronald Reagan that uses a fictional narrator to describe Reagan's life.

[4] Interestingly, during a semester I spent in Ireland in which I had limited access to computers, I found myself forced to go back to this system, and, having gotten so used to my new process, found it to be extraordinarily difficult to go back to my previous ways.

[5] One of my readers raised the objection that "sometimes the writing teacher is attempting to provide students with the skills to articulate their own view of the world." While I certainly agree that many writing teachers do attempt this, and that it is an admirable goal, I think that in such cases the "authorial relativism" (for lack of a better term) espoused by these teachers is in fact a worldview that they try to impress upon their students.

[6] A version of this story is found in *The Celtic Heroic Age* (Koch and Carey, 216–17).

WORKS CITED

Bartholomae, David. "Writing with Teachers: A Conversation with Peter Elbow." *College Composition and Communication* 46 (1995): 62-71.

Bowers, Neal. "No Secrets." *Narration as Knowledge: Tales of the Teaching Life*. Edited by Joseph Trimmer. Portsmouth, NH: Boynton/Cook Publishers, 1997: 107–115.

Bringsjord, Selmer. "Chess Is Too Easy." *MIT's Technology Review* 101(1998): 23–28.

Chang, Grace. "Contextualizing the Debates: A Historical View of Expository Writing." *Working with Student Writers: Essays on Tutoring and Teaching*. Edited by Leonard A Podis and JoAnne M. Podis. New York: Peter Lang, 1999. p. 334.

Cronon, William. "A Place for Stories: Nature, History, and Narrative." *Journal of American History* 78 (1992): 1347–1376.

Koch, John T., and John Carey, editors. *The Celtic Heroic Age*. Andover, MA: Celtic Studies Publications, 1997.

Narayan, Kirin. *Storytellers, Saints, and Scoundrels*. Philadelphia: University of Pennsylvania Press, 1989.

Sommers, Nancy. "Between the Drafts." *College Composition and Communication* 43 (1992): 23–31.

Stone, Kay F. "Burning Brightly: New Light from an Old Tale." in *Feminist Messages: Coding in Women's Folk Culture*. Edited by Joan N. Radner. Urbana: University of Illinois Press, 1993: 289–305.

Trimmer, Joseph F. "Introduction." *Narration as Knowledge: Tales of the Teaching Life*. Edited by Joseph Trimmer. Portsmouth, New Hampshire: Boynton/Cook Publishers, 1997.

Chapter 18

On the Use of "I" in Academic Writing

Samantha Sansevere

[...T]o achieve style, begin by affecting none—that is, place yourself in the background. (Strunk and White, 70)

In the interest of scientific objectivity, style requirements in technical and scientific courses [...] do not allow personal pronouns. [...] In papers for such subjects, you should write "Repeated experiments have shown," not "I found after repeated experiments." The practice in liberal arts courses [...] also is to avoid personal pronouns. (Yaggy, 25)

I think any student, myself included, is well aware of the warnings to avoid personal pronouns in academic writing. These warnings, I am sure, filter down from conscientious teacher to conscientious teacher, finally reaching the conscientious, impressionable student. I well recall my high school teachers as hell bent on using the red pen to excise *any* mention of myself in *any* of my writing. I was told that for writing to be mature, professional, and non-egoistic, "I" should not be used. Being the every-teacher's-pet that I was, I got into the habit.

Then there was college, where a professor quickly informed me that my writing would *not* be taken seriously if I did not claim my words by using "I." I was told that writing without "I" sounded weak. Characteristically, I changed again to meet the expectations, finding that I could slip easily into another habit. Aside from Dr. French, though, my college professors have, for the most part, been indifferent to the whole issue. They seem little affected by my visible presence in *or absence from* my writing. I wish I could be so unaffected. Left with no authoritative preference, I have been free to choose whether or not to use "I."[1]

As with anything, there are arguments for and against the use of I. Both sides of the inclusion/exclusion debate have their supporters. Could it be that writing *is* more mature, professional and "correct" when it avoids the personal? Or is writing that uses the personal stronger and more "correct"? Or is it just a choice, the outcome of which matters little? What is the student to do?

I venture to claim that both sides, though well intentioned, have it all wrong. The issues are actually much deeper than maturity, professionalism, and strength; and the choice most certainly matters—a lot. Whether or not one uses the personal in academic or any writing is, in one respect, really about our acknowledging our subjective place in this world. And perhaps more importantly, using the personal in academic writing has much to do with (what seems to be obvious) *personal* considerations. Using the personal is about self-identity and individuality; and it allows for a comfortable and welcoming environment whereby the emergence of a voice may be more likely. The decision to exclude the personal is one that, I believe, will adversely affect the writer's growth as an individual, a student, and a writer.

I begin this analysis with a rather philosophical explanation of my perspective on objectivity and how that relates to the personal pronoun in question. Then I give a more personal account of how it is that using "I" in academic writing is so inextricably linked to an individual's individuality. I want to narrow my claims to a very specific writer, especially concerning my claims in the section on individuality. Here, I am specifically concerned with student writers in academia.

Objectivity vs. Subjectivity: The "Real" Story

What is objectivity? What is the "truth" of things? Does either objectivity or truth exist? Philosophers have debated these questions for centuries. They have no answers. I think they have decided that the closest we can come to truth is mathematics, i.e. equations. The best they can do with objectivity is to try to define it. Theoretically, it is a perspective concerning the true state of reality.[2]

Objectivity is what we get when we get the "real story." I think of objective people as being those who have no vested interest in "taking sides" or of making a value judgment about something (an event or a story, etc.). They have nothing to gain by twisting or slanting a claim, so they "tell it like it is." There may not be a motive involved. I question if this can be done.

Whatever objectivity is, it must be free of subjectivity. Yet, people are subjective creatures. We all perceive differently. We are like little filters. We see, hear, smell, feel, and taste; then those perceptions are filtered through or processed by us. This processing is founded in our individual experiences. Such filtration results in what we call interpretation. Interpretation is a necessary result of experience. Experience is subjective. Interpretation is subjective. How then can people ever present an objective account of anything?

For example, consider two people, equipped with the same sensory capabilities, witnessing the same event. Say two brothers, John, an atheist, and Peter, a Catholic, while listening to a priest reciting the last rites, both observe a transparent figure hovering over their mother's deathbed, minutes before she stops breathing. Peter accepts that an angel came to take his beloved mother to heaven. The experience reaffirms his undying faith in God. He goes on to write an account of the experience, titling it "Heaven's Chauffeur."

John, who has experienced the exact same event, is amazed at the powers of the mind. He attributes the transparency to the glare of the hospital lights mixed with his overwhelming grief, coupled with the priest's words. He goes on to write an account of the experience, titling it "When Grief Consumes the Mind."

These perceptions are not inherent, and no one can prove they are. Rather, it is experience (environment, learning, etc.) that will color the way we "see" things. Further, each experience adds to our subjective perceptions. Each experience will form new perceptions. My point is, two (or a hundred) people can witness the very same event and perceive (see, process) it differently. So, everyone will "re-tell" an event differently as well. I call this phenomenon *subjectivity*. I believe this is the only perspective anyone can ever offer, since we can only ever speak from experience.

So, if no one can ever tell a story objectively, why pretend it can be done? I believe this is what happens when people "keep themselves in the background" in writing. By not using "I," one is in effect saying, "This is the objective, honest to goodness truth ... I in no way have contributed of myself to this account." It is impossible, considering the previous discussion, for this to occur.

Any type of writing is a form of expression, and essentially a re-telling, of what one has perceived. Everyone has something to gain (consciously or unconsciously) from a re-telling (description, writing) of a story, event, or happening:[3] a grade, publication, personal clarification, personal fulfillment. Writing is done for some purpose, and that is the author's slanted motivation.

To conclude, there are two types of subjectivity that occur in writing: (1) a person can offer only a subjective perspective; and (2) a person has something to gain from writing, and thus cannot refrain from "taking a side." With only this subjective accounting available to us, why avoid "I" in writing? If we know that there is a person behind the words, let us recognize that fact and accept the account as it is: subjective.

The Importance of the Personal to Persons

Retaining self-identity (a voice), in college writing is essential, if not logical, for students. Using "I" in college writing is also essential, if not logical, considering that "I" visibly inserts the author into the text, thereby almost forcing a voice, even if only suggestively. I want to expound upon these two ideas, first discussing the *necessity* of retaining individuality, herein referred to as voice, in writing. I will also touch on the difficulty of retaining a voice in academic writing. Not only do I suggest that first person viewpoint is preferable in light of subjectivity, but I urge using the personal to overcome pressures to resist voice in academic writing. I will also discuss other benefits of using "I" in academic writing.

What is a voice in writing? It is similar to a speaking voice, including tone, word-choice, verbal accent. Just as each individual has a speaking (or signing) voice, each person has a voice in her writing: a distinct, unmistakable, identifiable persona. Again, this has a lot to do with tone (be it a predetermined tone for a piece or the one most common for the author) and word-choice, and though a reader cannot "hear" an accent in writing, I think the equivalent would be something like certain phrases that are specific to, or used often by, an individual.

For example, I think voice in my writing is evident in many ways. The most common would be my constant references to philosophical ideas. This seems to be inescapable when I write anything academic. Being a philosophy major for almost five years, I am nearly haunted by the mental debates I've encountered. Somehow, it has become *part of me* to see philosophy in everything. Another factor would have to be my—also inescapable—swearing. Whether I am writing for pleasure or academia, for example, "pissed off" seems an appropriate way for me to express the notion of anger.

The point I am trying to make is that voice is part of identity. My friends can read something I have written and say, "I can see *you* saying this." No one else can put it quite the same way I can. That is voice. Everyone has or can have one in writing. Additionally, I believe a voice is unique. It is more than just similar to a person's speaking voice. There is a definite parallel between voice in writing and personality in personhood. A voice is to writing what a personality is to a person. It is inconceivable for me to imagine that my voice has not influenced my personality and vice-versa.

For example, when I moved from New Jersey to Florida at the age of twelve, I was as normal as any other twelve-year-old girl. But I was singled out instantly because of the way I *tawked*. My voice was the punchline for many jokes. My personality changed. It had to. I was now "The Joisey-Gurrl." I had to be ditzy around boys and tough around girls. It was the persona that went with the voice. Alternatively, when I got to college and learned words like epistemology and discourse, I had to shape up. I couldn't be a ditz using words like that! My personality shifted to accommodate a new vocabulary.

The words I use when I speak or write are very characteristic of me, and this use is bound to be influenced by my unique, subjective experiences. I live in Jersey, so when I refer to a group of people I say "Are yous okay?" But I have residual Floridian influences, so sometimes I say "Are y'all all right?" I am from a blue-collar family, so when I write about being angry I describe myself as "pissed off," but I am also an undergraduate at a fine institution so sometimes I say that I am "troubled." My accent when I speak, and the common phrases I use when I write certainly reflect parts of me, my past, my origin, etc. A (speaking and writing) voice is to a person *part of* her personality. Any writer should have a voice, if she has a personality. Not necessarily does one cause the other (though I can think of instances where personality is so similar to voice that it influences it enough to *cause* it), but they are inseparably related. I will use this relationship analogously throughout this portion of my discussion.

Aside from the fact that voice is part of a person and that excluding or extracting it from a person is just like removing a *trait* of that person, a voice has other importance in writing. A voice is the reason we can distinguish between one poem about lust and 300 other poems about lust. Not any one of these hypothetical poems will *sound* the same.

Additionally, in reading two separate pieces written by one individual, it should be clear that the pieces, though different, were authored by a single person. Aspects of the pieces will certainly vary. The purpose of the writing can be anything from persuasion to information to introspection. A different purpose will alter the piece. The expected audience will also alter the piece in some way, for example the amount of knowledge that will be assumed. The tone will vary according to the audience as well: Is the author addressing a group of laborers or a group of businesspersons? The rapport she will want to establish with either will certainly affect the way the piece is written. The type of writing will vary: Is it a course paper or a journal entry? Indeed many variants are at work. However, the certain voice of the author should be present in each case.

Why should we hear the voice of an author in each of her pieces? Stability. I think it is important to have a distinct identity to hold onto. To me, this is essential in maintaining a strong sense of self. If I allow my voice (my individuality) to vary according to the pieces I write, what then becomes of my identity?

Consider the unhealthy effects of an altering personality. If a person allowed her personality and/or identity to alter according to the situations she was in or the people she was around, upon being in a situationless state, she could find herself, I think, lacking a personality, thereby inviting continual identity crises.

Not only do I believe that a fluctuating voice threatens stability of self, but if one loses her voice, she becomes just another text. Voices make reading enjoyable. Voice allows us to differentiate among authors whose writing we like and those whose writing we do not like. Parallel this lack of voice in writing again to the lack of personality in persons. Without personality, how would we differentiate one person from the next?[4] Without voice, how will we distinguish among authors? How will we know we want to follow an author's work? How will we know when we read a novel by an author that we want to read another?

When a distinct voice is present in a work, it allows us to recall if we have read that voice before. I remember reading a couple of books by some author whose name I did not recognize as someone I had read before, Richard Bachman. But after reading the novels I was certain I knew the writer well. I learned subsequently that the books had been written by Stephen King, an author whose books I read faster than the library could get them in. It was his voice I felt I knew distinctly.

When we are familiar with a writer's work, we can connect various pieces to the same author and establish a coherent person behind the words. We can learn things about an author through her voice. These things we learn about the author may help us to attain even greater meaning within a text.

If we remove personalities from the persons we know, life would become quite a dreary prospect. I suggest similarly, if we remove voice from an author's writing, reading, too, would become a dreary prospect. Water and oxygen are of course necessary for living, but isn't it really *personality* that breathes life into an individual? Just as a pen and paper (or a stone tablet, or a computer) are essential for a text to occur, isn't it really an author with a voice who breathes life into a text? Without a voice, a piece becomes a dead thing. An example of a typical dead piece is a textbook. In most textbooks, we get no sense of personality behind the words. They are just … words. I tend to think textbooks are rather boring. There may be a "stoic" kind of voice there, but it is rarely distinguishable from other textbook voices.

If voice is a healthy, desirable aspect of writing, where then does the overtly personal presence enter this discussion? Can one have a voice while omitting the personal pronoun? Absolutely. Can one use the personal mode without having a voice? Probably. Where I see the need to connect them is here: voice is something that takes time to develop. Writers must have the freedom to explore their personalities on paper. They must have the freedom to include their personalities in their works. The most natural method seems to me to be the inclusion of the personal pronoun. By inserting "I" into a text, an author is forced to recognize her place in the piece. This will enable her to develop herself within a writing framework. By seeing herself in the writing, she will, over time, I believe, develop her style, her voice.

Using "I" does not guarantee that an author's voice will be present but it certainly suggests a person behind the words. This suggestion, though not the ideal, does establish the possibility of a personality, and that may be the more important goal. So while I believe a voice is the best way to make writing belong to a particular writer, using the personal is a good way to make writing belong to *somebody*, some *person* behind the words. I suggest that using the personal will help a writer to incorporate her voice. Using the word "I" is bound to "trick" the writer into letting more of her personality enter the writing, whereas totally depersonalizing writing allows for no individuality at all.

Voice is important: using "I" may encourage its development. Aside from the notion of subjectivity being evident in all writing, what are the other pressing reasons for the use of the personal pronoun? Individuality. I suggest that a writer, if forbidden the use of "I," may never develop herself or her voice. Instead, she will lose herself in academia and become a clone of those conscientious advisors of the past. Using "I" in academic writing is important in a writer's learning and growing process. Writing in the first person allows for a sense of accomplishment and a sense of opinion. It helps the writer to know that *she* is the one who came to a conclusion at the end of a paper. *She* is the one who did the research that she is presenting. *She* is the one who is arguing for something. She is *doing* something. *It belongs to her.*

Reader, imagine if after four or five years in college, you shuffle through all of the papers you wrote in that time and find that there is no indication that *you* wrote any of it, aside from the fact that your name appears at the top of each of the first pages. How can you feel that you learned anything if it was really "This Paper" who argued, or "This Paper" who proved, or "This paper" who concluded? How will it have affected the learning process while you were *in* college?

In a politics class I took during my junior year, I was taught to write memos. My professor explained the writing style for the class, and due to his careful instruction, I felt confident to begin writing even though I had never written a memo before. Considering that six memos over the semester would count for most of the course grade, it was important to learn to write them well. Memos have a very distinct format and the tone is not variable. They are "generally 'cold,' that is, [they] do not use rhetoric or emotion."[5] Use of the personal is forbidden. Not only was I not allowed to use "I" in these pieces, but for the purposes of the class, I had to write the memo *as* someone else, for example, the Prime Minister of Croatia. So, in effect, my voice and I were totally excluded from the writing for this class. I had to be ... *objective*. Or rather, I had to be someone else.

As a student I found writing these memos very difficult. In one sense, I was definitely appreciative that I was able to learn a new form, but actually I felt stifled. By memo number four, I caved in and included myself in the memo. I could not control myself. How could I possibly write a "cold" memo about the destructive power of nuclear arms after reading Carl Sagan's classic piece?[6] I knew I was taking a risk, but I had worked hard on the memo. The subject matter was powerful and the readings *affected* me intensely. My professor thought I had good things to say, and he gave me a deserving grade. He did, however, correct me in my use of the personal. He reminded me of the "cold" nature of a memo. Consequently, I did not include myself in the rest of the memos.

After this experience, I began to pay more attention to the types of writing that I was trying to mimic in the memos. I read an article on terrorism for the class. The author was a powerful man in the government who had a long, important title. It did not use the personal at all. I questioned my dogmatic approach to personal writing. Maybe "I" does not belong in every text. But then I decided there is indeed a difference between student writing and the work of established professionals. That difference again rests in learning and growing toward a stable identity. Student writers must have the opportunity to locate themselves within their writing for the reasons I have discussed, so that by the time they become people with long, important titles, they will have the confidence to express themselves skillfully, even if they have to do so without using "I." When I read the first line of the piece by the important man, there was a footnote; at the bottom of the page, a note about him, his achievements and his title. Therein lies another difference. On student papers, there are no such notes. In fact, if students do not include "I" in their essays, there is no indication of *who wrote the fucking paper*. Once a writer has a Ph.D. or a title or is an important author, he or she is established. The reader knows who it is. The credibility is evident.

It is possible that such writers exclude "I" because of convention. They may choose not to risk their publishability by rebelling against the system. It is also possible that those writers only get their long, important titles by remaining conventional, by playing the game. I suggest that for students, playing the game might hurt them in the long run. Not only might they suffer the consequences so far discussed, but they might forfeit the benefits of writing with "I."

Using the personal will positively affect how an author feels about her work and herself. A benefit of the personal is the sense of responsibility it lends. If it is the *author* who makes claims (as opposed to "This Paper"), she will feel more responsible for her words. More effort and care will go into the work if she has to own up to her words. Responsibility will yield dedication. The author will feel a positive pressure to defend herself, which will create a stronger paper. Using "I" declares authorship unquestionably, which is in itself rewarding.

This benefits the reader as well. The reader will never be left asking, "who says?" or "who thinks so?" A paper that states, "some would argue" is more open to question than a paper that reads "I would argue." There is no need to ponder as to who these "some" are.

So using the personal does not have only selfish rewards. There *are* benefits to the reader. Works using "I" tend to be less confusing, not only because claims are (well) claimed, but because the personal reduces wordiness. Compare, "It seems to be the case that" with "I have found that." "I" cuts down on excess verbiage. The more concise a piece, the better the chances that communication will take place.[7] A related benefit of using the personal for both the author and the reader is that it connects the two. This is especially important in persuasive communication. When the reader knows and can see a person in the words, there is a better chance that the reader will listen. A reader is more likely to "bond" with, or relate to, a person rather than a sterile sentence. This bonding is instrumental in certain situations.

Consider an essay where a student is trying to convince an oppressed audience that she will be the best representative for them because she too has experienced discrimination. Will the audience relate to her—believe her or have faith in her—if she does not include herself in the piece (by using "I")? If she does not use "I," I think the audience will not find her credible. Not only may the audience lose out on a potentially great representative, but also the author risks losing the chance of being a representative.

Opponents of the personal may feel that using "I" is redundant, that if the author is writing, we already know who is expressing himself—it is obvious, as in "The most important thing in life is money," instead of "I think the most important thing in life is money." However, I would note that, aside from the presumptuous nature of the first statement, it is presented as a fact, when it is of course, an opinion: it can never be proven objectively true. Moreover, when we speak, we use "I" all the time. If people didn't use "I" in speaking, they would sound ridiculous. Try it. Why should we not write the way we speak?

Considering the subjective nature of all writing, it seems reasonable, if not logical, to include the personal. Again, it seems that excluding the author of a text endorses a pretense of objectivity. Moreover, the use of "I" helps students to become stable, effective communicators. Not only will they take pride in their work, but their readers will recognize and appreciate their efforts. In my experience, it can actually hurt a writer to condemn her for including herself in her work. If a student is forced to exclude herself, she is not validated as having something to say. As evidenced by my memo-writing experience, the importance of the personal in student academic writing is monumental. It goes far beyond "professionalism" and "strength." Growth is key. Student writers need to realize their own voices. They need to feel stability in their writing. They need to feel responsible for their words. They need to feel worthy of their own expressions. Including themselves in their work will help them fulfill all these needs.

I think it is important not to lose one's self, one's voice, one's presence in academic writing. It is easy for us as students to let go, to let the discourse swallow us whole. It is easy to lose our personalities in the faux-objectivity of academic writing. It is hard *not* to give professors exactly what they are looking for. But I urge students to resist, and I ask professors to indulge our learning—just a little—because I believe the rewards are worth it.

Perhaps the best proof I could offer for the importance of using "I" in academic writing is this paper itself. If I had presented my arguments as objective truth claims exempt from any debate—e.g., "Both sides have it all wrong," *not* "I venture to claim that both sides have it all wrong," or, "Using 'I' will help a writer incorporate her voice in her work," *not* "I suggest that using 'I' will help a writer incorporate her voice in her work"—how would you, my reader, react?

NOTES

[1] For this paper, I reviewed all the papers I have written at Oberlin College. All used "I," except for the politics course memos (see note 5, below).

[2] I hesitate to get into what the hell reality is. I think, however, for the purposes of this paper, that the reader may assume reality is so linked with objectivity that reality can be seen as being similarly questionable.

[3] This is not to say that everyone's goal is selfish.

[4] I suggest that a name is to a text what a face is to a person; if no one had a personality, we could differentiate between people by their unique faces. In writing, if no one had a voice, we could distinguish authors by name.

[5] From a memo by Ben Schiff, Oberlin College Politics Department.

[6] The article referred to is "Climate and Smoke: An Appraisal of Nuclear Winter," and it was actually coauthored by Carl Sagan and four others: R. P. Turco, O. B. Toon, T. P. Ackerman, and J. P. Pollack. [Editor's note.]

[7] This assumes that communication is at least one goal of any writing.

WORKS CITED

Strunk, Jr., William, and E. B. White. *The Elements of Style*. Third Edition. New York: Macmillan, 1979.

Toon, O. B. et al. "Climate and Smoke: An Appraisal of Nuclear Winter," *Science* 247 (1990): 166–176.

Yaggy, Elinor. *How to Write Your Term Paper*. Third Edition. Scranton, PA: Chandler, 1968.

Chapter 19

Why Do We Write?

Dinah Shepherd

Writing.
What is writing
And why do we do it?
To find a voice
To say
I am here
Listen to me.
Writing.
What is writing
And why do we do it?
To connect with those before us
those after us
those standing beside us.
Writing.
To make our own history.
To make *my* own history.
To tell my story.
'Cause I've got one to tell.
And you might need to hear it.
Writing.
To make some sense of the craziness of a day.
To help someone else do the same.
To show me
and You
That I'm still kickin'—
Craziness and all.
Listen to me.

Jamal[1] is a friend of mine. I'd like to say we're real tight, but it's not like that. We greet each other with smiles as we rush in opposite directions, caught up in the hectic rhythm of a strangely intense place. Certain days—Tuesdays and Thursdays—our schedules seem to jibe, and I can count on bumping into him three or four times. Sometimes we hug, sometimes we hit a high five, and sometimes there's only an exchange of a "Whassup?" I recognize a light in him—a fire in the soul—and I am drawn to it. But other than that, I didn't know too much about him.

Until last Tuesday night, when the gods brought us together and said *Listen to each other. There is a story to be heard here tonight. And a story to be written.*

It was a slow night at the Writing Center, so I was excited when Jamal walked in, loudly announcing his entry, as per usual.

"No way, Dinah! You're the writing tutor?" he asked exuberantly.

We both laughed, and I pulled out a chair for him, next to mine. After asking him about his day, I moved on to the first "tutoring" question: "What class is this paper for?" Before responding, he took his head in his hands, flipped his dreads around, and rolled his eyes dramatically.

"Oh, man, D—it's for my Black Arts Workshop, and I'm freakin'. I'm all over the place in this paper, and nothin's comin' together like it should."

The assignment was open-ended. The gist of it was, I believe, "Write about what art means to you through your own culture."

I started to read the paper aloud, but somewhere between the third and fourth sentences, I turned Jamal's words inward, so I could hear them in his voice. This was his story, not mine. And I couldn't tell you how long I was immersed in Jamal's five-page draft. I would read one section, and then have to—feel *compelled* to—go back and read it again. It was simply too beautiful and too true to give it a quick once-over. My reading was interjected with spontaneous remarks—"whoas" and "wows" and "Jesus Christs" and "right ons." Usually, in reading someone's paper, I find myself nodding or saying "hmmm," but Jamal's paper brought out much more than that in me. In some parts, I would feel the tears coming. His tears, I could imagine, fell as he wrote this paper, and mine were shed right there on the spot.

> Writing.
> What is writing
> And why do we do it?
> To reclaim
> Unname
> Rename.
> Writing.
> Why?
> To circulate
> Reiterate
> Communicate.
> To keep the fluid motion in the circle
> *Will the circle be unbroken?*
> Yeah...
> If you tell your stories.

When I finally finished reading Jamal's glorious paper, I knew the only thing to do was to turn to Jamal and thank him. And I really, really meant it. He brushed off my reaction, again expressing his concern that the piece was "all over the place."

And it was. But it was supposed to be that way. Jamal wrote of coming to college from an African American family in Brooklyn, a family in which going to college after high school was not the norm. He wrote about feeling the need to "validate" everything said by his white friends. He wrote about his culture, rooted in the African Motherland. He compared his family and his way of life with that of those with a Western worldview and mindset. Time was a focal point for him—always rushing here, always planning the next day, the next vacation period, the next rest-of-your-goddamn-life. And he said that's not how he used to feel, that's not how he used to live. Jamal misses, he wrote, the more natural life he once knew.

Jamal's writing was all over the place. Which makes sense. Because, right now, he's all over the place, too. He's getting ready to graduate; he's feeling estranged, in some ways, from his family, and at the same time, estranged from a place he's been for the last four years. He's wondering where his place is, where his voice will fit. He's wondering in what part of the world he'll find himself at this time next year. Jamal is all over the place in every way you can think of.

We discussed this quite a bit after I recovered—literally—from reading his paper. Jamal was his paper, and his paper was Jamal. And I felt like I, too, was experiencing what he wrote about. When he spoke about time, I was invited to sit with his large extended family, "kickin' it" in the kitchen: chill, relaxed, being in the moment, talking, eating, breathing. Two lines later he jumps to the subject of his time at college, just as he actually jumped into it when he came here almost four years ago—and I'm feeling myself tighten up, wanting to back in the kitchen.

Our conversation broadened into an often-overheard one here on campus about the "evils" of the Western establishment. Jamal compared the whole Western approach with the Afrocentric approach. He broke it down by calling Western thought and discourse "linear," and African thought and discourse "circular." African writing, along with African American writing, often follows the form of traditional storytelling, involving morals, spirituality, connections to those *before us, after us, and beside us,* and the personal voice of the writer, unaccompanied by apologies for departing from Western conventions. African writing, along with African American writing, is often judged by different standards than those we so often use in the mainstream Western world. During the 1960s, Amiri Baraka, Calvin Hernton, and

Ronald Karenga headed up the Black Arts Movement, in which they set the precedent of judging art by how functional it is, how committed it is, and how collective it is. Functional: Will it help the cause of uplifting Black people? Committed: Is it true and real to the cause? Collective: Is it art by the people, for the people, about the people?

> Writing.
> Why?
> To say, Yo! This is where I come from.
> Writing.
> To say, Yo! This is where my ancestors come from.
> Writing.
> To yell, Yo! This is where we come from.
> So acknowledge
> Respect
> Accept
> Or step.
> 'Cause I'm teachin' you:
> Yo! This is where I come from.

I am often frustrated by the idea of writing in a strenuous academic environment. So much of what we are asked to write about in college does not seem to pertain to anything *real*, anything outside the realm of academia. My own writing here, along with the writings of my peers, often carries with it an empty voice, or a voice floating by itself. Floating with no connections. Often, the voice I read in a paper is not the voice of its author. I have come to believe the majority of academic writing is impersonal and, therefore, impertinent. What does a paper mean (i.e., Why is it even written?) if there are no following repercussions, no effect on the outside world, or more simply, on other people? Have we become a people who do not feel the burning desire to share our stories? Who do not feel it crucial for existence to reach out and touch others? Who believe that people must have an elevated level of understanding to appreciate our writing, or that our writing must be "dumbed down" to enable comprehension by the people with whom we coexist?

What's up with that?

What has happened to us that we are so afraid?

Or so arrogant?

> Writing.
> Why does one write?
> One writes to deconstruct the present paradigm.
> One writes to analyze the
> dichotomy

of relationships
in the era of post-modernism.
One may also write
to escape the confines of one's own internal structure.

I believe academia teaches us to remove ourselves from the big picture. The "school on the hill" thing is no joke. We are taught to keep a distance—from ourselves, from each other. We are taught to present ourselves as put-together VIPs, even when that's probably nowhere near what most of us are feeling. As we write, I believe we should feel as if we are learning about ourselves more and more every day and sharing ourselves more and more every day. We should feel that what we have to say is important—not because it sounds "good" or impressive, but because it is who we are. And *that* is good. Somehow, though, this does not seem to be happening.

It is sad that Jamal questioned the quality of his paper because it was "all over the place." Why should he think it's supposed to only be going in one place? And does he even know what one place that would or should be?

Last Tuesday at the Writing Center, Jamal brought me a living, breathing piece of art. Imagine that ... a paper filled with life, filled with a clear and pertinent voice. He had built no hiding places in his story and was therefore out in the open for all eyes to see. And I thank god he let my eyes see him. In the course of five pages, I was moved to tears, laughter, disbelief, rage, and joy right down to my core. His paper has been in the back of my mind ever since. And sometimes it moves to the front of my mind, and it's all I can think about. He had things to teach me, and I had things to learn from him. And I know he learned things about himself, too—he told me so. In his remarkable paper he was in touch with—and therefore connected with—his words, his story, himself.

Writing.
What is writing
And why do we do it?
I once heard Alice Walker say
She writes
so that she
can breathe.

NOTES

[1] A pseudonym.

Chapter 20

Demystifying the Discourse

Melissa Hoskins

I admit it. In a paper whose project is to demystify academic discourse by using resistant academic discourses to reveal the ways that it, like any language, includes by way of excluding—and by revealing its component parts, the way it is acquired, and what its limitations are—I don't know how to begin. Perhaps I will start by laying my cards on the table. This is an academic paper, for an academic course in a fairly elite institution of "higher learning." My audience is this academic discourse community of which I have been a part for almost four years. I considered writing this paper outside of the academy but balked at the difficulty of figuring out how to say "academic discourse" without saying "academic discourse." It is very telling that I choose not to take this challenge especially since this translation process was a large focus of the two interviews that I conducted.

What is also telling is that now this version is a revision of the original paper. And I had to revise that original text because, although on the comment sheet provided by the professor I self-identified the piece as both academic and personal/autobiographical, I came to realize the only way it was "personal/autobiographical" was that the subject was interesting to me and the views of the interviewees did reflect my views to an extent. But what was ironically missing from the earlier draft was any meaningful reference to myself, sadly letting down my readers if they expected the honesty of the opening paragraph to continue. So in this revised version I aim to maintain the integrity of my approach by including myself as a subject of inquiry.

What Methodology Did I Use?

I could not locate the book I was looking for, but I tried to conduct my interviews based on memory of the principles of *Experience Research Social Change: Methods from the Margins*, a book about feminist methodology. The idea of this method of interviewing is to break down the dichotomy of subject/object, making the researcher [me] less of an objective subject observing a research object, and more explicitly present in the research.[1] This is partly accomplished by examining how the researcher's [my] positionality (including position of power as the researcher) influences and shapes the research, and partly by making the interviewing process more of a back-and-forth, with both parties sharing information and making the purpose of the research clear.

I failed miserably at examining my positionality in the first draft of this paper. I supported my argument solely with the experiences of my interviewees. As I wrote in a journal entry, "By not making my experience and position explicit (even to myself) I am not doing justice to the conversation. I am an absent voice commenting on the struggles of others that so interestingly fit into my thesis without making it clear where my thesis came from in the first place."[2] The same journal entry also reveals something of my more honorable intentions: "It's a little more complicated, because as I was in a relative position of power as the researcher, I wanted to make sure I represented my interviewees in the most comprehensive and legitimate way, not aggrandizing my opinions, etc." But my efforts resulted in my leaving myself out of the discussion entirely while giving the impression that I was in there because I used "I" a few times.

Whom Did I Interview?

I interviewed Christa,[3] a Korean-Native American college student, someone who expressed how her acquisition of academic discourse alienated her from her home community. I also interviewed Danielle, a white working class Jewish lesbian college student who expressed the difficulty of translating political ideas to those outside of academic language. These interviews took place on October 16 and 17, 2001.[4] To remedy the omission of my own experiences in the first draft, I also answered the interview questions myself; my position is that of a lower-middle-class Cherokee and Caucasian college student. I asked ten questions (see Appendix) that covered our acquisition of academic discourse, how we translated what we learned from the language of the academy to the language of our communities, and what kinds of things, if any, academic language could not address or articulate. I also conducted a short discussion with my "Teaching and Tutoring Writing Across the Disciplines" class, for which I wrote this paper. I asked the class questions included in the Appendix. They replied to my email account with the answers to varying numbers of the questions. Since this part of my research barely scratched the surface, I have only included these responses in a limited fashion.

What Is Academic Discourse Anyway?

Language is a method and means of communication. Academic language, or discourse, creates subjects in much the same way a nation does through its official language (e.g., Spanish or English). The blank stare that Danielle and Christa got from community members when rattling off a phrase like "white supremist capitalist patriarchy" or "feminine constructions of desire and exotification in lesbian relationships" is very similar to the blank look my English-speaking brother gave a woman at the supermarket when she rattled off a string of French words.

Peter Elbow creates a path towards a clear definition when he breaks the goliath, Academic Discourse, into two more conquerable parts: (1) "sound argument" and (2) "stylistic conventions." (140–148) Further, he demystifies sound argument by recognizing that it is not particular to academic discourse alone. (142) This I believe to be a key concept, and here I feel it necessary to more clearly define the terms I have been using interchangeably, myself falling into the trap into which Bartholomae and many others have fallen by not dividing the discourse into parts as Elbow does. Academic *language* is the stylistic convention and jargon. Sound *argument* (supporting points following the statement of position) can be expressed using any kind of language. Argument carried out under the stylistic conventions with the field-appropriate vocabulary makes up *academic discourse*. As Beth, one of the other students in the tutoring course, put it, "I suppose [academic] language is about knowing the buzzwords, and then adeptly stringing those words together."

How Is Academic Discourse Acquired?

Elbow argues that students can better form strong arguments in a language with which they are already familiar, and that the stylistic conventions can be used better after the argument is in place. When I answered my own interview questions, I wrote that I enjoyed my Women's Studies classes because "I started getting feedback about my ideas [instead of stylistic concerns]; comments that either 'heard' my experiences or that pushed my argument further. [...] I think in the excitement of learning and utilizing new words to explain my experiences and ideas about life, I integrated everything, almost without realizing it." In Danielle's interview, she explained that her acquisition of the discourse began in the AP track in her mostly black high school:

> In AP there were about 35 students, made up of two Asians, one black, rest white. We were trained to learn and memorize traditional arguments and construct a thesis and a paper in order to compete in a college education. A paper was a 3-paragraph

essay that followed a formula, had clear and concise arguments, and responded
critically. This set of knowledge helped [me] at college.

Despite her knowledge of the form an academic essay should take, the
language and terminology were "alienating and turned me off. I still struggle
with the complexity of language used." (Interestingly, in my estimation, she
navigates the language quite well.) I wrote that I, like Danielle, learned "the
five or so basic ways to organize an academic paper" in AP English. It
wasn't until I took "Introduction to Women's Studies" that "a major part of
our exams would be to define these jargon words. So I learned them. Actually, I've come to really enjoy super thick academic writing if it is also a
scathing critique." Christa also seemed to make a distinction between structure and style by separating in which class she "had to learn how to restruc-
ture my papers" and in which she learned "to speak academically." In the
lived experiences of these two women, and mine as well, academic discourse
has at least two parts, and form seems to have been tackled before style.

Are there more than two parts to academic discourse? Various students,
writing instructors, and scholars have acknowledged definite differences in
the discourses specific to different fields of study. The same stilted language
is endorsed across them to varying degrees (science writing versus literary
writing), but it is still endorsed. Danielle began her interview with: "I have to
make a distinction between traditional, in the canon—which is oppressive to
me, and other marginalized people— and another language of resistance that
is still academic: the language of women's studies."

While Christa, Danielle, and I found the discourse of women's studies
useful, we still recognized the limitations it carries as an academic discourse,
"that it is both libratory and creates elitist hierarchies," to quote Danielle.
This statement is a self-conscious critique in the language of the discipline.
Perhaps women's studies is attractive to these women because it is "academic language that wasn't just buying into the canon and norms," as Danielle further notes. It was attractive to me as well because, as I noted above,
"in Women's Studies I started getting feedback about my ideas"; however, I
agree that this discourse does create its own hierarchies, as I have seen
fellow majors struggle with the "unpoliticized masses," in a similar way that
others from academe struggle with the "uneducated."

In the formation of my questions, I did not expect a distinction to be
made *between* discourses. I think the strength of that distinction has made
itself one of the most interesting, while unexpected, findings of this paper. I
did not expect it because having taken largely Women's Studies or related
courses, I didn't pay very much attention to papers outside of those disciplines. I did not realize immediately the significant perceived difference

between this and other academic discourses. The rise of alternative fields and ways of study has complicated the discourse of the academy, reminding me of the complexity of language and the numerous possibilities for resistance and transformation. Through the interviews and my own experience, I can see how these alternative discourses both transform the academy and are limited by the academy. Both Danielle and I have taken our Women's Studies discourses into other classes, for instance, using "I" and personal experience liberally. And Danielle, Christa, and I have all dropped the vocabulary when trying to relate our ideas to those outside of the academy.

The professionalization of alternative discourses such as Women's and Ethnic Studies is evident when Danielle talks about the double-edged sword of the difficulty of creating writing that can gain credibility and legitimacy, and writing that can be widely understood—writing with which listeners can relate. Note that the strings of words I referred to above that elicited blank stares (e.g., "white supremist capitalist patriarchy") were from feminist or women's studies discourse. It's important to note, though, that the same language can also critique itself in ways that traditional academic discourse could never dare to do. The most important aspects of my interviewees' acquired feminist discourse are its ability to be self-critical and its legitimization of personal story as an important way of knowing—aspects that they use in translating between discourse communities.

Translation

Though both Danielle and Christa experienced difficulty and challenge as they worked to use academic discourse, they did not expect the language difficulties they faced when they returned home from college. This difficulty seems evident across non-academic communities; the students in the Teaching and Tutoring course from less academic backgrounds had similar experiences. One of them, Dana, said in an email message to me, "I used to think that after four years of college, I would go home and everything would be the same. This [learning new ideas and new ways to express them] has completely changed how I will interact with people." And when Christa returned home to her blue-collar Korean and Native American family as a first-generation college student, "it was really hard, a big change-up in cultures. All of a sudden, I'm tryin' to throw around these big words and theories about race/class/sexism, etc., to my parents as if they didn't know what was up." To Danielle's two best friends from high school, she became a crazy militant lesbian. To Christa's family, she risked being a "pompous snot."

On the other hand, students who do not master and internalize academia suffer biting comments from professors, poorer grades, and find their opinions ignored. Says Christa: "I think some kids/profs might think I'm not so smart cuz honestly, some of those words I should know, I don't, and not being able to use these superfluous words is a bit of a marker y'know." These are different communities, each with their own methods of control and conformity. How does a student traveling between discourses make the connections?

Christa realized that just because her parents didn't use the same vocabulary, it didn't mean they didn't know what she was talking about:

> I just remember my dad being like, "um, I lived this stuff. Don't try to tell me what's going on." It kinda made me sit back and start listening to my parents instead of tryin' to think I knew it all cuz I'd read a few books or had a few experiences.

Her community emphasizes respect for elders, and so one strategy has been to listen to those people, "since they *know* the issues, and trying to re-verbalize what I learn in the classroom in a way that's not alienating." She faces a further difficulty in translation because she and her brother are "the only Asian-mixed grandkids"; most of her cousins are black and Native American, and so "culturally there tends to be some sense of alienation or unfamiliarity." And this is the side of the family she is able to speak with about these things. On her mother's side, there is an English/Korean language barrier. She stressed several times her fear of sounding like she had a big head, and her cautiousness when trying to engage in discussions with her family. In response, she has "worked towards not using any of these words/phrases" at all, trying to keep the "-isms and -ologies out," and this has made it easier to speak with her home community:

> I never *really* absorbed all the really academic sounding stuff, so it's not [...] a choice of which word do I use in which context, but how do I use the words I do know to fit these different conversations and still adequately describe the more difficult ideas/concepts.

For Christa, it seems to be less an issue of integrating herself into the academy than of integrating what she finds useful here into what she already knows.

Danielle has more fully internalized academic discourse—feminist academic discourse. "I've definitely absorbed and begun to use the terminology and style of writing that will be received well, or listened to [in the academy]." She exercises resistance both against and within traditional academic discourse when she writes even her traditional academic class papers using "I," feminist theory, and personal experience. She also uses a strategy taught in Professor A's feminist classes to connect the ideas behind the academic words with the lived experiences of her friends. "Professor A's feedback validated personal experience. She knew how to use individual experiences to bridge the gap between theory and life. This made knowledge real, alive, tangible, necessary and crucial for survival." The way she acts this out is similar to the way Christa described her strategy:

> listen carefully and critically to people, to draw out ideas that can be related to larger structures. [...] Just because someone doesn't have the language doesn't mean they don't know what you're talking about. It's really crucial and possible to make these connections.

My language-related experiences have been much the same as those of Christa and Danielle. I am more similar to Danielle in her internalization of feminist academic discourse and wrote in my survey answers that I even have come to enjoy it, though I understand its limitations. Both of my parents have been to college, and my family has strong convictions about the importance of education. It is mostly the politics I am careful about. In my interview I wrote:

> I think the political nature of my studies makes [translation of academic feminist discourse] a little different than others because a lot of my knowledge is obviously political, and the jargon I know expresses very political ideas some people are uncomfortable with. So the words can mark you and make people reluctant to hear what you have to say.

This is similar to some of the experiences expressed in our Teaching and Tutoring class where the student's use of academic words at home caused distrust. My strategy then, like the two women I interviewed, has been to drop the vocabulary. I too, am more likely to knock it when I am frustrated with its inability to apply to places outside the academy.

What Does This All Mean?

Here arises a very telling issue about context. When talking about feminist academic discourse in the context of the academy, we all seemed to value it, at least to some degree. Danielle experienced feminist discourse as a point for resistance and liberation within the college. I have found it *a way* to make sense of experiences that the dominant explanations could not address. Christa wrote of learning "terms like 'white supremist capitalist patriarchy' and other such *usefully* ridiculous terms [emphasis added]." But when talking about this language in the context of their home discourse communities, they devalued it. "If I want to talk about exotification in lesbian relationships, how desire is constructed, how it's affected by race, class, etc., all this *bullshit* we learn in women's studies [emphasis added]." Christa writes:

> I don't place any value on being able to use these made-up academic words, in fact, I'd say I place a negative value on them. Which has led me to feel more like academia isn't my world and that I wouldn't make it if I attempted to go on.

I, on the other hand, have had different difficulties in translation. I have found academic feminist discourse extremely powerful because, as I noted in the survey, "it has enabled me to put my experiences in a frame of many other similar ones. It makes them make sense within a larger structure, and explains many of the things that I thought were my fault, or my individual problem." I am frustrated by the lack of ways to share this knowledge with other people, impeded as it is by the specialized vocabulary that creates the commonplaces of academic feminist discourse.[5]

Words like "exotification" and "the public/private split" *are important* concepts used to explain a feminist view of the world. Because feminists are a marginal group inside and outside academia, words were created to explain the previously unnamed. Thus, "naming" is one of the most important bases of feminism. What is tragic (or problematic, to use the lingo) is that naming is only as powerful as the recognition of the names by the outside world. So unlike the traditional academy, which has a stake in keeping the doors closed and the nation small, feminism has a stake in letting in as many people as possible in order to challenge the dominant commonplaces.

The interviews also brought to my attention again the different parts that make up academic discourse. We seemed to have the most trouble/issues with the language, not the reasoning. We spoke of modifying our language from place to place but never of changing the reasoning. I think this occurs especially for us because we are talking about a resistant discourse. The conversation around making the discourse more accessible is most involved in tone and terminology. Christa also notes, as Elbow does, how "a lotta people get off on being able to say simple things complexly." The use of complex language to say "capitalist patriarchy" instead of "The Man," for example, has helped Women's Studies gain a foothold in the academy. Now that it has greater legitimacy in the academy, those of us involved with it are seeking ways to democratize its messages. Danielle stresses that "just because someone doesn't have the language doesn't mean they don't know what you're talking about. It's really crucial and possible to make these connections."

Both Christa and Danielle have not fully internalized academic discourse, nor do they express complete confidence about their command of it.

Christa speaks of being alienated, of academia not being "her world." Danielle doesn't come to this conclusion, but she does express doubt about her mental capabilities. The influence of both communities has created a split, perhaps more so in Danielle than Christa, at least as seen in these two interviews. Danielle seems to value the feminist academic discourse when speaking in context of the discourse but emphasizes its language limitations when speaking in the context of her home community. She completely rejects "traditional" academic discourse. Christa more completely rejects the academy's language altogether, though she still values the reasoning of resistant academic reasoning. The rejection seems to be partly caused by the academy's rejection of her home community's ways of speaking and, by extension, its rejection of her experiences and abilities. She "might not make it" if she goes on.

What It Lacks

While there was valuing and devaluing of academic discourse, the interviewees seemed to agree on what the discourse absolutely could not address. Says Danielle:

> Emotion. Fails miserably at addressing and dealing with emotion. Work done from a feminist perspective can be different. [Our Women's Studies professor] used emotion to help understand theory. She would tell us to feel the emotion *first*, and then theorize about it. Still theory falls way short of dealing with emotions/pain.

Christa refers to her answers to the other questions and requires quoting at length:

> I guess I find academia to be really cold. I think someone from academia'd read this and just think I had issues and just didn't have the stuff to make it in college/grad school. But I think these kind of conversations are the important areas of our life that "academics" mis-value (here's one of those ridiculous words), dismiss and ignore, and never understand. And I think it's by consistently doing this that most of their theories [...] don't relate to reality or people's lives. I dunno, I think academia misses the heart cuz it focuses too much on the brain.

Positionality seems to be key in the different ways these women ultimately absorb or reject all or part of feminist academic discourse. Danielle's and my AP tracking and parents well versed in dominant discourse gave us an advantage over Christa when she entered college. Danielle demonstrates awareness of this situation when she says, "Comprehension is connected to background, to whatever privilege you've had," and goes on to acknowledge her own fairly competent use of feminist discourse in the academy.

I would conjecture that not only does the academy lack an adequate articulation of emotion (perhaps what Elbow would refer to as "rendering") but a lack of discourse that serves the needs and wisdoms of students from a background other than the dominant. To the extent that mainstream discourse does concern itself with those on the periphery, the research focuses on problems and difficulties of marginalized students instead of strengths and then blames the problems on culture or family values rather than the deficiency of the schools. Further, as I wrote in the survey, "I think even [feminist academic discourse] misses the spiritual. There are just some things you can't explain and have to accept, and so in the language of proof and counter-proof, you simply can't go there." Christa sees this lack of the capacity to deal with the reality of people's lives, and understandably so, as she has seen it fail to deal with her family's life in a way that actually engages them in the conversation. More alarmingly, the critique is of a resistant discourse. Dominant academic discourse is an alien and unfriendly form to many people, while those who possess it wield it (perhaps at times unwittingly) in competition with and sometimes to the detriment of those who do not. Based on the interviews, my own experience, the work of certain sociologists and other researchers, even resistant discourses carry many of the problems of academic language and style.

The End and the Beginning

One of the ways students are instructed to write a paper is to say what they are going to say, say it, and then say what they said. That's one of the reasons why this section bears this title. But it is also because I hope that the end of my paper might lead to a continuation of efforts to demystify academic discourse. So what have I said?

In my interviews I found that while neither Christa nor Danielle—nor I—felt we had fully internalized and mastered traditional academic discourse, we had acquired resistant discourses to varying degrees. The difference in degree of acquisition seemed to be related to our class, race, sexuality, language, and gender position before ever entering the academy, and this position continued to affect our negotiation, and ultimately our acceptance or rejection of the academy. Further, our rejections of the academy stemmed from a perceived inability of academic discourse to address emotion, spirituality, and even everyday reality. Moreover, the simple use of academic terms does not make an argument valid, nor does it eliminate the pitfall of relying on "commonplaces."

These shortcomings of the discourse of the academy must alert us to the fact that the academy is not a monolith encompassing and addressing all "objective" knowledge. It is one language, a powerful language (as English itself is), but only one way of talking. It cannot lay sole claim to sound and supported argument, and it cannot address the entirety of human experience. It is a contested space, as resistant discourses struggle for footholds, attempting to use its legitimacy for transformative purposes. If we are able to realize these things, perhaps we can begin to open places for other discourses and allow our own to be transformed and improved by the multitude of voices academic discourse has so far largely ignored.

NOTES

[1] Wow, that's a lot of "obs" and "jects" and "subs."

[2] Journal entry for Rhetoric 401, Oberlin College, November 13, 2001.

[3] All student names are pseudonyms.

[4] All quotations from Christa and Danielle are taken from these interviews.

[5] A twist on Bartholomae's criticism of "commonplaces" in failed academic papers. Academia (including Women's Studies) has its own commonplaces. Further, creating alternative commonplaces is actually a radical/critical act, since commonplaces are the dominant logic taken for granted.

WORKS CITED

Bartholomae, David. "Inventing the University." *When a Writer Can't Write: Studies in Writer's Block and Other Composing Process Problems.* Edited by Mike Rose. New York and London: The Guilford Press, 1985: 134–166.

Elbow, Peter. "Reflections on Academic Discourse: How It Relates to Freshmen and Colleagues." *College English* 53 (1991): 135–155.

Kirby, Sandra and Kate McKenna. *Experience Research Social Change: Methods from the Margins.* Toronto: Garamond Press, 1989.

APPENDIX

Interview Questions

1. Please talk a little bit about how you learned to speak and write academically at this college.

2. Were certain classes key in acquiring academy-appropriate language?

3. What kinds of feedback, comments, grades, did you receive on your papers as you continued to negotiate the academy?

4. How does academic language, in your experience, differ from the language/s spoken in your community/s?

5. What have been some struggles in the translation of academic language to language spoken in your communities?

6. How have your communities responded to your use of language from the academy? What kinds of feedback have they given?

7. How does their feedback correspond/differ/relate to feedback given by students and professors?

8. What have been some of your strategies to translate political knowledge gained at Oberlin College to language that will be understood, accepted, and useful in your communities?

9. Are there certain things articulated in the language/s of your communities that academic language cannot articulate/address?

10. What other questions should I have asked?

Thank you so sincerely for your time and labor!

Section Seven

Online Writing and Electronic Communication

The first edition of this book was published a mere decade ago, yet the landscape of electronic communication has changed so drastically since then that the alteration can truly be described as breathtaking. We now exist in the world of Web 2.0, where the active role of content creator has supplanted the passive role of content consumer, and the runaway success of Wikipedia, carrying with it hordes of resistant academics, makes it the clear winner of the Internet popularity sweepstakes, for good or for ill the go-to site for fledgling researchers. Social networking sites such as MySpace and Facebook have to some extent supplanted email as the medium of choice, at least among the young, as has the proliferation of text messaging. Moreover, audio and video files may be created and shared with an ease undreamed of a scant few years ago.

Within this new environment come new opportunities for teaching and learning—and new issues for debate. Does Internet writing harm or encourage academic writing? Do all those wall posts on Facebook contribute to greater rhetorical flexibility or just provide another venue in which to use slang, incorrect grammar, and overall "bad" English? Do students learn how to express themselves concisely or become ever more distracted from their studies as they tweet their Twitter followers and surreptitiously text friends during class? What research data exist to answer these and other questions, and how are teachers of writing to select effective technology-based strategies from the myriad of those available?

Answers to these and other equally compelling questions about the impact of electronic communication and the Internet on pedagogy are well beyond the scope of this section. Putting "teaching writing using the Internet" into a search engine recently resulted in 114 *million* hits—so there is no dearth of discussion, research, and pronouncements to review.[1] By the time this book is published, substantial analyses of data from an extensive longitudinal study of students' writing that its authors hope will end the debate as to whether the effects of the Internet are salutary should be available, and one of them has already been quoted as saying that he believes the data will demonstrate that students "routinely learn the basics of writing concepts wherever they write the most."[2]

The three articles selected for inclusion here address a small piece of the very large Internet communication pie: one discusses online writing from the professor's point of view (JoAnne Podis), and two do so from that of the student writing associate (Elizabeth Weinstein and Aaron Miller), but all three offer strategies for teaching writing in the era of Web 2.0.

The Articles

The first selection in Section Seven, JoAnne Podis's "Authority Issues in Online Instruction" (Chapter 21), considers whether any changes in the "hegemonic academic paradigms" described in Miriam Axel-Lute's chapter in Section Five may result when the site of instruction becomes virtual. Podis, too, elicits the responses of peers—fellow professors—asking them to examine whether they have observed any changes in their relationship with their students as they have begun to teach courses online.

Many of Podis's respondents have, in fact, noticed changes, some subtle, some more obvious. Nearly all have observed increased communication with their students and also greater productivity as traditional status barriers have eroded. As a result, however, issues related to dealing with heavier work-loads have arisen, as faculty and students have begun to use the electronic media freely.

Podis updates her essay with current reflections from some of the original survey respondents and provides information from two recent articles reinforcing the notion that authority in the Web 2.0 environment may have to be re-negotiated.

In Chapter 22, "Internet Forums and the Writing Student," Aaron Miller identifies what he believes are the considerable similarities between academic writing and the writing found on Internet discussion groups. He contends that within groups whose members post regularly and discuss topics in depth, individual posts approximate academic essays.

Miller suggests that writing instructors may capitalize on their students' engagement with, and enjoyment of, Internet forums by incorporating participation into an actual course assignment. In the final section of his essay he provides specific suggestions on how to accomplish this.

Instructors may already be using the discussion forum feature of their college's course management systems; Miller's suggestion broadens the scope of student writing from the classroom to the wider world beyond.

The final chapter in this section (Ch. 23), "Writing in the Information Age: The Language of Email and Instant Messaging" is primarily a discussion of the development of Instant Messaging, including reasons for its popularity and potential positive and negative influences on users' writing habits. The author, Elizabeth Weinstein, ultimately sides with those researchers whose studies suggest that engaging students in any writing, IM included, may have a salutary effect, even if only to encourage writing in students who otherwise would not write at all. Weinstein's own informal study of IM as used by four teenaged boys provides her with a glimpse into actual users' motivations and habits.

Weinstein presents some statistics in her essay regarding the widespread use of IM by teens and young adults. More recent data from the Pew Internet and American Life Project show that while the percentage of teens using IM has dropped, it has kept pace with the use of "new" media such as Facebook—61% of teens report using Facebook, 60% use IM, and 58% use text messaging.[3] On a daily basis, a greater percentage of teens talk on their cell phones (51%), use social network sites to communicate (42%), or text (38%), but IM is still used daily by 26% of this study's respondents.

NOTES

[1] Www.google.com accessed 7/28/09.

[2] Quoted by Keller (2009).

[3] Lenhart (2009).

WORKS CITED

Keller, Josh. "Studies Explore Whether the Internet Makes Students Better Writers," *The Chronicle of Higher Education*, June 11, 2009.

Lenhart, Amanda. "It's Personal: Similarities and Differences in Online Social Network Use Between Teens and Adults," *Pew Internet and American Life Project*. <Http://www.pewinternet.org/ > Accessed 7/31/2009.

Chapter 21

Authority Issues in Online Instruction

JoAnne M. Podis

Language is a system of shared social relations, and communication imbricates us in those relations. Given then that medium does affect meaning and that discursive acts call us into subject positions, researchers must consider the meanings and subjectivities invoked by electronic publishing. If, as researchers, we view electronic writing simply as an efficient and neutral vehicle for the transmission of content, then we have no control over the ways it may victimize or empower us.   (Howard, 6)

In theory, at least, electronic environments potentially offer a free flow of information and ideas from all to all. (Kaplan, 21)

"Hey! JoAnne."

It is noon on Friday. I am walking through the crowded lobby of a downtown office building when I hear my name shouted. It is my online writing student, waving enthusiastically over the heads of other walkers.

"Have a good weekend, Carol," I shout back. "You, too," comes the quick reply, as we stride toward our respective exits.

This fleeting exchange became my motivation to explore in greater detail instructor-student authority issues in online instruction. It occurred to me that I knew an awful lot about this particular student, her family, and her recent good times as well as past difficulties. I knew that her current job was a promotion, and that a few college courses (which she took after being, basically, goaded into it by a co-worker) whetted her appetite for a four-year degree, one she will earn approximately thirty years after her high school graduation.

She also knew a great deal about me. She was quite comfortable hailing me in the middle of a crowd—by my first name, no less, although such informality does not, in general, exist between students and professors at the institution at which I was then teaching.

Although small and student-centered, the college offered only business degrees, and perhaps because of the conservative image that business programs connote, classrooms tended to be formal. Nevertheless, I knew my students fairly well, perhaps better than the average instructor, since I usually taught composition, in which a good deal of their writing was based on personal experience. But it seemed to me that I got to know my online students even better.

My curiosity piqued, I began to consider seriously and to research issues such as the following: From what sources does our authority as professors tend to derive? How do those sources change in an electronic setting? How do the students' contexts—social, educational, and personal—influence the authority relationship online as opposed to within the classroom? And finally, does the authority dynamic between professor and student change by design or of necessity as one leaves the traditional classroom? If the latter, what are the implications for professors contemplating online instruction?

To attempt to construct answers to these questions, I drew from my own (limited) experience as online instructor (and Internet junkie); from the (more substantial) experience of colleagues who regularly teach online, five of whom completed a brief questionnaire; and from published sources, both online and conventional. Not unexpectedly, I found both areas of consensus and wide divergence of opinion and experience. The instructors whom I surveyed, as well as myself, taught courses largely through email, and only a few provided opportunities for synchronous communication.

I began my research with some basic assumptions. Believing that "[...] authority, like voice, is situational and constructed," (Maher, 160) I felt sure that the context of the Internet and email would affect professor/student dynamics. My sense, too, was that the Internet might provide a vehicle for the "power-sharing critical pedagogy" Ira Shor says is "a process for restructuring authority, teaching, and learning." (147)

Certainly, electronic mail already has a reputation for potential egalitarianism that is inherent in the medium. After all, visual and other nonverbal cues as to the gender, race, or social class of the communicators are completely absent (let us disregard for the moment personal web pages with photos of the pages' owners and other graphics). Thus possible nonverbal sources of our authority as professors become non-existent or minimized. We do not, online, move into the power space at the front of the classroom or, for that matter, sit beside our students. Our students cannot see that we may wear ornamentation appropriate to our role as conservative professor or hipster scholar/mentor or any other identity we may choose to construct. Wherever our classroom environment appears on a scale from authoritarian to democratic, we cannot so easily use nonverbal factors to create it virtually.

One of my respondents is Suzanne, who has been teaching full-time for several years and online for two, and her experience reinforces my belief that informality is the email default. She notes that her online students "tend to act more friendly towards me. There isn't that same teacher/student barrier that often exists when you stand in front of a classroom." She considers herself "more of a tutor, mentor, or editor," as does Tim, another respondent, who is new to online instruction and who found that email's flexibility allows him to personalize instruction to a much greater extent than in conventional classes. In responding to his students' messages, he can provide "many individual responses to questions/comments by individual students." This personalization, he feels, can lead to greater informality in his relations with his online students. Joan C. Tornow echoes Suzanne's and Tim's experiences when she cites the example of a student who always addressed the instructor on a first-name basis when communicating online but never did when face to face. (54)

Within the conventional classroom setting, should we desire to exercise it, we have a degree of control that reinforces our authority: we may decide who speaks, for example, and for how long; we may establish the parameters of acceptable debate and discussion, as well as the topics for each session. The boundaries of time and space, set well in advance and memorialized in the schedule booklet, also apply. Thus the class meets in a particular room at a particular day and time; in general, we uphold those boundaries. We begin and end class, and doing so on time is generally held to be a virtue—in any case, certainly part and parcel of our authority is the right to officiate at the opening and closing of each class.

As we move into electronic settings, the various material qualities of our interactions with students, many of which combine to become seats of our authority as professors, disintegrate, with predictably major implications for those who contemplate online instruction. Tornow goes so far as to say that online instruction is "not for the faint of heart," noting that "In computer-network discussions, the teacher no longer mediates the conversation by calling on students and responding to their comments with a direct or indirect evaluation. He or she no longer controls the conversation." (54) And Michael Joyce comments, in referring to a networked class in American literature, "The learners truly take their place as co-equals in an interpretive community." (121)

What occurs, in effect, is that we are left with limited sources of authority. Our position as professors and our expertise in our discipline may convey credibility and authority. Although these may not disappear completely with the translation to a new medium, instructors may find that online they more quickly embrace the "tutor, mentor, editor" roles to which Suzanne refers. Joyce uses the term "multi-disciplinary specialist" (121) to convey the new, multi-faceted roles of the instructor who collaborates with her students rather than being the "head" of the class.

Verbal cues—the ways in which we use language, our diction, syntax, and other conventions of usage—may provide another, also limited source of authority for the online instructor as coach rather than player. However, I would suggest that the electronic context tends to mitigate professorial authority and that faculty contemplating teaching online may find their perspectives on their roles challenged in ways they may not expect. Patrick, a veteran in the conventional classroom, and an online professor for two years, comments as follows on the influence of the Internet, where all Web sites are created equal: "[...] with the Internet as a metaphor for the class (no single site being more important than another), the teacher with the more authoritarian approach may find him or herself swimming up the perceptual stream."

In fact, putting aside for the moment serious questions of access (such as those discussed by Ray and Barton and by Gomez), we can likely all agree that the Internet is potentially inclusive and egalitarian. Lewis J. Perelman asserts that its essence may lead to "the empowerment of human minds to learn spontaneously, without coercion, both independently and cooperatively." (23) This view of a democratic electronic community, as James Strickland notes, has been present from the beginning:

> In the best of all possible worlds, the teacher will be just one more writer on the network, a network linking voices across the room and across the country. This was the vision of the original hackers who began the computer revolution: a global village a la Marshall McLuhan/Buckminster Fuller. (Strickland)

While working on this article, I noticed that a TV commercial for an Internet Service Provider made the same point, using a montage of images of people—young, old, black, white, differently abled—to support the claim that socio-economic factors disappear as users log on. Faculty planning to teach online might bear in mind this natural inclination toward democracy.

At this point I will add that my survey suggests, not surprisingly, that professors tend, at least initially, to replicate their classroom style when they instruct online. Students themselves may react differently. For instance, Ed, an experienced instructor who by the late 1990s had taught Internet courses an impressive eight years, feels that his online students generally approach him more cautiously at first than they do in his conventional classrooms, seeing him as the disembodied voice of expert knowledge, with built-in authority—what Patrick calls the "Wizard of Oz factor." Patrick goes on to say that "students conditioned to think of teachers as authority figures tend to react fairly formally until the teacher reveals his or her personality." Ed, Patrick, and Suzanne are all in agreement that as the volume of email between and among students and instructor increases, so does the informality of the exchanges, and my own experience bears this out.

Another respondent, however, has a slightly different perspective. Donna's experience of over two years of online instruction, in the light of many years of classroom teaching, leads her to believe that "whatever approach an individual student would be using in the classroom will carry over pretty much directly to the online course." Similarly, she feels her approach to instruction does not vary significantly as she moves from the physical to the virtual situation. If anything, she notes, "I could make a case that I feel more in control online because I don't have to deal with the live, in-person presence of a roomful of people. There are actually fewer opportunities for the public challenge I think most teachers dread. If a student has an issue during an online course, it is much more likely to be handled privately."

Questions of personal teaching style or philosophy aside, electronic mail from its inception has not been a formal medium—quite the reverse is true. Talk to veteran Internet users, in fact, and you may very likely hear a lament for the days before the Invasion of the Newbies—the frontier days when such things as line editors and prohibitive online composing costs made revision anathema and questions of grammar, usage, and style moot. You simply typed out what you wanted to say—quickly. Whatever typographical errors were made stayed put, and format receded to make way for the gist of meaning you hoped would make it through. Today's Internet, these veteran users aver, is much too formal.

For most of us Janey- or Johnny-come-latelys, though, email tends to be supremely informal, and it may be harder than we might suspect to maintain the same level of formality of discourse customary in a classroom setting. Moreover, in addition to what might be called an ethos of egalitarianism, consider as well the various graphic conventions that have sprung up, all of which seem to contribute further to the essential informality of the Internet.

Emoticons are everywhere. The ubiquitous smiley face of the 70s, which perhaps should have been consigned to the same oblivion as other, equally forgettable products of that decade (e.g., polyester leisure suits), instead has exploded into the major substitute for the nonverbal nuances of interpersonal communication. Its variations appear infinite, to the point that dictionaries of smileys, now given the more dignified appellation, *emoticon*, are essential: how else to tell whether the sender is happy, sly, lipstick-wearing, or a Klingon? The use of emoticons may give an additional layer of feeling to verbal language, but it surely does not provide an additional layer of formality.

Acronyms, perhaps a throwback to days when writing messages as quickly as possible was a primary virtue—and perhaps a nod to the preferences of the engineers who designed the Internet (I think of the engineering majors I knew as an undergraduate and their propensity to label crises as FUBAR)—likewise contribute to informality of usage. They are essential components of Internet communication; they are impossible to avoid, and they form an essential core of knowledge for all Internet users. Sometimes they also substitute for the lack of visual and other cues, as for instance, LOL (laughing out loud). In any case they become habitual. If students are serious Internet cruisers, their inclination will be to continue to use them, and it may be that it is more difficult to cling to professorial authority when receiving and sending messages filled with :-) or :-(or a variation thereof.

Among the more carefree and whimsical aspects of email, however, there may also lurk the potential for miscommunication. Readers may interpret the tone of email texts in ways writers do not intend to a greater extent than occurs when texts are created non-electronically. Over and over again I have heard students and colleagues in communication with each other comment that they have received harsh-sounding or hostile messages that, following further dialogue with the senders, needed re-interpretation. Such a tendency may also affect professor-student authority issues.

Nearly all of my respondents point out that they have found that students tend to interpret online criticisms of their work more harshly than similar remarks made either orally or on paper. Suzanne comments, "[…] I never really intended my tone to be sarcastic or harsh, but some students read it that way at times," while Ed explicitly cautions, "I find strict approaches in comments and criticism are taken too seriously by students online. I purposefully try to temper my criticisms of papers, etc., for this reason."

On the one hand, students may be responding more sensitively to the "expert's" judgment; on the other, they may also respond with what they believe to be in-kind aggressiveness, depending on their sense of their own authority and, perhaps, on their experience with the Internet, where flaming is relatively common. There was some agreement among my colleagues and myself that students' online voices frequently seemed strident and aggressive, particularly when they emailed inquiries demanding rationales for grades on assignments. Most of us agreed that these requests, though private rather than public, were generally higher-profile challenges than occur in conventional classrooms. Tornow's research supports our experiences: "In this environment, students may readily dispense with the conventional stance of acquiescent and docile student." (101) In any case, whether on the professor's or on the student's part, misunderstanding can easily result. Adding a smiley to make attempts at humor more overt may help. Being aware of the potential for misinterpretation likely does as well.

As suggested above, students who are cyber-nuts will approach the online course with a good deal of confidence as well as enthusiasm, and they will have built-in expectations for the medium and their roles within it. I would suggest that this feeling of authority may carry over into their written assignments and other communications with their professors and peers alike.

Having said this, I will add that depending on course requirements, students' assignments may be submitted using formats as formal as would be expected in a conventionally taught course—i.e., no :-) appears in their research papers! I refer here more to the nature of the ongoing conversations between and among professor and students—the back and forth commentary in which an instructor or peer may query their texts, answer their questions, respond to their concerns, note their progress, and so forth.

As noted earlier, my sense, and that of my colleagues generally, is that online instruction may enable students and professors to become better acquainted simply by virtue of the fact that more, not less, opportunity for communication exists. Students seem inclined to do more work in online settings. The pressure is to perform, if for no other reason than it is glaringly obvious if no work is done. The situation in this way is far different than it is for students sitting in the back of the room hoping not to be called on to comment on work they haven't done or texts they haven't read.

How might greater informality of content and style affect the quality of students' work? In my experience, and that of my respondents generally, the quality of students'—and instructors'—communication may actually be higher. Both Tim and Patrick, for instance, point out that because they respond to their students at their own pace at times convenient to them, they can do so in a more measured way, giving rise, perhaps, to more thoughtful remarks. Tim has found that the quality of his online students' work remains as high, or higher, than that produced in class: "I do seem to get more probing questions and comments online from many of the students. [...] Questions lead to interesting discussions between student and faculty. Some of the thinking on the part of the students has been very high level." I would suggest that more capable performances by students may encourage instructors to grant more authority to them.

Online students are also likely to accompany their assignments with notes introducing the work, perhaps explaining why they have proceeded in a certain direction or asking whether they are on the right track. In this way a dialogue—the ongoing conversation to which I alluded above—begins and is sustained, and I contend that a less hierarchical professor-student relationship may result than is the case in many conventional classes. As Ed explains:

> [...] the students and I develop a closer, more personal relationship through email and chats. Many more online students contact me personally for advice. [...] I maintain relationships with students online far longer than in traditional teaching. [...] We all frequently share personal updates, ideas, jokes, etc. by email and through online chat. Many students from past classes also visit my tutorial labs, etc., just to check in or to have me give an opinion on their papers or articles.

I would also contend that the overtly dialogic aspect of online instruction causes professors to respond in readerly, rather than teacherly, ways. When I receive my students' email messages, there is something about going into my mailbox and opening the file that keeps the sender—my student—foremost in my mind; I am exceedingly aware that my student is speaking to me, in a very immediate sort of way, much more so than I am when I read text on paper. I read online texts much more as a reader, automatically reading for larger issues and meanings, with much less tendency to pause at typographical or other word- or sentence-level errors. For me, reading in this way lends more authority to the student texts. I feel that I read them, in a way, more seriously and differently from other texts. I feel very keenly what Joyce means when he says, referring to online instruction, "We face a new world when we teach <there>." (126)

The informal survey I have conducted raises more issues and opens areas for further inquiry. How, for example, may the discipline being taught influence the professor-student authority dynamic? Does classroom teaching style, or years of teaching experience, affect online instructional strategies? What about the type of software or hardware being used? Equally important, what are our students' perceptions of authority and other issues in online instruction? Informal student responses I have seen at two institutions during the past few years are overwhelmingly positive. Negative reactions have been limited to technical difficulties with software or hardware (or both) and complaints that not enough online courses are being offered. Given that all of the students taught by my respondents elected to take online courses, such positive response is perhaps unsurprising, but further interrogation may be both interesting and useful.

For example, earlier I have speculated that students' sense of authority may reflect their confidence as experienced, computer-savvy Internet users. But what of those students, many of whom tend to be older, who have no such level of competence? Lynn Sykes and Nancy Uber's study has already found anecdotal evidence that novice users may indeed feel disempowered in electronic settings, so this area of inquiry may indeed be another fruitful research path yet to be followed.

In terms of speculation on the future of Internet courses, Patrick's comments are perhaps the most intriguing:

> It will also be interesting to see how both the students' and teachers' attitudes change as we all become more sophisticated users of email, the Internet, etc. I think most of my students, both online and in class, tend to view email as a faster form of standard mail and they use the Internet passively as a kind of sexy encyclopedia. [...] I wonder what will happen when we see an entire generation of students who have spent their lives using these electronic wonders interactively: participating in Newsgroups, Usegroups, perhaps having put their own web pages on the Internet — in short, people used to the radically democratic, unhierarchical model that the Internet represents. Will they then take that model into the electronic classroom? Will they tend to think of the teacher as just one more node — perhaps one with a pretty clever webmaster — but just one more nonetheless?

Epilogue

Patrick's concluding words appear to be prescient indeed: at the time of this writing the Pew Internet and American Life Project contains the somewhat startling statistic that 64% of teens who use the Internet are not only *content creators* but also both *solicit* and *provide* feedback regarding their and their peers' electronic creations. (Madden, 2009) Further, as Elizabeth Weinstein's chapter later in this section makes clear, acronyms and emoticons continue to rule the linguistic landscape of Instant Messaging and texting, so the inherent informality of the Internet has also thrived.

The area of greatest change since I wrote the original chapter over a decade ago has been the ascendance of social networking sites, now ubiquitous and providing perhaps the greatest opportunity yet for users to embrace a new sense of authority. Two recent articles comment on pedagogical implications of the Web 2.0 world and support the idea that authority may indeed erode or, at best, need re-negotiation in online settings. Joseph Moxley comments that the Internet's new writing spaces "are all examples of collaborative, decentralized, online communities where crowds of people interact to construct knowledge. These are spaces that celebrate the values of sharing knowledge and the gift culture of the Internet." (Moxley, 184) Words such as "collaborative," "decentralized," "crowds," "sharing," and the like reflect an environment where authority is very far indeed from the zero-sum game of a hierarchical traditional classroom.

In a similar vein Rebecca Wilson Lundin focuses specifically on wikis: "they may make students feel more empowered to speak out, both against the teacher's authority and in response to their peers' writing. [...] Overall, the issue of online authority is greatly complicated by wiki use in ways that highlight how messy the process of balancing authority really is." (445)

Four of the respondents quoted above, including myself, continue to teach online and/or hybrid courses; we continue to enjoy our experiences, and our current responses to the questions that I posed then have not much changed from those we offered initially. Discussion forums, though, have become standard practice. They ensure that all students participate, and they offer students the ability to reflect before commenting. Tim thinks students may feel more freedom to disagree since they are not face to face with their peers, while Suzanne finds that the tone of the discussions has become more positive over the years and less apt to contain the flames of yore. Both Tim and Suzanne note that a democratic teaching style, providing some gentle guidance, enables these discussions to be largely student-led without their having to resort to lecturing as may occur in the conventional classroom.

We have all created strategies that we hope will enhance student learning. I use a rubric for evaluating discussion board posts to clarify my expectations and to maintain some formality in the writing while still encouraging open, wide-ranging discussion. Suzanne has found that using a short video to introduce herself helps to put students at ease and makes them more comfortable in working with her. Tim guides discussions by creating a central question or issue for each of their readings and to which he will refer as the discussions develop.

All of us feel that opportunities abound in the new media to engage students actively in their learning, and taking advantage of these new avenues for communication and composition will be the logical next step in our development as professors. As for myself, I've already decided that the next time I teach I may use text messaging in preference to email (assuming that the students agree). Such a move is appropriate given the results of a quiz I recently took ("What Kind of Tech User Are You?") that revealed me to be a Digital Collaborator. Let me add that said quiz was provided by the Pew project referenced earlier, and this is the full description of my result:

> If you are a Digital Collaborator, you use information technology to work with and share your creations with others. You are enthusiastic about how ICTs (internet collaborative technologies) help you connect with others and confident in your ability to manage digital devices and information. For you, the digital commons can be a camp, a lab, or a theater group—places to gather with others to develop something new.

Remarkably consistent with all I've said above, wouldn't you say? ☺

WORKS CITED

Gomez, Mary Louise. "The Equitable Teaching of Compositions with Computers: Case for Change." *Evolving Perspectives on Computers and Composition Studies*. Edited by Gail E. Hawisher and Cynthia L. Selfe. Urbana, IL: NCTE, 1991: 319–335.

Howard, Theron W. *A Rhetoric of Electronic Communities*. Greenwich, CT: Ablex, 1997.

Joyce, Michael. *Of Two Minds: Hypertext Pedagogy and Poetics*. Ann Arbor: University of Michigan Press, 1995.

Kaplan, Nancy. "Ideology, Technology, and the Future of Writing Instruction." *Evolving Perspectives on Computers and Composition Studies*. Edited by Gail E. Hawisher and Cynthia L. Selfe. Urbana, IL: NCTE, 1991: 11–42.

Lundin, Rebecca Wilson. "Teaching with Wikis: Toward a Networked Pedagogy." *Computers and Composition* 25 (2008) 432–448.

Madden, Mary. "Eating, Thinking, and Staying Active with New Media," *Pew Internet and American Life Project*, 6/2/2009. <Http://www.pewinternet.org> Accessed 8/3/2009.

Maher, Frances A., with M. K. Tetreault. "Women's Ways of Knowing in Women's Studies, Feminist Pedagogies, and Feminist Theory." *Knowledge, Difference, and Power*. Edited by Nancy Rule Goldberger et al. New York: Basic Books, 1996: 148–174.

Moxley, Joseph. "Datagogies, Writing Spaces, and the Age of Peer Production." *Computers and Composition* 25 (2008) 182–202.

Perelman, Lewis J. *School's Out: Hyperlearning, the New Technology, and the End of Education*. New York: Avon Books, 1992.

Ray, Ruth, and Ellen Barton. "Technology and Authority." *Evolving Perspectives on Computers and Composition Studies*. Edited by Gail E. Hawisher and Cynthia L. Selfe. Urbana, IL: NCTE, 1991, 279–299.

Shor, Ira. *When Students Have Power*. Chicago: University of Chicago Press, 1996.

Strickland, James. *Computers in the Classroom: A Look at Changes in Pedagogy*. ERIC, 1989. ED 315 791.

Sykes, Lynn, and Nancy Uber. *Reflections on Teaching in a Computerized Classroom: Knowledge, Power, and Technology*. ERIC, 1995. ED 388 984.

Tornow, Joan. *Link/age: Composing in the Online Classroom*. Logan, UT: Utah State University Press, 1997.

"What Kind of Text User Are You?" <Http://pewinternet.org/Participate/What-Kind-of-Tech-User-Are-You.aspx> Accessed 8/3/2009.

Chapter 22

Internet Forums and the Writing Student

Aaron Miller

In 1985, Orson Scott Card published his science fiction classic, *Ender's Game*, the story of an eleven-year-old strategic genius who wages a genocidal war on an alien race while believing that what he is doing is only a simulation. *Ender's Game* is a masterpiece of military adventure and a disturbing psychological study, as powerful and plausible today as it was at the time of its publication, even though some elements of the novel now seem dated. A major subplot deals with Ender's two older siblings, Peter and Valentine. Each as brilliant as their younger brother, Peter and Valentine (as would any two children with superhuman intelligence and too much time on their hands) instead set out to conquer the world. And how do two smart preadolescents go about conquering the world? The same way kids in contemporary times get anything done—the Internet.

Using their father's connection to Card's 1985 imagining of the 'net, Peter and Valentine create two anonymous personae for themselves and join in online discussion forums that are, presumably, frequented by adults of some political and social importance. With their false names and incredible minds, the two children are able to win themselves prestige, influence, and fame as great thinkers. Eventually their influence and cunning manipulations extend so far that they are able to seize power for themselves in a time of worldwide unrest, convincing the masses to follow them with nothing more than anonymity and the power of the written word.

Twenty-five years later, the Internet has arrived for real, and it has turned out not to be quite the engine of global pre-teen domination that Card envisioned. Online discussion forums, far from the almost-mystically potent venues of powerful and world-changing ideas that Peter and Valentine exploit, are simply another pedestrian part of online life. They exist everywhere on the Web, hosting discussion on anything from politics to philosophy to cooking to comic books. As Card envisioned, they offer their participants easy and anonymous access to discourse communities that can reach around the world. But, like anything else on the Internet, the quality of such democratic discussions can only be as good as the quality of the participants, and savvy "netizens" know when to take anything posted anonymously on the Internet with a grain of salt. When a million anonymous voices chatter on a thousand (mostly inane) topics, no single voice can be expected to change the world.

Given all this, why look at Internet forums in a course about teaching writing? Teachers of writing at the college level are meant to be turning out writers who *can* shape the world with their words and ideas, or at the very least, participate meaningfully in academic discourse. Of what use can the uncontrolled bedlam of Internet forums be toward that goal?

As an information resource, forums can be a powerful, if unreliable, tool, but most regular participants in Internet forums regard them as far more than that. For regular participants, the forum becomes a community, a major source of social contact and recreation. For members of such communities, the act of writing becomes an end in and of itself: writing no matter their level of education or writing skill, writing on subjects they care about passionately enough to get into heated debates with complete strangers, writing as a pastime, a hobby, even an obsession, writing in an environment where they are faceless and voiceless, knowable only by what they write and how they write it. There aren't that many venues, outside the academy, in which writing plays such a crucial part.

It would be an exaggeration to say that Internet forums refine these writers and improve their skills; in such a chaotic environment, few pause to examine their own writing and that of others, to understand how good and bad writing affects their fortunes in forum arguments, or to improve their own writing based on their observations. But Internet forums *could* refine and improve the writing skills of their participants if approached as a method of doing so. Examined seriously by writing teachers and incorporated as a tool in their repertoire of teaching strategies, Internet discussion forums have great potential both as a medium for practicing writing skills and as a gateway into the larger craft of writing.

What Are Forums?

By "Internet forums," I mean the broad family of formats for discussion over the Internet in which an author posts a new topic and his opening thoughts on the matter, after which the audience of the forum's other participants post their own replies, adding to the thread. That definition includes email lists (such as those found at http://groups.yahoo.com), LiveJournal communities (found at http://www.livejournal.com/community), and the site-specific discussion boards that almost any website of appreciable size, on any topic, will eventually include.

The distinguishing feature of what I will group under the heading "forum" is that they are not real-time; one takes one's time writing a message, posts it to the forum, and comes back later to see if anyone has responded. Forums often trade in one-line responses, making the forum little more than a very slow chatroom, but most of the time, a poster with an interest in the topic will take the time to write a lengthy reply. The posts can be accurately termed a "composition." A forum, therefore, is any Internet discussion format in which the participants *converse*, rather than merely type.

For purposes of this paper, I must also refine the distinction, mentioned earlier, between forums as informational resources and forums as venues for discussion. Forums can serve as no more than a clearinghouse for information on a specific topic: one finds a relevant forum, posts a question, and receives answers, or searches the forum's archives for similar questions. This mode of using Internet forums, though efficient, does not directly concern this discussion. As explained above, most forums are populated by a community of regular posters, interested in the forum's topic and in discussion for its own sake. To them, the forum is a hobby; they enjoy posing topics for discussion, answering questions, and (often) getting into arguments, merely for the sake of doing so. These regulars form the pool of the forum's knowledge and ideas; if not for them, more casual forum-users would not be able to gain answers to their questions so readily. For the remainder of the paper, I refer specifically to forums being used in this "community" mode.

Forums as Microcosms of Academia

Internet forums and academic discourse, for all that they seemingly belong to different worlds, bear enough resemblances to merit comparison. The heated exchange of posts on a forum thread and the stately discourse of academic papers differ in quality, in length, and in speed, but follow fundamentally the same format; forums, in a way, are tiny microcosms of the way that academic discourse works. Both academic journals and Internet forums discuss narrow fields of interest, specialized subjects with culture and jargon arcane to a member of the lay public. Writers for journals and forums alike write for an audience of peers who, like them, have a specialized interest and expertise in the subject at hand.

Readers of both journals and forums are also assumed to be participants. Certainly, it's vastly more difficult to have a paper accepted to an academic journal than it is to post to a discussion forum, but an academic journal is also assumed to have a more exclusive readership—academics, like the author of a given paper, who have a stake in debates within their discipline and who will be trying actively to publish articles advancing their own viewpoints. Writers of journal articles and forum posts alike write to an audience that can *write back*, and most writers are writing back themselves; that is, articles and forum posts both are expected to quote what previous authors have said on the same subject, either to reinforce and synthesize those points or to reject them.

And, in journals and forums alike, much of the really interesting discourse is oppositional. In their article, "The Rhetoric of Reproof," Podis and Podis question the ethics of the "conventional pugilistic approaches to academic discourse," in which the participants in that discourse engage in "scholarly self-promotion" by exercising a "professional obligation to be critical with a 'vanquish-the-opposition-at-all-costs' mentality." (Podis and Podis, 216) This is as accurate a description of Internet forums as it is of academic discourse; in both venues, participants bring strong ideas on topics about which they care passionately, and their advancement of those ideas, typically prompted by the statement of an opposing viewpoint, involves rebutting, attacking, dissecting, and otherwise negatively responding to that opposing viewpoint.

Depending on the forum, such attacks may be considerably less genteel online than in an academic journal, but the principle remains the same: the disputants compose and trade arguments, directed at one another's points but visible to the larger audience of the journal's or forum's readers. Whether each disputant addresses his points to the audience at large (as is generally the case in academic papers) or directs his statements specifically to his opponent (as is often the case on forums), the real goal is to convince the audience, not the opponent, of the superiority of his views. In either venue, the audience is not passive, but may jump into the debate on either side whenever they wish, by writing their own paper or posting their own message. And in both venues, "defeat" in such a disagreement is very rarely acknowledged or conceded; a viewpoint is considered to have won out when the majority of those interested in the dispute have decided and weighed in, in its favor.

These parallels between academia and Internet forums struck me as I read "The Rhetoric of Reproof" and realized that I had written a very similar piece not long ago, raising the same ethical questions, chiding other writers, as do Podis and Podis, for their unnecessarily harsh and negative way of advancing their positions. Podis and Podis wrote their piece for *College English* and cited important articles in the field of composition studies, while I cited several of the more active and vocal posters on a gaming forum, but the observations we made, and the prescriptions for improving the discourse, were identical. I noted the similarities, but more to the point, I noticed that my immediate reaction to the discourse described in the article was to think of it in terms of the forum debates with which I was familiar—a reaction that contextualized the article's point for me. I could approach the idea of such a discourse as something more than a complete novice. Forums can therefore be viewed as analogous to academic discourse, a useful introduction to the form—written argumentation as play.

Forums in the Classroom

To most students in high school and college, writing is a chore. They dread the prospect of sitting in front of another blank screen and churning out another formulaic paper on a topic of little interest to them. Nor are they much inspired by the paper's audience: the teacher or professor, who will examine their work as a finished product, slap on a grade and perhaps some perfunctory comments in illegible handwriting, and hand it back to them to be stuffed into a folder and forgotten.

These two elements, uninteresting subject matter and a lack of interactivity, work together to taint the act of writing itself in students' minds. When class writing never takes any form but that of formal essays to be handed in to the teacher, with no subject matter but what the assignment permits and no incentive to good writing but the threat of a bad grade, students come to associate writing in general with the boredom and lack of engagement inherent to that classroom format. To encourage students to write, the teacher must offer them the chance to write on subjects that interest them and must offer them the chance to write for a larger audience and experience writing as communication, rather than merely as mechanical exercise. Internet forums offer an opportunity to do both.

As technology becomes more integrated into the classroom, teachers are already beginning to experiment with the use of online forums as a novel format for class discussion. Courses at many, if not most, colleges use the discussion board feature of their course management systems to require students to create and respond to threads in order to augment discussion in the classrooms. This approach realizes many of the potential advantages of Internet forums. Students write for an audience larger than their teacher, write in a shorter and more informal format than that of an essay, and write for an audience that can respond, and to whom they respond in turn. This approach has great value in freeing writing from the narrowly defined, noninteractive boredom with which many students come to associate it.

For classes in disciplines other than writing itself, this approach to the use of forums may be concession enough to the need for diversity in writing assignments. However, class-based discussion boards still lack some traits that recommend Internet forums as a means of encouraging interest in writing. A true Internet forum is a community of strangers, known to each other only by the content of their writing. While this may come close to an accurate description of discussion boards used by large lecture-based classrooms, the fact remains that class discussion boards lack the anonymity of Internet forums. While writing obviously need not be anonymous to have value, there is something to be said for the freedom from self-consciousness that comes with knowing that one's work will be judged on its merits alone, not by prior relationships to the teacher and the other students in the class.

Furthermore, purely as an exercise in writing, class-based discussion boards still suffer from a predetermined topic on which the student may not be especially inspired to write. In an English or history or religion class, little can be done about this, but in a writing class, a further step can be taken to tap the potential of Internet forums as a venue for practicing writing skills. For a truly novel and open-ended exercise, writing teachers could open the entire breadth of the Internet to student writers, incorporating any forum that their students care to join. But, rather than asking them merely to take part in a forum of their choice, teachers could take the next step and challenge their students to follow the example of Peter and Valentine by writing effectively enough to sway the discourse.

A Writing Exercise Using Forums

Such an exercise might work like this: In the first stage, students search the Internet for a forum on any subject of interest to them. The subject need not be chosen from a vetted list of "academically appropriate" topics (and, indeed, the more specialized and obscure its topic, the better, so long as it is one with which the student is comfortable), but it must meet three basic requirements. First, the forum's topic, and the majority of its content, must be largely free of offensive or obscene material (controversial topics are fine; hate groups and porn sites are not). Next, a decent proportion of the posts to the forum must be more than a few lines in length, to indicate that the forum has a population of "regulars" interested in writing on the topic for its own sake (this can be verified with no more than a quick skim by the teacher; a few minutes per forum should be sufficient). Lastly, the forum should be overseen by moderators who conscientiously watch for and remove obscene posts or personal attacks (this is much easier for a teacher to check than might be immediately obvious—using the forum's search function to run a search for, say, the word "fuck" will, in general, give an immediate idea of the overall quality of the site's moderators). Students submit to the teacher the forum's URL and a brief description of the forum's topic, and the teacher then checks each forum chosen to ensure that it meets the basic requirements.

In the second stage, students must find or think of a specific issue or question relevant to their forum and must prepare a short report for the teacher, explaining the topic, providing background, and outlining their position in the argument as well as opposing views. Students who choose a forum on baseball might explain a disagreement over the relative merits of two teams, while students choosing a videogame forum might explain different playing strategies. The report must clearly and concisely explain the issue in enough detail that someone unfamiliar with the topic (the teacher, for example) will be able to follow a discussion. In this way, rather than limiting the assignment to a small list of topics, the teacher allows the students completely free rein to pick a topic of interest to them, while requiring them to show effective expository skills in explaining the material to the teacher.

In the third stage, students join in the forum's discussion of the topic they have selected and explained in their previous report. They make a lengthy post to the forum, either starting a new thread or joining an existing discussion in which they clearly and effectively lay out their side of the argument, marshal supporting evidence, and refute opposing viewpoints. When their post draws a response, whether agreement, comment, criticism, or rebuttal, they must respond in turn, clarifying, defending, or modifying their position. The goal of the students is not merely to write but to write persuasively enough to convince other forum participants of their point of view. When the thread has ceased to draw active attention from the forum or when it has reached a certain length (to be specified according to the individual teacher's needs) the student submits a transcript of the forum thread, along with the URL at which the thread can be found.

Obviously, reliance on the anonymous participants in a freely selected Internet forum creates constraints on the assignment which must be accounted for. Students should take pains in the early stages of the assignment to make sure that they have found a forum whose members can be relied upon to engage in an intelligent discussion and that the question or topic they select will draw interested and spirited discussion without being dismissed as "trolling" or "flamebait" (deliberately inflammatory or controversial posts made solely to provoke a response). To a certain extent, the reaction of a forum to the student's efforts will be out of the hands of both students and teachers; teachers should therefore evaluate the assignment with an eye toward the effectiveness of the student's writing in engaging the subject, without penalizing the student for the failings of other forum participants.

Conclusion

An exercise like this is only one possible way in which writing teachers could employ Internet forums to engage students in writing, offering them a chance to interact with a broader audience through their writing and to relate writing to subjects in which they are interested. By breaking down the association in students' minds between writing in general and stifling academic writing in particular, teachers can encourage students to look at writing as a powerful skill and an enjoyable activity, rather than simply as a requirement for school.

Although the Internet has developed very differently from Orson Scott Card's prediction in 1985, the basic premise of Peter and Valentine's story remains compelling. Internet forums may never allow children to conquer the world, but they do offer a place where the social constraints of age and gender and appearance fall away, leaving only the strength of one's ideas and the power of one's writing. As such, they provide an ideal venue for students to explore writing, and a gateway through which they can arrive at a better understanding of writing and an enjoyment of writing for its own sake.

WORKS CITED

Card, Orson Scott. *Ender's Game*. New York: T. Doherty Associates, 1985.

Podis, Leonard A., and JoAnne M. Podis. "The Rhetoric of Reproof." *College English* 63 (2000): 214–28.

Chapter 23

Writing in the Information Age: The Language of Email and Instant Messaging

Elizabeth Weinstein

I am not embarrassed to admit that I am a fan of all things "youth culture." I read all of the *Harry Potter* books and even did an honors project on them. I love children's television shows and movies, and I am addicted to MTV. I have also become immersed in yet another phenomenon that has its roots in youth culture: instant messaging, or IM. I was introduced to IM by my then-fifteen-year-old brother. He installed AOL's (America Online) instant messenger on my computer and set up my first screen name, ObieLiz02. At first I did not really understand the point of chatting with other people on the computer when we had a phone in every room of our house, and I had two email accounts. But against my better judgment, I too found myself hopping onto the ever-growing bandwagon of IM obsession.

Now an admitted IM junkie, I often wonder how my use of IM affects my writing in general, both in and out of the classroom. I love the way that IM allows me to express emotion while writing (through emoticons such as ☺, ☹, etc.), and I sometimes find myself wishing (hopelessly) I could use emoticons in my academic papers. Before IM and email, people communicated with one another mainly through face-to-face dialogue and phone conversations, supplemented by US mail. Teenagers spent hours talking on the phone with their friends and were often parodied in movies and television shows for doing so. Now, teenagers are more often parodied by the media for their online interactions with their peers. Instead of spending hours on the phone, they connect to the Internet from their computers or phones and chat with their friends at any given time (their parents being usually clueless as to how much time they actually spend online). This means that teenagers are writing more now than ever before. In fact, they probably type thousands of words every day just by sending emails and IM messages back and forth to other teenagers. The young consumers of IM have in a sense reinvented the English language by creating a sub-language, perhaps even a subculture, that I will term "IM-speak."

Why IM?

What exactly is the appeal of IM? And more importantly, how does it affect young people's writing? In this paper I will attempt to explain this phenomenon in a number of ways. First, I believe that in a sense, the Internet itself has become an incentive for literacy. Thanks to the Internet, young people literally have access to a whole world of information, but in order to access that information, they must be able to read and use a computer. Further, the youth and teenagers who participate in IM know that in order to carry on real-time conversations with people over a computer, they must be able to efficiently formulate thoughts into written words and to type quickly.

Second, I will argue that IM-speak, as a language, gives youth and teenagers a sense of empowerment that they do not feel over the phone or when speaking to someone face to face (in IM-speak written "f2f"). This is because IM-speak remains in large part a mystery to adults or to anyone who has not grown up around computers and the Internet.

In this sense, using IM is like using a secret language. There is even a code that children use to alert whomever they are talking to that a parent is monitoring their interaction—POS, which stands for "parent over shoulder." IM-speak is something teenagers have created largely on their own, and it is something they take pride in and feel comfortable using.

Finally, I will argue that the use of IM by youth and teenagers is largely a positive thing, because it encourages them to express themselves through writing and to make connections with other people using written language. Of course, there are numerous problems associated with the use of IM; some critics fear that because of the grammatically incorrect language used in most IM conversations, children will lose the few grammatical skills they have and never learn to write properly. Others fear that IM is a procrastination tool that eats away at time that could be better spent doing homework or socializing with people in person. Some parents also feel that IM detracts from the amount of time children spend with their families, because children would rather hole up in their rooms and chat with friends over the computer than converse with their families. I will discuss these issues as well.

What IM Looks Like and More

As I write this paper, the IM icon on my computer is present on the bottom right hand corner of my screen, signaling that I am online. Like many people who use IM to communicate with friends, acquaintances, and family members, I leave my IM turned on almost around the clock, and when I am away from my computer, I leave an "away message," signaling my absence. A friend, also a senior in college, has just messaged me with the greeting, "sup," slang for "what's up?" Our IM conversation is as follows:[1]

Histmajor08: sup
ObieLiz02: I'm starting my paper—my last paper of my college career
Histmajor08: god
Histmajor08: i meant good
ObieLiz02: sure
ObieLiz02: it's scary
ObieLiz02: I don't wanna graduate
Histmajor08: boo hoo
ObieLiz02: come on – you're not worried about the real world?
Histmajor08:no
ObieLiz02: y not?
Histmajor08: easy come easy go
ObieLiz02: u suck
ObieLiz02: can I take nonchalance lessons from u?
Histmajor08: nope cos it wouldn't help you
ObieLiz02: y not?
ObieLiz02: anyways…I gotta write my paper

IM works through something called a dialogue box. Unlike email, which is asynchronous, IM functions much like a phone conversation on the computer. When I sign onto IM, a little rectangular box pops up on my computer screen and displays my "buddy list," or a list of all my friends and acquaintances who are currently online. The sound of a door opening lets me know when a friend has signed on, and the sound of a door closing lets me know when that friend has signed off. If I want to "chat" with a friend, I simply click on her screen name, after which another dialogue box pops up, and I am able to talk with her, back and forth, for any length of time. Oftentimes, I will talk with more than one person at a time, switching frequently between dialogue boxes.

William Safire, *New York Times* columnist and a critic of English usage, describes the popularity of instant messaging in one of his essays:

Between superstar Britney Spears and 13-year-old singer Brittney Cleary, nobody will ever spell France's northwestern region of Brittany correctly again. But Miss Cleary […] in her song "IM Me," has engaged in text messaging, a combination of initialese and the euphoric use of the alphabet that deserves scholarly attention.

Apparently, IM is so much a part of popular culture that pop songs are being written about it (by teenagers of course ☺). After reading Safire's article, I logged on and downloaded Brittney Cleary's song, "IM Me." The lyrics are intriguing, to say the least:

TTYL [talk to you later]. No time to spell [...]
Hey, LOL [laughing out loud], G2G
I gotta go, but watch for me 'cause
I'll be right back, BRB
So sign on, and IM me

Mom thinks I'm doing homework
Yeah, research
But I can't help it, I've just got to surf
I gotta chat with my girlfriends on line...
This is just like passing notes
It's easier to type than use a pen

This song reads very much like an actual IM conversation—particularly revealing is the part where Cleary compares IM to "passing notes" during class. When I presented my idea for this paper to my teaching and tutoring writing class, the professor also made the comparison between IM and passing notes and lamented that teachers, try as they may, have never been able to tap into students' enthusiasm for passing notes in order to transfer their love of informal gossip writing into a love of all writing. But more on writing and the Internet in the classroom later.

Who Uses IM?

According to a study conducted in 2001 by the Pew Internet and American Life Project entitled "Teenage Life Online," approximately 17 million youth, ages 12–17, use the Internet, and nearly 13 million, or 74% of online teenagers use IM. In comparison, only 44% of online adults use IM. "Among the many striking things about teens' use of the Internet," the study notes, "is the way they have adapted instant messaging technologies to their own purposes. [...] Instant messaging has permeated teen culture to such an extent that for some 'message me later' has replaced 'call me.'" People use IM for a variety of purposes: 37% of IM-ing teenagers surveyed said they write things on IM that they would not say in person, and 17% of IM-ing teenagers reported using IM to ask someone out on a date.

In addition, the study found that many teenagers "use instant messaging to communicate with teachers and classmates about schoolwork or projects." This is definitely the case with my brother, who is now eighteen. I first got the idea to write this paper when I was home for spring break. One day, while I was hanging out in my brother's room, I watched him as he chatted with his friends online about homework assignments. Mostly, they complained to one another, but they also offered advice and support. What was really amazing about my brother's conversations, however, was not the content but rather the multi-tasking approach he took to communicating with his peers. I looked on, bewildered, as he fluently juggled a dozen separate dialogue boxes (most them ongoing conversations with girls in his class), surfed the web for a new computer part he wanted to purchase, computed math homework problems on his calculator, glanced at the television screen (which was tuned to MTV of course) next to his computer, fielded phone calls from friends who were not online, and downloaded electronic music files onto his hard drive, all at the same time. I cannot even concentrate on my homework when the radio is on, so how he functions in such a chaotic environment is beyond me. Apparently, however, my brother's scenario for doing homework is not uncommon among today's youth.

In their article, "But Will It Work in the Heartland? A Response and Illustration," Cynthia Lewis and Bettina Fabos describe "multiliteracies in New Times from the Midwestern U.S. 'heartland.'" (465) Lewis and Fabos interviewed one thirteen-year-old girl, "Sam," and her best friend, "Kerrie," about their IM use and discuss the implications of their findings in their article. An important part of their theory of multiliteracy is the same sort of multitasking I described above:

> [One] of us has teenage sons who admire both Woody Guthrie for the political messages in his music and Marilyn Manson for what they see as his critical stance on gender identity. They humor their English teachers' romantic visions of 'the writing process' and 'the writer's life' knowing full well that they will return home to multitask their way through their assignments with word processor and Internet open, phone and CD at hand, a book or two in their laps. (462)

Besides multitasking, Lewis and Fabos noticed two patterns that permeated Sam and Kerrie's IM usage: the negotiation of language, as well as the negotiation of social patterns when using IM. "Rather than speaking in one voice," the authors write, "Sam is conscious of choosing different tones and language styles depending on who she's Instant Messaging. [...] Sam and Kerrie use the technology to juggle numerous language styles and conversations at a time." (466–67) They continue:

> In the IM environment, the drama unfolds by way of multiple narratives and intersecting social discourses. IM communications, although typed, mimic face-to-face conversations. They are peppered with a distinct shorthand lingo (e.g., how r u?)—

often the shorter the better—and the norm is to type and send short, overlapping messages in the spirit of continuous interruption. (467)

This language, although it abandons almost all the constraints of traditional English, is highly evolved, and to speak it authentically is a symbol of status. For youth and teenagers, IM has become a vital social event. The length of one's buddy list is often indicative of one's popularity. For example, I only have around 25 names on my buddy list, but my brother has well over a hundred on his. Whenever teenagers meet nowadays, in addition to swapping phone numbers, they swap email addresses and IM screen names. "In general," write Lewis and Fabos, "Sam and Kerrie believe their IM relationships enhance their social status, establishing a kind of social currency that keeps them in the know." (468) Sam and Kerrie, like a lot of socially-conscious teenagers, carefully monitor the way they use IM to communicate with their peers. For example, they place importance on always appearing busy while on IM. They have created rules as to how long to wait before responding to an IM message—if they respond too quickly, it will look like they have no one else to talk to.

IM in Action: An Informal Study

In response to Lewis and Fabos's article, I decided to conduct an informal study of my own. I instant messaged my brother, who like me is always online, and asked him to create a "chat room" on IM for several of his IM buddies, so that I could ask them a few questions about the role of IM in their lives. At first, he resisted, calling my project "lame," but with some prodding from my parents, he reluctantly agreed, under the condition that I please not embarrass him in front of his IM buddies, and that I keep it under fifteen minutes, because he and his buddies have more important things to do than talk to me. The participants in my brief study were HotDog1 (my brother), and his three friends, screen names Maximus9, JimmyJ, and DJman. All were boys between the ages of fifteen and eighteen. Each of them stated that they had been using IM for around six years (since elementary and middle school) and that they thoroughly enjoyed using it:

ObieLiz02: so I am guessing you guys like IM

JimmyJ: fa sho (for sure)

DJman: im addicted—i don't like it ☹

ObieLiz02: how much time do you spend on IM a day?

DJman: difficult to say

DJman: id say 2 hours

Maximus9: close to 24/7

ObieLiz02: wow!
JimmyJ: an hour to two hours
ObieLiz02: how many people do you chat with?
Maximus9: actually, i use away messages a lot
DJman: up to 8 at a time
JimmyJ: usually about 5
HotDog1: 5 or 6...
Maximus9: 2-5

When asked (over IM) what they use IM for and what they talk about, the frankness of their answers, as well as their playfulness, struck me as unique to IM as a medium. Some of the things they wrote, I'm pretty sure they would not have written in a letter or a survey or said over the phone:

ObieLiz02: what do you like best about IM?
JimmyJ: ummmmmmm
DJman: it is universal—about everyone I know uses it
Maximus9: easy to communicate without going out of your way
JimmyJ: being able to talk to a lot of people at once
ObieLiz02: cool
ObieLiz02: has IM changed the way you communicate with others when you are not on IM?
ObieLiz02: like in email, over the phone
ObieLiz02: etc
JimmyJ: ya
ObieLiz02: how?
JimmyJ; i use different sayings, like LOL and BRB
JimmyJ; and TTYL
ObieLiz02: me too actually
JimmyJ: fa sho
Maximus9: yeah, i use the aol jive all the time (g2g, ttyl, np, lol)
ObieLiz02: what do you usually talk about on IM? (main topics, etc)
Maximus9: sex
JimmyJ: sex, drugs, rock and roll
DJman: how much i hate school
ObieLiz02: ok, gotcha – so IM is more for informal stuff
ObieLiz02: lol
Maximus9: yeah
JimmyJ: yep

At this point in the conversation I pretend to take a break from chatting, to see if and how the dynamic changes when I (an outsider studying IM culture), leave the discussion. Warning: uncensored language and incorrect grammar follow ;-).

ObieLiz02: just a sec
DJman: ...where are you going to school?
HotDog1: Miami
Maximus9: good choice
JimmyJ: there some fine bitches ova there
HogDog1: for shizzle
Maximus9: yeah
JimmyJ: fa sho
HotDog1: waitlisted over at Wash U
JimmyJ: hotter girls at Miami

As a feminist, I cannot take it any more and decide to butt back into the conversation.

ObieLiz02: do you use IM when you are doing other things? Like talking on the
    phone, homework, etc.?
Maximus9: i write papers while using IM
HotDog1: yeah
JimmyJ: watching tv, looking up stuff on the internet
JimmyJ: look for porn
JimmyJ: i mean
DJman: i do a lot while on IM
JimmyJ: researching
Maximus9: lol, sure JimmyJ
ObieLiz02: "researching" LOL
DJman: watch TV, do hw, avoid hw, talk to other people in my dorm room
ObieLiz02: so is IM the perfect procrastination tool?
Maximus9: hell yeah
HotDog1: definetly
ObieLiz02: do you think IM has helped your writing at all? Like papers for school?
DJman: LOL no way
HotDog1: nope
JimmyJ: ummmm hell no
ObieLiz02: has it made you more comfortable with writing for expression?
Maximus9: no
ObieLiz02: really?
JimmyJ: im a guy
JimmyJ: i don't need to write for expression
HotDog1: lol
HotDog1: thats my dawg
JimmyJ: I use grunts
ObieLiz02: do you worry about grammar when using IM?
DJman: naw, neva
Maximus9: no grammar for me
JimmyJ: grammar ain't important
DJman: some older people care about grammar
JimmyJ: ya, like my mom

ObieLiz02: like?
DJman: like the seniors in college

Now that I have been called old and essentially "uncool" for using somewhat proper grammar, I decide to wrap up the session. For a moment, I lament the fact that my brother arranged for me to talk with hormone-ridden teenage males, and I wonder why he did not ask at least one female. But then again, I am just honored that the boys were so brutally honest with me, a complete stranger. So goes the nature of an IM conversation.

IM and the Classroom

How does this conversation with my brother and his friends relate to my original hypothesis, that IM is actually a good thing because it interests youth and teenagers in writing? Was I wrong? After all, these boys admit whole-heartedly that they think IM has a negative influence on their academic lives. But then again, maybe it is good for them and they just do not realize it. Or if they do, then maybe they do not want to admit it (to themselves or others) because that would spoil the fun of IM—that is, writing without imposed rules and objectives. If this is the case, and writing IM messages can have positive long- and short-term effects on those who use it to communicate, then why wouldn't teachers want to try and incorporate certain aspects of IM culture into their classrooms? In their article, Lewis and Fabos hypothesize as to why it is often difficult to interest students in academic writing:

> When we compare the sophistication of Sam's rhetorical choices to the simple line-arity of the writing process as it is often represented in the classroom, we understand why so many students over the years have told us that they are bored by the pace and sequence of writers' workshop and that they fake their rough drafts after having completed final ones in a flash. (468)

If this is indeed true, then the New Paradigm might not be the best way to approach writing with today's youth. They are so technologically savvy that they crave variety and challenge in their assignments—not rules, repetition or an emphasis on process. More and more, it seems that today's students, like many journalists, thrive on pressure, speed, and deadlines.

While none of these articles I read for this paper talked about the incorporation of instant messaging into academic classrooms, several discussed what happens when emailing is incorporated into writing classrooms. Ruth Garner and Mark G. Gillingham, authors of an article entitled, "New Voices: The Internet Communication of High School Kids Who (Usually) Won't Write," criticize the traditional approach to writing instruction, especially on the high school level. They recall in vivid detail the way in which they were instructed to write when they were young:

> We got savvy enough to present events in chronological order for the history teacher and to sprinkle quotations throughout our literature papers, but we were seldom bold enough to propose many ideas of our own. No fools were we, for we did this writing so that our teachers could assess how much information we had acquired, not so that they could celebrate our fresh ideas or playful ways with words. (172)

Garner and Gillingham describe conversations they had with Dan Wilcox, a high school literature teacher in California, who "worries about students who, for one reason or another, won't write in school." (172) Wilcox's hypothesis as to why some of his students refused to write is that "adolescents have stories to tell. After all, they spend much of their out-of-classroom time [...] doing just that—telling other adolescents their stories about family, parties, work, and romance. [...] The problem is that traditional writing assignments [...] are usually about book and lecture topics, not about the drama in students' lives." (172) Therefore, to interest his students in writing, Wilcox assigned his students pen pals from America and Brazil, and required that they write at least two emails, at a minimum of 150 words each, per week to their new email buddies.

The emails were read but not graded, and the only requirement, besides length, was that the students not use profanity. To Wilcox's surprise, the students who wrote the longest, most detailed emails were not necessarily his best students. In fact, six of the students who wrote the longest messages were considered to be "at-risk" students, who were struggling academically and rarely turned in writing assignments. Ironically, they wrote far more than 150 words a week—one of these students sometimes wrote more than 500 words a week. In trying to understand why these typically "non-writing" students suddenly produced mass volumes of words when given the chance to email pen pals about their lives, the authors propose that "[to] some degree, it might have been the sheer novelty of the assignment or the near-novelty of the technology. We are fairly certain that it was partly the opportunity afforded them to tell out-of-classroom-like stories about themselves to other kids." (173) Analyzing the content of the students' emails, the authors note that the students (particularly the at-risk ones) wrote mainly of their troubles (home, school, romance). The authors also describe the email forum as a way of "owning" one's own life experiences and as a demonstration of the "power of personal narratives." Emailing for these students often took the form of journaling, although instead of simply recording their stories into a blank book, they were given continuous peer feedback via email.

Pokey Stanford and James A. Siders write about a similar scenario in their article, "E-Pal Writing!" The article describes "an e-mail pen-pal correspondence project and its possible effect on the writing skills of students with and without disabilities." (1) For a study, they paired university teacher education students with public school students for pen pal, e-pal and control groups. Students in the pen-pal group corresponded with the university students through US mail, while the e-pal students corresponded via email. "Of greatest importance in this study," the authors write, "was the improvement of all students' writing when involving e-mail, as compared to traditional correspondence." (2) It is also interesting to note that in another study conducted on 144 students at a Midwestern university, students preferred computer-mediated communication—chatting, electronic bulletin boards, IM, and email—to more standard forms of written and oral communications. (Merrier and Dirks)

However, there can be too much of a good thing. A big debate has emerged in the popular media in recent years, concerning whether or not IM and email are beneficial to children and teenagers. One article published in the *Minneapolis Star Tribune* quotes David Silver, a communications professor at the University of Washington:

> IM is just the newest phase of wanting immediate feedback and communication. [...] I don't think kids IM in iambic pentameter. They use the medium the same as the phone, to gossip, chat and insult. Teenagers, like all cultural groups that feel a little oppressed, develop their own cultural norms. It's in-group communication, with their own slang so they can promote their own coolness. (Von Sternberg)

Rick Bodemar, a writer for *Newsday*, is much more skeptical in his opinion of IM. He writes, sarcastically: "Our kids' writing skills are going to hell in a handbag. Or should I say a laptop." He describes the language his children use in email and IM as "cyber ebonics" or "computerese." "A good part of America has trouble putting together two sentences as it is," he laments, and continues with an anecdote:

> The other day, my 14-year-old daughter was carrying on separate instant-message conversations with two friends and her grandmother simultaneously. It was a sight to behold. Her mental gymnastics and frenzied work on the keyboard amazed me. But in the process she slaughtered the English language and wantonly ignored virtually every grammatical rule known to civilized man. [...] I guess I wouldn't mind so much if my kids were firmly grounded in the fundamentals of spelling and grammar. [...] But they're mere novices who are just beginning to learn how to write and express their thoughts in a clear, interesting manner. (2)

Bodemar makes a good point, but his argument comes off as defensive—he appears to be more alienated by IM than he is genuinely concerned about it. Parents have always worried about the things their children are into (e.g., rock and roll, telephone conversations, rap music). IM is simply another means for young people to create identities for themselves and to separate, figuratively, from their parents.

In concluding, I would like to return to Garner and Gillingham's article on email writing and at-risk students. They recognize that "the structure and content of the at-risk students' writing are, for the most part, unremarkable. What is remarkable is the simple fact that these students composed, mailed, and anticipated responses to their Internet stories, for they wrote little else in the classroom." (179) Youth and teenagers are in perpetual pursuit of a culture of their own, and their current means appears to be the Internet, or more specifically, email and IM. Whether they are talking about hobbies, gossiping, meeting new people or talking to old friends, when teenagers chat online, they are practicing written communication skills. Of course, Internet use, like anything else, can become excessive and interfere negatively in a person's life, but in most cases, IM and email are simply enjoyable activities that enable teenagers to stay in touch with one another and to have a sense of control over their social environments. Parents ought to be thankful that when their children are spending hours in front of a computer screen, at least they are at home (or at school, or another place with a computer), instead of out wandering the streets. Maybe teenagers' love of IM will eventually transfer to other forms of writing. Judging from the IM conversations I have read and have had myself, there is a lot of inventiveness and creativity involved, which in my mind is a positive thing. Who ever worries about correct grammar in creative writing any way? Well, G2G. TTYL! ☺

NOTES

[1] All screen names are pseudonyms.

WORKS CITED

Bodemar, Rick. "Life in Cyberspace/Sup with U Kids? 2 Much Computerese," *Newsday*. New York: December 20, 2000.

Garner, Ruth, and Gillingham, Mark G. "New Voices: The Internet Communication of High School Kids Who (Usually) Won't Write," *The High School Journal*. 82, no 3: February/March 1999: 172.

Lenhart, Amanda, and Rainie, Lee. "Teenage Life Online: The Rise of the Instant-Message Generation and the Internet's Impact on Friendships and Family Relationships," *Pew Internet & American Life Project*. 6/20/2001. http://www.pewinternet.org/

Lewis, Cynthia, and Fabos, Bettina. "'But Will It Work in the Heartland?' A Response and Illustration," *Journal of Adolescent & Adult Literacy* 43 (2000): 462–469.

Merrier, Patricia A., and Dirks, Ruthann. "Student Attitudes Toward Written, Oral, and E-Mail Communication," *Business Communication Quarterly* 60 (1997): 89–99.

Stanford, Pokey and Siders, James A. "E-Pal Writing!" *Teaching Exceptional Children* 34 (2001): 21–24.

Von Sternberg, Bob. "Where Fingers Do The Talking," *The Minneapolis Star Tribune*. January 20, 2002.

Section Eight

Discourse Communities: Issues and Problems

Accompanying the "process revolution," with its emphasis on teaching writing as discovery, was the writing across the curriculum movement (WAC), which took root in many colleges and universities in the 1980s. Educators and critics alike viewed WAC as an attractive option because it addressed critics' complaints about perceived declines in the quality of student writing and responded to writing teachers' perennial lament that composition courses lacked content. However, WAC was more than a practical solution to problems; it was also an idealistic effort to enhance the educational experience of students across the curriculum. As an editor of this book noted in an unpublished speech at a university adopting a WAC program:

> When students must *write* about their understandings of, say, personality theory or cell division or emergency cooling systems for the cores of nuclear reactors, when they must explain these things in their own words, they [...] understand them more profoundly than when they are merely asked to read textbooks and attend lectures.

This dimension of WAC is "Writing to Learn," as distinct from "Writing in the Disciplines" (WID). (Purdue) Herrington and Moran note, "The 'writing to learn' strand focuses on [...] writing to engage in exploratory thinking and learning in ways assumed to be useful [...] in any discipline." (7)

The impetus for the second strand, WID, arose when proponents of WAC recognized the need to teach the specific conventions of writing in diverse areas of study, or as Herrington and Moran put it, to teach "the ways of writing and reasoning assumed to be characteristic of academic contexts" (9). However, when English composition teachers tried to teach students to write for various disciplines, they weren't familiar with or adept at writing those forms (e.g., a physics laboratory report). Thus, in many WAC programs, instructors in various disciplines were urged to teach writing in their regular courses, since they (as physicists, sociologists, economists, etc.) were members of the *discourse communities* in which their students were trying to write papers. As one WAC scholar notes, "students best learn the specialized conventions, standards, and processes of writing in their chosen fields when they do so in the context of their own majors. [...] Teachers of all subject matters are [...] best prepared to help students write in their own fields." (Anson, ix) It is in this context that the "writing intensive course" came into being, and writing associates were often assigned to work with such courses.

As teachers and tutors undertook responsibility for initiating newcomers into disciplinary discourses, the idea of "entering discourse communities" gained significance in composition studies. In particular, scholars and teachers not only sought ways to help novices negotiate complex discourses but to interrogate the nature and purpose of students' entry into academic discourse. Many compositionists began to observe the existence of injustice and inequality in the practices of academic discourse communities in that students of diverse backgrounds might be marginalized by discourse conventions and forced to accommodate or assimilate. (Zamel, 515–16) While many scholars defended academic discourse on the grounds of its intellectual power and integrity and its potential for self-critique, others maintained that it tended to exclude students on the basis of such factors as gender, race, class, and sexual orientation. Thaiss and Zawacki, in a research study on academic discourse and "alternative" writing, note that the latter may "be employed for political purposes in order to call attention to those voices that have historically been marginalized or silenced by dominant discourses, as most notably, feminist and African American scholars have done" (9)

The Articles

Chapter 24, Anita Stone's "Scientific Writing: What's So Difficult About It Anyway?" is very much in the reformist spirit of the WAC movement. Stone wrote her essay for writing associates wishing to help students enter scientific discourse more effectively. A biology major and peer writing associate, Stone augmented her own views with the observations of three science professors and twenty-one science students at Oberlin College.

At one level, Stone is concerned to clarify aspects of scientific writing itself, which she says requires "mastering a whole new discourse," a discourse that "makes use of an entirely different language," and which "demands that we, as science students, learn to write all over again." At another level, she seeks improvement in the teaching of science writing; as she notes, "scientific writing 'instruction' is being carried out in a very fragmented way, mostly through students' outside exploration of writing manuals. If scientific writing were emphasized in a classroom setting [...] students would probably show greater improvement in their writing abilities."

In the second article (Chapter 25), "Defining a Persona Within the Boundaries of Academic Discourse, or, God, I Sound Like a Pretentious Ass," Elizabeth Schambelan tells of her attempts to rebel against what she considers the soul-deadening strictures of academic writing. In recounting her struggles to assert some sense of self within this kind of writing, Schambelan chronicles her battles with an authoritarian English teacher who required her to write in a stilted and artificial manner that she learned to master all too well, but which she found herself increasingly unable to accept. She states, "Academic writing is problematic to me because it asks me to construct a persona that I dislike. [...]" In writing a critical essay for a college literature course, she notes, "my persona became, not the Intellectual-as-God, but the student dutifully affecting that convention in deference to the powers-that-be." Unfortunately, her attempts at rebellion ultimately strike her not as positively subversive, but as spitefully self-denigrating, so she continues the effort to "find a voice" that will balance her warring selves.

Chapter 26, Holly Thompson's "Traveling the Middle Ground: Bridging the Dichotomies Between Academic and Personal Discourse," continues the quest for balance begun in Schambelan's essay. Like Schambelan, Thompson is troubled by her warring selves: in this case by her tendency to be *either* "emotional" *or* "orderly," *either* "reflective" *or* "analytical"—but not both at the same time. Attributing her emotional voice to the influence of her mother and her orderly voice to that of her father, Thompson observes:

> I see now that these two voices were cultivated in response to one another, and that just as I am a product of my parents' genes, I also represent a hybrid of the two voices I have constructed for them in this paper. I have felt for a long time the separateness of these distinct voices and strive for a more intermediary meeting place that blends these dual voices. [...]

Thompson goes on to identify her analytic persona as a "public" voice associated with the stereotypically "male sphere of rationality and emotional detachment" and her emotional mode as a "private" voice associated with "feminine stereotypes." She concludes by questioning the private-public "dichotomies [that] are artificially imposed in academic communities." Academia, she believes, should question these dichotomies and welcome more personal elements in its written discourses, thus achieving "a richness of perspective that a balanced middle ground permits."

In the final essay, "Academic Papers Within the College Discourse" (Chapter 27), Kanupriya Arora critiques how students across the curriculum are asked to write their course papers. As a student and as a writing associate who has tutored many others, Arora believes that student essays are too often "walled off" from the serious intellectual discourse of the classrooms for which they are produced. Noting the great importance that papers usually have in determining a student's grade, she finds it ironic that they are "never introduced into the academic discourse at all." Arora laments that "this most important and hallowed of academic exercises" takes place largely in isolation from the classroom and from classmates. She is dismayed that "academic papers seem to exist in some kind of surreal place where each student is alone and on her own, working on her papers and receiving them back with secret markings and evaluations that are rarely communicated with fellow students." This process, Arora feels, is "like throwing pebbles into a pond. Except it's not pebbles, but the pearls of our hard work and analysis." She urges greater appreciation for the contributions student writing can make to the ongoing conversations of disciplinary discourses. Of paramount importance, she believes, is that "papers must be discussed openly within the classroom," so that students can learn from what other students write.

WORKS CITED

Anson, Chris M. "Introduction: Reflection, Faculty Development, and Writing Across the Curriculum." *The WAC Casebook: Scenes for Faculty Reflection and Program Development.* Edited by Chris M. Anson. New York: Oxford University Press, 2002: ix–xiii.

Herrington, Anne, and Charles Moran. "The Idea of Genre in Theory and Practice." *Genre Across the Curriculum.* Edited by Anne Herrington and Charles Moran. Logan, UT: Utah University Press, 2005: 1–18.

Purdue University Online Writing Lab. "Writing Across the Curriculum and Writing in the Disciplines." Accessed 8/7/2009. < http://owl.english.purdue.edu/handouts/WAC/>

Thaiss, Chris, and Terry Myers Zawacki. *Engaged Writers and Dynamic Disciplines.* Portsmouth, NH: Boynton/Cook Heinemann, 2006.

Zamel, Vivian. "Strangers in Academia: The Experiences of Faculty and ESL Students Across the Curriculum." *College Composition and Communication* 46 (1995): 506–521.

Chapter 24

Scientific Writing: What's So Difficult About It Anyway?

Anita Stone

Introduction

Learning how to "write well," whether trying to develop a strong command of the language or simply improving mechanics, is a challenge most students have to face when they come to college. Science majors may be particularly overwhelmed upon finding they not only need to build up their general writing skills but must also master a whole new discourse, one that appears to be completely different from other forms of writing. The first impression many students (myself included) get about scientific writing is that it makes use of an entirely distinct language and demands that we, as science students, learn to write all over again. As a tutor I have often noticed that students' dread of writing papers doubles (if not triples) when they have to write a scientific paper. Most students I have encountered would actually rather write a five-page English paper than a two-page lab report.

But what makes scientific writing so elusive? How exactly are scientists supposed to write? One could say that the main characteristic of scientific writing is its specificity, which is required in every aspect and at every step. First of all, like much acceptable academic writing, any piece of scientific writing must have a definite purpose. However, in science writing, that purpose may be even more sharply focused and narrowly restricted than in writing for, say, the humanities. Scientists usually do not write about something in general; in their research articles they try to answer a specific question to which they severely confine themselves. Anything that does not directly relate to the main question must be excluded. Furthermore, generally speaking, in science there is little room for striking opinions or creative interpretations, only for "safe" evidence. Scientists are reluctant to state any theories unless they are supported by considerable data. In addition, although many scientists write for the public in books, magazines and newspapers intended for a general audience, their professional work is published in scientific journals and aimed at a particular readership: other scientists with a background in the subject. In other words, the audience that scientists most often write for is highly specialized.

Even more striking is that scientists appear to write in a language of their own. Its uniqueness can be seen in its terminologies, format, and even sentence constructions. Because scientific writing serves a narrowly specific purpose and *must* be focused and concise, the language has been developed to convey meaning with crystal clarity. In trying to avoid ambiguity, writers end up using sentence structures that have been tested over the years (e.g., "The purpose of this experiment was to [...]"; "It is well known that [...]").

The format of research papers is also highly specific and consists of six distinctive sections: abstract, introduction, materials and methods, results, discussion, and literature cited. (Note: in this non-scientific paper about scientific writing, I make use of only sections two through five.) Again, the format of a scientific paper reflects scientists' obligation to make their assumptions clear, their methods repeatable, and their interpretations separate from—albeit heavily supported by—the actual data.

These constraints make scientific writing quite difficult to master, and even after years of practice, some scientists still feel insecure about their abilities. Given that scientific writing is so challenging, it is only natural that students should face frustration when trying to learn it. Accordingly, *the purpose of my paper* (pardon the allusion to scientific style) was to determine and analyze some problems students' (myself included) experience with scientific writing. The conclusions of my informal "study" may be useful in determining how these problems can best be addressed by writing associates, teachers, and student writers themselves.

Materials and Methods

Because I was interested in obtaining both students' and teachers' perspectives on the topic, I spoke to some students and faculty of Oberlin College. I interviewed a total of three science professors (one in neuroscience and two in biology). The biology professors both teach writing-intensive courses in their disciplines. The interviews lasted approximately half an hour and were conducted in a very open-ended spirit. Typical questions were

- What main problems do you perceive in the writing of your students?
- Are the problems specific to lab reports, short papers, or research papers?
- Why do you think these problems occur?
- Do many students come to you for help? What do you think would help?
- What do you consider a "good" scientific paper?

To get students' responses, I conducted a written survey in Biology 205 ("Plant Ecology"). The course itself provides writing credit, and most students who returned the survey had some previous experience with scientific writing in other classes. Twenty-one students returned the survey. Also, as a student in the class, I filled out a survey and later asked friends not in the class to do so, for a total sample size of twenty-three students. Most students were either biology or environmental studies majors, many with a double major in English. Most had experience with scientific writing through biology, neuroscience, and geology classes. The following is a summary version of questions asked on the survey:

1. How many science classes have you taken involving writing? In what areas?
2. What kinds of writing did the classes involve? (lab reports, papers, etc.)
3. Did you feel you got a lot out of such classes, or was writing a "nuisance"?
4. Do you like to write for science classes more than for humanities classes?
5. What differences in your writing processes do you perceive between science writing and "other writing" (e.g., English papers)?
6. What problems do you typically encounter in writing science papers, which you do *not* normally experience in other papers?
7. What helps you when you are having trouble writing a science paper? Do you talk to other students? Do you go see the professor?
8. Have you ever been to a writing tutor for help with a science paper? If yes, did it help? Have you ever been to a writing tutor for help with any paper?

Results and Discussion

From the faculty interviews and student surveys, I was able to detect eight main problems students have with scientific writing.

1. The most striking (but not most frequently mentioned) problem I noticed was the misconceptions students have about scientific writing—both content and language. Many students wrote that they don't enjoy scientific writing because it does not allow for creativity at all. As one student put it, "science writing requires precision, not creativity. [...] It is less thought-provoking." A similar misconception is that scientific writing must be dull and uninteresting to be precise: "I don't feel science writing involves ideas and I think it's pretty boring."

Despite students' general impressions, I have become convinced (and professors have assured me) that in reality scientific writing *does* involve some amount of creativity, because scientists have to present unique ideas, not just passively accept and repeat what others have done. If we view scientific writing as an extension of science, we realize that because science itself must be original and thought provoking, the writing needs to follow suit. Initially I was surprised at the negative characteristics that students associated with writing. However, I realized that they would naturally come to the conclusion that scientific writing has to be boring and uncreative because no one has told them otherwise. Moreover, it is true that many of the professional articles we read in science classes seem rather boring and obscure, and so students don't get much exposure to examples of engaging scientific writing. Even though professors would like to see students become more engaged in their science writing, they seldom try to dispel the myth that dull writing is preferred in science, perhaps for fear that students will get "carried away" with their own thoughts and opinions while writing. Indeed, in science courses much attention is given to enforcing the "rules" of scientific writing, an approach that probably intimidates some students and alienates others. To address this problem, faculty members should probably try to correct the misconceptions and emphasize that it is acceptable, even essential, to be creative to a certain extent.

2. The most frequently mentioned problem was frustration with expressing ideas in a clear and understandable way in science papers, even if the ideas themselves come easily. As one student put it, "my ideas come easily enough and I *know* what I want to say, it's just difficult to say it with the correct words." I myself find it difficult to be concise in such papers, yet also accurate enough that someone else can repeat the study. It is likely that these problems result from lack of practice with scientific writing. If students aren't actively practicing these skills—and aren't receiving feedback—it becomes all the more difficult to get comfortable with this "new" kind of writing. I have found that by the end of a semester, my scientific papers are quite competently done, whereas in the beginning they strongly reflect my lack of practice.

3. Adhering to the many rules and restrictions of scientific writing can also be quite frustrating. Especially for students who are used to writing humanities papers, the shock of being subjected to rigid formats can be severe. I noticed this complaint especially from biology/English double majors. A typical comment was that "there are so many constraints on your writing and you have to be so careful about terminology that sometimes it becomes difficult to focus on the actual content." Another student observed that "some of these rules seem pointless to me. [...]" I think a large part of the problem is that students aren't really told exactly why these rules are necessary. Most of the time, we are given a specific format to follow, but we aren't made aware of the *reasons* for such standardization. The main reason is the necessity to avoid misinterpretation of data and to keep complex ideas from becoming too confusing; scientific writing cannot be completely "free-form" because people are dealing with specific facts in specific ways. One

professor actually called the existence of so many rules a "protection mechanism." However, since students don't know the logic behind the rules, it becomes more difficult to appreciate and follow them.

4. A critical problem, noted by both professors and students, relates to developing a discussion and interpretation of scientific data. Although students called it "drawing my own conclusions from the studies," while professors called it "summarizing vs. interpreting," I believe that both groups are really talking about the same issue. Indeed, this is a difficulty that is common to humanities papers as well—students many times find themselves repeating or summarizing a book or an argument rather than analyzing it. However, I find this problem especially obvious in scientific writing. I believe the main reason for the trouble is that students are "scared" of scientific data and are operating under the misconception that they are not supposed to include any of their own conclusions. In fact, one student said she liked scientific writing because "there is no pressure for you to come up with your own ideas," which, as I mentioned above, is a common myth that professors, for one reason or another, seldom attempt to dispel. In the words of another student, "I don't know whether I am right or have the authority to throw in my own ideas."

Students feel the need to be very careful about anything they say, such that they try to cite other studies to back them up. Once, for instance, I was writing a long research paper and found myself cautiously attempting to cite a source for everything I said. I finally realized that it was ridiculous for me to back up obvious facts, such as "plants need light for photosynthesis," with citations. Ironically, however, I found that while students are complaining that "there seems to be less respect for opinion in scientific writing," professors are complaining about students' failure to include their ideas in their papers. I suppose that lack of communication is part of the problem in this case. In addition, many students don't know how to go about drawing their own conclusions because "sometimes it's hard to come up with your own interpretation when the topic has already been thoroughly researched and it seems that all the viewpoints have been explored."

Students should realize, however, that their ideas need not be totally original, as long as they attempt to offer a valid interpretation. They should also realize that there is room to discuss the work of previous researchers and to examine whether their own findings are consistent with earlier ones. For example, I noted in a lab report that "Heinrich (1976) has demonstrated that bumblebees do in fact spend more time on 'hot' patches of *Impatiens*." Students might also include statements such as "these results appear to differ from those obtained by *x*." Another approach I find useful is to admit that I cannot make assumptions based on unclear data or that my ideas are only speculations that need further testing: "Smaller flower patches could therefore be associated with less pollinator movement. Further comparisons of small and large patches of *Impatiens* may reveal whether these patches do indeed differ in nectar production levels."

5. Scientific writing often requires a detailed knowledge of scientific facts. The problem arises when students don't yet have this knowledge, but are nonetheless required to use it. Professors noted that many times students appear to be writing without a very firm grasp of the subject. Understanding the topic is the first step in ensuring that the writing itself will have a clear focus. However, often students are required to write on a topic in which they are not interested, and this discourages them from properly researching the topic. Since all science writing, at least in my experience, requires research at some point, this can be an obstacle to producing a good paper. Students also complained about being overwhelmed with all the information in the scientific literature, which is probably another reason why they have a hard time getting familiar with a topic. Finally, it is important that professors (and students) avoid unreasonable expectations about writing. Within the span of only a few weeks, students are typically required to obtain considerable knowledge about topics scientists may have been researching for years, and then they are expected to write incisive papers about those topics. Everyone's expectations should be adjusted accordingly.

6. A related problem, identified only by the professors in my study, is that students usually don't allow themselves enough time to write well. This is a classic problem with any form of writing, but in science, especially if students are not very familiar with the subject, they really need all the time they can get. It is impossible to research background material, interpret data, draw conclusions, and so on, and still produce a clear and orderly text in one or two nights. The "night-before" approach does not work well with scientific writing. However, some students insist on following this pattern, especially with lab reports, since they are not extremely long and do not appear to require much work. In reality, though, they are among the most frustrating types of scientific writing because of the need for clarity and precision.

7. Another problem pointed out by the professors concerns mistakes in the actual mechanics of the writing (grammar, usage, etc.). While this problem is clearly not limited to science writing, it would seem that science professors are especially mindful of such errors because of the importance of conveying information accurately, without ambiguity. One professor estimated that about 80% of the time he spends grading a paper is devoted to correcting mechanics. The biggest problem seems to be the use of long,

murky sentences that could be reduced to "express ideas in a less convoluted way." On the other hand, students sometimes take the rule to be precise too far and produce abrupt, choppy, telegraphic sentences that lack flow. Therefore, they end up producing texts that are far from readable. Again, I think that such mistakes can be avoided with practice.

8. Finally, some students realize that a major problem related to all those discussed above is that there is little instruction given on science writing. Many wrote in the surveys that they feel practice and feedback are important: "If professors asked for multiple drafts, focused on group processes, and did a careful, thoughtful critique, that would really help. But if professors just set students loose and are only interested in the product, scientific writing becomes less enjoyable and less useful" (interestingly, this was said by a biology/English double major). I believe many problems students have with science writing are aggravated by the lack of instruction in this skill. Unfortunately, although most science professors realize how important it is that students learn to write scientifically, scientific writing does not play a prominent role in the curriculum.

Conclusion: What Can Be Done?

In essence, becoming an effective science writer takes a lot of practice and hard work. Scientific writing, then, is a specific skill that can only come with experience. Science students generally seem to be aware of the importance of writing for scientific work and of the difficulties associated with its mastery. When asked what they usually do when faced with scientific writing problems, students gave a variety of answers.[1] However, I was surprised that not many students actually go to professors for help (to turn in drafts, talk about the paper topic, etc.). This is unfortunate, since all professors I spoke to said they *do* emphasize to students that they are available for help on any stage of a paper. They regret that few students actually take advantage of the opportunity. I myself had never turned in a draft of any paper (humanities or sciences) until this semester. When I finally did so (for a lab report), I was amazed at how much it helped me in producing my final copy.

While these practices are helpful, I feel that students are often not motivated to follow professors' suggestions. A reason may be that the scientific writing "instruction" is being carried out in a very fragmented way, mostly through students' outside exploration of writing manuals. If scientific writing were stressed in a classroom setting (e.g., setting aside a class for peer response groups), students would probably show greater improvement. I feel that we are constantly reminded of how crucial it is to write well and bombarded with scattered, vague information on how to do so, yet we are not really given the right tools to accomplish the task. In simple terms, most of us are frustrated because we *want* to become good science writers but just don't know how. Somehow, the guidelines provided in writing manuals just don't seem to do the job. The reason for this is very simple: the manuals tell us what to do but do not *show* us. I often find that a simple classroom example is worth ten pages of explaining from a manual. However, I do recognize the challenges of including science writing in the classroom. Another overlooked option is the help available from writing associates. Professors said they recommend that students see a writing tutor only in "extreme cases." In other words, tutoring is not being viewed as a generally helpful, interactive process through which students can grow. By the same token, science students may be reluctant to be tutored, since writing associates are usually not science majors and may not have much experience with science writing. Although this is a concern, tutors could still provide relevant guidance. Alternatively, more science students could be encouraged to be writing associates. Since many times professors are unable to offer extensive individualized attention outside the classroom or to spend time on writing *in* the classroom as previously mentioned, it seems that tutors would be a practical alternative. Science students would certainly benefit from this approach. As a writing associate and a science major, I hope that this alternative will be viewed more seriously in the future, both by science professors and students.

NOTES

[1]Thirteen students said that they have a friend or roommate read their papers; nine that they read a paper aloud; nine that they submit drafts to the professor; four that they listen to music; five that they take a walk; seven that they procrastinate; five that they read other scientific papers; and none that they see a writing associate.

Chapter 25

Defining a Persona Within the Boundaries of Academic Discourse, or God, I Sound Like a Pretentious Ass

Elizabeth Schambelan

When I was a senior in high school, I took Advanced Placement English with an instructor whose pedagogical method was, to put it kindly, "traditional." For her, the five-paragraph essay was not just a possible method of approaching critical analysis; it was a sacred icon which we, the students, were not to desecrate.

For half a year I doggedly churned out five-paragraph essay after five-paragraph essay. I never got a grade lower than A–. Then, at the end of the first semester we read *Invisible Man*. I really liked it, and my enthusiasm carried over into the paper I wrote on it: rather than searching my brain for a serviceable topic, I found there were things I actually *wanted* to say. And, since what I was saying did not lend itself to the five-paragraph structure, I didn't employ it. My teacher commented that she found the paper "confused" and gave me a C.

I spent much more time than usual on the next paper; it was a sterling example of the five-paragraph theme. There were exactly nine points, each well supported; I never used the same transition or verb twice, and so forth. Although I usually wrote my papers on a word processor, I composed this one on an old typewriter that dropped t's and always printed g's, for some reason, in red. I used single-spacing, and typed it with no margins, on lined notebook paper with ragged edges. I corrected typos with a black pen and, when I felt the need to move whole paragraphs, I cut them out with scissors and used masking tape to reinsert them. I turned it in that way.

My teacher wrote a rather scathing comment on this paper—something about how, when I got to the state university, my professors might not tolerate such an "awful-looking manuscript." (It was particularly scathing because she knew that the state university was my "safety school" and that I was hoping to be admitted to a more competitive college.) Despite all this, she gave me an A on the paper, and I felt very clever.

I have recently come to regard this incident as more than just a passive-aggressive play for revenge. My deliberate physical destruction of my "manuscript" was not solely motivated by my desire to annoy the teacher. The most basic motivation, I think, was my desire to do with the paper's appearance what my teacher, and my own concern about grades, would not allow me to do with its form and content: make it different; make it my own. I still have that paper, and I really do think it's a neat-looking object: the dense, black, idiosyncratic print, spotted with red, divided into blocks by the yellowish masking tape, now turning brown with age.

I have gone on at such length about this incident because that paper, that "awful-looking manuscript," functions absurdly well as a symbol of my entire relationship with academic writing—that strange vacillation between wholehearted appropriation of the accepted mode of discourse and desperate attempts (often characterized by a vaguely psychotic sort of glee) to thwart that very mode of discourse.

I think that this vacillation comes about due to the conflicting pressures that I feel when I write academic prose. These pressures are my desire for acceptance and success within the academic community and my sense of self-integrity—that is, my desire to reject the academic community (this desire deriving not from any particular political gripe against academia, but from a strain of knee-jerk individualism). In other words, the conflict is between my desire to go to grad school and my desire to move to some city, get a disreputable job, define myself as an "artist," and try to have unexpected things happen to me (my culture's idea of "conformity" vs. my culture's idea of "iconoclasm").

But I should make clear that I'm not speaking of a "real" conflict; rather, I am speaking of a battle enacted entirely within the parameters of the page. In my *life*, I know what I am: a future grad school student. Indeed, with each word of this very paper that I'm writing, that path becomes a more probable reality. And at any rate, somehow, in real life, the choices do not seem as opposed as they do on paper. But it is precisely what is on paper that is at issue. The conflict is one of textual personas made manifest through textual voices.

Academic writing is problematic to me because it asks me to construct a persona that I dislike: the persona inherent in student-written, traditional academic discourse. Peter Elbow speaks of "author-evacuated" (145) prose characteristic of traditional "high" academic discourse. In such discourse, there is no "I." Instead, there is a detached and abstract voice that is meant to assert a claim on objectivity, on a quest for some "essential truth" that would be distorted by any personal involvement, any subjectivity on the part of the textual persona. Such prose purports to contain *no* persona at all; it purports to be generated from a void of pure objectivity. But, even as I believe that there is no such thing as an "essential truth," I believe that there is no such thing as a text without a persona. Every text has a voice, and so, every text has a persona. The persona of such "author-evacuated" prose is an implicit one, but it is still there. When the text is authored by a privileged member of the academic establishment and is published in a scholarly journal or appears in some other accepted arena, then the persona is that of the Intellectual-as-God, the judge on high who is able to sort the wheat of reality from the chaff and to present it to us, distilled into print.

Now everyone knows that no such entity exists, but still, the persona of the Intellectual-as-God has become such an embedded convention in academia that there is a strong compulsion to adopt it. In fact, it is a persona that I have often been known to adopt, as in this passage from a paper I wrote six months ago:

> Milly Theale is the title character of Henry James's novel, *The Wings of the Dove*. Her metaphoric identification as a dove is overt. Kate Croy christens her as such, and Milly seizes upon the appellation as if it is a "revealed truth." James generally takes subtlety to the point of dissimulation; it is uncharacteristic of him to convey so directly a metaphor so significant that it serves as the work's title. However, James's overtness in this respect can be explained: it is itself dissimulation. [...]

When I read this passage over, I am reminded of a Sartre quote that I came across as a first-year student:

> Shortly after semi-automatic machines were introduced, investigations showed that female skilled workers would allow themselves to lapse while working into a sexual kind of daydream; they would recall the bedroom, the bed, the night and all that concerns only the person within the solitude of the couple alone with itself. But it was the machine in her which was dreaming of caresses. [...] (Sartre, 290 in Marcuse, 27)

Herbert Marcuse uses this quotation in *One-Dimensional Man* to explain how it is that factory workers can live out their lives going through the same tedious motions, day after day, hour after hour: They become hypnotized by the "drugging rhythm" of the work; they derive a strange satisfaction from the very gestures themselves. (Marcuse, 26)

When I first read this passage, I copied it down, taped it over my computer, and became strangely obsessed with it. I could never understand this obsession—but I should have found a clue in the fact that I placed the quotation near my computer (as opposed to, say, my bed); I placed it at the site of all my endeavors to engineer academic discourse.

Although I didn't realize it at the time, I think I was fascinated by the passage because I and students in general are susceptible to the same process that Sartre and Marcuse describe. When I wrote the passage on Milly Theale, as well as the ten additional pages that followed on its heels, I derived a strange satisfaction from it: the satisfaction of appropriating that inert syntax, those phrases ("as such," "it is itself"), and all of those gestures which go into creating the persona of the Intellectual-as-God. I was a skilled worker in a factory, and that factory is the academic establishment, and its product is "high" academic discourse—author-evacuated, "objective" text. The "caresses" I was dreaming of were not the satisfaction of creating a paper that expressed something I wanted to say, and which said it well, but the caresses of approval of the academic establishment. And I got an A on the paper.

But, because I was a *student* writing to a *professor* in such a voice, and probably affecting it somewhat awkwardly at that, my persona became not the Intellectual-as-God, but the student dutifully affecting that convention in deference to the powers-that-be. The persona became that of academic worker bee.

I do not like to think of myself as an academic worker bee, and so this particular persona is one that I have been struggling to leave behind me. The first real attempt in this struggle was the "awful-looking manuscript" I mentioned before. Later on, I grew a bit more subtle. For example, in my first year of college, I wrote a very dry and academic paper on Lewis Carroll. However, in the paper I used quotes from the Marquis de Sade to help illustrate what I called "sadomasochistic imagery in *Alice in Wonderland*." In a very deadpan tone, I introduced the most obscene and violent quotes from *120 Days of Sodom*. It was just like the awful-looking manuscript: instead of using masking tape and smudged ink, I was using "bad words" and images of sexual mutilation.

But it was the same method. I produced a very conventional text and then *superimposed* the "subversive" elements upon it. Those quotations from Sade were not an intrinsic part of my text. They were even physically separate from it: They were block quotations, set apart from the main body of the text by double spaces and indentations, surrounded by clear white space.

Those quotations were like graffiti; I had profaned my own paper in much the same way that another teenager might have profaned the walls of her school or neighborhood. The quotes had the same benefits that graffiti yields: an eye-catching sensationalism. They had the same purpose that graffiti has: to express defiance of the situation in which you find yourself. And they had the same flaw: In defying your situation, you find yourself desecrating the place where you live.

Graffiti is generally an adolescent thing. This semester I have tried to define my voice within academic discourse in a way that does not rely so much on shock value, and this transition of voice, I suppose, parallels the transition from disgruntled, shock-value-loving teenager to adult with a more mature and temperate disposition. But like many people on the cusp of adulthood, as my stage of life is often cloyingly called, I am a bit reluctant to let go of my old ways, because I fear turning into my vision of the archetypal Bad Grown-Up: dull and fusty, boring and bored. I fear taking on too often the persona inherent in my Milly Theale paper because I fear that persona will become ingrained. This fear itself, I know, is silly, one of the final shreds of my adolescence, but it is still disquieting.

And so what I am trying to do is strike a balance, somewhere between the Marquis de Sade and Henry James. This balance, as I've said above, will come about when I've succeeded in *integrating* personas (honor student vs. discipline case, conformist vs. iconoclast, adolescent vs. "twentysomething," etc.), rather than simply smearing one on top of another. A new persona will emerge, I hope, one which satisfies all the conflicting parts of myself.

The attempt to find a voice, which I have described above, is of course very personal to me; it has to do with my personal background, biases and predilections. But the struggle is one which every college student must go through; we are all faced with the paradigm of the Intellectual-as-God, and we all must defer to him to some degree if we want to survive, and we all (because of our *voluntary* presence in the ivory tower) must find a way to justify this deference to ourselves.

I was originally hoping to end this paper with a ringing conclusion that would further point the way ("We must all . . ."). But that would be something that the Intellectual-as-God would do. I don't know if my struggle to find my own voice in academic discourse can be instructive to anyone else, for it is so very personal; for example, others might not *care* about all this, or others might feel more pressures owing to cultural differences than I have had to grapple with. But in a way that's just it, because I think that it is only in looking at the very personal nature of my own particular problems with academic discourse—by writing with those problems in mind, by writing, in a way, *from* those problems—that I am able to begin to define my own persona.

Works Cited

Elbow, Peter. "Reflections on Academic Discourse: How It Relates to Freshmen and Colleagues." *College English* 53 (1991): 135–155.

Marcuse, Herbert. *One-Dimensional Man: Studies in the Ideology of Advanced Industrial Society*. Boston: Beacon, 1964.

Sartre, Jean-Paul. *Critique de la Raison Dialectique*. Vol. 1. Paris: Gallinard, 1960.

Chapter 26

Traveling the Middle Ground: Bridging the Dichotomies Between Academic and Personal Discourse

Holly Thompson

The Personal Context

I was seven years old when my parents divorced and my father left home. I stayed in the house I had lived in all my life. When my dad left, he took with him my brother, Erik, who was sixteen and could walk to high school from my dad's new apartment. Heidi, my sister, left too, because she was eighteen at the time and started attending college in Vermont. Living in my house with just my mom and my older brother, Mark, was like living in a brand new place. My mom found herself in a new role of leadership since my dad, Heidi, and Erik were no longer around to help her run the household.

From this new household emerged a distinct "emotional" voice that I believe my mom, through her commitment to the process of self-reflection, helped cultivate. Home was often a hotbed for emotionalism. The three of us bickered on a regular basis, and when we were not spatting, mom would often press us for our emotional reactions to situations and share her own. She loved to hear our stories, giggled at our goofy antics, and was always quick to cry when something either moved or disturbed her, or when she became consumed by insecurity. For ten years, my mother was my primary female role model, and so in many ways I learned to adopt an emotional voice like hers. Looking back on those years, I see that while my mom's emotionalism may have helped me to better understand my own emotional self, the parameters of her emotional expression were often loosely drawn. Though she did reflect later upon her emotional outbursts, she often acted in the moment from her impulses and would lay everything on the table. She thus lacked an analytical lens through which to view and reflect upon her emotional expression. I modeled this behavior for many years, and it was not until I separated from my mother and went to college that I achieved enough distance to view my childhood critically, to learn the value of self-consciousness and self-reflexivity as opposed to the kind of unmediated self-exposure that my mother relied on.

My father, on the other hand, created a very different atmosphere in his home, and it was not until he moved out of the house that I began to feel the distinctions between the voices of my mother and my father. My dad's homes were fairly empty and stark. He remarried to Anna, an obsessive-compulsive housekeeper who adored glass tables, fine china, and a clutter-and-dust-free living environment. In their house, I never felt that I could use anything unless I asked because I was afraid of creating a mess and thus offending my dad and Anna.

Our conversations were as orderly as the house. We never argued, nor did I ever hear them fight. When they asked me factual questions about the goings-on in my life, I answered in a heightened voice, assuming a maturity I had not yet achieved. At meals, I would listen to their intellectual conversation about current issues, but I never voiced my opinions because, again, I did not want to "mess things up." They never asked for my opinion—my father rarely invited ideas or reflections about any aspect of my life, particularly my "inner life" of feelings, images, and stories. In my father's house, we kept these private thoughts to ourselves. Life in this household was about order, facts, and reason. I did not feel there was room for my emotionalism, nor for the voicing of a reflective, "inner" voice. I swallowed my tears when Anna looked at me funny, or I sat in the bathroom with the fan on when I could no longer hold them in.

To avoid confrontation, the frightening possibility of knocking over a vase, or some unspoken signal of disapproval, I spent long hours alone in my basement bedroom, doing schoolwork, writing in my journal, imagining. In that sanctuary, I enjoyed privacy. I retreated into my own compartment where I held close the ideas and images that went unspoken, unshared. Occasionally, I would write mini-stories or scribble pictures with Magic Markers, but I often tore up these sheets and threw them away so they could never be seen by anyone. I poured myself into my journal, which I kept hidden in my overnight bag. I recognized a personal need to reflect on my experiences in order to understand them. However, in the context of my father's house, I felt a sense of shame about this voice that was only given full expression in my locked-up diary.

On Sunday nights, I'd zip up my bag, hop into my father's beige Camry, and head back to my mother's home. When I arrived, I would leave my defenses at the door and immediately purge myself of the festering frustration, often by picking petty fights with my mother. Sometimes these collisions would burgeon into extended outpourings of anguish and anger that started in the foyer and traveled throughout the whole house, lasting as long as a few hours. I usually ended up in my bedroom with the door slammed shut, but, without fail, Mom soon would open the door (never knocking first), with "one more thing to say." There in my bedroom we would battle each other for the final word, regardless of how irrational these words may have been. These sessions would end with both of us apologizing in tears, promising one another that we would drop the subject and move on. However, we never looked back on our fights to ask why they arose or to analyze how we could work together to change our behavior.

I see now that these two voices were cultivated in response to one another, and that just as I am a product of my parents' genes, I also represent a hybrid of the two voices I have constructed for them in this paper. I have felt for a long time the separateness of these distinct voices and strive for a more intermediary meeting place that blends these dual voices, which, as I have discovered through the process of writing this paper, are impossible to completely separate. However, I do believe that in each of these homes I struggled with the tensions between a "public" voice and a more "private" voice. Mom's house was a space where the private became public, where we drew few lines and where feelings were exposed, invaded, and rarely reflected upon. In Dad's home, the private remained private as we bottled up our emotions and remained isolated in our individualized compartments. Additionally, I felt alienated from the cold, detached intellectual conversation, which, in the context of my father's home, was "public" discourse. Looking back, I can see that I used my journal as a rest stop between the two voices. I could *publicize* my inner world in that book *privately*, without intrusion. And, residing in my overnight bag, it traveled a middle ground between the two extremes that these homes have come to represent.

Bringing My Voice to College: The Academic Context

I carried my overnight bag with me to college, and since I arrived four years ago, I have gradually unpacked the journal from its hiding place. This process involved identifying the voices I constructed for myself and reflecting upon my struggle to achieve a balanced voice. It has also involved giving meaning to these voice constructions by contextualizing them theoretically. Through taking women's studies courses in college, I have come to partially define myself as a "feminist thinker." Calling on my working understanding of feminist theory, I can see how my construction of my parents' voices—of the private and the public, as well as how I located myself within these constructions—fit into essentialized gender categories.

My father's home, for example, can be seen as a particularly male sphere of rationality and emotional detachment within which I felt my private voice alienated and silenced. Similarly, my description of my mother plays into feminine stereotypes that characterize women as being hyper-emotional, irrational, and hysterical. I am a female located on the continuum between these two points, and I feel there are implications to the fact that my position is, indeed, a female one. Growing up with the dual voices of my parents, I have internalized certain conceptions of gender as well as an understanding of how I, as a woman living in a society that has historically subordinated women, fit into these constructs. I see that I have cultivated my private voice in reaction to my father's more public voice, while my mother affirmed and encouraged the growth of this private voice through making it public.

In constructing these voices, I recognize the limits involved in identifying such constructions. To some feminist theorists, feminist pedagogy that teaches students about gender categories is "reductive and dangerous," encouraging feminist thinkers to "operate within a binary perspective." (Ritchie, 249) In my reflections, was I in fact essentializing my experience by tailoring myself and my parents to fit rigid gender dichotomies? Am I forcing (and reinforcing) these stereotypes, or is it the case that they are already there, and I am simply naming them? In my quest to make sense of my own struggle for voice, I feel I have been compelled, on some level, to essentialize my experience and to rely on gender dichotomies in order to understand the points of tension and my position in relation to them. I am thus "taking the risk of essence" (Gayatri Spivak, cited in Ritchie, 256), recognizing that essentialism, like the constructions themselves, is not a fixed position but rather can be viewed as a temporary point on a developmental path, a view I share with Ritchie and Spivak.

This discussion has encouraged reflection upon my education and my experiences as a female student in the academy. My academic experiences in college have indicated that the dominant discourse of academia, as I have come to know it, encourages the use of the public voice over the private one, often without recognizing that the two are invariably linked. I consider academia to be a socializing force that shapes assumptions, beliefs, standards, and, thus, voices and identities. Through reading academic texts and observing the often heightened discourse of lecturing professors, students become versed in an academic language, one that was shaped fundamentally by men. This public discourse has the power to alienate and marginalize women, often silencing them and rendering them invisible. Dale Spender takes up this issue in *Man-Made Language*:

> The male control of meaning extends to the registers of public discourse so that it is
> both the meaning and the form in which that meaning is expressed (in public dis-
> course) that has been encoded by men and controlled by men. (78)

Often, this discourse does not resonate with female experience, for women
have traditionally been relegated to the private sphere:

> [Women] have not been in the public arena, they have not been the "culture" mak-
> ers, with the result that any meanings which they may wish to encode, but which are
> different or at odds with those [...] generated by men, have been tenuous and transi-
> tory: They have been cut off from the mainstream of meanings. [...] (Spender, 52)

Historically, public discourse in academia has been a male-dominated
realm. Even "progressive" institutions such as Oberlin College, credited with
being the first college ever to admit women, were founded on exclusionary
practices. According to *The History of Oberlin College*, "The young men in
all departments wrote compositions, delivered declamations and engaged in
discussion regularly throughout their course. The 'misjudged sex' only wrote
compositions." (Fletcher, Vol. 2) These misjudged women wrote about
dreams, visions, tales, descriptions, and metaphysics—subjects deemed
"appropriate to the feminine mind"—while men wrote speeches articulating
their opinions on subjects they studied in men-only courses such as "Compositions and Extemporaneous Discussion," "Composition and Exposition
Discussion," or "History of Theological Opinions." Once a month, these
young men took part in public declamations which female students were
permitted to attend, but at which they were to remain silent. No woman had
voice at these sessions nor ever delivered a speech. However, if a woman had
written an exemplary essay, she was afforded the privilege of having a man
read her paper for her. The gender dichotomization of the public and private
spheres was thus instituted from Oberlin College's inception. (Fletcher, 716–
739)

Although over time these gendered dichotomies have been subverted and
while there are, of course, exceptions and overlaps inherent in these categories, I mean to suggest that, because most women have historically been
excluded from the public arena, it has been harder for them to break into this
male-generated definition of academic knowledge and discourse. At Oberlin,
I have oftentimes experienced difficulty in trying to locate myself within this
defined discursive space that I feel does not always speak to my experience.
This is the case because I feel that the academic conception of knowledge
within the college community goes so far as to *delegitimize* the private and
personal voice. Although some professors and scholars in the fields of
women's studies and composition studies are working to disrupt and chal-

lenge the dominant discourse that privileges the use of the public voice over the private, it is my belief that the academy continues to reproduce a system that clearly distinguishes these voices, the academic and the personal, to the detriment of the latter.

In the more "traditional" academic classrooms, I have not felt encouraged to integrate my life experiences with what I read, write, and discuss.[1] As an English major at Oberlin, I have struggled in classes where the discourse, for example, demands a purely textual reading of a literary work. In many of these classes, I have remained silent in discussions and have written perfunctory "one-draft" papers that I do not feel reflect my voice or experience. The language of these papers mimics the detached, academic, and public discourse to which I felt little intellectual, emotional, or bodily connection during or after the writing process. In rereading some of my academic papers, I find it nearly impossible to locate my position in the writing. Rarely do the papers voice any criticism or opinions; rather, in these essays I stick closely to interpretations of meaning and symbolism, relying on the text for support and authority. In these papers I assume a more public persona that does not embody my private, personal voice. Both in class discussions and in my writing, I have been the girl sitting at her father's dinner table, afraid to break into the discourse in any meaningful way by voicing emotions and opinions. Instead, I have retreated into "silence," so as not to "mess up" the neat, rational, orderly discourse I have been trained to adopt.

My conception of knowledge and of an "ideal" education encompasses a continuous exchange between one's work and one's self, between intellectual pursuits and life experiences, between theory and praxis, the public and the private, the "academic" and the "personal." Only in my women's studies classrooms and in the teaching and tutoring writing course have I been able to explore these connections in depth, and both Women's Studies and Expository Writing happen to be marginal programs within the institution. These "marginalized" learning environments have encouraged and affirmed a self-reflexive learning process by requiring weekly journal entries as well as writing assignments such as the one I am fulfilling by writing this paper. Such assignments are open-ended, allowing room for the exploration of the autobiographical voice, the positioning of the self in the course material. In "Introduction to Women's Studies," I wrote two autobiographies—one in the first week of the course, and another revised version as the final writing assignment that interwove themes from the assigned course readings. These spaces have not served merely as venting places used exclusively to air and expose the private, personal voice. Rather, they have functioned as meeting places for a more emotional, personalized voice that is contextualized both theoretically and historically in a reflective, analytical voice: an "academic" voice. The journals and the autobiographies are, then, examples of assignments that I feel have invited the integration of these dichotomized voices.

Implications and Reflections

Is there a place for such an integrated voice within the dominant discourse of the academy? Though I feel grateful for having the opportunity to blend the public academic voice with the private personal voice in the context of women's studies and expository writing classes, I have felt, overall, that the college academic community has not recognized this middle ground and continues to clearly dichotomize the personal and the academic, privileging traditional definitions of "academic" discourse. I want to suggest that there is a danger in dichotomizing. By grasping onto dichotomies, we deny ourselves a richness of perspective that a balanced middle ground permits, closing our eyes to the nuances, subtleties, and rich diversity that are created along a continuum.

Furthermore, because they are nothing more than constructions, these dichotomies are, I believe, artificially imposed in academic communities. Through my own constructions of writing voices in this paper, I have tried to show that these voices do not have to be separate. Though I have spent a considerable amount of time revising and restructuring this paper, I found that my tendency during the writing process was to write in a voice that, in my mind, combined both academic and personal elements. The "Personal Context" section is done largely in a narrative mode, but it is also analytical, and the more theoretical sections of the paper are also grounded in experience and self-reflection. I discovered that, in writing this paper, I was quick to label and categorize, to push themes into definite analytical compartments. Composing this paper, then, can be seen as an enactment and a working through of the tensions that lie between the constructed dichotomies of public and private, academic and personal.

I am a *woman* who is *academic*. I cannot and do not wish to separate the two. I am a hybrid, a whole person striving to write holistically, to create a fluidly defined space for myself in which to write, to act, to be. I look forward to creating, through continued work in teaching and tutoring, future spaces for myself and for others in which we can travel and enact this middle ground.

> The goal will no longer be to eliminate the risks of temporality by clutching to guaranteed space, but rather to temporalize space. [...] The universe is revealed to me not as a space, imposing a massive presence to which I can adapt, but as a scope, a domain which takes shape as I act upon it. (Pierre Furter, cited in Freire, 26–27)

NOTES

[1] Traditional classrooms, based on my experience, are those that promote textual approaches to learning rather than putting subjects in a socio-political or self-reflexive context. For me, this definition applies mainly to college courses that I have taken in English and theater.

WORKS CITED

Fletcher, Robert Samuel. *The History of Oberlin College*. Vol. 2. Oberlin, OH: Oberlin College, 1943.

Freire, Paulo. *Pedagogy of the Oppressed*. New York: Continuum, 1970.

Ritchie, Joy S. "Confronting the 'Essential' Problem: Reconstructing Feminist Theory and Pedagogy." *Journal of Advanced Composition*. 10 (1990): 249–273.

Spender, Dale. *Man-Made Language*. London: Routledge and Kegan Paul, 1980.

Chapter 27

Academic Papers Within the College Discourse

Kanupriya Arora

Introduction: Problems in Writing

One of my hardest tutoring experiences at the Writing Center was with a student writing a paper for an English class. She came in flushed, clutching a pile of loose papers and notes which, she informed me, she was finding it impossible to turn into a coherent paper with a thesis and argument. We went through the draft, such as it was, and the various notes and post-its she had scribbled ideas on. I had not read the book she was writing about, so she explained it to me as best as she could, her voice coming alive with genuine interest. We talked about her disconnected ideas and tried to carve out some kind of cogent argument. I could see her struggling with her analysis, struggling to take in the things I was saying, struggling to convey her ideas in appropriate words. I could practically see the way she was rushing around inside her own head, trying to arrange everything she felt or thought about the book into neat piles of presentable material. By the end of the session, we had made some headway: she had a thesis and a structure for her supporting ideas. But I knew that when she actually sat down to write the paper, the final product would not reflect the amount of work she had put into it; that her professor was likely to dismiss her argument as poorly structured or "awkward"—that favorite adjective of many college professors—and the student would face the consequences of being a mediocre academic writer.

I couldn't help feeling a sense of privileged guilt. Writing usually comes naturally easy (or, at least, easier) to me; the distance between the ideas in my head and the words on my screen is but a bridge that I have to cross every time I sit down to dish out another academic paper. The length and slope of the bridge vary from paper to paper, it's true, but I have always been able to see the other side, to know that I'll come within acceptable, even impressive, proximity of the goal, and that I will be awarded accordingly with an "A" or a commendation. I wondered how it felt to write a paper that just seemed like an endless upward climb. To struggle on, the way my tutee did, without sight of a satisfactory end, and then, even after the many hours of clambering up, to be greeted at the end of the day, not by cheers or empathy but by some words on a paper pointing out all the things you did wrong.

Another one of my tutees came in with ten poised, carefully researched pages about the origins and practices of the Unitarian Church. I commended the clarity of the paper and noted the objective, detached, impressively academic tone in which it was written—and the unfortunate absence of insight and interest underneath. Then I asked him what specific areas he was interested in working on. He said he didn't know; the paper was due in a few hours and he couldn't really think of or make any big changes. The paper was more or less ready to hand in, he said; he was just, somehow, dissatisfied with it. Unfulfilled, I think in retrospect.

We talked about the paper for the next half hour, as I tried to probe deeper into his thesis and his reasons for choosing his topic. He had interesting things to say, and I suggested that he add them to his paper, take his research to the next level. But he was hesitant to do so—he wasn't really sure that was what his professor wanted. At this point we were both somewhat resigned to the paper as it was, and he left soon after. It was a 100-level religion class, and I was fairly certain he would receive at least a fair grade on it, but I couldn't help thinking what an unfulfilling experience it was for the student as writer, for me as a tutor, and likely for the professor as reader.

Questioning Students' Problems

Writing papers is hard. I don't know of any student who doesn't struggle with, stress about or lose some sleep over them. Writing associates exist because paper writing is difficult. In a college environment that hopes not only to encourage but necessitate critical thinking, it is to be expected that articulating our ideas and defending them would be a difficult and exhausting process. This raises two questions. First, are papers hard for the right reasons? In other words, do we as students get enough out of our papers considering the time and mental effort we put into worrying about, planning and writing them? Second, since writing is so difficult, why don't more students come to the Writing Center? Why is the dreaded difficulty of writing papers ignored or inadequately addressed by students and professors alike?

There is a general assumption—at least in institutions that are attempting to abandon the mechanistic model of multiple choice questions and correct answers to instill a more perspicacious way of thinking—that papers are difficult because of the amount of critical thinking they require, and that they are therefore worthwhile. Yet, over and over again during the course of this semester, I have read about or come across students who are able to circumvent the intended challenge of writing a paper by learning what "works" in academic discourse. I too have written such papers. The right kind of vocabulary, the appropriately academic persona, the prescribed format of presenting the argument—if you can learn these basic skills, you can get by with minimal engagement with the subject and earn a satisfactory grade. Of course, work is still required, and grades can only matter so much—such papers end up simply being a waste of time and energy for all involved.

At the other end of the spectrum are those students who face a lot of difficulty presenting their ideas in the correct format, and that becomes the crux of their struggle as well as a great source of stress. Many students also suffer in grades and self-esteem from not being able to tackle these issues successfully, even if their ideas might be interesting, unique, and assiduously conceived. Such papers can involve too much input and not nearly enough returns for the student, intellectually or academically.

Admittedly, the value and effect of any argument depend a great deal on its articulation. In any kind of writing, form and content are inextricably linked and should both be the subject of discussion and attention. But far too often, neither of them is the subject of any discussion at all (with the notable exception of rhetoric and composition classes)—and this is my main problem with the status of academic papers in college discourse.

In my five semesters at college, I have taken many writing intensive classes, and all of them have followed the same model: the class is invariably based on a discussion of ideas based on prescribed reading, and every now and then—three or four times during the course of the semester—we must write analytical papers. In most cases, the flow and format of the class are uninterrupted by this exercise—usually the class is far past the subject of the paper—and students are required to hand in their individual papers to the professor. The length of the paper is specified, as is the general subject in most cases; while some professors narrow down the focus of the paper and provide detailed instructions, others simply want something that is relevant to the course. Of course, a student can always approach the professor for more clarification, but this in itself is difficult for many and does not significantly affect the position of the paper in the context of the classroom.

The Classroom and the Paper

The classroom is the site of nearly all of the academic discussion that takes place in a course; even online discussion venues like Blackboard try to simulate this setting. The academic paper is far removed from this place; it is something we write in the privacy of our rooms or in quiet lounges, spending long hours hunched over our computers, attempting to organize our thoughts into coherent and impressive arguments. We have the time to develop our thoughts and the resources available to research and test our arguments, and, ideally, create a paper that is relevant, compelling and rewarding.

The problem with this scenario is that in reality, it doesn't always work out that way. We *don't* always think of particularly insightful things to say (especially by the due date), and if we do, there is no guarantee that we will be able to convey them perfectly or even commendably. I suppose one could argue that the point of writing papers is to develop critical and analytical thinking, not necessarily original thinking. But the fact remains that students are under tremendous pressure to produce some startling and original insights and then to defend them in a prescribed manner, limiting themselves, in so doing, to a certain kind of voice, vocabulary and attitude. An honest survey of any cross-section of college students is certain to reveal that what most students care and stress about in paper writing is quite different from the sacred goals of learning and analytical thinking. And while our personal motivations—grades, graduate school or earning the esteem of our teachers—do drive many of us to write "A" papers and learn the ropes of analytical writing, the two questions I raised earlier (Are papers worth all the effort put into them? Why don't more students visit the Writing Center?) still seem both crucial and largely ignored within the broader academic discourse.

This pressure to write a particular way and produce certain results is greatly—and, I would argue, misguidedly—compounded because the paper isn't really a part of the classroom discourse at all. Such a situation is ironic because most professors give papers inordinate importance in a student's final grade. And yet, this most important and hallowed of academic exercises not only takes place outside the classroom but is never introduced into the academic discourse at all. In most cases, I have no idea what my fellow students write about; I am left to my own devices as they are to theirs; we finish our own papers in our little private spaces and hand them to the professor; we receive them individually with grades and some comments. Instead of partaking in a constant volley of ideas and arguments, writing an academic paper in college is more like throwing pebbles into a pond. Except it's not pebbles, but the pearls of our hard work and analysis!

This set of circumstances not only makes the paper tremendously important to our academic careers—so much of our grade and merit as students depends on it—but also makes it an almost unnatural part of our academic lives. The classroom and the constant engagement with students form the bulk of our experience in college, and the too-important academic papers seem to exist in some kind of surreal place where each student is alone and on her own, working on her papers and receiving them back with secret markings and evaluations that are rarely communicated with fellow students.

The Implications

First of all, imagine the wealth of ideas and interesting insights that are never shared between students studying the same subject and going to the same class. I could be sitting next to a student with the exact same (or the exact opposite) opinions about a particular play or book, and I might never know. Especially given the fact that we write papers on subjects that have already been discussed and dealt with in class, our individual written investigations and conclusions may never inform or engage with others.

Furthermore, relegating paper-writing to this weird alternate reality greatly exacerbates the difficulty of the actual writing. Since papers are not a healthy part of the classroom discussion, students rarely have a forum to discuss the process of writing about a particular subject and the problems that they might face in doing so. Not only do we miss learning from comparing our similar and different ways of thinking and forming arguments, but those of us who need the most help might be the least willing to step forth and ask for it. I believe that this is also one of the reasons why the Writing Center isn't able to reach as many students as it might. In an academic environment where the process of writing a paper is as little discussed as the final outcome of it, where the process of writing rarely merges with or emerges naturally from the course of a classroom discussion, and where the outcome is given so much importance, an academic paper becomes too personal, too important, and too unnatural a thing to take to a room of writing "experts."

Moreover, the Writing Center can only really focus on the form and presentation of a paper. Even if, as tutors, we are able to discern and comment on the content of the paper, we can't be on equal footing with the student in terms of our knowledge or insight nor engage with the idea in the way a classmate might. As opposed to a democratic workshop of ideas and arguments that can happen in class, the writing center might seem more like a place where you go to "ask for help." If the attitude toward paper writing is so closed in the classroom, it is likely that coming to the Writing Center might require the extra step that many students would not be keen to take.

Such a disconnect between the flow of ideas in the classroom and the walled-off area of paper writing not only fails to advance disciplinary discourses, but, in some ways, also creates a notion that discourse has "ceased" or arrived at a conclusion for the student. Much of our most important research and analysis for a class comes at the end of the semester and is supposed to culminate in our "final papers," which seldom provide much chance for discussion between the student and the professor, let alone among the students themselves. At the start of a new semester, one can see unclaimed final papers in the folders of many professors, sad testimonies to the actual "place" of papers in the discourse and their value to those who write them.

Of course, there are exceptions in all the above cases. As students in a residential college, we do engage with fellow students outside of class, continuing classroom dialogue and learning from the perspectives of friends and teachers. Professors also are invariably helpful and accessible. My point is that the academic paper is not incorporated naturally into the classroom discussion; it is not part of the discourse but rather considered the culmination of it; and the process and challenge of writing are very rarely and only briefly acknowledged, and even less addressed. All this makes paper writing a much more difficult and daunting process than it needs to be and considerably diminishes the returns we could be getting on the work we do.

What Can Be Done

In taking this class on teaching and tutoring students, I have had the chance to read the papers of fellow students and share my own with them. This has been a novel and incredibly enriching experience for me, and I cannot overstate the value of being able to engage with the refined and thoughtful ideas of my peers. I have been led to many new avenues and have watched my own thinking develop in response. Even more startling is how completely natural and "but of course!" such a discourse feels, and this paper is an extrapolation of that very sentiment.

The papers we write as students need to be a natural and active part of the academic discourse. They should serve to further the dialogue established in the classroom, not to mummify forced "conclusions" and sustain hollow paradigms of format and presentation. I think the goal of students' academic writing within the disciplinary discourses needs to be constantly reiterated so that we don't lose sight of it, and so that we as students are able to write not only more easily but more rewardingly.

Foremost, I feel that papers must be discussed openly within the classroom, free from and ideally prior to a graded evaluation, which should take this discussion into account. If the subject assigned by a professor is specific and focused, there should be a place for detailed discussion of a student's research, analysis and thesis—and the opportunity for other students to respond to or question it. If, however, as in many English classes for example, the subject is wider or simply unspecified, there can still definitely be a platform for students to share their theses and present some basic background or arguments. I am not suggesting that every class turn into a writers' workshop; however, even a simple, informal sharing of students' theses with the class can go a long way to validate the importance of academic writing and make it a process and tool of engagement, rather than a wall of words that each of us must carefully build and crash into at the end of each semester.

This would not only make paper writing a much more logical and organic part of academic discourse but also, by "liquefying" and in a sense demystifying the paper, relieve some of the tremendous pressure student writers feel to write something perfect sounding and perfectly structured. To refer back to my two tutees: it would make it impossible for students to hide under the garb of academic voices and impressive vocabulary and make it necessary to really delve into the subject. It would also give the professor a clearer sense of the kind of work and thinking a student puts into her paper, and lessen the importance of the final "finished product."

Another way of making academic papers more valuable is to provide students with the opportunity of responding to and revising their work in light of the discussion and commentary on it. This already happens in different ways in some classes, and there can certainly be any number of other means to make academic papers an organic part of classroom discourse—but the point remains that papers need to be brought into the classroom and argued, deconstructed, and shared to whatever extent they can be. Bringing the academic paper into the classroom discourse validates and rewards the amount of energy we expend on our papers. This particular all-nighter, for example, has certainly been worth it.

Epilogue: A Graduate's Perspective

Reflecting on this paper four years after having written it and two years after graduating, I find that the two questions I posed in it have gained new significance and clarity for me. As a graduate who chose not to reenter academic life (at least not yet) or otherwise make much use of my transcript, it is now far easier for me to distinguish between those academic papers that furthered my learning and those that were merely chores, fillers or exercises in the propagation of the great liberal arts tradition. Since I do not write papers for a living or for grades any longer, the value of my academic writing career has become easier to examine, if not to define.

The word that now jumps out at me is "liquefying." Indeed, I can separate all my college courses in terms of liquid and solid papers (!)—papers that were, to refer back to my essay, solid and obdurate like pebbles or walls, and those that were organic, malleable, not nearly as needlessly difficult and far more rewarding. The latter type were, without exception, integrated into the course to a degree that affected and transformed my writing process, be it through engagement with professors and fellow students in class, over Blackboard, or in study groups. And where the paper was liquid, so, invariably, was the grading process and the discourse—and the lessons learned from such courses have flowed into many other aspects of my life and learning.

As a graduate who has chosen to continue working with student writers—*is* there any other kind of writer?—in various contexts, from underprivileged children skeptical of or indifferent to the value of writing, to highly ambitious professionals applying to American and European academic institutions, I find that writing well can apparently serve radically different purposes in different contexts, but that as teachers and tutors, as people who attempt to help others *compose*, it is crucial for us to stay focused and to reiterate the value of writing in exploring, organizing, distilling and communicating thoughts. All other values proceed from and must be secondary to this value.

It is possible that the above seems self-evident to some readers, especially those in academic institutions, but in a broader context, in the world beyond college, where the value of quantifiable parameters—grades, professional rungs and wealth—has become monolithic and has global consequences to boot, it seems to me that it is no longer sufficient for institutions merely to teach in the traditional sense; rather they must constantly examine and communicate to their students the moral underpinnings and implications of their own evaluative traditions. Writing, especially, throws such underpinnings into stark relief because it neither abides thoughtlessness nor submits to quantification—and the place of writing in an academic discourse ultimately comes to signify a great deal more than the difficulty and value of writing a college paper.

Section Nine

Empowering Marginalized Learners

In Chapter 26, "Traveling the Middle Ground: Bridging the Dichotomies Between Academic and Personal Discourse," Holly Thompson considered some of the ways in which academic discourse has traditionally been at odds with personal language. Although not all students who are prohibited from writing personally or autobiographically in their college courses are truly "marginalized," many of them are. Marginalized or excluded students are typically those differentiated from the mainstream by virtue of certain characteristics or attributes, including the following: gender, race, class, sexual orientation, ethnicity, learning disability, or the use of English as a second language.

Holly Thompson's essay explored in some detail the problems faced by one category of historically marginalized learners: women. As she noted, feminist scholars and teachers have convincingly argued that the academy has, from its inception, been largely the province of men—men who have, not by simple chance, established academic discourses to be in harmony with the kinds of inquiry and expression that are held to be stereotypically male. Academic discourse is frequently characterized by a writer's use of the following specific methods or techniques: employing specialized vocabulary (often polysyllabic), setting up linear structures (e.g., arranging texts through the use of logical progressions rather than associational leaps), providing solid, factual evidence for support (as opposed to relying on appeals to emotion), documenting sources (incorporating footnotes or parenthetical references), and keeping oneself in the background (sparing use of "I" and no obviously autobiographical material used for evidence). Women, by contrast, according to such a view, are stereotypically assumed to engage in discourse that is not so relentlessly driven by the dictates of linear argument and "objective" analysis.

As Thompson noted in Chapter 26, there has been much discussion to the effect that drawing such "dichotomies" based on supposed gender attributes is problematic. To classify discursive features as "male" or "female," she observed, is to "essentialize"—i.e., to oversimplify and misrepresent the categories of "man" and "woman" by rigidly and reductively attributing stereotypical qualities associated with a gender to all its members. Those who voice such cautions about essentialism are sometimes called "constructionists," for they believe that people's identities are forged and created—constructed or put together—and that they are a result of their interaction with various social and environmental influences rather than a result of their possessing some supposedly universal essence of femaleness, maleness, blackness, etc. Thus, when we look at groups that are considered marginalized within academia, we must remember that it is dangerous to make similar assumptions about all individuals within those groups. Still and all, as Thompson concludes in considering her own dilemma, there is often important truth contained in essentialist positions, and they do make for effective political rallying points, positions from which people can work for reform.

As we turn our attention to working with marginalized student writers, it is important to recognize that traditional or mainstream academic discourse is generally unreceptive, even hostile, towards *difference*, specifically as that difference is manifested in features of discourse that deviate from the accepted conventions. As we know, the differences that occur in a diverse, multicultural society and student body are numerous.

The Articles

Chapter 28, Emily Ryan's "Attention Deficit Hyperactivity Disorder and the Writing Process," examines the plight of student writers struggling with ADHD. Through research and personal narrative, Ryan identifies specific problems and attempts to offer solutions. In order to present a clear picture of a disability about which there are many misconceptions, Ryan incorporates the story of her own struggle with ADHD. Although she was a bright student and even a gifted writer, she struggled not only to complete her written work but also to overcome the harsh and judgmental comments she received from some teachers who assumed she was simply "lazy." Overall, her goals for the piece include efforts to "pinpoint the difficulties academic writing presents to ADHD students, [...] locate the role of the instructor in this process, reevaluate my own history as a writer with ADHD, and emphasize the immense importance of approaching writing with one's *own* process." This latter point is crucial, Ryan believes, for it is her strong conviction that "process" is actually a weak point of students with ADHD, such that compelling them to follow a rigid, predetermined writing process is a recipe for failure. She also cautions teachers and tutors about the stigma surrounding the disorder, noting that efforts to build students' self-esteem are warranted.

Chapter 29, "Writing Beyond the Words: Language Minority Students and School Discourse," by Maria Barajas-Román, focuses on the problems faced by bilingual students in the English classroom. Like Ryan, Barajas-Román approaches her topic by combining research with personal experience. As the child of an immigrant family in Nebraska, she and her family encountered prejudice because they were not "Anglo" like the majority of the population. Earlier in her education, Barajas-Román found this difference embarrassing and simply wished to conform and assimilate. Even in college, she was reluctant to acknowledge the existence of discrimination and social injustice. However, as she wrote her honors thesis, she began to develop greater consciousness of the forces that create prejudices and hamper the efforts of bilingual students to succeed. In order for "language minority" students to prosper, she asserts, teachers must "understand linguistic diversity with a sensitive multicultural attitude." For this to happen, she believes, "more research must be done to help teachers identify their preconceived biases and develop an approach to redefine their efforts" and to allow students "to tap into the underlying power structure of discourse." Ultimately, Barajas-Román was herself able to tap into this discourse, and she understandably urges teachers to "consider students' cultural and linguistic heritages as valuable resources [...] thereby including language minority students as active participants in their own advancement."

The final article in Section Nine is Chapter 30, Emma Nolan-Thomas's "Theory and Practice: Integrating ESL Scholarship and Peer Tutoring Pedagogy." In this piece, Nolan-Thomas, a tutor at her college's writing center, looks at possible ways in which writing associates can improve the tutoring assistance they offer nonnative speakers of English, often referred to as ESL students (English as a Second Language). Although Nolan-Thomas sets out to establish clear guidelines to offer writing associates, her examination of the research on ESL issues and of the survey responses she received from a range of peers leads her not so much to definitive answers as to open-ended "pedagogy puzzles" that teachers and tutors might profitably explore. In attempting to answer the question, "Should writing associates change their tutoring styles when working with nonnative English speakers?" Nolan-Thomas explores such issues as the authority dynamics of tutoring sessions with ESL students, the prioritization of "form versus content" in advising tutees on their papers, and "balancing positive feedback and constructive criticism." In concluding, she aptly observes that ideas "about how to tutor [ESL students] best must be constantly reassessed through an ongoing process of dialogue between tutor and tutee and reframed through the dual lenses of theory and practice."

Chapter 28

Attention Deficit Hyperactivity Disorder and the Writing Process

Emily Ryan

Getting thought to paper has always been hard for my son. In first grade, he had to do book reports and I almost lost my mind! He would tell me the entire thing, then write a few words, tell me the ENTIRE thing, write a few words, and so on until he had the last words on the paper.

—Anonymous forum post, addnews.com

Although your ADD/ADHD student may seem to be verbally expressive (he may talk a lot), he may still be poor in putting down his ideas in written form. Sometimes it is a long journey from the brain, down the sleeve, to the hand, and finally to the pencil and paper. The mouth is a lot closer to the brain.

—addinschool.com

Home Work

It's 2:30 a.m. and I'm writing a paper.[1] I'm sitting cross-legged on my bed staring at my blank-screened laptop. I'm surrounded by handwritten notes, highlighters and pretzels; an indecipherable chaos extends from my mattress to the floor, where my academic clutter begins to bleed into a landscape of washed and unwashed clothes, overturned shoes, lip-gloss. I can hear my roommate snoring. By morning I'll have a solid introduction.

It's 3 a.m. and I'm writing a paper. It's been a productive night. I've plucked my eyebrows, clipped my nails, and reorganized my iTunes collection. I've opened and closed the window six times. I've examined my face for twenty minutes, squeezed five blackheads and counted my pores. I've planned an outfit for tomorrow, written my mother an email and read a poem by e. e. cummings that has nothing to do with my paper. I've read the prompt for my paper twelve times. I've checked my email 25 times. I've trimmed my bangs. I've walked seven circles around my room. I've showered.

It's 6 a.m. and I'm writing a paper. I can't think straight. I have two pages, three paragraphs, and I'm not positive they're in the right order. I

have five different documents open on my desktop, filled with notes, quotations, and tangents. I refer to the assignment sheet again. I stare at the screen
for ten minutes. I think of a sentence, but I forget it before I finish writing it
down. I think about how when I was twelve my brother wanted a dog. I
realize that I'm thinking about dogs and violently shake my head, clearing
the thought like an Etcha-Sketch. I reread the last three sentences I've written, trying to imagine where my argument was going. I look out the window.
The sun is rising. I try to remember what we're learning about the sun in
astronomy. I think about how my astronomy professor wore a purple shirt
yesterday, and how he only wears purple shirts on Wednesdays. I wonder if
he has obsessive-compulsive disorder. I wonder why I was so much better at
science when I was sixteen. It's now 6:30 a.m. I'm writing a paper.

At nine o'clock my roommate's alarm goes off, and I start crying. I have
a class in an hour, and it's in the way of my plans to finish my paper. I think
about skipping. I think about asking for an extension. I've done these things
before. Today, I don't. In class I write out a paragraph by hand instead of
taking notes. Later, writing my conclusion, I pause to check the assignment
sheet and realize that I've lost it. I spend fifteen minutes looking for it, but
instead find my wallet. By 4:30 the paper's finished, and I'm waiting for it to
print. I have to run to Rice in order to turn it in ten minutes late. I know my
professor won't know the difference, but I write a note in the margin apologizing for being late. I slip it under my professor's door. Done.

During dinner I realize that I forgot to write and sign the Honor Code. I
start crying. I take a magic marker out of my purse and make a large note on
my hand to e-mail my professor later. My friends turn to ask what's wrong
and I cry harder, mumbling something about my nonsensical conclusion and
a shaky thesis. I swear right and left that my paper was utter crap and moan
about how I haven't slept in at least 36 hours.

I get an A.

Self-Control

Hallowell and Ratey, in *Driven to Distraction,* define ADHD[2] as "a
neurological syndrome whose classic defining triad of symptoms include
impulsivity, distractibility, and hyperactivity or excess energy." (6) In terms
of biology, evidence suggests that ADHD is associated with a depressed
activity in the frontal regions of the brain—the areas that control the interpretation of sensory and cognitive information, regulate behavior, attention and
impulse, and which scientists speculate interact with the sections of the brain
that determine decision-making capacity and that access working memory.
(276) The simplest way that I've found to characterize ADHD to someone

who does not have it is as a developmental delay in self-control. (Goldstein) Self-control, rather than inattention, may make more sense neurologically as the core symptom of ADHD. Goldstein explains, "children [with] ADHD possess the self-regulation or self-control of children approximately two thirds their chronological age. It is not that their self-control isn't developing, it's that it is developing at a much slower pace." Life with ADHD is chaotic and inconsistent, marked by disorganization, poor time-management, inattentiveness, speeding thoughts and physical restlessness. Shopping for groceries, paying bills, keeping dental appointments, sitting still in church—activities most people take for granted—become painfully difficult ordeals.

If the New Paradigm approach to writing emphasizes *process* over product, and ADHD represents a struggle with self-regulation, it is easy to see how students with ADHD might lose their way. The process is long and arduous, and process isn't exactly their forte. It requires focus and follow-through: extensive brain-storming, planning, layers of drafts and revisions, coordinating one's schedule to share and receive feedback with others—all before revising yet again, proofreading, and producing a final product. In attempting to pinpoint the difficulties academic writing presents to ADHD students, at any age, I also hope to locate the role of the instructor in this process, reevaluate my own history as a writer with ADHD, and emphasize the immense importance of approaching writing with one's *own* process.

"Mad" Distraction

My dear reader, I should warn you that this section is a bit of a digression. I find it, however—and I hope you agree—quite a necessary one. You see, after completing the first draft of this paper, I sent it out into the world to see how it would fare. I quickly discovered that there was one looming question in the minds of my readers that my paper left unresolved: "What's the difference between having ADHD and just being *mad* distracted?"

It seemed that everyone who read my paper could relate to some part of it; they had "been there," and wanted to know what the big deal was. Most college students have messy rooms, pull all-nighters, and have their confidence shaken once in a while. Most college students are plagued by the tempting force of the Internet in all its evil manifestations—Facebook, blogs, Instant Messenger; Direct Connect—and most college students seem to know at least one person downing amphetamines without a prescription in order to squeak through finals. So what makes kids with ADHD any different?

In truth, I'm not really sure. I've done my research; a testament to my vanity, I've been reading up on ADHD ever since I was diagnosed at age ten. The problem is that it's become so ingrained in my sense of identity that I interpret nearly every unproductive or undesirable behavior I exhibit as a symptom of my disorder. Lost keys? ADD. Bad mood? ADD. Missed period? I'd probably find a way to blame *that* on ADD, too. Apparently, I'm not alone. As Hallowell and Ratey explain, "Many of the symptoms of ADD are so common to us all that for the term ADD to have any specific meaning, rather than just be a scientific-sounding label for the complex lives we lead, we need to define the syndrome carefully. The best way to understand what ADD is—and what it is not—is to see how it affects the lives of people who have it." (3) I have thus included the following section.

History

In kindergarten, we had vocabulary workbooks with the words organized by length and difficulty. I remember whining loudly to my teacher, with the three-letter-word workbook unfinished in my lap, that I could read all the words in the five-letter workbook, and being told I could not move on until I had completed the three- and four-letter workbooks. So I would sit, bored and frustrated, wiggling my loose tooth, thinking about Tony North in the corner who I was secretly in love with, and wonder why, so suddenly it seemed, we were moving on to a new activity, when I had just barely started.

In second grade we would write daily journal entries, which I took very seriously. I would sit for about ten minutes and stare at the large, beige-lined paper, thinking about anything and everything that came to mind. Finally I'd start writing, but it seldom related to the prompt. I would begin complex fictional narratives, which I could never finish on time. One week I was seven journal entries behind, because I was still working on a story I'd started a week ago.

My teachers tolerated these behaviors with some sighing, but for the most part, no real objections. My kindergarten teacher did express concern to my mother that I seemed "so bright" and yet my handwriting was so "dark and messy," and I kept talking out of turn. My second-grade teacher didn't hassle me much, although an incident stands out in my mind where I was chastised in front of the whole class for dropping my pencil—my guess is I had been dropping it all afternoon, and she assumed I was playing a game.

By fourth grade I had quit playing outside after school altogether. My homework would take me hours. The smallest things would distract me: a ticking clock in another room, the hum of the air conditioner, the lure of my box of Barbie dolls. Often my mom would check on me and I would be doing something completely unrelated—playing with dolls, reading a book, looking at old photographs—that had suddenly grabbed my attention and lured me away from the task at hand. That year I was diagnosed. I remember being put off by having to see a psychologist but relieved by my label; there were other kids like me. I wasn't "lazy" or "weird." I wasn't alone.

In middle school, things got both better and worse. My classes were easy, except for math, so it didn't matter that I couldn't sit still in them or pay attention to save my life. In sixth grade I had a teacher who pulled me aside and threatened that she could remove me from the "Gifted" program if I didn't soon "shape up" and "start caring" about my work. I had no idea what she was talking about. The subject was language arts, and I cared immensely. I would spend hours at night beginning our short story assignments—they would just never be finished by morning. I suppose, too, that to her, it looked like no more than a half-hour's work for a child my age. I didn't think to tell her that I had ADD, since it wasn't something I thought about most of the time, but my mother did. I'm not sure what she said, but after they spoke my teacher's demeanor toward me completely shifted; she was very sweet to me, almost doting, for the remainder of the year.

In seventh grade, the director of the Learning Disability program—yes, I worked simultaneously with the Learning Disability and Gifted teachers—encouraged me to try out for our school's writing team, Power of the Pen. The prompts were timed, and I didn't finish either of my audition pieces, but somehow I was selected for the team of seven. By the end of the two years I spent in those weekly meetings, I had learned two extremely valuable things: that there was something I could be successful at—something I hadn't believed since early childhood—and that I could effectively combat my ADHD with a powerful stimulant: stress. Through this channeled anxiety, not only could I get things done on time but also quickly.

In high school my struggle with the writing process became its most severe. The process was not merely encouraged; it was mandatory and defined in very specific ways. Brainstorming, rough drafts, and peer revisions were usually required, stapled to my final drafts as part of the grading rubric. This was bad, because I had learned that I could feed off the stress and urgency of the night before in order to quell my symptoms and achieve a state of hyper-focus,[3] a surprising symptom of ADHD that can be extremely helpful but difficult to trigger. In the worst case of forced process, I was required to draw on my non-existent time-management skills to turn in my project in mini-steps leading up to the due date. Brainstorm worksheets were due week one, note cards weeks two and three, a works cited page week four, a rough draft week five, a revised rough draft week six, and finally a paper in week seven. Following this structure proved impossible for me. I'd forget which day things were due. I'd leave my note cards at home. I'd stay up until 3 a.m. researching and then fidget in class during the designated work-on-your-project time, too distracted by my peers, the test I had next bell, the birds out the window, to focus. That quarter, I got a "C" in English, since the only work we were graded on was our participation and apparent progress on the research paper. The actual grade on the paper was averaged into the next quarter. Even though to my teacher I appeared to be slacking off the whole time, I received a 95% on the final assignment. She was shocked.

Process

Many factors contribute to the ADHD student's difficulty conforming to the writing process. Poor time management skills are perhaps the most detrimental. If you have little sense of time—if hours pass while you shuffle unfocused from activity to activity, forgetting where you began or what you set out to do, if you space out in the classroom following a tangential train of thought unaware that twenty minutes have passed, if you have little ability to assess your work load and prioritize, if on some days an assignment will take you twenty minutes and on others it may take four hours, if you're constantly overestimating and underestimating your own efficiency, confused by the mixed messages of being scolded for sloth and praised for creativity, if you've lost every planner, every calendar, and every post-it note you've attempted to utilize—how do you begin to manage your time? People with ADHD tend to shuffle from moment to moment, giving priority to whatever is most immediate, often in a state of anxiety, wondering what appointment they've forgotten will spring up next or where the time has gone.

Without effective time management, it is difficult for the writing process to begin. As a child, brainstorming never happened for me pen-to-page, as my teachers required, but took place more covertly: during math class, while watching TV, in the empty minutes before committing each word to my rough draft. If a student has managed her time ineffectively, she may not have time to get peer feedback. I've often thought that an ADHD student would not make it to the writing center; it doesn't stay open until 5 a.m.

Another skill essential for strong academic writing, and closely related to time management, is organization. The ADHD student may struggle with organization on two fronts: the organization of *things* and the organization of *ideas*. My mother is always advising me that if I were just able to keep my room clean, I would save so much time and energy in not having to search every day for what I need. The problem with this theory is that for me, organizing my things takes such an effort that whenever I've tried it, I didn't have time to do anything but pick up. This physical disorder of one's environment can hinder paper writing in more ways than are at first apparent. For example, it's difficult to start a paper if you've lost the binder for the class, or the assignment sheet or if your primary sources are hidden under a pile of laundry. It's difficult to leave your room and go to the library if you can't find your purse or take notes while you research if you've lost all of your highlighters and pens. Persons with ADHD may live in an environment of such complete chaos that when they sit down to write, they're too anxious to begin. If your life seems physically chaotic, how can you think creatively?

Organizing one's ideas is also challenging. It requires, like time management, an ability to step back, see the big picture, and prioritize. People with ADHD tend to be caught up in details because they've learned that keeping track of them is important to their survival; forgetting or remembering the wrong one is often the difference between success and humiliation. Organizing one's thoughts may take an exceptionally long time, if it's accomplished at all. On many papers I've gotten back over the years, instructors have praised my mechanics, my ideas, and my analysis, but they also complain that I jump from point to point with no apparent connection,

The last two symptoms that I view as significant obstacles to the writing process are inattentiveness and impulsivity, which I believe are inextricably linked.[4] While inattentiveness is often seen as the core symptom of ADHD, this is slightly misleading, since it is often coupled with a tendency to hyperfocus. Impulsivity, which is usually used to describe outward ADHD behavior, is perhaps just as apt when applied to the ADHD thought process: distraction is the manifestation of inner impulsivity. ADHD thoughts are associative (boyfriend, boy, blue, sky, skyline, chili, Cincinnati, home, mom, teacher, school, grades, success, money, bank statement—where is my bank statement?), and your decision to follow these thoughts, or to act on them (e.g., abandoning the computer where you had been doing homework—until your friend emailed you and asked about your boyfriend—to get up and look for your bank statement) is impulsive. My behaviors as described in the opening section were largely the results of inattentiveness and impulsivity.

The ramifications for writing are obvious. Good writing requires patience, meditation, and focus. It's hard to maintain an uninterrupted inner dialogue with a subject matter, plotline, or idea if you can't keep thinking about what you want to think about, and it's even more difficult to translate this inner dialogue to words on a page if you can't keep doing what it is that you're trying to do. These difficulties can be alleviated slightly by the natural stimulant of stress, but this is dangerous when the student begins to work too close to the deadline. Work might not be completed on time, and extensions are requested or grades lowered. Prescription stimulants may be a wise choice for some, but finding the right match between medication and student is often a frustrating search. Even then, stimulants can only help so much—

they will never do the work for you—and some students with ADHD may find that without their mental impulsivity, their creativity suffers.

Stigma and Other Students

After finishing the first draft of this paper, it seemed that the next logical step was to find other students with ADHD and ask them questions. I didn't want this paper to just be about me; I wanted it to be true in a larger sense. If in sixteen pages all I'd accomplished was an analysis of my own relationship with the writing process and what had gone wrong, what use would it be to anyone else? If I were to discover if I were making this up, I needed the point of view, and cooperation, of other students. So I began contacting friends.

What I encountered surprised me. I expected, I suppose, a mini-celebration at our acknowledgment of our shared struggles, a coming-out party of sorts. What I found was hostility and evasiveness. One friend went to great lengths to make clear to me that she was not as ADD as I; she'd quit taking her medication soon after she'd been diagnosed (three years ago) and didn't "cheat the system" by asking for basic accommodations such as extended time on exams. Another student I know agreed to talk with me, but only if I promised she could remain anonymous. Even though I'd already mentioned anonymity when I asked for her help, this was her first, and most urgent, demand. She, too, made an effort to downplay the disorder's effect on her life: "I'm medicated," she told me, "But I probably don't have to be. I don't think I even have it anymore. It was just a temporary thing."

I contacted others on campus without response. It was clear that my study wasn't going to get very far. I began to wonder why my friends' reactions had been so hostile and why they had come as such a surprise to me. Then I remembered what a big secret I had made of my own situation in middle school. Because I've been diagnosed for half my life at this point, I've already overcome the stigma they are just now feeling and fearing.

I emailed one of my best friends from home, a guy who was diagnosed this year, although I've been telling him he had ADHD since we were sixteen. When asked if he had told anyone else about his diagnosis, he replied:

> I still harbor the notion that if I mention it to most people, they will think I'm faking as an excuse or that it doesn't exist and I'm just lazy. I mentioned it casually one night to explain why I'm so spacey, and at the mention of the letters ADD my friend's girlfriend promptly and unapologetically responded with "That's bullshit." I'm sad to report that she's going into education.

It seems that college students with ADHD still encounter stigma, internal and external, about their disorder. It is possible that many students allow this stigma to become a roadblock to receiving the assistance they need *and* deserve. The first friend I spoke to had such severe reservations about receiving assistance that she used the words "immoral" and "cheating" to explain why she has not told the college that she has ADD. When I first approached the student services director at my college, I had the same trepidations, but she reassured me that when these same advantages (extra time, medication) are offered to students without ADHD (or a comparable learning disability) their performance does not approve, while the performance of an ADHD student does. Accommodations are simply a leveling of the playing field. The second girl I spoke to was concerned primarily that her reputation be kept intact; she didn't want to be "outed" as having a "disorder," as if ADD would brand her defective in the eyes of her peers. Students who believe that their disorder is shameful or fake will find greater difficulty in coming to terms and coping with the challenges it presents. If there were greater awareness of ADHD and its prevalence, perhaps it would be easier for students to accept it as a part of their lives without fear of being judged.

Self-Esteem and the Role of the Teacher

Writers must possess a certain amount of confidence before they can even start writing. Many students with ADHD suffer from low self-esteem. Years of being called lazy, of being singled out as a behavior problem, of hearing demands to shape up, begin to collect in one's psyche. Inattention, disorganization and impulsivity all come together to make eager, intelligent children with ADHD appear as irresponsible, lazy troublemakers. I remember teachers asking me why I didn't try, why I didn't care. I was chastised for not sitting still, for talking out of turn, and for being disruptive. I was given detention for not bringing my book to class. I received large eye-rolls and painful sighs when I'd ask my teacher—yet again—if I could borrow a pencil. The longer children go without being diagnosed with their disorder, the more likely the damage to their self-esteem will become irreversible. They'll begin to believe that they are lazy, that they're not good enough, and that they will never do well in school. They'll actually begin not to care, because that's safer than caring and getting let down. This problem is especially prevalent in women, since young girls with ADHD often go undiagnosed, or undiagnosed longer, because their symptoms—quiet distraction, daydreaming, and social awkwardness—are not as apparent as those of their male counterparts who tend to be more hyperactive and cause greater classroom disruption. Even with a diagnosis, blows to self-esteem persist. Many teachers do not "believe" in ADHD, while others simply don't know enough about the disorder to approach their students with accommodations and sympathy. School districts tend to ignore the problem, rationing IEPs and 504 plans[5] only to those students with the worst academic struggles. "Your child is doing fine," my high school told my mother, "why should we give her extra time on tests or extensions on papers?"

When I sit down to write, I sit down with all of these selves, all of these voices I've heard over the years. The kindergartener. The middle-schooler. The writer, The failure. *You're lazy. You're irresponsible. You're never going to make it in college. Why don't you try harder? Why don't you care? Why can't you live up to your potential?* I'm swept up with fear. Panic. Ghosts of discouragement. And, until I've drunk several gallons of water and set this fear aside, I cannot begin to write.

I should mention that I have had good teachers; the role of the educator in the life of a student with ADHD is not necessarily negative. My experience with the Learning Assistance Program at my college has been tremendous; it took their office less than a week to accomplish what my high school refused to do for four years. But even in high school I had several understanding teachers who—once they realized how dramatically my test scores improved with an extra half-hour—allowed me extra time to complete timed tests, even though the school did not require them to do so. For every teacher who made an effort to get to know my situation, however, there was another who pried the test from my hands with five questions left unanswered.

I believe it is an educator's duty to be up to date in scientific and psychological information regarding many learning disabilities, so that they may be patient with students who operate a little bit differently, instead of dismissing their problems as "fake" just because "they didn't exist forty years ago." An encouraging teacher is invaluable in the life of a struggling student.

How Far I've Come

As a double major in creative writing and English, as well as a Writing Center tutor, it seems that I've mastered the writing process somewhere along the way, despite all the discouragement and *mad* distraction. Returning to the personal narrative which began this paper, it seems like a fairy tale: the princess trudges through the treacherous swamp of paper writing and emerges unscratched and with the golden A. If this is what emerges, I apologize, because along with many of my negative self-conceptions, this view is a falsehood. My paper-writing history is littered with extensions and hyphenated grades. Even when it works out well, there are still the hours of physical and emotional exhaustion, the uncertainty, the shattered confidence, and the feeling that, after all the hysterics of my process, my success is so surprising that it can't possibly be deserved. So, while the writing process and I don't quite fit, I'm still trying to work out the kinks in my current system. But it's mine. And improvement is always, well, a process.

A Process of One's Own

I'd like to conclude with some suggestions for students with ADHD tackling the writing process, but the reader should keep in mind that I am not an expert, and this is only my opinion. Students with ADHD must first accept that they are smart, that they are capable, that they can write. They must educate themselves about their disorder, about coping mechanisms, about structure. They must utilize planners and visit their college's learning center, their therapists or counselors, and their professors. They must utilize every resource they can—extensions, prescriptions, computers, post-it notes, visual reminders, expert advice. They must try and try and try to prove naysayers wrong, to prove they can be organized, they can be accomplished, they can write. Then, they must toss everything they know out the window, and start over from scratch. They should create their own writing process.

It may involve notebook paper and a bag of chips; it may involve writing a rough draft on scraps of paper all day long for a week as ideas come to them; it may involve dictating out loud to a tape-recorder or a friend; it may involve hours and hours of little sleep; it may involve taking a bath before beginning every assignment in order to relax enough to begin, or it may involve drinking five cups of coffee in order to be so over-stimulated that there is no need to compensate with wandering thoughts or fidgeting. It may involve thinking while you walk, talking while you think, or moving to new surroundings to focus. It may involve scrapping brainstorming and revision or fusing brainstorming, revision and writing all into one simultaneous step.

Whatever the process is, it should come from within, and it should be considered legitimate. Only then can the creative benefits of impulsive, associative thinking and the mind in search of over-stimulation begin to emerge and find their way onto the page, and only then can writers with attention deficit hyperactivity disorder begin to express themselves, not with their disorder, or in a state of disorder, but through an order all their own.

NOTES

[1] This paper does not remain in first, second, or third person for very long. I have written in first person to emphasize that this paper is based, predominantly, on my experience and opinions. The third person is used conventionally, as the situation under discussion does not apply solely to myself. Finally, my slips into the second-person "you" are not accidental, as I am trying to help the reader empathize with students who have ADHD as much as possible.

[2] Attention deficit hyperactivity disorder used to be a distinctly different label from Attention deficit disorder, which recognized that not all ADHD patients are noticeably hyperactive. Today, medical experts tend to use ADHD to encompass both cases with and without hyperactivity. For the purposes of this paper, ADD and ADHD are used interchangeably.

[3] That is, to become so engrossed in an activity that the rest of the world melts away. A student who is hyper-focused on an activity does not notice people coming and going and probably won't respond to his or her name. I think that being hyper-focused is very similar to "spacing out," when I become so entangled in a train of thought that I forget where I am. However, I haven't read anything to suggest psychiatrists have made the same connection.

[4] This is solely my opinion. Many scholars, in fact, view hyperactivity and impulsivity as closely linked, while inattention is left floating in its own category. I think the problem here might be in the definition of "impulsivity," which seems more than slightly malleable.

[5] These are legal plans of action in the state of Ohio for dealing with students with disabilities and special medical conditions. The state is required to give qualifying students special accommodations. Many schools resist compliance because of financial strain.

WORKS CITED

Goldstein, Sam. "Is ADHD Really a Problem Paying Attention?" April 2002. <http://www.samgoldstein.com/node/54.> Accessed 8/11/ 2009.

Hallowell, Edward M., and Ratey, John J. *Driven to Distraction: Recognizing and Coping with Attention Deficit Disorder from Childhood through Adulthood.* New York: Simon and Schuster, 1994.

Chapter 29

Writing Beyond the Words: Language Minority Students and School Discourse

Maria E. Barajas-Román

Language is not just another thing we do as humans; it is *the* thing we do. It is a total environment; we live in the language as a fish lives in water. It is the audible and visible manifestation of the soul of a people.

—Robert Bunge

This paper combines fact and feeling. On the one hand, I've researched second language learning for almost two years in conjunction with my senior honors project in sociology. So I have a great deal of scientific and historical data to support my conclusions about teacher perception and its effect on language-minority students. However, I have also experienced English as a second language (ESL) as a child. I therefore have much personal data to support my conclusions. For the most part, I've become accustomed to relating my academic findings on ESL education and omitting my personal experiences for fear that colleagues would oppose my efforts, claiming that my emotions made me "incapable of conducting pure research."

The present essay, however, gives me the flexibility to explore both the academic and personal aspects of ESL/bilingual education. I believe the schism often imposed between personal and academic experiences with language creates an artificial setting that could never be "pure research." I will try to combine the facts I have uncovered about ESL/bilingual education and my encounter with second language learning to provide a more complete picture of this crucial topic that affects nearly every school in the U.S. today.

First, a little history. When the founding fathers signed the Declaration of Independence, they envisioned a nation as John Jay described it in 1788:

One united people—a people descended from the same ancestors, speaking the same language, professing the same religion, attached to the same principles of government, very similar in their manners and customs. (Perea)

However, people of many different nationalities representing different language groups settled in the colonies. Therefore Jay was defining the U.S. as an Anglo-only society based on the exclusion of other groups.[1] Benjamin Rush who also signed the Declaration of Independence saw dark skin as a disease similar to leprosy, and Thomas Jefferson wrote a plan to expel all people with dark skin from the country. (Perea, 583–95)

The early record is overflowing with similar sentiments about non-Anglo people. Leaders of the time turned their feelings into blueprints for expulsion, isolation, enslavement and extermination. This plot took greater shape when the United States annexed part of Mexico. Rufus B. Sage, a journalist, expressed the common view, describing residents of New Mexico in 1846:

> There are no people on the continent of America, whether civilized, with one or two exceptions, more miserable in condition or despicable in morals than the mongrel race inhabiting New Mexico. [...] To manage them successfully, they needs be held in continual restraint, and kept in their place by force, if necessary— else they will become haughty and insolent. As servants, they are excellent, when properly trained, but are worse than useless if left to themselves. (Sage)

This view of Mexicans is still embraced by many today. It is therefore not difficult to understand why the electorate supports current ESL/ bilingual policy and reform that perpetuates the image of Mexicans as "other" or "foreigner." In their minds, Mexicans are an insolent "mongrel" race whose only abilities include cutting grass and changing diapers. Hierarchy and relationships of power are reflected through the expression of ideas. Who gets to express ideas and express them first, and which ideas get expressed are also relevant to this power dynamic. Foucault identifies the crux of the political debate on bilingual education:

> History constantly teaches us, discourse is not simply that which translates struggles or systems of domination, but is the thing for which and by which there is struggle. Discourse is the power which is to be seized. (Foucault, 110)

How people of color feel they relate to the hierarchical power structure has an affect on their ability to insist that American society include cultural and historical diversity. The groups with access to the channels that offer mass distribution of their ideas will subjugate those who do not assimilate to their way of thinking, acting or speaking.

Consider Benjamin Franklin's comments in a letter to Peter Collinson, a British Member of Parliament, dated May 8, 1753:

> Those [Germans] who come hither are generally the most ignorant stupid sort of their own Nation [...] few of their children learn English [...] the signs in our streets have inscriptions in both languages and in some places only German. In short, unless the stream of their importation could be turned from this to other Colonies, as you very judiciously propose, they will soon so out number us, that all the advantages we have will not, in My Opinion, be able to preserve our language, and even our government will become precarious. (Franklin, 19)

Likewise today, those in control of American discourse persist on demonizing citizens who speak a different language or come from a culture that does not reflect the values of an Anglo-dominated society.

Significantly, in 1974 the federal government began to address the issue of civil rights of language minority (LM) students as a form of national-origin discrimination. Previously, the right to an equal education for these students simply meant that they were allowed the same books and facilities as the other English-speaking children. Language minority children were left to "sink or swim" in the English-only waters of the monolingual classroom.

In fact, most educators, accepting that LM students were "culturally deficient," subscribed to one of two views; either they needed to be forcefully assimilated into the "American way," or they could simply be abandoned to learn nothing, as illustrated in the attitude of a California school official during the Great Depression:

> Most of our Mexicans are of the lower class. They transplant onions, harvest them, etc. The less they know about everything else, the better contented they are. [...] If a man has very much sense or education either, he is not going to stick to this kind of work. So you see it is upto the white populations to keep the Mexican on his knees in an onion patch. (Weinberg, 146)

Over the years, such attitudes contributed to increasing dropout rates among LM students, low self-esteem and inferior ability to communicate in English.

Along these lines, it is not hard to understand why my siblings and I found it difficult to attend a majority white school in Lincoln, Nebraska, where teachers classified me with a "language problem" and placed me in a remedial class. The principal seemed to laugh at my mother when she requested conferences to discuss the treatment my sisters and I were receiving.

I remember sitting in the principal's office, my feet dangling from the fake leather seats, as he looked above his small circular reading glasses and responded to my mother sternly. He told her that "teachers were professionals," and "how dare" she "tell them how to do their job." I used to count the tiles on the floor as he seemed to humiliate my mother with explicit criticism and implicit threats. I remember wanting nothing more than for her to stop making trouble. I was different at the school. I looked different, spoke different and teachers would point to me and say to each other, "Watch her, she will steal from your desk and then her mother will come and yell at you in that jungle language."[2]

Some researchers have focused on the miscues that occur between teachers and students due to cultural background. Student behaviors such as attention-getting strategies, ways of responding to questions, and ways of interacting are examples of actions influenced by cultural background. For some African American, Native American, and Hispanic students, collaborative learning activities may be more effective because they parallel the context for learning found in their cultures. Another factor to be considered is the extent to which the literacy tradition of the home and culture closely resemble that of the school. If there is a strong emphasis in the culture on the oral tradition, then knowledge may be transmitted through "verbal usage and memorization" as in the cases of Moroccan and Western Samoan cultures. This is different from the highly literate tradition in the U.S. and presents problems if the teacher expects certain types of classroom interaction based on reading text. (Bennett)

Every school morning was a battle of nerves for me. My mother therefore devised an incentive to help my sisters and me enjoy our education. My mother continued to teach us our ABC's, basic spelling and math. In addition, we all looked forward to what became a tradition in our family: the "after school fiesta." Each spring, when school let out for the summer, if all of us had passed on to the next grade level, my mother would make a cake with all of our names on it (usually it also said "Great job Kids!"). We would then receive little colorful bags full of gifts and candy. I remember my favorite gift of all was a little notebook that had dotted lines and instructions on how to write cursive letters.

Because of my mother's efforts, I never fell completely behind my grade level and eventually moved into the "gifted" program when I scored perfect marks on a national achievement test. A journal entry dated October 6, 1986 describes how I felt about this official transition (I corrected the spelling):

> I'm not sure if they really want me here. Everyone in the class is very smart and they remember me from the other slow class last year. [...] I just want to be good at everything so they will know that I am also smart. When Ms. Flowers comes by my desk I always smile at her, I never touch anything I am not supposed to. I can't wait until they get to know me and know that I can speak well, I wish I never knew Spanish at all.

My mother's dedication and tenacity to my education taught me to take responsibility for my own learning. However, as the last sentence of the entry shows, I could not escape the feelings of inadequacy and shame fettered to memories of my native language and history.

Language-minority children need to feel accepted and a part of their educational environment. A great deal of the responsibility of shaping these students' attitudes is placed on teachers. But teachers have a tendency to prepare their lessons with content materials based on what is familiar to them. As a result, their preferences are often conveyed in the subject matter, including preferences about cultural and linguistic backgrounds. The empowering role of teachers may seem obvious to an audience of successful college students. However, the real-life classroom presents socio-political challenges beyond those of theoretical pedagogy:

> It is also a painful irony that when the schools ignored the existence of nonAnglophone students, they were universally credited with Americanizing generations of immigrants, while now, as schools finally struggle with the formal teaching of English to non-English speakers, they are bitterly attacked for failing no matter what method they try or how genuine their intention to succeed. (Baron)

This indicates that there is much more to educating language-minority students than just creating an academically sound program. Further, language-minority students need special consideration from teachers to make sure that hidden biases are not conveyed to impressionable young minds.

Much of the progress in LM education cannot prevent the likelihood of the appearance of students in schools where teachers are not trained to teach English as a Second Language. The Bilingual Education Act of 1984 provides guidelines for education and transitions for language-minority students. However, bilingual education is logistically impossible for many areas with a large variety of language groups represented in their classrooms. In addition, federal funds are only available to schools that meet numerical qualifications, thereby leaving thousands of LM students without bilingual materials or services by trained professionals. Interactions of language, culture, minority group membership and literacy in American schools go hand in hand, and have, evidently, spelled success for some children, but not for all.

According to DeStefano and Kantor, one important contribution that anthropological studies of schooling have made is providing strong evidence that LM students experience difficulties in learning English partly because of cultural differences. (115–24) Reyhner and Garcia note that culture influences behavior and psychological processes, creating shared meaning in how a group sees the world. (84–91) Bowman reports that children have "acquired scripts," sequences of actions and words that they learn from adults which they internalize. (118–20) LM students seem to be at a disadvantage once immersed in classroom discourse. Clearly, the dialogues they encounter there are unfamiliar and incongruent with their own experiences. Many teachers, it seems, are unaware of this, expecting LM students to demonstrate competence in reading and writing to be considered acceptably bilingual.

As a first-generation Mexican American, I grew up listening to the stories of my young father's journey to the United States, his hardships and discoveries, and most of all, his dream to have children that were educated American citizens. I am the second oldest of five American-born children. This May, I will graduate and become the first in my family in over seven generations to earn a college degree. Moreover, I will be continuing on to graduate school at a prestigious Ivy League institution.

When I look at my work over the past four years, however, I am dissatisfied with almost every paper I submitted for evaluation. Though the content in the papers is academically sound, looking back, I can read between the lines and see my intense struggle for validation. Each sentence is a shovelfull of acquiescence burying what I knew to be true about life and learning. For instance, the following is an excerpt from a history paper I wrote sophomore year:

> In the British colonies, 2.5 million Africans were brought to be slaves between 1619 and 1807. By the 1700s in Brazil historians estimate no more than a few thousand slaves had landed in Amazonia. The demographic make-up of the slave population was one of several differences between Iberian and Anglo/Dutch colonial systems. Other differences included variances in state government, religion, and the economic nature of slavery. Each of these components contributed to the formation of each colony's slave environment either to a more hostile or favorable degree.

The professor of this class gave me an "A" for my examination of "the economic nature of slavery in the colonies." I quoted facts and figures that applauded murderers and thieves for having the industrial wherewithal to subjugate entire races and nations. I listed these cases under a heading that read, "Successful Colonial Pursuits."

Successful? The bitter taste of that word still lingers in my throat. The material for the course haunted me with images of human suffering and indignity. I wanted to write about slavery as a perversion of humanity; I wanted to write about how it disgusted me to break down history in terms of economic goals and appropriation. However, I realized as I was staring at the blank computer screen that thoughts about anything other than the assigned topic were no use to me.

I wrote the paper, buried my feelings and allowed myself to feel proud of the strides I was making in the world. I was becoming more than my father or his father ever dreamed of being. My feelings confused me. I was doing what I was supposed to do, trying my best not to cause any trouble. On the other hand, I couldn't shake the sickening feeling that I was betraying myself. The honesty of this recognition reminded me of an experience I had that frightened me when I first encountered it, one that took me four years to synthesize. The experience began when I was 17 and on the verge of getting my high school diploma.

A long bus ride took me into the hot dusty country surrounding the city of Tijuana, Mexico. I was going to stay with my father's family for the summer in order to help arrange the legal immigration of one of my cousins to the United States.

The bus was crowded, and the stench of chemicals and poverty in the landscape around me slowly crept into my hair and fingertips. At one stop, I noticed a small girl and boy board the bus with little dilapidated shovels in their hands. The little girl's feet were bare, and her cheeks were stained with tears. I overheard their conversation as the boy comforted his sister. Apparently, the two were sent out every morning by their mother to work by the roadside. The children would run in front of the cars and fill in potholes with their tiny shovels for money. Their work usually yielded enough to pay for their eight family members to eat at least one meal. That day the children had toiled till dusk; however they had barely been compensated enough to ride the bus back to their hut.

From the children's conversation, I learned that this was the third day the family had not eaten. When I heard this, the weight of despondency nestled on my shoulders, and the flies circling my face took the opportunity to prick my motionless hands and feet.

Then the children began to sing. They sang with their eyes closed and their mouths wide open like chicks crying in a nest. The words of their song were from an old corrido[3] that was happy and playful, but the sounds their voices made tasted like sorrow and quickened like desperation.

Fortunately, the other riders were as moved as I was by the recital and were therefore quick to fill the children's arms with portions of the fruits and meat they were carrying.

I bowed my head to acknowledge these children in my own history. Only luck had narrowly placed me on the other side of the border, where streets were paved and houses were more than four cardboard walls and a tin roof. I had escaped hunger and disease, illiteracy and injustice. If one moment in my life could sum up my faith in human dignity and courage, it would be this dusty bus ride where I literally felt the tangible presence of hope.

It was this moment, this truth, which subconsciously urged me to the hallowed halls of a selective liberal arts college with a long tradition of social consciousness. I wanted to help change the world; I wanted to change the realities I had seen. Unfortunately, it soon became clear that changing the world was a vague mission tainted with greed, self-loathing and arrogance. Though I no longer had the same language barrier I had struggled with in my youth, I nonetheless found myself drowning in words I was expected to write and say. These words had no relation to what I felt or knew.

Progress can be achieved by helping teachers understand linguistic diversity with a sensitive multicultural attitude. However, more research must be done to help teachers identify their preconceived biases and develop an approach to redefine their efforts. This understanding of the social context of language in the classroom will help teachers better facilitate LM students by allowing them to tap into the underlying power structure of discourse. The racial, ethnic and linguistic composition of classrooms continues to become more diverse. Undeniably, the unity that once characterized all-white schools is no longer stable, making it quite dangerous for teachers to continue to assume a uniform educational stance.

Fortunately, my situation eventually improved my junior year when I became involved with volunteer programs in the local Latino community. My work resulted in a Community Action Fellowship award in education. The responsibilities of the fellowship included recruitment and mentoring of other campus community volunteers. I helped place volunteers primarily with a new school developed to redirect high-risk middle school students. The children at the school presented a challenge to all involved; many had been convicted of violent crimes and required constant supervision and guidance. With the combined assistance of the teaching staff and regular meetings used to redefine our efforts, the volunteers and I were able to make connections with the students.

Most of all, the Community Action Fellowship allowed me to rediscover the clarity I felt after that bus ride in Tijuana. I realized that my mother wasn't subjecting herself to humiliation when she confronted the educators at my school; she was fighting. My mother fought for what she believed just like those children in Mexico fought every day for food and shelter.

I needed to write about what I knew, whether or not it would be academically accepted. This past summer, I got the opportunity to research bilingual and ESL education through a Mellon Minority Fellowship. This fellowship allowed me to examine extensively the complications of teaching English language while simultaneously building math and other basic skills in public schools across the U.S. Combining research on the philosophical, policy and program planning levels of bilingual and ESL, I gained a wide perspective of possible solutions to English as a second language teaching.

This research was the key turning point in my college career. Not only was it important to my community, but it allowed me to reconcile the difficulties I went through as a child. I was writing and reading about a reality I knew well; I was personally connected and invested in my work. At the very least this research redeemed my academic confusion between just "toeing the line" and risking disapproval by writing about what was important to me. Teachers must consider students' cultural and linguistic heritages as valuable resources as they try to create the classroom experience, thereby including language minority students as active participants in their own advancement.

NOTES

[1] By "Anglo" I am referring to people of English descent. Therefore, "non-Anglo," in this context, includes white Mediterranean people, Eastern Europeans, and people of color.

[2] I would like to emphasize that putting my personal experiences in italics was meant only as an aesthetic device for the reader, to make the transition from "personal" to "academic" easier to read. It should not be interpreted that I meant to devalue or separate the two aspects of this piece. I feel that both personal and academic experiences should hold equal value and legitimacy in college and university settings.

[3] A corrido is a Mexican folk song.

WORKS CITED

Baron, Dennis. *The English-Only Question. An Official Language for Americans?* New Haven, CT: Yale University Press, 1990.

Bennett, Christine I. *Comprehensive Multicultural Education.* Boston: Allyn and Bacon, 1990.

Bowman, Barbara T. "Educating Language-Minority Children: Challenges and Opportunities." *Phi Delta Kappan* 71 (1989): 118–20.

Bunge, Robert. "Language: The Psyche of a People." *Language Loyalties: A Source Book on the Official English Controversy.* Edited by James Crawford. Chicago: University of Chicago Press, 1992: 376–80.

DeStefano, Johanna S., and Rebecca Kantor (1988). "Cohesion in Spoken and Written Dialogue: An Investigation of Cultural and Textual Constraints." *Linguistics and Education 1.* Columbus, OH : Martha L. King Language and Literacy Center: 105–124.

Foucault, Michel. "The Order of Dicourse." *Language and Politics*. Edited by Michael J. Shapiro. New York: New York University Press, 1984.

Franklin, Benjamin. "The German Language in Pennsylvania (1753)." *Language Loyalties: A Source Book on the Official English Controversy*. Edited by James Crawford. Chicago: University of Chicago Press, 1992: 18–19.

Perea, Juan F. "Death by English," *The Latino Condition*, New York: New York University Press, 1998: 583–95.

Reyhner, Jon, and Ricardo L. Garcia. "Helping Minorities Read Better: Problems and Promises." *Reading Research and Instruction* 28 (1989): 84–91.

Sage, Rufus B. *Rufus B. Sage: His Letters and Papers, 1836–1847*. Edited by LeRoy R. Hafen and Ann W. Hafen. Glendale, CA: A. H. Clark, 1956.

Weinberg, Meyer. A *Chance to Learn: The History of Race and Education in the U.S.A.* Long Beach, CA: The University Press, 1995.

Chapter 30

Theory and Practice: Integrating ESL Scholarship and Peer Tutoring Pedagogy

Emma Nolan-Thomas

During my first week at the Writing Center, I was intrigued to discover that a high percentage of the students who sought help with their papers spoke English as a second (or even third or fourth) language.[1] Working with my first nonnative English speaking tutee, I was excited to read his paper and try my new tutoring skills, but I was also concerned. Although I hoped the session went well, I found myself troubled: should I perhaps have modified my tutoring approach when working with this student? Should I have focused more on grammar, perhaps—or would such a focus be condescending?

As I worked with nonnative English speaking students, I found myself drawing on my own experiences as a nonnative speaker of the dominant language during my time abroad in Morocco last spring. I do not speak French or Arabic fluently, and my experiences of immersion in these languages were exciting, but at times also extremely frustrating. I recall trying to explain a simple question to my teacher one day, realizing that I sounded like a kindergartener and wishing I could fluently inform my teacher that, in English, I was a reasonably well-educated and intelligent person. The moment passed, but that memory of frustration made me wonder what it would be like to be a nonnative English speaker at my college.

Through conversations with students at the Writing Center, I soon discovered that the Writing Center, the Department of Rhetoric and Composition, and the First-Year Seminar program were the main resources available to these students on our campus. Recognizing that the Writing Center is a crucial resource for many ESL students caused me to wonder if we, as writing associates, needed to know more about working with them.

To gain further insight into these issues, I began to research the fields of ESL and composition studies, drawing on both primary and secondary sources, hoping to blend the voices of college students with those of scholarly experts. Much of my student feedback derives from two rounds of surveys completed by Writing Associates enrolled in "Teaching and Tutoring Writing," discussion with ESL tutees at the Writing Center about their experiences with English academic discourse, and some surveys filled out by both ESL and non-ESL students at the Writing Center. The writing associates included in these surveys reported different amounts of experience with ESL students, from rarely working with them to working with them about a third of the time. Unfortunately, the pool of survey responses from those using the Writing Center is the smallest; only six tutees, two of whom are nonnative English speakers, completed the surveys.[2]

My research also draws on secondary sources from composition studies and TESOL studies literature. In particular, I am indebted to two articles that directly address the issue of peer-tutoring ESL students: Muriel Harris and Tony Silva's article, "Tutoring ESL Students: Issues and Options" (1993), and Mark-Ameen Johnson's article, "ESL Tutors: Islands of Calm in the Multicultural Storm" (2002). Both contribute significantly to the small field of scholarship on peer tutoring ESL students' writing and form a core of secondary research that I relate to my own exploration of tutoring ESL students. I discovered a great deal of overlap in the issues addressed in these articles and discussed by Writing Center tutees and tutors. In this essay, I aim to bring these disparate sources into dialogue with each other.

Bridging the Schism between Composition Studies and ESL
Another central reason for my choice to explore ESL pedagogy is my desire to work towards bridging the gap between composition studies and TESOL work. This gap is closely examined by Paul Kei Matsuda in "Composition Studies and ESL Writing: A Disciplinary Division of Labor," where he charts the historical reasons for the continuing disciplinary division between Composition Studies and ESL studies. Matsuda terms this distinction a "disciplinary division of labor," which he argues has resulted in "a lack of concern about the needs of ESL writers among composition theorists even today." (Matsuda, 788) At the same time, Matsuda argues that TESOL theorists have similarly tried to set themselves apart as a discipline, envisioning TESOL as "applied linguistics" rather than writing pedagogy. (778) Still other foundational theorists of ESL pedagogy have argued that, in the words of William Slager, "to teach English to native born Americans, and to teach English as a foreign language, are as widely different as two tasks can be. The first in many ways deals with language as an art. The other deals with

language as a science: its subject matter and its classroom techniques require special background and training." (Cited in Matsuda, 785)

At the same time, authors like Vivian Zamel have drawn attention to the many similarities between ESL studies and composition studies. In "Strangers in Academia: The Experiences of Faculty and ESL Students Across the Curriculum," Zamel argues that these disciplines share a "marginalized" position within academia: "these courses are thought to have no authentic content [...] the work that goes on in these courses is not considered to be the 'real' work of the academy." ("Strangers," 515) Similarly, Sarah Benesch argues that ESL studies, like composition studies, faces an academic environment in which pedagogy is inherently political, as ESL and composition teachers alike must make ideologically-charged decisions. (705–17) While these fields might have much in common, relatively little scholarship has been done to compare the research about them. The Writing Center, as a site of assistance for both Ll and L2 English speakers, brings these disparate fields together through practice, raising the question of how tutors should adapt tutoring styles to work with students of varying linguistic backgrounds.

Writing Associates Reflect

As a group exercise to begin discussion about ESL issues in the Writing Center, I asked the Writing Associates in the Teaching and Tutoring class to reflect on their own experience in unfamiliar language settings. This discussion not only opened dialogue on this issue but illustrated how tightly connected ESL, composition, and tutoring pedagogy can be. Every writing associate in the course could think of a time they had been steeped in unfamiliar language, from living abroad to learning a new type of academic discourse. This familiarity with unfamiliarity is a shared experience that writing associates can use to relate to their ESL tutees; while working with nonnative English speakers in the Writing Center, I have found that my own experiences of being a nonnative speaker serve as a helpful reference point.

One theme of our discussion that seems to relate directly to tutoring is that of the frustration that may result from being surrounded by unfamiliar discourse. Many students in the class discussed how difficult it is to express one's *voice* in a nonnative language; one tutor used the term "inert prose" to describe his voice in his second language. Another student commented that this unfamiliarity led her to feel self-conscious and reminded me of my own experience of feeling "stupid" because of my limited vocabulary and knowledge of grammar in Arabic. One tutor reflected on this feeling of frustration at length, describing how, in Introductory Spanish,

> I had no identity as a writer. I said what I knew how to—if I came up with an idea but didn't have the vocabulary for it, I would usually just write something else [...] sometimes I feel that [ESL tutees] at the Writing Center have to "dumb down" their paper because of the language barrier.

Another tutor articulated her own experiences with writing academic papers in Spanish, which is not her first language:

> Although I almost always understood what was going on, I couldn't participate in discussion the same way I usually do. This was troubling for me, [since] being able to verbally express my thoughts is crucial to developing a keen understanding of any subject matter. I also struggled—and continue to struggle—with writing papers in Spanish, because my piecemeal understanding of the language prevents me from maintaining the same impulse and free flow of ideas that is usually indispensable in my other [English] papers.

As a writing tutor, keeping these challenges in mind is key to setting appropriate expectations. Recognizing that ESL students may be aiming to express complicated ideas with more limited means than they have in their first language may make their efforts appear all the more impressive.

Another student's comment brought us back to the important role that Writing Center tutors can play in the English-learning process for ESL students. Relating his experiences of learning French, one writing associate reflected that "having someone to discuss mechanics with is useful, so native speakers or at least proficient speakers are very important." Writing associates are perfectly placed to play this role, as native (or near-native) speakers with a firm grasp of the English language. As yet another tutor pointed out, becoming aware of the "standard" practices in a new language takes a lot of time and practice, and having someone to explain linguistic norms can be extremely helpful. Aside from helping with papers, writing associates can assist ESL students as discussion partners, joining their ESL tutees in practicing academic discourse out loud. As *peer* tutors, it is just as important in working with ESL tutees to be able to identify with them (as with non-ESL tutees) and to recognize that we can and do have helpful feedback to offer.

Integrating Research, Feedback and Experience

When I originally chose this topic, I hoped to compile a simple set of pointers for writing associates working with nonnative English speakers. My Teaching and Tutoring professor thoughtfully predicted that my findings would probably be less conclusive than I anticipated. Sure enough, rather than a strict set of "guidelines," my exploration into the world of ESL pedagogy has led to more questions than answers.[3] Accordingly, rather than oversimplify the complexity of research in this field, and to avoid essentializing the feedback I received from tutors and tutees, I have decided to list my "findings" as pedagogy puzzles, thought-provoking dilemmas faced by both tutors and scholars alike that have no simple answers. It is my hope that, although these "puzzles" offer no straightforward advice, they might be helpful as a starting point for readers to work toward their own answers.

Research on ESL versus Non-ESL Student Writers

Several ESL theorists argue that ESL students' writing processes are more similar to those of native English speakers than they are different. Studies have demonstrated that both L1 and L2 students use a "recursive composing process, involving planning, writing, and revising, to develop their ideas and find appropriate rhetorical and linguistic means to express them." (Silva, 675) In other words, both L1 and L2 students rely on writing as a process to compose papers. In keeping with this "more similar than different" hypothesis, the surveys completed by ESL Writing Center tutees included feedback that was strikingly similar to that of non-ESL students. Furthermore, many theorists emphasize the vast diversity among ESL students, and caution readers against drawing too many essentializing conclusions about the diverse group of individuals in this group. Both L1 and L2 tutees stated that they came to the Writing Center for grammar and paper structure, said they felt free to ask as many questions as they wanted, and found tutors knowledgeable in the field of their paper to be most helpful. This similarity raises an initial puzzle: Should writing associates change their tutoring styles when working with nonnative English speakers?

Some ESL theorists have rejected the argument that ESL students should be taught exactly like native speakers, acknowledging that expectations should be reassessed for nonnative speakers as well as recognizing subtle but crucial differences in the writing process for these students. Harris and Silva emphasize the importance of "pre- and post-writing discussion sessions" for ESL students. They point out that these sessions are an excellent opportunity for nonnative speakers to practice the language and solidify their arguments. My own experiences in the Writing Center corroborate this conclusion. I have found with several tutees that verbal discussion of the paper at hand can clear up a lot of confusion. Some of these students had difficulty explaining their point coherently on paper but were able to articulate it very clearly verbally, often without even noticing it. ESL students may be less likely to realize that talking with a peer will help them with their paper, but I have found that repeating their points orally can help them to realize that they do know how to express their point. While this technique has also been helpful with native English speakers, I find that I use it more often with ESL students, and that it can be even more helpful in this context.

Similarly, most of the writing associates stated that they usually alter their tutoring style when working with nonnative English speakers. In response to a question about their tutoring styles with nonnative English speakers, one student mentioned that with ESL students, "I think I do more listening and repeating and make sure we are on the same page." Another tutor described making greater use of grammar terminology with ESL students, since "I feel that the 'rules' give language [learners] something to grab onto while developing linguistic skills." The degree to which a tutor will need to alter his/her style will most likely differ considerably, even among ESL students; one tutor's advice to "try a variety of tones and approaches" is highly relevant to this particular "puzzle."

Confidence and Working with ESL Students

Several of the tutors surveyed reported some anxiety about working with ESL students. One writing associate commented: "I feel unsure [working with ESL tutees]. They ask for grammatical help, but sometimes I think they want more but are too shy to ask for it. I think this arises because of the language barrier." Another student noted that, although she had been "nervous at first," with greater experience, she became "increasingly more confident." Yet another tutor explained that, although he has grown more comfortable working with ESL students, "I think I have a harder time integrating a process model tutoring with ESL students." While ESL literature offers no easy answers, the words of the writing associates are instructive: experience, in addition to having a number of techniques and approaches to try, is probably the key. With this dilemma, as with others, it is important to remember that tutors can always ask tutees what *they* would like to focus on; all of the tutees surveyed said they were comfortable asking for further help if they felt unsatisfied with the session.

Authority Dynamics and ESL Peer Instruction

In his classic article, "Peer Tutors and Institutional Authority," Jeremiah Dyehouse addresses the power dynamics of unequal authority that can arise in a tutoring session. In my own experiences at the Writing Center, I have found that these power dynamics can be exaggerated when working with ESL students since the tutor is in a position of authority not only by virtue of her position but also her status as a native language speaker. This challenge was also reflected in several tutor surveys. One student asked, "how can I make [ESL students] feel comfortable and respected despite the barrier between us?" Particularly given the feelings of frustration and ineptitude that may arise when one is in a linguistically unfamiliar situation, this question seems particularly relevant.

An equalizing technique practiced by one tutor is "to emphasize my own ignorance more than I usually do." Again, this writing associate is relying on the shared experiences between them—both have less experience with languages other than their first language, and examining idioms in one's first language may help one better understand the arbitrariness of most languages. When I felt too "in charge" of a tutoring session, I also found it helpful to switch to asking more questions rather than making absolute statements, since answering questions can put the tutee in a position of authority.

Creating a Hierarchy of Needs

Choosing what aspect of a paper to work on is often a challenge for writing associates; this decision-making process can become even more overwhelming when working with nonnative speakers, since there are often more grammatical and convention-based issues to consider when working with such tutees. One writing tutor, who specified that she had never worked with an ESL student, expressed this anxiety particularly clearly: "I don't really feel prepared to be in this situation [tutoring ESL students...] my anxiety lies in [not] knowing what *kind of* help to provide, how picky to be, what to let go of, etc., within a paper."

Different tutors offered different perspectives on which aspect of a paper they usually focus on most. One tutor admitted, "I try to correct everything. After all, I want them to do as well as possible." This tutor's ambition to create a nearly perfect paper is admirable; however, as is discussed above, pressure to fix *every* "mistake" in a paper can leave tutors feeling frustrated and overwhelmed, anxious about tutoring ESL students in particular.

For an opposing perspective, Harris and Silva urge tutors to "withstand the pressure to correct every error." (530–31) Acknowledging the wish of some nonnative English speakers that tutors correct *every* error, they identify this as "editing" more than "tutoring." They encourage tutors to adjust expectations by pointing out that it is unrealistic to expect nonnative English speakers to write with the exact same "written accent" of native speakers.

Harris and Silva also suggest that tutors try to make a distinction between "global errors" and "local errors" when working with a student on a paper. They define global errors as those that directly "interfere with the reader's understanding of the text" while local errors do not. (526) In creating a "hierarchy of needs" tutors and tutees have to find a middle ground between perfecting the paper and helping the tutee learn to write a better paper. Even if a tutee leaves a session with only a couple of new writing skills, it may be more valuable in the long run than a tutor fixing every detail of a paper without complete explanation. Again, tutoring is a balancing act.

Form Versus Content: A Continuing Debate

One recurring question when making a "hierarchy of needs" for a tutoring session is the question of whether to focus more on form or content, another issue that occurs in many tutoring sessions but is often pronounced in sessions with ESL students. This is an issue that elicits particularly contrasting viewpoints in the literature. Zamel argues against the notion that nonnative English speaking students must learn grammar before moving on to content, challenging the assumption that "belief and knowledge are two separate entities, that language must be in place and fixed in order to do the work in a course." (509) Zamel problematizes the traditional view:

> an essentialist view of language in which language is understood to be a decontextualized skill that can be taught in isolation from the production of meaning and that must be in place to undertake intellectual work [...] supports the illusion that permanent solutions are possible, which releases faculty from the ongoing struggle and questioning that the teaching-learning process [...] involves. ("Strangers," 510)

According to Zamel, this view of ESL instruction emphasizes the "deficit model of language and learning," a pre-process conception that has lost currency in the field of Composition, at least for L1 students. (510)

The writing associates surveyed differed as well in their approaches to this puzzle; however, many more talked about focusing on grammar than on structure or content. According to one tutor, "I almost never talk about flow or argument [when working with nonnative speakers] because I'm too worried about grammar. I think that since the papers are usually for ESL classes they are much more focused on learning English rather than learning how to write." One student explained this decision, stating that "becoming more familiar with the English language [...] is necessary before [a nonnative English speaker] advances to improve her argumentative skills in the English language." Ann Fathman and Elizabeth Whalley similarly place emphasis on grammar correction in their article, "Teacher Response to Student Writing: Focus on Form Versus Content." This empirical study implies that students make more changes in their writing when presented with grammatical feedback, but the study draws no conclusions about the effect of these different types of feedback on student work as a whole. While it is important to be sensitive to the ratio of feedback about form to that about content, the needs of each student and each paper will probably differ dramatically.

Making Suggestions versus Asking Questions

One ESL student I have worked with several times at the Writing Center commented to me that tutoring would be more helpful if writing associates gave more concrete suggestions for improving papers rather than merely identifying problems. He was often able to understand the problems they identified, but he still struggled to put these suggestions into practice.

This suggestion introduces the dilemma of supporting a student's agency in writing their own paper or of satisfying their desire for a "correct paper," a tension that is also embedded in the process of choosing what part of the paper to focus on most. One possible middle ground would be offering several alternatives that would be clearer or more grammatically correct, thus enabling students to choose on their own within a framework of "correct English." Again, the issue of authority and power is at play in this situation; as in many tutoring scenarios, the tutor and tutee must balance critique with open-ended suggestions, responding to the student's writing while acknowledging his final control over his own work.

Balancing Positive Feedback and Constructive Criticism

One way in which ESL and non-ESL student writers may be more similar than different is in their need for positive feedback in addition to critique. Katie Gilmartin, for example, reminds beginning tutors that "Most tutees come to the Writing Center because they are upset with the quality of their writing [...] Commenting on promising areas, as well as those that need work, is vital; the majority of tutees I surveyed wrote that they were thankful for encouragement and motivation, as well as criticism." (20)

Similarly, Mark-Ameen Johnson reminds tutors to be aware that nonnative speakers need positive feedback, too, especially if they are revising a paper for resubmission. This can be particularly crucial if the student has gotten negative feedback from a professor who expects him or her to write with a "native accent": "They may need to hear someone say, 'This paper got an F-, but *you* are not an F-!'" (203) Encouragement can be vital to a sense of confidence, as anyone who has received a scathing comment on a paper will understand. As peers, we know that experience of needing positive feedback intimately, in addition to realizing the value of critique, and so we are able both to empathize and strategize with our tutees.

Balancing Risk-Taking, Theory, and Practice

The dynamics of peer tutoring ESL writers have been largely unexplored by composition theorists and TESOL specialists alike, and there is significant room for further analysis. Due to constraints of time and a dearth of anonymous feedback, my examination of this topic has not focused closely on the experiences of ESL students themselves in the Writing Center; this is an area that certainly warrants further study to better address the puzzles raised here.

While I have drawn few conclusions, Vivian Zamel does offer some advice that applies to tutors, tutees, students and teachers alike. Zamel reminds teachers that writing in a nonnative language inherently involves risk-taking, and that this risk taking is a natural part of the learning process that should be encouraged. ("Composing," 165–87) Tutoring ESL students is, in many ways, unfamiliar linguistic territory that must be continually researched. Conclusions about how to tutor best must be constantly reassessed through an ongoing process of dialogue between tutor and tutee and reframed through the dual lenses of theory and practice.

NOTES

[1] Throughout this paper I use several descriptive terms for students who do not speak English natively, including "ESL." I realize this term is not always correct, since English is often not a "second" language but rather an additional one; it is, however, a term widely recognized and used throughout the literature. For the sake of variety, I also employ the term "nonnative English speakers," which is more correct, and the terms "L1" (first language) and "L2" (second language), since these terms can be more succinct in certain circumstances.

[2] This low response rate may be instructive for future projects; concrete incentives to complete surveys may be necessary to get a better response rate.

[3] Jennifer Wewers draws a similar conclusion in her article "Writing Tutors and Dyslexic Tutees: Is There Something Special We Should Know?"

WORKS CITED

Benesch, Sarah. "ESL, Ideology, and the Politics of Pragmatism." *TESOL Quarterly 27* (1993): 705–17.

Dyehouse, Jeremiah, "Peer Tutors and Institutional Authority." In Podis and Podis, 54–57.

Fathman, Ann, and Elizabeth Whalley. "Teacher Response to Student Writing: Focus on Form Versus Content." *Second Language Writing: Research Insights for the Classroom.* Edited by Barbara Kroll. Cambridge: Cambridge University Press, 1990: 178–190.

Gilmartin, Katie. "Working at the Drop-In Center." In Podis and Podis, 15–21.

Harris, Muriel and Tony Silva. "Tutoring ESL Students: Issues and Options." *College Composition and Communication* 44 (1993): 525–37.

Johnson, Mark-Ameen. "ESL Tutors: Islands of Calm in the Multicultural Storm" in *Dialogue on Writing: Rethinking ESL, Basic Writing, and First-Year Composition*. Edited by Geraldine DeLuca et al. Mahwah, NJ: Lawrence Erlbaum Associates, 2002: 199–212.

Matsuda, Paul Kei. "Composition Studies and ESL Writing: A Disciplinary Division of Labor" in *Cross-Talk in Comp Theory: A Reader*, Victor Villaneuva ed. (Urbana, Illinois: National Council of Teachers of English, 2003), pp. 773-796.

_____. "Situating ESL Writing in a Cross-Disciplinary Context." *Written Communication* 15 no. 1 (January 1998): 99-121.

Podis, Leonard A., and JoAnne M. Podis, Editors. *Working with Student Writers: Essays on Tutoring and Teaching.* New York: Peter Lang, 1999.

Silva, Tony. "Toward an Understanding of the Distinct Nature of L2 Writing: The ESL Research and Its Implications." *TESOL Quarterly* 27 (1993): 657–77.

Wewers, Jennifer. "Writing Tutors and Dyslexic Tutees: Is There Something Special We Should Know?" In Podis and Podis, 229–37.

Zamel, Vivian. "Strangers in Academia: The Experiences of Faculty and ESL Students Across the Curriculum." *CCC* 46 (1995): 506–521.

_____. "The Composing Processes of Advanced ESL Students: Six Case Studies." *TESOL Quarterly* 17 (1983): 165–187.

Section Ten

Class Background and Writing:
Teaching, Tutoring, Learning

This section might be seen as a continuation of Section Nine, "Empowering Marginalized Learners," because that is indeed a theme of the articles collected here. However, the focus of this section is a subset of that larger topic, for the concern of all three essays is the impact of socioeconomic class background on student writing, including relevant implications for teaching and tutoring. Like students of other groups who face marginalization, working class students often find themselves struggling to employ the conventions of academic discourse. In many cases, working class students have not had the same level of preparation for college writing that students with greater class privilege have had, and so they lack the mastery that is expected of them. In other cases, working class students may find themselves resistant to what they see as the academy's implicit rejection of the languages—and cultural values—of their home communities, and so they balk at the requirement to tailor their writing to fit the acceptable academic modes.

Whatever the case, the situation is complicated by the stigma surrounding class in U.S. society. Because the American ideal is that of a classless society (nearly everyone claiming to be "middle class") with unlimited social mobility, students may be slow to recognize that their class backgrounds may have affected their level of academic success. Those on the lower rungs of the socioeconomic ladder might harbor feelings of shame for their situations, while those on the upper rungs may experience guilt for their privilege. In any event, class is often overlooked as an issue of importance in matters of teaching and learning, and it is only within the past fifteen years that researchers in composition studies have begun to explore its effects. The articles in this section should raise awareness of the issues and also clarify approaches that teachers and writing associates might use when tutoring students from working class backgrounds.

The Articles

In Chapter 31, "My Hidden Class Consciousness and the Impact of Socioeconomic Class in Academia" Monica Bielski Boris explores problems facing students from working class backgrounds attempting to enter the academic mainstream. As she notes, while scholars and social activists have recently focused much attention on "racial and gender inequalities," marginalization due to socioeconomic class differences is often ignored. One reason for this oversight, she says, is that signs of membership in a particular class may not be overt or obvious. Perhaps the most crucial hardship that working class students face in seeking to succeed in college is the need to compensate for their weak high school preparation. According to Bielski Boris, working class people generally have "lesser educational opportunities" because "America's public schools are still segregated by class as well as race." Using her own education as an example, Bielski Boris talks about the shock she experienced upon first arriving at a highly competitive college:

> I was frightened and frustrated. I felt as if I was deficient, that I was just less intelligent than my classmates. I felt like an impostor that Oberlin had let in by mistake. [...] I just could not digest that even though I had graduated valedictorian of my high school, I did not have the academic "tools" to easily assimilate into the Oberlin curriculum.

Speaking specifically of her initiation into academic discourse, she notes, "I struggled with my writing skills and my reading speed. I plodded through dense scholarly texts that seemed to be written by aliens."

Bielski Boris looks beyond questions of underfunding of public schools to examine "the class culture" in which she grew up and the ways in which its values clashed with those of the academy. To supplement her experiences, she draws on responses solicited from fellow writing associates and from her tutees in a writing-intensive course, some of whom talked of the stigma and shame that surround discussions of class. She concludes by considering practical approaches to help working class students succeed. For this edition of *Working with Student Writers*, Bielski Boris, now a professor of labor studies, provides an epilogue discussing how issues of class status have remained an important aspect of her life and career.

Virginia Pryor's "Writing in Academia: The Politics of 'Style'" (Chapter 32) examines how student writers, especially those from "marginalized sectors of society," are "faced with a constant tension between the sense of being coerced into using specific language [...] and their own compulsion to attempt to assimilate into the system by following its rules. [...]" Pryor's remarkable essay both explores this tension analytically and enacts it materially and emotionally by dramatically juxtaposing two different voices. The opening section, written in a "high academic" register, talks about a profound need for changes "in the way academic institutions consider student writing—changes in the standards that would allow for a plurality of voices. [...]"

The second section, by contrast, is a narrative in the colloquial speech of Pryor's community language—the English of the working class South. Chronicling the details of her background, she notes that she made the decision early to assimilate: "I was real young when I decided, out of respect for my mother and my family, and all they had done for me, I wanted to give myself as many chances as I could to do well with my life." An obstacle to upward mobility surfaced, however:

> I began to notice that all the people on T.V. that sounded smart, like the people on the news, didn't talk like me or anyone I knew. I found out that that's how, in America, you're supposed to sound like if you want people to listen to you. And I thought I had a lot to say, so I studied the newspeople like I would a book, memorizing and practicing their speech.

Not surprisingly, when she practiced her standard English, her friends "made fun of" her and her mother pronounced her "uppity."

However, Pryor was tenacious, and she made it into a high school where she studied "for the first time with rich kids." Speaking of this new atmosphere, she says, "I still worked on my talking. It was funny, the accents in the school were different, less twangy, more serious, partially erased. Lord knows I scrubbed and scrubbed at mine until I thought there was almost nothing left." In this school, her "secret" practicing could come to the surface and merge with official course work. Ultimately, Pryor, a once-marginalized student who became empowered within academia, asks "What price did I really pay?" While she has mastered academic discourse and finds it useful and worthy of respect in its own right, she remains troubled by its tendency to exclude speakers of other, less rarefied, discourses. She concludes with the forceful "insistence that her [mother's] language, as well as many others, has [...] a right and a place in the exchange of knowledge."

Chapter 33, Desirae Sweet's "Rural Blue-Collar Identities and the Writing Process," completes this section by examining the impact of a rural blue-collar background on students' efforts to produce academic discourse. Like Bielski Boris and Pryor, Sweet incorporates her own experiences into her essay. Describing herself as "Fresh off a farm," she recounts the "culture shock" she experienced as a new student at a selective liberal arts college. According to Sweet, "The combination of cultural and class differences that sets these two types of communities apart can create a sense of dissonance and even inadequacy in students from rural and blue-collar backgrounds."

Like Pryor, Sweet is concerned that such students—who are, for the most part, outsiders with respect to the academy—must make uncomfortable accommodations to fit into the discourses most valued in higher education. Like Bielski Boris, she worries that these working class students may remain largely hidden from view, waging their silent struggles to gain a discursive foothold in their college or university. In analyzing the specific problems facing this group of students, Sweet identifies "discomfort with academic discourse" as well as problems with professor-student power dynamics and also what Miriam Axel-Lute (Chapter 16) calls contextual writer's block. To alleviate these problems, Sweet urges teachers and tutors to strive for a "heightened awareness of the issues" facing these students and also encourages students to retain pride in their rural blue-collar voices by channeling them "in productive and soul-nourishing ways that affirm the value of a student's background." Essentially, Sweet does not call for a reform of academic discourse to accommodate working class language as Pryor does but rather recommends a celebration of such language outside the classroom.

Chapter 31

My Hidden Class Consciousness and the Impact of Socioeconomic Class in Academia

Monica Bielski Boris

At Oberlin College, a place awash with defiance against norms of personal appearance, a stranger to the campus would most likely have a difficult time determining whether or not a given student comes from a well-to-do family. Although there are many wealthy students on campus, most students, including those "with money," adorn themselves in casual clothing and often wear thrift store ensembles of ripped jeans and faded T-shirts. Outward appearances may not reveal any socioeconomic class differences. However, the truth is that class divisions do exist on campus, and the fact that class distinctions remain hidden only contributes to further difficulties for Oberlin students with working class backgrounds. Even though people at Oberlin, which boasts a history of promoting diversity, frequently engage in discourse about racial and gender inequalities, when it comes to socioeconomic inequality, the discussion is non-existent. Despite the lack of discourse about class, for many Oberlin students, including myself, class differences are an important issue that centrally affects our educational experience.

One's class is not easily definable because "class" is multidimensional. Class definitions can be used to denote the amount of money one has. (This is probably the most common usage in the United States, but class means so much more than just money.) The type of work one does plays a large role in establishing class identity. For example, my father is an autoworker, and he earns what would be considered by most a middle class wage. However, he does not view himself as truly middle class because he did not attend college and because he works in a blue-collar job, where he gets his hands dirty and doesn't know if his job will be there tomorrow. On the other hand, many white-collar workers who have college degrees earn less than my father but consider themselves middle class because they possess a marketable skill based on their education and because they feel some sort of professional prestige about their work. Class viewed in this way is not merely economic but societal; it is based on work descriptions, skill levels, and educational backgrounds. Because of these reasons, class affects people in multiple ways.

From my perspective as a college student, class impacts much of a student's life. The most obvious effect is economic. At Oberlin, students with economic hardship have difficulties paying the extraordinarily large term bill every semester, but this is not the only place where working class students face challenges. We also face considerable cultural friction, stemming from our class-specific experiences. Although I do not want to essentialize the "working class experience," I do believe that in a capitalist society like that of the United States, in which one's class status often determines one's opportunities, working class people deal with some common hardships. One of the most common is our lesser educational opportunities. Although there have been attempts at supposed "school choice" programs and busing programs, America's schools are still segregated by class as well as race.

Like most working class students, I attended the local public high school—in my case it was in a blue-collar suburb. While attending high school, I never thought much about the quality of my education because I did not have a standard for comparison. Attending a private college-preparatory school was totally out of the question and not just because of the cost. The only private schools located near my town were Catholic parochial schools, and they were basically teaching the same curriculum as the public schools, except for their religious focus. I did have a faint idea that private schools and wealthier public schools were somehow better than my school, but that world was so far from me that I never presumed to question my education.

The first time I realized that my education may not have been "up to par" with the schooling of other American high school students was when I came to college. I remember attending my first college class ever, a politics course, and when the professor said that we would have to write a ten-page paper for the course, I had my first of many "Oberlin-induced" anxiety attacks. I had never written a paper of more than five pages in high school. Beyond that, I had never written a paper for any class other than English. I didn't know how to use a computer, even for word processing. I was frightened and frustrated. I felt as if I was deficient, that I was just less intelligent than my classmates. I felt like an impostor that Oberlin had let in by mistake. After blaming myself for the problems I encountered in my first semester of college, it slowly began to sink in that it wasn't my own personal stupidity that left me unprepared for college work; I wasn't inherently less intelligent than the other students. My problem was that my high school had not provided me with the basic writing, reading, and study skills to prepare me for the curriculum of a selective liberal arts college. I just could not digest that even though I had graduated valedictorian of my high school, I did not have the academic "tools" to easily assimilate into the Oberlin curriculum.

I could argue that the reason for my inadequate high school education was that my school was underfunded or did not have the caliber of teachers that other, more prestigious or wealthy schools had, but I don't believe that this is the only reason. My high school was certainly not the wealthiest of the Ohio public schools, but it was by no means struggling like many inner-city schools. My school had fairly new textbooks, a few computers, a decent library, and more extracurricular activities than most public schools. So why did my education fail to prepare me for Oberlin? I think it had a lot to do with the class culture of my community and the expectations that both teachers and the residents of my town had for what a high school education should be. Most of my high school classmates, like me, were the children of blue-collar factory workers. Our parents had not attended college, and many times I got the impression that most families, including my own, did not value the skills needed to succeed at a highly selective college. The focus was not on academic discourse or scholarly research; such things were seen as frivolous, even by most teachers. The focus was rather on personal responsibility, respect for authority, and acquiring life skills that would help students move into the work force. Most of my high school classmates, if they attended college, went to the local public university to study fields such as education, health care, engineering, and criminal justice. They went to college to train for a job, not to study art history or anthropology.

Because of the class status of my hometown, people view college as practical preparation for a career. Thus, they often do not perceive the value of a selective liberal arts education. However, there are other reasons why many working class families do not send their children to private colleges. Attending a private college is an expense that drains most working class families. Beyond the price of tuition, many families cannot easily afford to provide the necessary living expenses for students in college, particularly for the four years or more it takes to receive a bachelor's degree. Of course there are exceptions. I am from a working class family, and yet I have been able to attend Oberlin. I also know other working class students on campus. Financial aid does allow students without much money to attend Oberlin and similar colleges, so why didn't more students in my high school graduating class attend highly competitive colleges? I already mentioned the expectations of many families that students should acquire job skills in college, not just scholarly skills, but there is more to it than this.

Working class students often receive inadequate preparation for a private college education, and the reasons do not just stem from the lesser quality of public schools in working class communities but also from the lack of *informal preparation* they receive from their families. Academic skills and educational priorities are not just transmitted in the schools; parents play a large role in forming the educational background of their children. I am certainly not arguing that working class parents have lesser parenting abilities. However, if one's parents have not attended college, they often do not understand the process of preparing and applying for college, which then gives the children of professional parents an advantage. Beyond that, some working class parents may not see the importance of a college education because they themselves did not need one to reach their present status.

Neither of my parents attended college, so in many ways they were not able to provide me with the academic skills I needed when I first came to Oberlin. My parents, particularly my father, encouraged me to do well in school because he knew as I was growing up that education would be integral to my success. They knew I needed to go to college, but they were not certain how to get me there. In my house, my parents never read academic books. The only books in my house were the Bible and a series of Time-Life books about World War II that my father occasionally skimmed through.

When I was young, like most kids, I thought my parents were smart people. It was not until I reached the sixth or seventh grade that it became evident that my parents did not have "sound" academic backgrounds. It was at this time that my father could no longer help me with my math homework, and my mother could no longer spell-check my writing. I know they were in some ways ashamed, and because of this, I felt awkward in discussing school with them. They were, however, extremely proud of me, even more so than many of my friends' parents, who were from upper class backgrounds.

At that time, my teachers became the model for what an intelligent person was supposed to be like. I became increasingly concerned about how they perceived me and more conscious of the working class vocabulary and grammar I had inherited from my parents. I vested my self-esteem in the grades teachers gave me. It was disastrous for the development of my inner voice because I merely molded my thoughts into the standard presented by my teachers. Needless to say, my public high school teachers adhered to the "Old Paradigm" method of teaching, and I mastered their tests for knowledge. I became an expert at the five-paragraph paper. I learned to memorize historic dates and math formulas with the skill of a human computer. What I didn't learn was how to think or even how to speak my mind. All of this stemmed from my embarrassment surrounding my parents and my working class roots, which prodded me to "make it" in school.

I really thought I had escaped my background when I graduated from high school. I was at the top of my class. I had an impressive student resume that included speech and debate championships. Most important, I had been accepted to Oberlin College. I thought all of the embarrassment would fade away and I would blend into this new scholarly environment. My hopefulness about college, however, could not wash away my class background. On the day my father dropped me off at Oberlin, I remember being overwhelmed by my first impression of the student body. Although the other students looked like me, they somehow seemed different. They were more confident. Their obviously professional parents seemed more helpful and concerned than my father, who was as lost as I was on the first day of orientation.

It has been a painful journey through Oberlin since that first day. In my first year, I struggled with my writing skills and my reading speed. I plodded through dense scholarly texts that seemed to be written by aliens. At first, I was too proud to seek help because I felt that it would only draw attention to my working class status. However, I truly wanted to succeed, so I dropped my defenses and enrolled in study skills classes as well as an expository writing course. I began visiting professors in their offices for advice and guidance and utilizing tutors for my more difficult courses. By the end of my sophomore year, I felt much more secure in my academic abilities.

With my newfound confidence, I have even tried to share my experiences. I now work for Student Support Services as a peer liaison for first-generation and low-income students. I really enjoy my job and want to help others in my situation. However, my job is challenging in that often first-year students do not want to concede that they need extra help; they merely want to blend in, as I once did. I learned you cannot simply "blend in" without the threat of "drowning." Just as we cannot and should not ask students to ignore their race and gender, we cannot ask students to hide their class backgrounds.

Many studies have shown that women and people of color face barriers when they enter the academy, but I never hear discussion of the obstacles that working class students must overcome. Why is this? To get a larger perspective on this issue, I decided to distribute questionnaires to the other writing associates in my teaching and tutoring class and to the students whom I tutor in a composition course. I found some conclusions similar to those I had reached. Many people admitted that class is something more easily hidden and that both working class students and students of middle and upper class backgrounds are ashamed to reveal their class status.

Of course, the embarrassment stems from different sources. For working class students, there is a real embarrassment about our class status, especially when we enter the academy, which has traditionally been a place for the elite. For middle and upper class students, the shame comes from guilt about being privileged. One of the tutors described this kind of shame at Oberlin:

> People here are ashamed to talk about class—the privileged because they were privileged and the poor because they're poor. The rich don't want to talk about it [...] it's guilt. [...] I know I've just been ridiculously lucky [...] and that's the thing about class—it's all luck at age 0–22 [because] you've done nothing of personal integrity to deserve or legitimize why you have what you have. Around less rich people I feel the need to hide the fact that I've had it so good, and I can try and make it sound otherwise, but I guess mostly I'm not sure how to respond—no one wants pity (I don't think) and I certainly can't join in any bitch fest so it leaves me silent, shrugging and listening. [...]

I think this is how a lot of Oberlin students with "privileged" backgrounds feel, and I know that dealing with this unease and guilt is difficult because as a white woman, I have felt it whenever racism has been discussed. However, this guilt and shame must somehow be overcome if we are to address class and racism or any of the other factors of discrimination within the academy.

This brings me to another important question that I asked in my questionnaire: "What are some practical ways that tutors and professors can sensitize themselves to issues of class in order to assist students?" All of the tutors who responded to this question admitted that none of their tutees have ever discussed their class status with them. Still, class does affect students in their academic preparation and therefore often affects their writing skills. Virginia, one of the writing associates, had a very practical suggestion:

> A tutor can ask a tutee about his/her class background in a way that expresses genuine interest and concern, and an awareness that this issue might pertain to specific academic difficulties in this environment.

Virginia does concede that this can be a risky piece of advice, if the question appears to the tutee to indicate "patronism or hostility." She also notes that, at a school such as Oberlin, professors must be wary about making the assumption that all students are middle or upper class.

The tutees who responded to my questionnaire also offered valuable insights. One advised tutors and professors "to get to know the students and their backgrounds better and realize that if a paper is written badly, it doesn't always mean that the student was lazy and didn't try." Another stated:

> I think that the tutors and professors should get to know students and what they have done or what they are used to in high school. I don't mean that they should accommodate to each student, but they should take this into consideration in order to help these students to get used to the "college scene."

This may seem like a simple solution, but it truly would make a difference. Too often, professors and tutors at Oberlin make assumptions about what a student *should* know when they first come to college. The reality is that high school educations vary a great deal, and the quality of preparation has a lot to do with the student's class background. If those in the academy could see the whole student and not just the product in the form of their papers and exams, progress would be made.

Len, a writing professor, sees the solution as the empowerment of students and the implementation of a more inclusive curriculum:

> [...] I'd say that it's important for us to be sensitive to *all* issues and kinds of marginalization and oppression. While experiences with oppression clearly vary, I believe that a predisposition towards wanting to empower excluded students of all sorts will prepare people to be sensitive, at least in principle, to class issues as well.

I also agree that addressing class and other forms of oppression will help students come to terms with their own class status. I do, however, see class as being more difficult for students to address than race or gender. In American society, where capitalism reigns, class status is not viewed as a form of oppression or discrimination; it is viewed as a measure of one's effort and worth. We absorb the idea that we are somehow to blame for our "lower" class standing because we and our parents "did not work hard enough."

Such self-blame and shame are destructive, for they keep working class students from addressing their class status and possibly seeking assistance with their studies. I know it is painful to face class issues, but I urge everyone connected with the academy to acknowledge the impact of class and to begin talking honestly about it. I understand the crucial role of class firsthand. While I have achieved a certain level of academic sophistication at Oberlin, I remain intensely aware of my class background, even if I can hide my status among a seemingly homogeneous student body in ripped T-shirts.

Afterword and Epilogue

1997: In writing this essay, I struggled with whether or not to use my personal narrative to address class issues in the academy. Like many others, I tend to devalue my experiences. How could *my* life prove anything? I then began to realize that discussions of class status within the academy are primarily conducted at the theoretical, factual, or objective levels. I rarely see anyone writing about their own struggles with class in making arguments or drawing conclusions about class structures and discrimination, and I feel that more personal and autobiographical writing needs to be done in this area. It was difficult to write this paper at first, but I increasingly felt more liberated by the experience. Finally, I realized, I was writing about socioeconomic class and was actually able to include myself.

2009: I wrote this essay as a graduating senior trying to understand class status and reflect on my experiences as a working class student at an elite private college. Since then, I have wrestled with the definition of class and have continued on in academia. After college, I enrolled in a Ph.D. program in industrial relations at Rutgers, The State University of New Jersey. Being in a graduate program with the intent of establishing myself as an academic challenged me. I still struggled to find my voice in my writing. Having to criticize the experts in my field and assume the authority to provide my own theoretical analysis daunted me. I again was able to find inspiration and assistance from some of my teachers who recognized my struggles and patiently advised me.

My research focuses on diversity issues in labor unions and the workplace, and my experiences with class identity have influenced my work. It has been an advantage to be able to draw on my background as I write about workers and labor unions. Still, even though my field addresses working class issues, my working class roots at times cause me to feel like an outsider among my colleagues. I have the degree, the academic job and accompanying salary, but class is not only about education, career and income. It is also about culture, and culturally I have not assimilated into the class culture of academia. It might sound silly, but it is a big deal to me that, for instance, I prefer beer to wine or blue jeans to business suits. Sometimes I feel again like an impostor, especially when I am at events like academic conference mixers or parties with senior administrators. At such times, I remember how I felt during my first semester at Oberlin or while pushing myself to write my dissertation. It is at these moments that I have to overcome my self-doubts and fears in order to find my place in academia.

The process continues, but it has really helped me to be a better teacher. I teach labor studies courses to undergraduates with diverse class backgrounds at a large public university. The advice I found useful as a tutor to never assume a student's class background or prior educational preparation still holds true as a professor. A student's ability to perform in college depends on many factors including the quality of K–12 education, the skills instilled by parents, and for some—particularly nontraditional adult students—their own experiences in their workplaces and communities. Having less preparation does not mean students cannot be successful. It just means they need to acquire essential skills, and this is where a helpful and understanding professor or writing associate can have a real impact.

Chapter 32

Writing in Academia:
The Politics of "Style"

Virginia Pryor

Since the development of "English" as a formal area of academic study in the past century, a conventional mode of thought has regarded this discipline, and often academia itself, as an entity separate from politics and everyday lived experience. Despite the facts that these assumptions were prevalent at the time English was founded in a Western context limited exclusively to white males of the upper classes, and that the last half-century since World War II has seen a dramatic rise in "acceptance" of various marginalized sectors of society into institutions of higher learning, the insistence that academia is or should be separate from and immune to political and cultural issues is still prominent. A clear illustration of this belief appears in a letter written by a disaffected teacher to the editor of the newspaper of the National Council of Teachers of English. Mark Albrecht, an English teacher from Ukiah, California, charges that NCTE

> capitulated to feminists [...] and became more and more the province of education-
> ists [...] who believed in such tripe as women's studies, black studies (and black
> English) and "process." Now their offspring offer us multiculturalism, collaborative
> "learning," and whole language—all of this a retreat from hard, individual work and
> traditional values. [...]   (Albrecht, 17)

While Albrecht's tirade represents perhaps an extreme position, recent years have witnessed an increase in neo-conservative attacks aimed at educational reform. The implications of such debates for the teaching of writing, specifically in reference to discourse within departments of English, are crucial in relation to issues of multiculturalism and questions of difference in grammar, usage, and ultimately, writing "style."

My assertion is that these differences are formed and influenced, but *not* solely defined or easily categorized, by differences in economic, cultural and linguistic backgrounds. Further, because of the hegemonic[1] nature of the standards for academic writing, a large proportion of student writers are faced with a constant tension between the sense of being coerced into using specific language, grammar, and style and their own compulsion to assimilate into the system by following its rules—appropriating and incorporating these standards into their own writing.

In the past twenty years, and even today, conflicts within academic institutions concerning the need for diversity and a plurality of modes of thought in education have brought forth many needed changes in the curriculum, such as African-American, Women's, Judaic, and East Asian Studies departments. There are still several multicultural departments being pushed for by activists with concerns of underrepresentation of other marginalized cultures, such as the Queer and South Asian communities. Also, debates are ongoing as to whether there should be an umbrella department deemed "Cultural Studies." All of these progressive changes in the structure of the departmental system have been necessary to address the specific concerns of the growing number of students from diverse cultural backgrounds as well as to provide a means for all students to gain exposure to, and education about, the many cultures and communities around them.

While I want to make clear that these new programs are sites of incredible struggle and that they stand as examples of effective change and improvement in the curriculum, it should be pointed out that they are also examples of the willingness of academic institutions to make curricular changes *on their own terms*. Specifically, within these emerging fields of study the notion that there is only one "standard" means of academic writing remains, for the most part, intact and virtually uncontested. The particular forms of discourse vary from one department to another, but the basic ideas about what constitutes acceptable writing still remain. Thus, the fundamental issue of the need to appropriate mainstream academic discourse, even within culturally diverse fields of study, continues to be crucial for many students.

It could be argued that changes in the way academic institutions consider student writing—changes in the standards that would allow for a plurality of voices and for acceptance of diverse uses of language and style—directly threaten to disrupt the hegemony exerted by the dominant code of academic discourse, thereby undermining its rigid enforcement and the eager willingness of students to assimilate to its rules (or beliefs). There is a direct correlation between this kind of discursive control and the ideological control that functions in society. That is, the language of discourse prominent in, for example, the English department, grew out of traditions formulated by the largely white male elite class that originally constituted the whole of academia. Although these kinds of class boundaries are perhaps not so prominent today, it can still be said that discourse arising from the dominant class inherently serves its ideological purposes, i.e., excluding the members of other communities that are not incorporated in the discourse.

The argument in this paper is not a radical or revolutionary one; there is no desire or intent to eliminate traditional academic discourse. It should be recognized that in many respects, academic discourse is quite useful, especially if writers feel comfortable using it to communicate their ideas, or if academic readers find highly specialized discourses conducive to their comprehension of the ideas being communicated. I am asserting, however, that there is a profound need for the incorporation and inclusion of other ways of thinking and self-expression in academic writing, specific to individual abilities and interests within the wider community. Conventional academic discourse is not so problematic in itself; yet the insistence that it is the *only* acceptable style of writing within academia—whose members come from varied communities and backgrounds—must be challenged.

The topic of this essay is very personal to me, for a lot of reasons.

I was born and raised in Memphis, Tennessee, the daughter of a woman from the country, whose father (my grandfather) built their house after the War. He made his living in construction, building bridges for the betterment of the community. My grandmother took her joy in raising her children and taking care of the garden, where they got a lot of their food (and also grew produce to trade with other people who had gardens, like my great-aunts and uncles, who all lived nearby). Neither one of my grandparents finished high school. My mother did but did not get a chance to go to college. She met my father in Memphis, where she had begun to work and start her own life.

My father's family likewise was from a rural area—in Mississippi—where his father served as a Baptist preacher and his mother as a school-teacher. Though he had no money to go to college, he worked three jobs and spent more than a few years getting his degree in accounting at Mississippi State, and then moved to Memphis. This story he has told me all my life has given me a strong sense of the importance of working real hard to be able to do better for yourself—no one's gonna hand it right to you. In my father's way of looking at things, "If you want something, you have to earn it." When we had hard times growing up, my mother's way of explaining to me was, "Money don't fall off trees, Virginia. You can't have everything—you get by on what you need."

Both my parents wanted to move up in the world, and the city was their place of opportunity—more freedom and choice, they figured. They got divorced when I was just over a year, and my father moved to Little Rock to marry my stepmother and live. I spent a lot of time between both places and ways of life, which kept on getting more and more different as I got older. As my father got to doing well for himself, my mother had a harder and harder time making ends meet. She started going to college at night, working by day. Those were all trying times. I was real young when I decided, out of respect for my mother and my family, and all they had done for me, I wanted to give myself as many chances as I could to do well with my life.

I took the lessons both my parents had taught me and kept them with me all the time, especially at school. School was the only place I had for hope of moving up, changing my situation. I resolved to always work and study as hard as I could, to learn everything I was taught. In second grade, I saw the light at the end of the tunnel for me, that maybe if I got smart enough I could make it to somewhere else, because Memphis had no hope for my life. As I got older, I started to realize that we didn't have enough money for me to go far, and I would have to be smarter than most to get a scholarship. I worked extra hard.

When I was in sixth grade, I began to notice that all the people on T.V. that sounded smart, like the people on the news, didn't talk like me or anyone I knew. I found out that that's how, in America, you're supposed to sound like if you want people to listen to you. And I thought I had a lot to say, so I studied the newspeople like I would a book, memorizing and practicing their speech. I was always real good at grammar, memorizing. I was the only one in the class who could recite all the prepositions in alphabetical order on command. I can still do it without recollecting up until … "down." That's not very far, but it's been ten years. (I'm obliged to demonstrate for anyone who asks me politely. My method was by learning them to the tune of commercial jingles until the words got their own rhythm locked in my head.)

Anyway, I had always done well on grammar tests, but I realized that I wasn't using it when I talked, so that was really hard to practice, because I couldn't in front of my friends or they made fun of me, and my mother wondered why I was being so uppity. I started my own private lessons. This later proved to be a good idea, because I made the decision to transfer to a better school, in a better neighborhood. I knew I wasn't getting the education I would need to get scholarships to places far away. We couldn't afford any private school, but luckily Memphis had a public "magnet" high school, where they took your standard test scores, and if they were high enough, you could go in the honors program they had, no matter where you lived. 'Cause I had studied hard for so long, I did really well on those tests, since they were also all about memorizing. It was weird going to school the first time with rich kids—the way they talked, dressed, everything. And I couldn't believe that everyone studied a lot. In my old school I was one of a few. I was scared at first that I wouldn't be smart enough, because all these kids had learned and read so much I hadn't even heard of. But I studied all the time, knowing if I worked hard enough I could do it. I read stuff on my own to kind of catch up, from time lost during fights in the hallway, from being with disruptive kids who wouldn't let anyone else learn, and the fact that at my old school we learned the same stuff every year anyway.

I still worked on my talking. It was funny, the accents in this school were different, less twangy, more serious, partially erased. Lord knows I scrubbed and scrubbed at mine until I thought there was almost none left. Acting classes and plays helped, too, where I could learn to have lots of accents by imitating. By this time I was already good at this. And at the same time, they were teaching us in our honors classes how to write our essays in these formulas so we could pass all kinds of tests and get into colleges. The magnet school was considered a public college-prep school. It was to my fortune that they also passed out all kinds of lists of words to use, where and how to use them right, definitions, tricks of the trade. The best part was that I didn't have to practice on my own, because we were writing them all the time for every class, and these were our tests, too. No more multiple choice, which I thought was a negative at first, but then I realized I was doing real well after a while, and it got real easy. For a while I stopped sleeping as much so I could study more, but after a couple of years I was much better at it, and didn't need near as much time.

In my first year, though, I started to feel I was losing something of myself, we all felt it at home too. I didn't talk or act the same, I felt different. My mother and I stopped getting along at all, and our relations weren't good again until about a year ago, after I spent a lot of time getting to know her better. So in high school this was tough, and I didn't have my own voice anywhere I could hear it. This is when I started writing poetry. But I started winning all these contests, and my teachers encouraged me so much that when my mother was in hospital with surgery they made me compete in this essay contest. To be spiteful, I wrote an essay about how bad it hurt that my father left when I was so young, a real depressing essay. Then it won—can y'all believe that?—they announced my name on the news. Momma was watching in the hospital, and that made her proud, so I reckon it wasn't so bad after all. But people at school started to think of me as some weird, big-shot writer or something, because a piece of fiddle I once wrote got in an anthology too. I thought this has to stop, I sent that essay in as a joke to see what would happen, and my voice is not here if they're gonna keep taking it away from me. And if I just write to myself, why, what's the point of that? And how can they judge my writing? I felt like a phony, so I stopped caring about that, for a long time. Even now.

By the end of high school, I could churn out those formula essays on any topic before I could blink an eye, and that's what I did to pass all the A.P. exams with flying colors, so I could get college credit to help me out later. I still can't figure if I knew what I was talking about, I mean I guess I did, because I definitely studied it all, but I came to think that sometimes it didn't make no difference. When I got into a fancy college due to my test scores and grades, I came with the same idea in mind: Learn the formula, listen to whatever the teacher wants and do it, memorize anything that will help. That has worked for me a lot, but this semester especially, I've come back to asking myself where am I in all this mumbo jumbo? And I realized that I have learned to make some of it fit me, that I talk through it, and not the other way around, most of the time. I do believe there is a difference. But how much hard work has it been for? What price did I really pay? Why are our lives always used in phrases to do with work and money? Is that all there is?

I think not, because there's my mother in Memphis, waiting for me to come home and tell her about all I have learned, the kind of learning she couldn't get when she was young. I have to change my accent to go home, make it natural or real or Southern so she can understand me, and so I don't hurt her feelings too bad for being so distant all the time. I get to share what I have learned, the real things, the ideas that help me understand the world and how it works. To help me understand myself, maybe one day tell me where I am. Or maybe I'm the only one who can know that, on my own. Maybe where I say I want to be is where I should go.

I want to make a few comments about the two types of writing I used in this essay. They are both extremes in my writing style, in their language and voice. However, I distinctly hear or read my voice in both of these extremes. There are a multitude of voices on the continuum in between, including the one I'm using right now. Those who know me will recognize that I do not speak completely in either of the two extremes. In both cases, any vocabulary or phrasings I do not normally use were incorporated for their value to me as means of communicating more effectively and powerfully. Rest assured that nearly every word was considered with respect to as many of its possible implications as I could think of. I make no claims to total intentionality, but at least partial.

I'm sure, in reading the first part, that some of you might have been offended or felt alienated by some of the terminology or style that I used, possibly passing it off as "academic crap," with the additional irony that I was simultaneously seeming to argue against this exact type of style. I wrote this way to give further impact to my statements that I am not against academic discourse, only the fact that it's seen as the only way to communicate scholarly issues in writing. Possibly, some of the language or grammar I used in the second part was offensive or annoying to some. Maybe the abrupt split between the two styles represented more a site of mental devastation than anything else. I don't know.

One thing I can say is that my mother would be more highly offended than any academic reader would by my using some Southern rural figures of speech that she knows I damn well never used in my life, but borrowed from sources such as herself and my grandparents. At the same time, I think she would be more than appreciative of the consideration I've given these issues, and of my insistence that her language, as well as many others, has just as much of a right and a place in the exchange of knowledge. Unlike most things these days, knowledge is not something that can be owned or stored or rationed out.

NOTES

[1] My use of the term here is taken from Gramsci: Hegemony describes the situation in which the ideology (systems of beliefs) held by those in power asserts complete authority over those subordinate to it. The kind of power involved is one that is able not only to exert control, but to win and shape consent of the controlled, so that the authority is maintained and seems logical or "natural," even to those who might, from an outsider's perspective, seem to be oppressed by it. Further, all conflicts within the dominant modes of thinking and all "alternatives" are negotiated and framed within the range of the system. (Gramsci, 206–276)

WORKS CITED

Albrecht, Mark. "To the Editor." *The Council Chronicle* 2 (Nov. 1992): 17.

Gramsci, Antonio. *Selections from the Prison Notebooks.* Edited and translated by Quintion Hoare and Geoffrey Nowell Smith. New York: International, 1971.

Chapter 33

Rural Blue-Collar Identities and the Writing Process

Desirae Sweet

These days there's dudes gettin' facials, manicured, waxed and botoxed/ With deep spray-on tans and creamy lotiony hands, you can't grip a tackle box/ With all of these men linin' up to get neutered, it's hip now to be feminized/[...]/ Oh, my eyebrows ain't plucked/ There's a gun in my truck/ Oh thank God, I'm still a guy.
—Brad Paisley, "I'm Still a Guy" (2008)

Some people look down on me, but I don't give a rip/ I'll stand barefooted in my own front yard with a baby on my hip/ 'Cause I'm a redneck woman/ I ain't no high class broad/ I'm just a product of my raisin'/ And I say "hey y'all" and "yee-yaw" /[...]/ And I know all the words to every Tanya Tucker song/ So here's to all my sisters out there keepin' it country.
—Gretchen Wilson, "Redneck Woman" (2004)

The songs quoted above have both reached number one on the Billboard country charts in the past few years, as mystifying as their rigid constructions of masculinity and femininity may be to many. While it may be very tempting for some to write off the success of such media as proof of the large number of people who dwell in our country still ignorant, still unenlightened, I think the popularity of such cultural emblems merits a closer analysis of the ways in which they construct identities. Fresh off a farm, I myself experienced a sort of culture shock upon arriving at a selective liberal arts college that had a distinctly metropolitan flavor despite its bucolic surroundings.

The combination of cultural and class differences that sets these two types of communities apart can create a sense of dissonance and even inadequacy in students from rural and blue-collar backgrounds. In the following, I will examine these cultural and class differences and their potential to disrupt the writing process, manifested as discomfort with the academic discourse, exaggerated student-professor power dynamics, and exacerbated writer's block. Then I will reflect on possible means of assuaging this sort of student turmoil and ultimately attempt to offer some practical coping mechanisms.

Concepts of Class

Class is difficult to define in America today. I suspect that, like other categories of social definition, class is an ever-changing, fractured, and multifaceted concept. As Monica Bielski points out in "My Hidden Class Consciousness," the term "class" is used to describe the combination of one's wealth, level of education, skill level, and job type. (213–14) Nomenclature, hampered by the truly American fallacy that "everyone" is middle class, is one of the central difficulties in probing issues of class. Subsequently, it has even been difficult for me to pin down linguistically the segment of the American populace I want to discuss. There is in fact a plethora of labels one might affix to this American subculture, including blue-collar, working class, lower middle class, redneck, or even white trash.

Some of these terms, especially "redneck" and "white trash," have strong negative connotations and are particularly degrading when used in a purportedly objective context, from the outside—whether or not the community or individual would apply the term to itself in a spirit of underdog pride. The term "Middle America," which refers to "the middle class in the U.S., especially when regarded as a conservative political force," (Oxford) can also be perniciously misleading. It blurs the real distinctions that exist even within the so-called middle class, presenting a fictitious, monolithic majority "real America," reminiscent of the vice presidential nominee Sarah Palin's rhetoric during the election campaign of 2008. The term "working class" also seems inaccurate because it refers only to "people who are employed for wages" (Oxford) excluding farmers and all others who are self-employed.

The term that seems most apt is "blue-collar." This label describes "workers who wear work clothes or specialized protective clothing, such as miners, mechanics, etc."—people who "get their hands dirty"—as contrasted with "white-collar" workers who "work in an office or other professional environment." (Oxford) It seems that this term and its surrounding ethos resonate with people, as is evidenced by the popularity of the "Blue-Collar Comedy Tour," whose performers include Bill Engvall, Larry the Cable Guy, Ron White, and Jeff Foxworthy. In this paper, I mean to deal specifically with rural blue-collar identities, although the issues probed here will obviously have implications for blue-collar people who do not live in rural areas. For this segment of the population—rural blue-collar people—class and culture mingle to the extent that they are nearly indistinguishable from one another, producing a somewhat widely accepted set of values and symbols. This subculture has a very particular ethos, infused with all the pretension of domestic beer and country music. I am confident that related stereotypes are familiar to most, so I will not enumerate them here.

As complicated and fractured as concepts of class are, I am not quite sure how to classify myself or my family, but there are vital points of identification with this segment of American society that have shaped my self-definition and my college experience. Both of my parents hold bachelor's degrees (from state colleges), so I am not a first-generation college student. However, being from a farm family, the vast majority of adults I am familiar with from "back home" engage in occupations that involve a great deal of mechanical and physical labor, which would seem to classify them as "blue-collar." Both of my parents worked on our family farm for an extended period of time, and my dad is now an independent agricultural consultant who works as a tow truck driver during the winter to make ends meet. Nonetheless, my more fortunate grandparents paid for me to go to a private, college-preparatory, girls' Catholic school from 7th through 12th grade. Thus even my story may be used to emphasize the fractured nature of conceptions of class and to complicate the idea of class identity.

Class and Culture

This rural blue-collar culture as I have experienced it has a whole slew of associations and values that I have found are foreign and even distasteful to many of my college peers. Political conservativism, an emphasis on religious beliefs and morality in everyday life, and rural slang and colloquialisms all play an expansive role in rural blue-collar culture. Also integral to this worldview is the acceptance of largely patriarchal gender relations that, while changing slowly, continue to emphasize women's domestic and nurturing roles. (Little, 401) Each of these components is challenged—sometimes in a way that fundamentally degrades rural blue-collar culture—at my self-described "liberal" college.

An important class difference for students in particular is the view of the purpose of education. In blue-collar backgrounds, as Bielski rightly asserts, college is seen as the means of attaining a good job after graduation more than an opportunity "to study art history or anthropology." (215) Influenced in large part by economic necessity, academic discourse is often viewed as "frivolous" (Bielski, 215)—the antithesis of real-world pragmatism. Reflecting upon the instruction she received in writing at a state agricultural college with just such a view a few years ago, my cousin noted, "It was [...] a vocational-type atmosphere. They didn't care as much about your [essay] structure, just that you knew how to feed a cow." (Stokoe) This mindset about the purpose and function of education can wield a great amount of influence, as it has in my own educational journey. I have struggled continually with the worth rural culture ascribes to a technical education. During the summer following my freshman year of college, I very nearly chose to enroll at a state-funded agricultural school near home but ultimately decided to continue pursuing my liberal arts degree. This tension resounds within me still as my dad sighs, "I just want you to be able to get a good job when you graduate," exhaling a mixture of anxiety and bewilderment every time we discuss my plans (which now include graduate school in religion).

Two Worlds, Two Modes of Discourse

These points of cultural dissonance can be challenging and even debilitating for young adults trying to establish their identities as individuals as well as promising student writers because "every word, discourse, 'betrays the ideology of its speaker.'" (Parker, 148) As Miriam Axel-Lute rightly posits, "marginalized students may face, or be aware of, more personal conflicts with the dominant discourse, rather than merely intellectual disagreements." (158) Consequently, "they may be less comfortable expressing themselves in the dominant discourse." (158) In Min-zhan Lu's case, negotiating between two conflicting worlds caused her internal turmoil whenever she read or wrote. Her effort to separate the two ideologically charged discourses in which she communicated—English (the "language of the Bourgeois") and Maoist Standard Chinese ("the language of the working class")—made "writing... a dreadful chore." (443) Each mode of discourse had its own rhetoric and often diametrically opposing values.

While Min-zhan Lu's case of growing up in Communist China is undoubtedly an extreme example, her difficulty in bridging two cultural spheres and its effect on her writing process are instructive. By communicating in either discourse, a student caught between two worlds is forced to legitimize one at the expense of the other. This inner struggle can only escalate when combined with unfamiliarity with one of these modes. Students entering college from a rural or blue-collar background in particular may have had limited exposure to academic discourse, and the added complication of cultural dissonance could make writing and discussing in that academic discourse even more of a chore than it may be for their peers.

By the same token, upon returning home for breaks, I have to watch my own use of language carefully. My academically refined self usually won't let me say "ain't," but communicating in terms that are seen as too technical or flowery for a casual conversation marks me as pretentious and ridiculous, as my cousin and little sister are always quick to point out. In my home community, I have to elide some words, throw in a few key terms like "cellar" and "downtown" (referring to the Dollar General, stoplight and two gas stations in town), and use "real" as an adverb. Conversely, remarking that someone is "living high on the hog" at college would likewise render me an object of ridicule. As a result of this class and culture gap, I struggle with what will sound "appropriate" in the academic sphere, negotiating how much of my rural self I can allow in my comments and contributions, sometimes choosing my words with excruciating care—so as not to sound like a "dumb redneck." This is still a problem for me in terms of contributing to class discussions off the cuff, but in writing the conflict can be lessened a bit, if only due to the extended amount of time one is given to mull over the wording and concepts involved in a paper. Even as a junior in college, from time to time I still fear I won't sound intelligent or promising enough—as a kid only recently "off the farm"—to my professors or classmates.

Exaggerated Student-Professor Power Dynamic

Class insecurity and a more traditional sense of gender roles resulting from a small-town background can exacerbate the student-professor power dynamic. The academy, as we all know, has traditionally been the realm of the elite—those who have the intellectual and financial capacity to delay income while undergoing years of higher education. Students who come from humbler backgrounds, Bielski reminds us, can experience "real embarrassment" in the face of their more confident and privileged peers, whose parents are able to offer empathetic support during the important college and graduate school processes. (217–18) If rural blue-collar students experience "embarrassment" with their peers, it is easy to see how those students may feel outright intimidated by some of their professors, who are agents of this academy traditionally dominated by the elite.

I experienced such intimidation with one professor in particular who had been at my institution for decades. A physically imposing man whose teaching style employs little positive reinforcement, this professor terrified me with the power of his academic position as well as the exercise of what I perceived as his masculine authority. I was so intimidated by his authoritative demeanor, decades of establishment within the academy, and gruffness that the course made me feel inadequate, as if I had nothing to contribute to its academic dialogue. Very much a product of rural blue-collar America, I have found that the lingering influence of hyper-traditional gender dichotomies can be harmful. With this particular professor, I was intimidated to the point of silence in class and disillusionment with the subject matter. While I have empathized with other students who were intimidated by this professor's abrasive demeanor, I have never heard any sort of accusation of sexism against him and indeed have never felt specifically devalued by him on the basis of gender. Consequently, I am inclined to interpret the gendered aspect of my intimidation to my rural blue-collar background.

In rural communities in general, there is still a broad acceptance of stereotypical gender roles, which encompass the types of work that men and women "should" do as well as the ways in which members of each gender "should" behave. (Little, 401) In farm households in particular, even when women participate in what is seen as "men's work," they construct new gender boundaries within which to clearly distinguish themselves from their male counterparts. (Pini, 1, 8) For many, as the changing economy forces more and more family members to find work off the farm in settings where there is less of an overt distinction between men's and women's work, I suspect that this principle comes into play. One manifestation is the passivity and relative silence of women in mixed situations—whether or not they carry a formal tenor. One male head of a town board in the Ozarks described his sole female colleague as "a good ol' gal" who "pretty much jest sets there— hardly ever says nothing" (Parker, 149), alluding to the purportedly innate connection between femininity and passivity.

Although my home community is nowhere near as isolated or economi- cally depressed as the Ozarks, as a rural young woman I too have felt the pressure to defer to male authority figures such as my grandfather, father, or even my cousin's boyfriend in a broad range of situations—from practical judgments (like car repair) to accompaniment when going out at night. This nearly subconscious connection between femininity and passivity, combined with class insecurities, has at times made me feel less than comfortable contributing to class discussions. In this sense, gender can indeed be "a prestige system, a set of positions that result through processes of social evaluation in [a] community." (Parker, 149)

Exacerbated Writer's Block

Writer's block can be a manifestation of authority relations in the class- room as much as a manifestation of a writer's underdevelopment when students "are denied the authority that practicing writers usually have." (Podis and Podis, 140) In that sense, the class insecurities, cultural disso- nance, discomfort with academic discourse, and the exaggerated student- professor power dynamic described above can all contribute to writer's block. Even outside the realm of class or gender role issues, Jenny Love's survey of student writers who were also writing tutors led her to conclude that "clearly, writer's block *can* come from the feeling that we are inade- quate, unknowledgeable, and that we will be exposed, to ourselves to our readers, as 'failures.'" (Love, 146)

Axel-Lute's survey results led her to conclude that authoritarian class-room power dynamics can induce and exacerbate writer's block for students. To this I would add the caveat that such a dynamic does not have to be the sole creation of the professor. It may in fact be related to such factors as the class insecurities or patriarchal patterns and expectations I described earlier. I experienced writer's block with each assignment for the course taught by the aforementioned professor. Sadly, I never felt comfortable setting up a conference with the professor, even though he encouraged students to do so and made time in his schedule accordingly. I ended up hastily writing those papers at the last minute, awash with feelings of inadequacy.

In the Aftermath

Culture clashes and class and gender inequalities are large-scale social issues—complex and woefully persistent—for which there are no simple fixes. Min-zhan Lu cogently urges educators to encourage students to form their own readings from their interaction with both discourses and to "see themselves as responsible for forming or transforming as well as preserving the discourse they are learning." (444, 447) I, however, lack the ingenuity and insight into pedagogical issues to develop a concrete suggestion based upon her exhortation. Nevertheless, what may be more readily achieved on the individual and institutional level is an increased awareness of the issues that plague students from rural blue-collar backgrounds. This set of issues may be difficult or uncomfortable to approach since "many unconsciously embrace the American myth that everyone is middle class." (Tokarczyk, 165) Furthermore, one's social class and whether or not one hails from rural America are not as apparent as one's race, ethnicity, or gender (Bielski, 218), so these issues receive less attention. Indeed, as Tokarczyk points out, "while people will acknowledge racial or gender difference, they often are only vaguely aware of class inequality." (165) The challenges that non-minority students from blue-collar backgrounds face may not be acknowledged institutionally due to "a societal assumption that whites are not represented in the lower socioeconomic classes." (Tokarczyk, 166)

For peer writing tutors as well as professors, acknowledging that a rural blue-collar background may contribute to a student writer's difficulties can be extremely instrumental. After all, problems that student writers encounter (such as writer's block) are often spurred on by contextual factors as Axel-Lute proposes. It is important for professors as well as tutors to "be wary about making the assumption that all students are middle or upper class" (Bielski, 219) or that all students come from a metropolitan, politically liberal household. As one respondent to Bielski's survey suggested, professors and tutors should "get to know the students and their backgrounds better and realize that if a paper is written badly, it doesn't always mean that the student was lazy and didn't try." (Bielski, 219)

I sincerely wish that every rural blue-collar student who is struggling or intimidated by academia could have the sort of mentor I found the spring of my freshman year. I was lucky enough to have a professor who actually grew up in my hometown and was able to provide me with some guidance, encouragement, and much-needed perspective. However, such mentoring may be very difficult to implement on an institutional level, as students may very well feel too stigmatized to self-identify and be part of such a program of their own volition.

Rural blue-collar discourse may not be ranked alongside academic discourse in colleges, universities, and peer-reviewed journals and books, but these voices need not be entirely lost or suppressed. Those voices can still be channeled in productive and soul-nourishing ways that affirm the value of a student's background. Now whenever I go home, I cherish more than ever before the clever "redneck" banter I share with my much-loved grandpa. My educational and career trajectory may be increasingly opaque to my father, but we can still bond over the country music that speaks to the deepest yearnings of both of our beings. Indeed, listening to country music—at least for me—helps close the gap between where I come from and who I feel I am in a way that is somehow both comforting and empowering.

Although students from a rural blue-collar background do not usually stand out at first glance in a college setting, the cultural and class dissonance these students experience can produce discomfort with academic discourse, exaggerate student-professor power dynamics, and exacerbate writer's block. This counterforce to the ideally egalitarian nature of a learning environment, thorny though it is, need not be left to rage unabated. Through heightened awareness of the issues faced by students who enter highly selective liberal arts colleges from the world of rural blue-collar America and the channeling of background-specific discourse into other arenas of expression, the anxieties of this segment of student writers may be somewhat alleviated.

WORKS CITED

Axel-Lute, Miriam. "The Making of Contextual Writer's Block" *Working with Student Writers: Essays on Tutoring and Teaching*. Edited by Leonard A. Podis and JoAnne M. Podis. New York: Peter Lang, 1999: 151–168.

Bielski, Monica. "My Hidden Class Consciousness" in Podis and Podis, 213–20.

Little, Jo. "'Riding the Rural Love Train': Heterosexuality and the Rural Community." *Sociologia Ruralis* 43, (2003): 401–417.

Love, Jenny. "Learning from Writer's Block" in Podis and Podis, 143–50.

Lu, Min-zhan. "From Silence to Words: Writing as Struggle," *College English* 49 (1987): 437–48.

Oxford American Dictionary Version 1.0.2, Apple Computer, Inc., 2005.

Parker, H. Jane. "Engendering Identity(s) in a Rural Arkansas Ozark Community." *Anthropological Quarterly* 65 (1992): 148–55.

Pini, Barbara. "Farm Women: Driving Tractors and Negotiating Gender," *International Journal of Sociology of Agriculture & Food* 13 (2005): 1–18.

Podis, Leonard A., and JoAnne M. Podis, Editors. *Working with Student Writers: Essays on Tutoring and Teaching*. New York: Peter Lang, 1999.

Stokoe, Sarah Ann. Personal Email, October 29, 2008.

Tokarczyk, Michelle M. "Promises to Keep: Working-Class Students and Higher Education." *What's Class Got to Do with It? American Society in the 21ˢᵗ Century*. Edited by Michael Zweig. Ithaca, NY: Cornell University Press, 2004: 161–167.

Section Eleven

Issues of Identity and Power in the Classroom and the Academy

This section continues the conversation on identity, marginalization and empowerment, including essays that explore the relationship between race and writing and the impact of sexual orientation on composing. Since the identities involved—those of race and sexual orientation—are not unique to these authors but apply to groups in society, these explorations of self and discourse also carry larger social significance. In this section we also include two chapters that examine the marginalized position of the teaching of writing within the field of English studies and the academy at large. Often viewed as a service discipline and as the site of pedagogical activity that many consider "drudge work," composition is generally accorded second-class status in higher education. Although these two chapters focus on the situation of faculty members more than students, they have important implications for all who are committed to working with student writers. After all, it is ironic that while writing teachers, teaching assistants, and writing associates work to improve the abilities and the status of others, their own status is low. In linking essays about students working through issues of identity and marginalization with essays about faculty members working in a marginalized field, we hope to suggest that there is a connection between the circumstances of writing students seeking academic legitimacy and the circumstances of teachers and tutors who are committed to helping them.

The Articles

In "Caught Between Skin Color and Dialect: A Non-Essentialist View of Black English" (Chapter 34) Monica L. Davis challenges the assumptions regarding terms such as "Black English," which in her view only heighten social divisiveness. She uses her own experiences to illustrate what she believes to be a destructive fallacy: the essentializing of racial identity.

Growing up in a predominantly white neighborhood, she is unaware that others will assume or expect her to speak the "Black English" that she herself never uses and hears infrequently. During her college experience she finds that her attempts to "fit in" with other African-American students by adopting "their language" ultimately fail; her struggle to reconcile her identity as an African-American woman who chooses to use "standard" English forms the core of her essay. She also uses the experiences of two friends, both black, to exemplify different responses to the issues raised in considering self and language. Taken together, the three women's views illustrate the complexity—and the volatility—associated with such issues.

Rebecca Phares and David Schwam, in "Writing Inside Out: Issues of Sexual Identity in the Writing Classroom" (Chapter 35), consider whether, and to what extent, students who do not identify as heterosexual may fully participate in the writing classroom and to examine "some of what queer students face in the classroom, and how this affects the ways in which they act, write, and speak." In composing their essay, Phares and Schwam, in addition to researching their topic, interviewed nine students and circulated a questionnaire to more than a dozen others (not all of whom were queer). Theirs was not a scientific study, but rather they wished to include in their writing reactions from others and to include anecdotes beyond those they discovered in their research. Some of the specific issues emerging from Phares and Schwam's work were not, as they might have expected, a lack of any reference to queerness (although that did occur), but rather the lack of *in-depth examination* of queerness, and the essentializing of queer experience— similar issues to those raised by Monica Davis in her essay on racial identity. In classrooms where queer issues were addressed, on the other hand, students stated that the discussions often led to productive considerations of other, equally controversial subjects. They conclude by acknowledging the difficulties inherent in establishing "safe" spaces within the academy, yet they affirm that writing teachers may benefit from providing such spaces "to broaden the discourse of the classroom, both by including the queer student in the discussion and by adding to the general level of understanding and empathy of the class as a whole."

In Chapter 36, "No Voice, No Vote," Lauren Podis explores the marginalized position of composition—particularly basic writing instruction—by reviewing issues related to the status of expository writing at Oberlin College and by placing this discussion within a larger national context. Podis, a peer tutor in the Oberlin program, interviewed the long-time director of composition there (who also happened to be her father and an editor of this book). It is from this segment of her essay that the title—suggesting the disenfranchisement of writing instructors—emerges. In the second part of her chapter, Podis extends the discussion outward, citing authorities as diverse as Wayne Booth and Mike Rose to the effect that the disparagement of composition—its students and its instructors—amounts to nothing less than a national "scandal." In connecting the Oberlin situation with the national picture, Podis theorizes that the disdainful attitudes aimed at composition arise at least partially from concerns that those who work with basic writers may be "opening the floodgates" to people who "have no business" in the rarefied regions of academe. In other words, she believes that political, cultural, and socioeconomic class issues are involved.

The final article in *Working with Student Writers* (Chapter 37) is Grace Chang's "Contextualizing the Debates: A Historical View of Expository Writing." Chang, a peer tutor, originally wrote this essay in conjunction with her honors research for her English major, and it is richly documented with material from the Archives of Oberlin College. As a student member of the Expository Writing Committee during her senior year, Chang helped with the filing of the committee's request for permanent status for a composition faculty position that had been filled on a temporary basis for twelve years. As a participant in the discussions and debates conducted during this process, she had direct exposure to the issues raised, and she was able to observe for herself the various attitudes and assumptions held by members of the faculty, administration, and student body with regard to the teaching of writing at Oberlin. Based on her archival research, Chang was able to dismiss the oft-repeated belief of some faculty and administrators that permanent slots in writing at the college level are unnecessary because some day "the high schools will start doing their job":

> [As] my research in the Oberlin Archives shows, the argument being advanced that one day the high schools will finally "get it right" so the college will no longer have to assume the burden of teaching writing skills is wishful thinking. Exact echoes of this hopeful wish can be seen in historical documents from well over fifty years ago.

Questioning that the need for college composition results from poor preparation in high school, Chang observes that the need is rather "a reflection of the fact that new students (of whatever skill and preparation) need time and instruction before they can adjust to the foreign discourse communities of higher education."

With the benefit of her research perspective, Chang debunks other myths about the teaching of writing, demonstrating that the view that composition is inferior to literature is not based on any legitimate assessment of worth but is rather the result of historical and political developments. Indeed, at end of the nineteenth century, she notes, the situation was reversed: "During these early years of professionalization when the academic merits of English literature were being contested, composition, in effect, helped to legitimize the new discipline." Asserting that there is important professional and pedagogical work going forward in composition, she concludes with an exhorttion to give teachers of writing "the full professional consideration and support that they deserve."

Chapter 34

Caught Between Skin Color and Dialect: A Non-Essentialist View of Black English

Monica L. Davis

If only the world we live in was like the world we see on *Star Trek*. In the United Federation of Planets, people don't have to deal with issues such as classism, inequality, sexism, and racism. All the horrendous social ills that plague us have long since vanished in their society. They've even got Universal Translators so that everyone can speak their parent language and everyone else can understand them perfectly because the technology makes them all sound the same. I wish we had little pins we could wear on our clothing that would make everyone sound the same. Then we would not have to have debates over things such as "Black English" and "White English."

I hate those terms. They're so divisive. Their dichotomy embodies within its very existence the root of division, separation, and opposition. What is "Black English" anyway? Many books have been written by various learned individuals explaining the West African/Creole/Southern American origins of the African American vernacular, its emphasis upon body language and elision, and its usage, so I will not repeat. Instead, I will give the definition of "Black English" of my nine-year-old niece, Mallory, when I put the question to her: "It's English that black people speak." Obviously, this is a much too simplistic definition. However, it is that definition—tinged with the innocent frankness of a fourth grader—that people accept, instead of the book-length expositions given by linguists. "It's English that black people speak."

But, as Ari Jones and Kelli Lane point out in an unpublished paper written for our teaching and tutoring course, "researchers [...] cannot justifiably apply a unique label to the Black linguistic style when clearly what is implied is that those features defined as Black English are not confined to Black speech." What the writers are referencing is that linguists have discovered that numerous aspects of "Black English" have been found to be a part of the language patterns of non-blacks. However, what they don't point out is that not all black people use Black English. Instead, Ms. Jones and Ms. Lane follow the same essentialist progression of the authors of the many books they doubtless consulted in the course of writing their paper. Their suppositions are erroneously universal to all black people. For instance, they say:

> [N]o matter how well the person of color masters the "master's" language, s/he will never [be] afforded the same or total degree of power within his society. Still, many Blacks strive to master the white language for any relative power afforded them. The very phenomenon proves unique, however, for the person of color. S/He must negotiate with the two languages, depending upon the situation faced.

No, "S/He" Mustn't!

It is difficult to express in words the levels of offense and anger to which I ascended when I read that passage. I poured a great deal of it into my journal entry for the week:

> I utterly, completely, totally, wholeheartedly, and unquestionably reject the use of the term "white language" or "white English." It is not "white" English; it is English, or, if you must, it is "standard" English. That does not necessarily make it "white." To call it so only shows that [Jones and Lane] have bought hook-line-and-sinker into the bigoted tenet that "standard" and "correct" are synonymous with "white." That's total bullshit. You don't see all White people using standard English, do you? If you're silly enough to think that, I suggest you spend some time in rural America. My point is that everybody deviates from the standard no matter what color your skin happens to be.

I still think that it is flat-out wrong to refer to mainstream English as "white English." True, there is a form of English that is accepted in mainstream America as the "standard." However, it is a fallacy to believe that because what we call "standard" English is mainstreamed, it is, therefore, "white." An element of common sense seems to be lost when people equate the terms "mainstream society" and "white society." The former refers only to the prevailing direction of the activities of contemporary America. The misappropriation of the latter as analogous to the current flow of the public arises from the fact that white Americans comprise a staggering 83% of the total U.S. population and 96% of the middle class from which the mainstream gets its direction. If the demographics were reversed and black Americans made up 83% of the population, then "black society" would determine the mainstream—and standard English.[1] And, as I stated in the journal, not all white people use the standard. What kind of English, then, are they speaking, if they are white and don't use the "standard" dialect?

My other big problem with the passage from the Jones/Lane paper is the essentialization of "the black experience." They make a sweeping generalization that black people are predisposed to speaking Black English when they say that "many blacks strive to master the white language." What they seem to have forgotten is that the language one speaks is not innate. The sole basis upon which language is shaped is environment. Therefore, for example, black children will not grow up using the black vernacular unless it is a part of the everyday environment within which they function. In that case, Black English is not their parent dialect, contrary to the essentialist view.

Despite being black, when I was growing up I was only marginally exposed to Black English. My mother spoke standard English, and I had five older siblings who all spoke it as well. I went to schools where I was taught the grammar of standard English. I was addressed by my teachers in standard English. What other kind of English was I supposed to use?

I grew up in the suburbs of a major city, in a predominantly white, middle class neighborhood. I went to schools that were 90% white, and a lot of my friends were white. Hence, the language I was raised with was that of the white middle class. Most of the other black children who attended my schools didn't speak Black English, either. There were some who used the black vernacular to an extent; that is, only in a social setting, not in the classroom. However, because my social life included as many white people as black people, and because my home language did not include the Black vernacular, spending a few hours a week listening to people using Black English proved to be insufficient exposure to affect my own speech patterns.

Even though I was aware of the existence of Black English, it never occurred to me that people might expect me to use it. Amazingly, I didn't discover that until I went off to inner city Cleveland for college. Prior to this experience, I had little exposure to the city, despite living a mere forty-five minutes away. I had no way of knowing that the black people in the inner city would speak differently than I or the black people that I grew up with in the suburbs. I found out pretty quickly, though.

Before the first semester of my freshman year, I took part in the Minority Scholars Program, designed to facilitate the transition of minority students from high school to college. The participants comprised approximately twenty-five black students and two or three Latinos. We were all housed for five weeks in a single dorm. This was my first real exposure to black people outside my suburban experience. The majority of the students were from Cleveland, with a few from other large cities. Almost all used Black English heavily. Hence I, with my "white girl voice," stuck out like a sore thumb.

I have to admit that I tried to fit in. I immediately recognized that something about me was different from almost everyone else, so I started to change myself to be more like them. I tried to be "down." Therefore, I entered what I refer to now as my "gangsta" phase. I ditched my classical and soft rock tapes and started listening to rap music. I tempered my vocabulary, stopped using big words that my new friends frowned upon. The awful word "nigga" somehow insinuated itself into my vocabulary and nearly every sentence ended with the tag-on "an' shit." I don't think I had said the word "motherfucker" twice in my life before that summer, but soon I was using it as often as I would "and" or "the." I was attempting to make myself "more black" by doing all this, but it didn't work.

My "gangsta" phase lasted nearly all of the two years I attended that school and lived in Cleveland. By the end of my sophomore year, I had decided I was too unhappy to continue my education there. I left the school for a variety of academy-related reasons, but in an attempt to be totally honest here and, at long last, with myself, I should say that I also left because I knew I was a social misfit. I have remained friends with only two people of my many acquaintances from those days: Sonya and Michelle.[2] Both of them have now told me what I suspected was true all along: when I was attempting to "be black" by "acting black" and "talking black," I was like a white person trying to be black. The voice, the music, and maledictions did nothing to mask my "white" suburban upbringing. I was play-acting, and everyone knew it, so I was never really accepted. Things were said behind my back, and I was being laughed at. I was making a monumental fool of myself.

Don't I sound like the bloody victim? I wasn't really. I was young and misguided. I'm better now.

However, I would be horribly remiss if I didn't acknowledge that this less-than-pleasant experience left an indelible impression upon me. I know that it affected my views on Black English and those who speak it. I'm not saying that my experience is solely responsible for my rejection of and enmity toward Black English, but psychologically I know that I will forever associate the language with a painful and nearly humiliating experience. Still, that cannot fully explain the feelings about Black English that I expressed in the following excerpt from my teaching and tutoring class journal:

> I have to admit that even as a Black American, I consider the "Black" vernacular to be ignorant-sounding and embarrassing. Every now and then I find myself watching one of those afternoon talk shows, and inevitably there's a Black person called to speak on national television in that broken, slang-ridden, incomprehensible gibberish, and I feel the embarrassment for my whole race at what I see. I don't feel that I've given up my "Blackness" by speaking the way I do (in tone and manner as well as in language); nor do I feel that I've been brainwashed into believing that standard English is the correct way to speak.

Aside from the anger and disgust, I think I should point out two important points. First, after my initial college experience, it took me a while to accept that I am not any less black for speaking the way I do. I had to come to terms with the notion that although I am a black woman, I am also an individual, and I don't have to define myself by my race. I also learned that I don't have to "earn" my race or embrace all aspects of black culture (i.e. Black English, traditionally black music, etc.) in order to be proud of my heritage. Second, I don't think I've been brainwashed into rejecting Black English in favor of standard ("white") English. I don't buy into the "white is right" philosophy. What I do believe is that from my point of view, as with anyone, I see my parent dialect—standard English—to be correct and deviations to be incorrect, but not necessarily inferior. It's a point of contention, to be sure, given what I have said above in my journal entry. But the situation carries an element of uniqueness in that I feel that when anyone who looks like me uses Black English it reflects on me.

For instance, my best friend, Sandy, was born and raised in Southern California. She's six feet tall with long blonde hair and blue eyes. What image comes to mind from that description? Let me guess: a big-breasted, empty-headed, flaxen-haired surfer babe in a red bikini, like one of those girls on *Baywatch*. Sandy is tall and pretty and does have blonde hair, but she is also very intelligent and articulate. She resents being seen in media-based "California surfer girl" terms because that's not who she is. When I turn on my television, I often see the media's representation of a black woman and too often it's the stereotypical eye-rolling, head-swaying, loud-mouthed type with four-inch long fingernails, braids, a warm-up suit and a million pieces of gold jewelry. Or, it's a single mother with a crack baby on the news or a whore in a movie. This is what mass media is teaching non-black people to expect from black women, but that's not what I am, and I resent that the preconception is extending to me, especially since I've worked so hard to stay clear of being stereotyped.

I'm not just imagining that people expect me to act a certain way and to talk a certain way because I'm a black woman. I explained it in my journal:

> In the past, I have been criticized by other Black people for not speaking "Black" enough. I remember two such occasions. The first was when I was living in Cleveland and a girlfriend of mine (Black) had given my phone number to a friend of her new boyfriend. This guy, Tyrone, […] called me up and in the course of talking to him, he said something to the effect of "I've got to tell you that I ain't never dated no white girl before and I kinda wish Sonya woulda told me you was white." When I informed him that I am a Black person like him, it took a few minutes to convince him and finally, Sonya's boyfriend had to verify the fact for him. In another instance, I was working in a retail store in downtown Cleveland on the week-

ends. It was during the holiday season and when we answered the phone we were instructed to say "Happy Holidays from Structure. This is _____, how can I help you?" One day, a woman (Black) from the Urban League called with a complaint that she had been to the store and didn't see any minority employees. She wanted to know why the store discriminated against minorities. I told her that there were several minority employees in the store and identified myself as one of them. "You?" she said incredulously. "To what minority group do *you* belong?" To which I responded, "I'm African American." Again, this lady acted as if she didn't believe me. I suppose I should have answered the phone like this to prove I am Black: "Hey, wassup, peeps! Merry Christmas and all that fro' Structure. Dis Monica; whatchu be needin'?" In both cases, these individuals made assumptions about my race because of how I speak.

My friend, Myra, recently reminded me of another instance when this happened to me. I used to work the front desk of a local hotel with her and one day some guy called to make a reservation. He thought that he should get preferential treatment because he was a semi-regular. He tried to "sweet talk" me into giving him an expensive room at a discounted rate. "I know who you are," he said. "You're that cute blonde." I said, "No, I'm not the blonde." He tried again. "You're not? Then you must be the brunette with the pretty green eyes." I was too exasperated to even tell him that he was wrong.

To people on the other end of the telephone I don't sound like a black woman because most people already have a preconceived notion of what a black woman should sound like, which includes the use of Black English. It's an essentialized view that doesn't allow much room for individuality even though all black women do not sound the same.

Las Tres Amigas

When I was thinking about how to approach this paper, the idea came to me to include some comparisons between my speech patterns and those of other black women. But I didn't want to do it in the form of a survey with people I didn't really know. So I called my two friends from college, Sonya and Michelle, and asked them if they would be willing to help. They agreed to come down to my house for the weekend so that we could talk about Black English and our individual and collective experiences as young black women. While the weekend didn't progress as smoothly as I would have hoped, the information I gathered is extremely relevant to my own questions, anxieties, and expectations concerning my race.

Ostensibly, Sonya, Michelle, and I are very similar to one another. We are all about the same age; we all have college degrees; we are all pursuing, or intending to pursue, graduate degrees. That's where we are now; however, our backgrounds are very different.

Like me, Michelle also grew up in a suburb of Cleveland. However, she grew up in an eastern suburb, with a higher percentage of blacks, as opposed to where I live in the west. The schools she attended were more racially integrated and all of her friends were black. In addition, and most significant, Black English was spoken in her home. Michelle's parents are code-switchers. Code-switching is what linguists call the "ability to use different [dia]lects in appropriate contexts." (Hall, 201) Michelle's parents have always used the black vernacular at home, yet they switch to a more main-stream form of speech at work. Hence, Michelle does the same thing. She uses Black English when she's in a social setting, but when she's at work or in the classroom, her speech is almost exclusively standard.

In contrast, Sonya grew up in the public housing projects of inner city Cleveland. Her home language completely excluded standard English, and her social circles were comprised of only black people from her own neigh-borhood. She attended substandard inner-city schools where there was little or no emphasis on learning standard English, much less using it. So, until she started college, Sonya had very little exposure to the standard dialect. She's now in the process of earning her master's degree in social psychology. A few weeks before she visited me, she had called me and told me that her academic advisor informed her it would be wise for her to attend speech therapy to make her speech more appropriate to an academic/professional setting. The rationale was that she was going to have a difficult time getting through her master's orals with her speech so heavily laden with black vernacular. She was very upset and offended with the suggestion, so when we started talking about these issues in my bedroom over chips and beer, it was like rubbing salt in a gaping wound. The effect was explosive.

I was foolishly optimistic about how I thought our conversations would progress. I thought we'd joke our way through it. But I was wrong. Almost immediately feelings started rising to the surface that I never knew any of us had.[3] One of our very first discussions began when we were talking about using Black English in college classrooms and ended as follows:

Monica: Don't you feel, I don't know, out of place when you're talking sometimes?
Sonya: What do you mean by that?
Monica: I mean don't you think you stand out? Sound different?
Sonya: I know I don't speak standard English, Monica. But I don't think I "stand out"—you know what I'm sayin'?
Monica: But, Sonya, you're a grad student. Look at the spheres you operate in. People don't talk like that.
Sonya: So what, you tryin' to say I sound ignorant?
Michelle: She didn't say that, Sonya. Can't y'all talk for one fuckin' minute without doing this shit?

Sonya: She thinks I'm ignorant because I don't talk like a white girl from the suburbs.
Monica: Fuck you, Sonya. I can't help where I grew up.
Sonya: No, but you can help how you act.

Sonya and I were the primary participants in the majority of the intense arguments over that weekend. Sonya was constantly accusing me of "trying to be white," and I kept getting angry and defensive. Here, we had been talking about my "gangsta" phase at college.

Monica: You really think I changed that much from school?
Michelle: Well, Chipmunk, you are a little different. I think it has a lot to do with your need to fit in everywhere you go. See you're gettin' pissed. You asked, Monica, I'm just tellin' you what I think. You like to blend into the crowd, Chipmunk. You don't like to be different. You don't like to stand out. You rather operate in the grey area than the black or white.
Sonya: Yep. And you think that black and white don't matter.
Monica: You know, I asked you all to come down here to talk about Black English and help me with this fuckin' paper, not to use your half-ass psychology degrees to gang up on me.
Sonya: Why you bein' defensive? You know it's true. You like to think that you so smart that when white people look at you they don't see you[r] skin. I got news, girlie, they see BLACK no matter how white you try to be.
Michelle: Wait a minute, Sonya. I wouldn't go that far.
Sonya: I would. She rejects almost everything black. Look at that shit on her wall [referring to my autographed poster of Adrian Paul]. You like white boys now? You in denial, girl.
Monica: Keep it up, Sonya, and you can take yo' ass home. Is that black enough for you?

Throughout the whole weekend, Sonya kept backing me into a corner and I had no effective counterattack because, truth be told, I was wondering if there was an inkling of truth to what she was saying about me. Do I somehow look for validation from white people that I'm not like "the others"? Is that why I have such contempt for Black English?

Michelle, who, completely in keeping with her ability to code-switch, was trying to negotiate between diametric opposites, had a theory.

Michelle: I'm serious, Chipmunk. Your dialect is changing the more you talk.
Monica: Is it?
Michelle: Yeah. And it goes back to what I was sayin' before about you tryin' to fit in everywhere. You subconsciously manifest a new you to fit every situation. To an extent, we all do it, I guess, but this is the first time I've ever observed the actual transition between two phases, especially in you. The more Sonya and I speak to you using Black English, the more you incorporate it into your own speech patterns.

Monica: But you do it, too. You just did. You switched codes.

Michelle: I know; I do it all the time. When I'm hangin' wit my girls, I relax and talk like this. But I know when I need to use the standard.

Monica: So you do recognize a need for standard English?

Michelle: I don't know if there's a need for standard English, but I do know that there is a need for me to speak it.

Monica: In order to be taken seriously in white America?

Michelle: Probably. Yeah. White people think Black English sounds ignorant and unintelligent.

Monica: So do I.

Michelle: Why, Chipmunk? I know you grew up around mostly white people, but you knew black people, too. Why can't you see any value in it?

Monica: I'm not really sure. I think, partly, that I want to distance myself from the stigma surrounding "acting black," you know. I don't want to be associated with—

Sonya: —black people.

Michelle: Shut up, Sonya! Monica, how many foreign languages have you taken? Three? Four? Do you remember when we were taking Spanish in college and had to eat Mexican food, and read about Hispanic culture? We thought it was fun. How come you can't see Black English like any other language? You condemn it, and it's part of your own culture.

Monica: Wait a minute. There you go doin' the same thing the chicks in the paper did, essentializing. Just cause I'm black doesn't mean that Black English is a part of my culture, Michelle. I didn't grow up with that dialect in *my* household. My mom spoke standard English, so all us kids did, too.

Michelle: Okay, but Monica, you are black and Black English is a part of black culture. It's part of your roots.

Monica: So I should embrace it? No, thank you.

Michelle: You are so goddamned rigid. Not "embrace it," tolerate it. Look, I reject some aspects of black culture, too. Like I don't like to eat chitlins, but I don't look down on the people who do.

Monica: So you're sayin' that I look down on people who speak Black English?

Sonya: You do.

Monica: I think that as far as mainstream society goes, it holds black people back. We have enough obstacles in our path, since you say, Sonya, that all they see is black, the way we talk is one barrier we can remove relatively easily.

Michelle: But shouldn't we be fighting for the acceptance of all ourselves? I mean, shouldn't we demand that white America accept us from A to Z, from skin color to dialect?

Monica: In a perfect world, yeah. But we all know, even as young as we are, that shit will never happen in our lifetime. You were right, Michelle, I wanna operate in a grey area. I wanna take the best of both worlds and discard the unwanted trash.

Sonya: When it comes down to race, happy mediums don't exist, Monica.

Monica: And they never will as long as people like you perpetuate division. You're the only black in your graduate [school] class, right? So how do you think your fellow grad students view you when you talk?

Sonya: I don't give a flyin' fuck how they view me. I know what's goin' on up here. I don't need them to validate me.

Monica: Very eloquent, Sonya. How the hell do you expect to get through your orals—you need your professors to validate you. That's a part of the academy that has nothing to do with black and white.

Michelle: Except that her professors are all white.

Monica: True. So are you gonna go ahead with the speech therapy?

Sonya: No, but I'm sure if I hang around you long enough I'll learn how to talk how they want me to.

Michelle said she knows she needs to speak standard English to be taken seriously in white America. Like many white Americans, I think Black English sounds "ignorant and unintelligent." While writing this paper, I have done research that has shown me it is a valid and effective mode of communication. However, knowing that does nothing to negate my contemptuous feelings toward the black vernacular. It still sounds unrefined to my ears. I can only imagine how it sounds to the average uninformed white American.

Michelle's "need" to speak standard English is an issue of societal perception and power. In a way, Jones and Lane were right when they said that "many Blacks strive to master the white language for any relative power afforded them." While I disagree with their terminology, I have to concede their point. Eighty-three percent is a nearly insurmountable number. In this country, we live under a majority rule, and the overwhelming majority is white. In order to gain power in this society, we all have to play by white rules. As much as most of us wish things were different, they're not and they're not going to be for a long, long time.[4] Michelle, Sonya, and I are aspiring professionals, but as black women, there are racial obstacles in our path. Contrary to what some believe, being black and female doesn't guarantee smooth sailing into the upper middle class on the Affirmative Action wave. If anything, we have the greater challenge of proving ourselves because of our "inferior" sex and "inferior" race. For me, and for Michelle as well, language variation is an obstacle that is within our power to remove. But it's not about "mastering the master's language." It is about opening doors for ourselves and those who come after us. Cue the uplifting music.

I'm not a pioneer and I'm not making excuses for myself. I'm just a young, ambitious black woman trying to climb my way over the barriers that centuries worth of racism have placed in my path. Sonya says my attitude implies that I think the ends justify the means; that is, as long as I satisfy my ambitions and end up where I want to be, it doesn't matter that I've abandoned "my people" and my culture in the process. First, I think her idea of black culture and mine are incongruent, and, second, as much as I tell her that's not what I have done, she contends that she would prefer not to have to choose that road. Sonya has always had a propensity to think in all-or-nothing-at-all terms, and it is only now that she is beginning to feel a tension between her attitude and society at large. Sonya wants to hold on to every aspect of her heritage and fulfill her ambitions. I commend her for her tenacity, and I admire her and respect her for resisting the pressure to conform. However, she is in danger of derailing her career. I'm not saying that if she refuses to give up the black vernacular in her professional life, she's forever condemned to the projects, but I don't think she'll get as far as she might if she were to become a bit more mainstream. She is an intelligent young woman, but in the ears of her white professors and peers her brilliance is muted by the way she talks. Sonya is aware of this, even if she's resistant.

In her own words, Michelle says "I have conformed." She explains that she doesn't speak Black English anywhere outside her home because it doesn't sound "good enough" to use in her academic/professional spheres. As for me, in a way I didn't have to conform at all because my parent dialect is the one that is deemed "good enough." However, after forcing myself to think about the issue—and given some of the racist attitudes I have developed in regard to my own race—I'm not sure that is necessarily a good thing. But that's something I'll have to work out over time with everyone else.

In the end, it all boils down to racism. Until people can see past the color of a person's skin, language barriers will never be surmounted. If racist attitudes weren't such a large part of the American social fabric, none of this would matter. We would have a society like the one on *Star Trek*, maybe even with little Universal Translator pins. Egalitarianism would render divisions obsolete, and black, white, brown, yellow, and red would all accept each other "from skin color to dialect." Sonya could be a successful social psychologist using Black English in an upper class community, and no one would think twice about it. I would stop believing that negative racial stereotypes extended to me because those stereotypes wouldn't exist. We would all accept people for *who* they are, not *what* they are. Unfortunately, that world may never exist outside of science fiction, but it's comforting to hope things will improve. Otherwise, we're all just wasting time.

Notes

[1] The population statistics were obtained from the U.S. Census Bureau 1995/1996 Population Profiles. [Editor's note: By 2007, the percentage of white people had dropped to just under 80%. (U.S. Census Bureau, "Annual Estimates").

[2] The student names in this piece are pseudonyms.

[3] Prior to commencing our discussion, I asked Sonya and Michelle for permission to tape our conversations. They agreed. I transcribed the excerpts from our talks directly from the tapes. I should mention that I did not overly emphasize the use of Black English when I was transcribing. Given the background information on all of us, it's obvious which dialects each of us was using. Also I felt that what was said was more important than how it was said.

[4] According to the U.S. Census Bureau PopClock, the population of the U.S. as of 2:51 p.m. December 16, 1996 was 266,304,415. Of that number, 82.7% represented white Americans; 12.7% represented black Americans, while another small percentage encompassed everyone else. According to the 1995 population profile, it is estimated that the percentage of black Americans will have risen by only one-tenth of a percentage point to 12.8% by 2000. [Editor's note: As of 5:16 p.m. EST on August 19, 2009, the Census Bureau's PopClock estimate for the U.S. was 307,218,814. The July 2007 estimate of population indicates that blacks comprised 12.85 % of the total. (U.S. Census Bureau, "Annual Estimates").]

WORKS CITED

Hall, William S. "Black and White Children's Responses to Black English Vernacular and Standard English Sentences: Evidence for Code-Switching." *Black English: A Seminar*, Edited by Deborah Sears Harrison and Tom Trabasso (Hillsdale, NJ: Lawrence Erlbaum, 1976): 201–208.

U.S. Census Bureau. "U.S. and World Population Clocks." Accessed: August 19, 2009. <http://www.census.gov/main/www/popclock.html>

_____. "Annual Estimates of the Population by Sex, Race, and Hispanic Origin for the United States: April 1, 2000 to July 1, 2007." Accessed: August 19, 2009. <http://www.census.gov/popest/national/asrh/NC-EST2007-srh.html>

Chapter 35

Writing Inside Out: Issues of Sexual Identity in the Writing Classroom

Rebecca Phares
David Schwam

LIBERATION   of any sort can be PAINFUL   COSTLY
but also   EXHILARATING   FULFILLING.
My journey is CONNECTED to my sense of myself
as   TEACHER
—Christine Robinson (79)

It is only recently that sexual identity has begun to be discussed within the academy. As students and teachers start to shape this discussion, it is important to look at the many factors that influence whether or not a student decides to come out or speak on queer issues in the classroom. In this paper we seek to investigate the place of lesbian, gay, bisexual, and transgendered (LGBT) students in the writing classroom. How has the mainstream classroom been constructed to silence queer students and queer experience? What place should issues of sexual identity occupy within a multicultural classroom? What steps can be taken to bring queer experiences into the classroom? How does the traditional definition of the personal as irrelevant to intellectual work and classroom discourse affect our approach to such issues? These are some of the questions we seek to explore.

Queer Studies is a new and evolving discipline, and "the queer student" is a term that, in some ways, masks the diversity of the people it encompasses. Queer students, as we will use the term, are lesbian, gay, bisexual, or transgendered. They may or may not be closeted. The people who fit under this label include men, women, transgendered, African American, white,

Latino/a, Asian American, of different class backgrounds—in other words, very diverse. There is no one "queer experience." The people this term describes live their lives within a matrix of inseparable identities. So, as we begin this paper we want to establish that we are not writing about any monolithic "queer student." At the same time, while this term is broad, it is not devoid of meaning. In some ways, the presence of homophobia in all of our lives draws us together. This is not to say that all queer students experience homophobia in the same ways, but that we must all mediate its existence in our lives. In this paper we are trying to describe some of what queer students face in the classroom and how this affects the ways in which they act, write, and speak.

Methodology

It is not our purpose to compile statistical data or even, necessarily, to make broad generalizations. In fact, if there is one generalization we can make based on our research, it is that difference pervades the queer experience with, and the queer response to, the inclusion (or exclusion) of issues of sexual orientation in the classroom. While some students may describe similar experiences, frustrations, and revelations, it is a recognition of the diverse ways in which individual students have negotiated these situations that is the most potentially useful information to come out of our research.

For these reasons, our research methods were designed primarily to elicit personal experiences and opinions relating to the interaction between sexual identity and academic work. Our primary sources, aside from our experiences as queer students, writers, and writing associates, included (1) readings in the areas of education, composition studies, and queer theory, (2) personal interviews, and (3) questionnaires.

We conducted nine interviews in all. The subjects encompassed a fairly wide array of backgrounds. We will try to highlight these differences as we discuss individual interviews. All the subjects' names, except those of professors, have been changed in order to maintain confidentiality. One or both of us conducted the interviews, and the tone was generally conversational. We encouraged subjects to talk about their experiences in classes at Oberlin and elsewhere. We requested actual writing samples when appropriate.

We also received sixteen responses to a questionnaire that was handed out in two classes: "Teaching and Tutoring Writing Across the Disciplines" and "Lesbian, Gay, and Bisexual Issues in Language." The questionnaires presented an interesting challenge in that we distributed them in classes in which there was no expectation that even a majority of respondents would identify as queer. Questions were, therefore, geared toward more generalized notions of risk in academic writing and experiences with how queer issues have been brought up in classes, two of the areas in which we were particularly interested. It was our goal to encourage queer students to write about their experiences, though also to ask questions to which anyone could respond without much difficulty. Indeed, some of our most insightful and useful responses came from straight students. We also decided to make the somewhat controversial move of asking respondents point-blank: "Are you straight?" We did this because we felt it was information vital to our study. We were also able to justify this question because it reverses the almost universal assumption that everyone is heterosexual and that it is the special responsibility of queer students to "come out" and make their position known. Fortunately, no one responded to this question in an overtly hostile manner (though one student responded ironically, "Yes, I suppose so").

The paper we present here is a joint effort. It is a collaboration that draws on informative resources, experiences, and shared goals. However, as we have each brought our own distinct interests and perspectives into this project, we have decided to write the two main sections of the paper independently. We hope that by taking this approach, we will be able both to present a unified work of (queer) scholarship and to stress the diverse paths of inquiry in this relatively untapped area of study.

The Classroom Milieu (Rebecca)

Let us begin by looking at how some students perceive the ways in which LGBT issues are handled in the classroom setting. Several students remarked that if sexual orientation is mentioned at all, it is usually by way of homophobia being attached to a list of "-isms." James wrote about how queer experiences have been brought up in his classes:

> They have not been represented at all. If mentioned in context of discussion or reading, queer experience is attached to the long list of "isms" without any in-depth exploration or even concrete reference to events or personalities. When a specific issue concerning a specific community is discussed in context of a general discussion revolving around some philosophical question, the writing that comes forth usually treats the experience as merely another category of experience (racism/ sexism/ classism) and glosses over it.

James' comment points out how a multicultural classroom can obscure difference rather than examining the many forms of oppression that exist.

Another student, Ben, remarked that queer perspectives have been brought up in his classes:

[...] but it usually takes the form of assuming authority i.e.: "well I'm gay, so I know what Oscar Wilde's talking about in this poem. [...]" I know that sounds caddy [sic], but it's the way sexual orientation has been brought up in many of my classes, and I think this sort of use of the personal is unproductive.

The kind of comment Ben seems to be reacting to is part of the legacy of identity politics, which involves using parts of one's identity to give authority to what one says. If what Ben says is true, that people whom he has observed raising queer issues are doing nothing more than stating that their sexual orientation gives them authority, then this kind of gesture does seem fairly unproductive. However, it is interesting to contrast Ben's characterization of his classes with those of the many other students who said they had never participated in discussions of sexual orientation within the classroom nor dealt with issues of sexual orientation in academic writing.

For instance, a senior woman who describes herself as bisexual wrote of occasions where sexual identity has been brought into the classroom as "a sort of side issue. You read a book or an article dealing with queer experience and then it isn't even discussed or it is discussed briefly." In this case, though queer issues have clearly been included within the scope of the class, students and teachers have failed to engage such issues in any meaningful way. Why would students avoid talking about these subjects in the classroom? Perhaps they do not feel it is proper or appropriate. Many unspoken rules exist as to which subjects are or are not appropriate for classroom discussion. Lesbian, gay, and bisexual issues can be assumed to be inappropriate unless teachers and students work together to redefine what kind of discussion is allowed.

Kim offers another perspective on what role the inclusion of LGBT issues can have in the classroom:

In one English class, queer issues opened the door for other modes of expression. I guess what I mean is that by addressing those issues other "controversial" issues came to the fore.

While Ben noted that sexual orientation was raised to establish authority and did not further discussion, Kim describes a more substantive use of queer issues leading to the possibility of inclusion of other "controversial" issues. She gives us a glimpse of the liberatory potential of including these issues.

Michael makes a distinction between classroom reaction to sexual orientation as it is brought up on a general level and on a personal level:

Generally, when people bring up sexual orientation in a mixed group setting the tension level in the discussion goes up a notch. When someone draws attention to his/her own homo/bisexuality, it goes up maybe five notches. People [...] often don't feel comfortable with the issue, especially when they are forced to think of it as a personal one.

This phenomenon could reflect the traditional idea that the personal has little place in academic discussion. Ideas considered "objective" are privileged over those seen as "subjective," and ideas drawn from personal experience are often linked with the subjective. Personal revelations of sexual orientation are even more counter to the unspoken rules of the classroom than are more abstract statements. But, as many scholars of Expository Writing assert, the use of personal experience can often tap a depth of analysis inaccessible through more abstract or impersonal statements.

Andrea remarked that issues of sexual identity have not been brought up much, "but in the context of Women's Studies class discussion—I've heard several people address their sexual orientation there. Somehow that context is not as threatening, I think, or maybe sexual orientation issues seem more relevant there." Perhaps this is due to the links between women's studies and the women's movement in this country. While the mainstream women's movement in the U.S. has a checkered past in its treatment of lesbian and bisexual women and the issues particular to them, this is also one of the first places where lesbian issues were brought to the fore. More recently, the discussion of lesbian concerns has occurred in the context of queer studies, but for many years, they were most openly discussed in women's studies writings and classrooms.

Andrea also wrote:

Far more often than not, queer experience has been left out of classes not directly concerned with gender issues/ women's studies. The only paper that I can think of where I have addressed sexuality at all (and LGB issues as well) was for a women's studies class. Otherwise it doesn't come up and I don't bring it up. Either it doesn't feel relevant or I feel funny as a mostly straight person appropriating queer issues.

Andrea's lack of comfort with bringing up sexual orientation seems to again reflect the idea that issues of sexual orientation are personal issues that are outside the sphere of the classroom. Andrea also expressed discomfort with "appropriating queer issues." Perhaps this response is informed by the idea that one must speak only from one's own identity, a main tenet of identity politics. This vein of thought kept Andrea from perhaps opening the classroom up as a place where LGBT issues could be discussed openly.

While most students have read literature by gay, lesbian, or bisexual authors and learned of famous LGBT figures in history, the queer aspects of these lives are often specifically ignored. I can recall an English class in which the professor lectured for a full hour and fifteen minutes on the life of Gertrude Stein, never mentioning that she had long-term lesbian relationships, and even referring to Alice B. Toklas, Stein's lover, as Stein's "friend." The professor's portrayal effectively erased all queer aspects of Stein's life. If students did not have prior knowledge of her life, they could have left that lecture believing Stein to be heterosexual. It is not surprising, then, that in the discussion period of Stein's *Three Lives* later in the week, no one brought up obvious queer themes and characters in the novel. Such omissions are extremely common, even the rule.

In an interview, a sophomore women's studies major described a class in which a queer subtext was discussed, but when she mentioned that Shakespeare may have had a male lover, the professor explicitly dismissed her comment as irrelevant and outside the sphere of the class. This is another example of how defining the personal as irrelevant in the classroom can strategically erase queer history. Professors or students in English classes in which I have participated often bring up biographical information about authors. However, information related to lesbian, gay, or bisexual matters is often dismissed as merely personal. Generational differences in how we speak about queer issues may have played a role in these situations. If a concerted effort is made to break this silence, it could dissipate over time.

Enforced silence on these issues causes a stronger sense of isolation for many queer students. It also teaches students that the classroom is not a place where they can expose their identity or apply explicitly lesbian, gay, or bisexual perspectives on the subject matter. These feelings are not easily unlearned. Even in classrooms that are specifically constructed to include lesbian, gay, and bisexual issues, this factor, in addition to fear of homophobia, can work to silence queer students. This dynamic is reinforced by the "Current Traditional Paradigm" of teaching composition, which assumes that the creation of knowledge is an individual act that occurs in a social vacuum. The idea that personal experience (usually interactive) is irrelevant to the formation of knowledge helps to maintain dominant paradigms.

During a conversation with Visiting Professor of English Elizabeth Freeman, she described, in the context of Queer Studies, the manufacture of knowledge from experience as follows: "If there is a lack of theory, you have to use your own experiences to make theory." If personal experience is not seen as a valid source for academic knowledge, then such theory can be easily invalidated. Many teachers of expository writing are now calling into question the exclusion of personal experience. This process is the first step in bringing the lives of queer people into the classroom. Even in classrooms where the personal is seen as relevant, there are many barriers to LGBT students' expression of the personal.

Attempting to break the silence which has traditionally surrounded sexual orientation is not a simple task. In looking at lesbians in literature, we see some similarities to lesbian students writing today. Many early 20th century lesbian writers "coded" lesbian content into their published texts. That is to say, these writers knew that they could not write directly about these issues and wrote about them in a kind of a code. Only those who were part of the desired discourse community could decode the texts. Also, Julie Abraham, in an article on writing about lesbian writers, asserts that these writers may not have had the language to express their ideas more directly:

> [The idea that writers only avoided homosexual subject matter from fear of retribution] glosses over the more complicated and deeper effects of oppression—that the problem created by social taboo is an absence of cultural structures for conceptualizing, understanding, and representing what is forbidden, not just fear of punishment that forces silence. (264)

Because their own history and identity has been strategically hidden from many queer students, they may not have the words to effectively describe their experiences or articulate ideas about being queer. In this way they are similar to writers who wrote in the early part of the century. While there is a lesbian, gay, and bisexual discourse community, many queer students may be just coming out, closeted, or be otherwise isolated from this community. They may lack the tools to talk about or write about their experiences because of the silence that often surrounds such experiences.

While writing for an audience has significant implications for what a queer student will write about his or her life, many students can find writing for themselves to be a useful tactic in clarifying feelings and stating what cannot be freely stated elsewhere. My own experience [Rebecca's] provides an example of how writing can be a liberatory experience for queer students. Early in my high school career I was taught many of the techniques and strategies extolled by New Paradigm composition professors. I learned to freewrite, and this tactic made me much more comfortable with writing in general. During my junior year of high school, I took a creative writing class in which I found these freewriting techniques to be quite useful. Soon I found myself writing love poems about women. I was quite surprised at this as I had not yet come out to myself. Before I gave the poems to my teacher, I changed the gender of the women I wrote about, but writing these poems helped me to realize what I had been hiding from myself, that I was attracted to women. I came out to myself in writing. For me, coming out to myself, while it was a difficult process, eventually had an extremely positive effect on my mental health. Thus, I found the technique of freewriting to be liberatory, even though I censored myself because of perceived homophobia.

It must be acknowledged that queer students have the opportunity to hide their identity, which is a choice many other historically oppressed groups do not have. Edwards, Myers, and Toy describe the predicament of many queer students. While such students have the choice of "passing" and avoiding some forms of oppression, this choice can have significant ramifications:

> Thus, concealment of one's homosexuality can serve as a refuge that others, particularly most people of color, lack. However, choosing to remain invisible brings its own stresses. Being forced to compromise one's integrity by misinterpretation, withholding information, or manipulating language to hide one's sexual identity and intimate relationships often results in self-hatred, alienation, suicidal depression, substance abuse, and physiological impairment. (251)

The ability to hide sexual orientation can clearly be a double-edged sword. Queer students can choose to blend into the classroom and never bring their particular perspective into it. This choice, however, has significance both for students who make it and students who never have the opportunity to hear this perspective.

Many people espouse the idea that while it is fine for someone to be lesbian, gay, or bisexual, "what someone does in the bedroom is their own business, but it should stay there." This ignores the reality that queer people do not have the option of cordoning off issues pertaining to their sexuality. These issues spill over into the workplace, the courtroom, and the classroom. In some ways this cordoning off of lesbian, gay, and bisexual issues, and the fight within various discourses to resist this, echoes the battle many feminists fought to declare the personal as political. Sexual identity is inherently a personal issue, but how can it help but become political when in some states, what queer people do in their bedrooms is still considered to be illegal? The religious right certainly considers queer issues to be political issues, and to avoid facing up to this fact is to ignore a very real war that is being waged in the American political and religious arena today. In a climate in which our lives as queer people are at stake in so many ways, the issues we face and the heterosexism that pervades our society must be recognized and discussed outside of the bedroom. Silence is not neutrality. As queer people have known for many years, silence can be stifling, painful, and dangerous.

Silence can also cause a kind of invisibility that is especially damaging to young queer people struggling to find a place where they can be accepted. These young people are searching for voices that will speak out against the many hateful messages that often go unchallenged in the hegemonic discourses of the church, the classroom, and the family. Unfortunately, queer youth commit suicide at rates far higher than their heterosexual counterparts, and these young people are often students. How could these students' lives be improved if they knew that they were not alone, if they had positive images of the lesbian, gay, and bisexual people who came before them?

The classroom is too often defined as a space in which LGBT students and teachers are expected to be silent about their experiences, in which queer political issues are deemed irrelevant, and in which lesbian, gay, and bisexual biographical information about authors and historical subjects is excluded. It is important to explore the ramifications of this silence in the lives of students and teachers.

Contemplating the Gulf (David)

For lesbian, gay, and bisexual students, the choice to come out in academic writing or class discussion can be extremely daunting. While the goal of such a choice may be to affirm a position of authority or construct a more authentic and honest identity within the classroom, the result is often the opposite: negation of all other facets of identity, mistrust, even the threat of verbal or physical harassment. This paradox leads naturally to a question: given the pervasive violence and prejudice against LGBT people in our society, is it ever really possible to construct a classroom that is truly "inclusive" or "safe" for queer students?

Risk is, after all, a combination of perceived and actual danger. While it is unlikely that queer students at Oberlin College would be harassed or punished for simply divulging their sexual orientation in a class, it is also important to remember that such students have probably had a wide range of experiences with homophobia before coming to Oberlin (and I am not suggesting that Oberlin is free of homophobia). If we haven't all experienced direct verbal or physical abuse because of our sexual orientation, we surely have all overheard the jokes and slurs against gays and lesbians that are part of the everyday discourse of school cafeterias and locker rooms. We have become almost deaf to the damning words of religious leaders and politicians. And we are all familiar with the stony silence that surrounds queer issues in virtually all mainstream classrooms.

In *One Teacher in Ten*, an anthology of gay and lesbian teachers' personal narratives, Kevin Jennings describes the impact of an early brush with homophobia in a junior high gym class:

> Mr. Hooker stopped in midsentence, fixed his gaze on me, and said very slowly and clearly, "stop looking at his legs."

As my classmates [...] turned to look at me amidst the dead silence of the wrestling room, I felt as if a stake had been driven through my heart. A few moments of silence passed, and Mr. Hooker then went back to his lecture.

I never went back to being the same person I was before that moment. I never played on an organized school team again from that day forward, even though playing sports was (and is) a source of great joy for me. I never again felt like I belonged at school. I never forgot Mr. Hooker. (20)

The frequency of such paralysis-inflicting experiences among queer students is frightening. The scars they leave behind are largely interior and, therefore, often overlooked. What teachers might construe as shyness or apathy on the part of the student might actually be a kind of defense mechanism: the results of an experience like the one described above.

Common modes of pedagogical intervention must also be reconsidered in light of the queer experience in the academy. Ellen Louise Hart, in her article "Literacy and the Lesbian/Gay Learner," aptly points out that expressivists such as Peter Elbow, when expounding on the liberatory function of freewriting, fail to take into account the case of the writing student who is in the closet. The potential of freewriting cannot be overstated in any discussion of a New Paradigm approach to teaching writing. However, for this student, the threat of having to share one's freewrite with the class—which Elbow describes as the "essential human act at the heart of writing" (33 in Hart)—prevents the writing from ever truly being "free." Jan Cooper, who teaches a queer studies-oriented composition class at Oberlin, lends credence to this assertion when she speaks about a sort of non-specific writer's block she has observed among many of her queer students. Clearly, the obstacles facing queer student writers go beyond the dilemma of writing about sexuality.

Most experienced queer writers have at some time or another had to come up with highly creative ways of negotiating and skirting around a direct approach to issues of sexuality—while at the same time attempting not to compromise their unique points of view. One bisexual religion major has consistently chosen topics that deal with "gender and the nature of love." "My goal is to work on the prof slowly," he says of his unstated, though omnipresent goal of shifting the "natural paradigms" of his discipline. A lesbian math major recounts a series of "issue" papers she wrote for a high school government class focusing on topics such as same-sex marriage and domestic violence in the lesbian community.

In certain ways, these examples seem to highlight the creativity and adaptability required of the queer writer in the straight classroom; however, they also lead us to speculate on what the writing might have been had it not been so carefully excised from the realm of the personal. What new directions might have been pursued and what discoveries made? What was left out for fear of exposing too much? Hart puts her finger on the problem when she states, "specificity is at the root of critical thinking." (36) This is not to say that all writing about sexual orientation should contain or would even benefit from the inclusion of the author's personal experiences. Rather, I am suggesting that, while most forms of academic writing are, by convention, not explicitly *autobiographical*, most writing on issues of sexual orientation is inherently *personal*. At the time of our interview, the math major mentioned above, now out of the closet, was grappling with whether or not to write her final paper for "Popular Piety and Christianity" on gays and lesbians in the bible. Even though the paper would be firmly grounded in traditional methods of academic research, she still felt it would be a major risk to bring such issues into a classroom which, if not outwardly hostile to her way of life, is at least politically/morally ambiguous.

The enforced denial of one's personal experience or way of life is what queer students must deal with over and over again, both inside and outside the classroom. Peter Elbow is correct when he writes, "in *using a discourse* we are also tacitly teaching a version of reality and the student's place and mode of operation in it. In particular we are affirming a set of social and authority relations." (146) The fact is that the discourse of the academy is by and large a heterosexual one. And for students to operate within that discourse, they must, if not explicitly hide their sexuality, be quiet enough about it that no one would assume they were challenging heterosexual norms.

A senior sociology major describes an experience he had while participating in the Oberlin-in-London Program. As the "resident gay" in an intensive discussion class about racism and other forms of discrimination, he felt the need to speak up in almost every class about discrimination against queer people. One particular student began "rolling her eyes" whenever he would make such comments, as if to say, "Don't you have anything *else* to talk about?" This made him uncomfortable, and eventually he began to censor himself in class. One student in the "Lesbian, Gay, and Bisexual Issues in Language" class responded on a questionnaire: "It feels like the Queer experience has consumed our class—to the point that the heterosexual [...] has little room left to speak." To me, this statement is more than a little ironic, especially considering how many classes are consumed by the heterosexual experience and how rarely the queer student is given room to speak at all.

More than anything else, however, this example illustrates the unfeasibility of the "classroom as safe space" for queer students. Even in the context of a queer studies course, even though the student who made the statement wouldn't likely fit anyone's stereotype of what a homophobe looks like, it can only be read as an assertion of the student's very real heterosexual privilege. The basis of queer studies as a discipline is, arguably, rooted more in making sense of homophobia than it is in making sense of same-sex love. How is it possible, then, both to acknowledge the pervasive homophobia that exists in society at large (and among almost any given group of students) and, at the same time, to actively combat it in the classroom? If we don't have safe spaces, what are we left with?

In "Arts of the Contact Zone," Mary Louise Pratt defines contact zones as "social spaces where cultures meet, clash, and grapple with each other, often in contexts of highly asymmetrical relations of power [...]" (34) Students who are out as lesbian, gay, or bisexual inevitably find themselves in the midst of just such contact zones. If handled correctly, the teacher can use such situations to broaden the discourse of the classroom, both by including queer students in the discussion and by adding to the general level of understanding and empathy of the class overall. However, the question remains: what constitutes *correct handling*?

There is, of course, more than one answer to this question. One student said simply that for him the ideal class is one in which the professor has the attitude, "This is me and whoever you are is fine." There seemed to be a general feeling that an atmosphere which fosters open-mindedness and free expression is preferable to one in which any opinions, even controversial ones, are explicitly censored. One sophomore lesbian who took Jan Cooper's LGB "Issues in Language" class her first semester at Oberlin was impressed when Cooper made her own heterosexuality known on the first day of class. This seemed to imply, like a *Se Habla Español* sign displayed in a store window, that *sexual orientation is discussed here*. This made the student much less anxious about coming out herself. No longer did she have to wait for the opportune moment that might never come. Elizabeth Freeman takes a more casual attitude, often using her own life as a case study in class discussions ("So I had this girlfriend ..."). Freeman also echoes the sentiment that any discussion of identity should be an inclusive discussion: "White people can talk about race because they have to; straight people can talk about sexuality because they have one."

The first time I [David] came out in any academic context was in a paper I wrote for "Gender, Race, and Language," a composition class taught by Wendy Hesford. I think I did this not because it felt like a particularly "safe" environment (though I knew from the readings and films in class that I would not be condemned for coming out). I did it because I felt it was a step I needed to take in order to raise my writing to a higher level. How was I to write effective autobiography without integrating into it this essential part of my being?

Another student who was in the class with me and who was also interviewed for this paper took an even bigger risk by having an essay she wrote about a personal experience with homophobia workshopped in class (a class, I might add, which was quite heterogeneous as to sexual, ethnic, and political identity). The essay begins:

> One Friday night, my partner and I went for a walk through Tappan Square. We decided to head towards the Apollo theater to see what was playing that night. We were holding hands like we normally do in the safe, comfortable environment of the Oberlin campus. In a flash a car whizzed by and we heard, "DYKE," screamed by young males. Immediately Erin and I tensed up, and there was now a foot of space and tension between us when there used to be none.

She goes on to observe how "unsafe" Oberlin actually is and how the level of diversity within a community cannot necessarily be equated with the level of tolerance. The discussion that ensued was an eye-opening experience for everyone involved. Certain students disagreed (vociferously) with her assessment of the Oberlin community. Others shared similar experiences with harassment based on stereotypes and social stigmas. The professor acted mainly as a discussant and only rarely as a facilitator or referee. If not always comfortable, the discussion was productive in that the author came away with many suggestions for an effective revision (ostensibly, the primary purpose of the workshop), and the class was given the opportunity to delve into the very sorts of issues which, as we have argued, have for so long been silenced. For me, this experience highlighted the tremendous potential of coming out in an academic setting: for the writer, for other queer students in class, and for the learning process in general.

Afterword

When we began thinking about this project, we wanted to explore how being queer affects writing and, more specifically, writer's block. In doing our research and writing the paper, however, we realized how little information there is on the particular aspects of queer students in the classroom, especially the writing classroom. Hopefully, with the advent of queer studies, more research will be done in this area. As a result of this lack of published resources, we ended up doing a more general exploration. This led us to the conclusion that a liberatory pedagogy must be informed by issues specific to queer students. Thus, it follows that teachers and tutors should be aware of these issues, especially as students start coming out earlier and earlier in their educational careers.

WORKS CITED

Abraham, Julie. "History as Explanation: Writing About Lesbian Writing, or 'Are Girls Necessary?'" *Left Politics and the Literary Profession*. Edited by Lennard J. Davis and M. Bella Mirabella. New York: Columbia University Press, 1990: 254–84.

Edwards, Billie L., Patricia Myers, and Jim Toy. "Combating Homophobia Through Education." *Multicultural Teaching in the University*. Edited by David Schoem et al. Westport, CT: Praeger, 1993: 249–59.

Elbow, Peter. "Reflections on Academic Discourse: How It Relates to Freshmen and Colleagues." *College English* 53 (1991): 135–55.

Hart, Ellen Louise. "Literacy and the Lesbian/Gay Learner." *The Lesbian in Front of the Classroom*. Edited by Sarah Hope Parmeter and Irene Reti. Santa Cruz: HerBooks, 1988: 30–43.

Jennings, Kevin. "I Remember." *One Teacher in Ten: Gay and Lesbian Educators Tell Their Stories*. Edited by Kevin Jennings. Boston: Alyson, 1994: 19–28.

Pratt, Mary Louise. "Arts of the Contact Zone." *Profession 91*. New York: MLA, 1991: 33–40.

Robinson, Christine. "You Can't Tell by Looking at Me." *One Teacher in Ten: Gay and Lesbian Educators Tell Their Stories*. Edited by Kevin Jennings. Boston: Alyson, 1994: 78–85.

Chapter 36

No Voice, No Vote:
The Politics of Basic Writing

Lauren Podis

Looking back on my childhood, I have come to realize that many of my experiences were somewhat abnormal compared to those of my peers. Both of my parents are educators at the college level, and this fact has colored almost all of my memories. Instead of playgroups, during the summers I was schlepped to the office with my father. While he compiled reports and syllabi, I would draw on blackboards or pester his colleagues who happened to be in. Spring or winter breaks did not mean family trips to Florida, but a journey to whatever city the MLA or CCCC had chosen as a conference site. I have spent hours running through the hallways of various Westins and Hiltons or sitting in the back of Carnegie rooms reading Laura Ingalls Wilder while the grown-ups slugged it out over discourse communities and paradigm shifts. This all seemed normal to me, and I seldom thought much about what my parents did unless it was brought up by others. Even then, not much contemplation on their profession was sparked, as the subject was usually broached very specifically, e.g.: "Boy, English must be your favorite subject!" or "Good writing must be in your genes!" or, my favorite, "I'll bet you have to watch how you talk when you're at home!" More recently, however, I have become increasingly interested in my parents' positions both as teachers and as advocates of progressive basic writing curricula.

Although I certainly didn't think about it at the time, those years spent sitting quietly in conference halls and hearing my parents discuss a never-ending array of work-related woes over the dinner table wound up having a profound effect on me. From my experience, which is by no means vast or complete, I have gleaned two things: first, that expository writing programs are of vital importance, and second, more often than not, they "don't get no respect." Although performing a great service to a large number of students, programs that serve basic writers are often looked upon with suspicion and the professors who teach them seen as somehow sullied by working in a more applied discipline. In this paper I'd like to explore why these beliefs hold and take a look at the complex social and political underpinnings of courses that travel under the name of "basic" or "expository" writing.

For a lesson in the politics of basic writing, I turned to my father, Professor Len Podis, who has been with Oberlin since 1975 and was one of those who oversaw the creation of the Expository Writing Department. Len started out teaching Developmental Writing, which was administered under the Equal Opportunity Program (EOP) and intended to replace a required composition course that had been phased out in 1972. The position was renewed on a year-to-year basis without faculty rank and was seen as carrying little status. Indeed, before starting out Len was warned that the previous hire had felt so mistreated that she went to the President's office to complain nearly every day and after being fired was escorted to the campus border by college security officers. Although the veracity of the story was never ascertained, it made him consider seriously the commandment he had received from his dean to "not make waves." Since the EOP program was viewed with some suspicion by the faculty at large, he was "lent" to the English Department to teach composition classes as a way of making the program seem less alien and threatening. Adding insult to injury, he found that in College faculty meetings he had only a "voice" and no vote. (Still, his position was better than that of a fellow EOP instructor, who was dismayed to discover that in meetings he, for some reason fathomable only to the powers that be, had been accorded neither voice nor vote.)

After the idea of a separate writing program was suggested, it took eight years of committee work (1976–1984) before the Expository Writing Program was established. Originally, the only tenured position was Len's—it would take more than another decade for both of the other two positions to become permanent, although an estimated 15 to 20% of any given class at Oberlin will at some point take an expository writing course. Basically, the Expository Writing Program has had to fight for every concession granted by the administration. Even though the program has a good reputation among students and is generally deemed useful by the faculty, there is still an innate bias towards its existence.[1]

Unfortunately, Oberlin is not an isolated case. It would appear that, in general, institutions regard composition as necessary but view it as "intellectually second-class." (Rose, "Language." 342) The often shabby treatment of writing professors underscores this attitude. In addition to having to constantly defend the existence of their programs, writing instructors find themselves, like Len and the unfortunate EOP colleague mentioned above, robbed of a voice. They often must endure such conditions as lower pay, part-time or temporary status, and larger-than-average course loads, and they may be given little (if any) say in faculty issues. According to Mike Rose, "The people who teach writing are more often than not temporary hires; their courses are robbed of curricular continuity and of the status that comes with tenured faculty involvement." ("Language," 342)

Calling this marginalization of composition teachers "the worst scandal in higher education today" (Booth, 57), critic, professor, and essayist Wayne Booth offers support for his point with this quote from a former student working two part-time composition jobs:

> I have no office, no telephone [...] at one place I do not even have a place to hang my coat. I am not a groaner by nature [...] but I groan because I am a professional, an experienced professional [...] and I have no voice, no rights, no benefits [...] I have no right to speak. I am specifically excluded from faculty meetings at one college and only politely informed of meetings at the other. (Booth, 58)

Indeed, the situation was thought serious enough on a national level that in 1987 the Wyoming Conference Resolution was drafted and later passed. A response to the widespread unequal treatment of composition teachers, the Wyoming resolution unequivocally states its opposition to the unfairness of the salaries and working conditions of writing teachers at the post-secondary level. Furthermore, the resolution goes on to propose formulation of professional standards for post-secondary teachers and advocates the establishment of procedures for hearing and acting on grievances brought by teachers against institutions that fail to comply with them. Although this was an important step, old habits die hard, and it is yet to be seen whether the resolution will have any long-term, far-reaching effects on practices that seem to be firmly entrenched.

All of this begs a fairly obvious question: why is such a bias present in the first place? In my mind the most salient reason for distrust towards basic writing programs is the idea of remediation that they seem to imply, one which strikes a chord with the public. Within the past few decades the mass media and various political jeremiads have been ringing alarm bells and screaming to anyone who will listen that American education at every level is, pardon my bluntness, going down the shitter. According to such reports as *A Nation at Risk* and *Newsweek's* landmark piece of alarmism, "Why Johnny Can't Read," and more recent books such as *The Closing of the American Mind*, we as a nation are heading towards mass illiteracy or at least towards a population who couldn't identify a split infinitive if hit over the head with one. The presence of basic writing programs at the college level ties in with such national hysteria. If secondary schools were doing their job, such courses wouldn't be necessary, or so conventional wisdom seems to go.

A new and disturbing idea that these classes are keeping "unfit" students in school has emerged out of such doomsday rhetoric, and this outlook is manifested in the academy through a marginalization of composition as a discipline and the labeling of students who take advantage of it as deficient. Even in situations where such programs are tolerated, it appears that some within the academy perceive them as a temporary burden—something that can be phased out when our national literacy crisis is solved. According to Mike Rose, head of UCLA's Writing Program, such a mindset "keeps writing instruction at the periphery of the curriculum." (Rose, "Language," 341) He mentions that students in UCLA's basic English A are disparagingly referred to by one dean as "the truly illiterate among us" (Rose, *Lives*, 2), and it seems to be an unfortunate but inescapable fact that this is not an uncommon perception. Of course, as Rose makes clear in *Lives on the Boundary*, such dire predictions about the abilities of students and the state of education have been around for a long time, but the frenzied tone of the prophecies seems to have increased in recent decades.

Another reason for the distrust of basic writing programs is the perceived split between the lofty pursuit of literary criticism and theory and the more applied (and hence barbaric) field of composition. Although composition is rife with weighty theory of its own (see James Berlin or Paulo Freire, for example), this fact is usually ignored, and composition classes are perceived as the university equivalent of vocational education. This rather odd notion seems to stem from the belief that writing is a skill or tool—a means to an end, not the end itself. It is "something one develops and refines and completes in order to take on the higher-order demands of purer thought. [...] It is absolutely necessary but remains second-class." (Rose, "Language," 347)

Though there was once a time when I would have dismissed notions of the "ivory tower" as anti-intellectualism, it would appear that such a designation is not altogether uncharitable. As Rose argues, one of the reasons why the field of composition is looked upon with suspicion is because it has immediate, real-life application. Paula Johnson goes further with the literature-versus-composition argument, saying that:

> Literary scholarship does not strive to effect anything, except maybe an advancement in academic rank for the scholar. Composition research, on the other hand, tries to do something to what it studies. The social analogue is plain: the leisured elite and the rude mechanicals. (Johnson, 15)

While Johnson may come down a bit hard on the field of literary studies, her frustration is understandable. Her assessment of the situation is correct, and it is unbelievably disheartening to see a field from which so much vital theory (educational or otherwise) is emerging be treated as a necessary evil that many would like to see phased out.

All of these negative statements concerning the need for basic writing programs are disturbing in and of themselves; however, when one begins to unpack what is behind them, they become even more so. Although this may sound melodramatic, what I have seen, heard, and read leads me to believe that much of the controversy surrounding the issue stems from the fact that such programs are seen as serving students who are believed by some to have no place in a traditionally-defined academy—non-native speakers, students of color, students from different socioeconomic backgrounds, mature students, etc. Following this line of reasoning, the next part of the argument would seem to be that such students are hogging more than their fair share of academic resources. If they truly belonged in the university in the first place, then they would not need such frills as writing centers and peer tutors. Therefore, these students are obviously unfit, and "remedial" programs are keeping "undesirables" in positions that could be occupied by abler, more deserving students. Clearly, this is nonsense based on age-old prejudices which seem to be alive and well in academia, supposedly a bastion of free thought. As Rose puts it, "Class and culture erect boundaries that hinder our vision [...] and encourage the designation of otherness, difference, deficiency." (Rose, *Lives*, 205)

Another reason that Expository Writing programs are viewed with suspicion and outright hostility is that their goals and methods often present a challenge to traditional ways of teaching. "What we [the Oberlin program] are doing is working against the myth of English as elitist grammar study, and that upsets a lot of people," says Len Podis. With an emphasis on such ideas as the importance of collaborative learning and empowerment through control of one's own ideas, the New Paradigm-styled writing class is a radical departure from traditional pedagogy and is hence perceived as a threat by some segments of the academy. While certain ideas are becoming gradually more accepted in the writing classroom and even other disciplines, such as the sciences, for the most part traditional pedagogy prevails. Process over product, error as a necessary and healthy part of writing well, the idea that anyone can become a competent writer—all of these New Paradigm tenets represent a way of teaching that could potentially open the academy to a larger and more diverse group of students than ever before and a curriculum which would no longer "blind us to the true difficulties and inequities in the ways we educate our children." (Rose, *Lives*, 7) In order for this to happen, writing programs must be viewed as a permanent, viable part of the academy instead of a stop-gap measure to ferret out deficiency, and writing instructors must be given the benefits of tenure and influence that their colleagues in other departments enjoy. But until the theory coming out of composition studies is given the consideration it demands and professors in the field are taken seriously and given the respect they deserve, basic writing will not progress out of the academic ghetto that has been constructed for it.

NOTES

[1] In 2005, the Expository Writing Program at Oberlin College became the Rhetoric and Composition Department. [Editor's note]

WORKS CITED

Booth, Wayne. "'LITCOMP': Some Rhetoric Addressed to Cryptorhetoricians about a Rhetorical Solution to a Rhetorical Problem." *Composition and Literature: Bridging the Gap*. Edited by Winifred Bryan Horner. Chicago: University of Chicago Press, 1983: 57–80.

Johnson, Paula. "Writing Programs and the English Department." *Profession 80*. New York: Modern Language Association, 1980.

Rose, Mike. "The Language of Exclusion: Writing Instruction at the University." *College English* 47 (1985): 341–359.

_____. *Lives on the Boundary*. New York: Penguin, 1990.

Chapter 37

Contextualizing the Debates:
A Historical View of Expository Writing

Grace Chang

At Oberlin College the Expository Writing Program was instituted in 1984 as an entity separate from the English Department, which had historically taught the bulk of composition courses. In the program's founding legislation, the college faculty stipulated that the program would have a minimum of four FTEs (full-time equivalents)—three in the program and one contributed by the English Department in recognition of its historical role in teaching writing. Despite the force of this legislation, the college was for many years reluctant to provide full and stable staffing for the Program. It was only in 1989, five years after its inception and after much struggle, that the Program attained the level of two permanent FTEs. The third FTE was not made permanent until 1996, twelve years after the original legislation.[1]

The College's reluctance to stabilize staffing for so many years appears to have been rooted not in financial reasons, but in prejudicial assumptions about the academic merits of composition by the larger faculty. Despite much respect for the program by external evaluators and many faculty and students alike, there has persisted a suspicious attitude toward Expository Writing in the College as a whole. Even though the College established the Program as a way of ensuring certain general education services, ironically enough, it is devalued precisely because it is viewed as a service program.

This devaluation has occurred due to an inherent structural conflict within the college between its professional and service claims. Even as the college maintains its commitment to teaching, it also esteems and rewards professionalism over teaching. General education teaching is considered to be less professional and, consequently, is equated with remediation. Because the expository writing faculty serve writing across the curriculum for the College, they are not often seen as true research scholars and thus are accorded less professional status than faculty in other more self-consciously specialized disciplines. The subject matter is dismissed as remediation and the staff regarded as second-class citizens.

Even as the Expository Writing Program has been devalued because it is viewed as less specialized and less scholarly than other departments, there is, paradoxically, a resistance on the part of the college to let it become more specialized. Expository Writing is one of the very few (if not the only) curricular units discouraged from developing advanced courses or a major. This may be due to a general fear that advanced courses will impair or detract from the service functions of the Expository Writing Program. Ironically, the Program has continually been asked to reassure the College that it will not teach advanced courses at the expense of the basic writing courses, at the same time that it is intellectually disregarded for not doing so.[2]

Since the teaching of composition has generally been seen as remedial, the reluctance to support full staffing was premised on the hope that high schools would "finally bring students up to date," thereby eliminating the need for more faculty.[3] There has been, in other words, little willingness or desire to maintain the teaching of expository writing for its intrinsic value. The new pedagogy and theory in expository writing are little acknowledged, and composition is regarded primarily as a skill rather than a demanding intellectual mode of inquiry. Despite new theoretical developments in composition, there exists a belief that the proper place for teaching writing is in high school, and that expository writing in college is a form of remediation.

But as my research in the Oberlin Archives shows, the argument being advanced—that one day the high schools will finally "get it right" so the College will no longer have to assume the burden of teaching writing—is wishful thinking. Exact echoes of this wish can be seen in historical documents from well over fifty years ago, as the following excerpt from minutes of the English Department (May 11, 1944) shows: "The high schools should be somehow held responsible for teaching English Composition." Obviously the high schools have not been "getting it right," for some time now, and the need to improve student writing at the college level is not a temporary problem that will magically disappear one day when the high schools miraculously improve. Since its earliest days, the college has *always* found student writing to be unsatisfactory.

> We have gone too long upon the assumption that because students were admitted to college, they must know the elements of composition. The fact is that, for whatever reason, many of them do not, and we propose to teach them those elements or confess that there are students who cannot be taught to write. (Oberlin College Annual Report, 1912–1913)

In composition the department still lays its strongest emphasis upon accurate writing, a course thrust upon it by the inadequate preparation of at least a third of its students. The general level of writing in the college is growing constantly higher, but every now and then there is something like illiteracy in upper classmen that seems to call for desperate measures. (Oberlin College Annual Report, 1928–1929)

Contesting the notion that the high schools have simply failed to meet their obligations, composition theorists consider it inevitable that institutions of higher education will find the writing of new initiates to be unsatisfactory because the discourse communities of college are quite different from those of high school. Not surprisingly, new students are often unable to begin writing at the level desired by faculty within a given specialized discipline. Sometimes, this may be in part due to a lack of preparation, for whatever reasons. But just as often, it is a reflection of the fact that new students (of whatever skill and preparation) need time and instruction before they can adjust to the "alien" discourse communities of higher education.

Because professors are already working within the discourse of a particular discipline and usually have been doing so for some time, it can be hard for them to realize just how jarring and intimidating their specialized discourse appears to someone unfamiliar with it. As the historical documents indicate, whether or not the high schools significantly improve, there is always going to be an institutional need for writing courses to help high school students make the transition to college writing. As one student put it, "High school writing is just different from college writing."

Even in 1963, when the Introductory English Composition requirement was abolished at Oberlin, ostensibly because student writing had improved dramatically, there was an overall uneasiness on the part of the general faculty that student writing was not completely up to par and could use further improvement. In fact, the requirement was abolished not because student writing had suddenly improved, but because of pressures from the English department to be freed of their service duties to the College. The detrimental consequences of abolishing the composition requirement, however, became readily obvious over the years as the quality of student papers declined. And in 1984, as I have detailed above, the college created a separate Expository Writing Program independent of the English department, as a way of protecting its service interests even while paradoxically requiring the English department to contribute one FTE to maintain the program.

In the rest of this chapter, I would like to clarify the contemporary debates about the status of expository writing by contextualizing these debates within the backdrop of institutional history. I will be examining the relationship between Expository Writing and English on two levels: (1) the theoretical overlap in the two disciplines in terms of subject matter and pedagogy and (2) the bureaucratic relationship between the two departments.

Before the Industrial Revolution, when the contingent of students going on to higher education consisted of the wealthy gentry and would-be theologians, the primary mission of American colleges was to cultivate and enlighten gentlemen. In many ways, the traditional college, with its Classical humanist "liberal studies" curriculum, was defined in opposition to the market place; pre-professionalism was openly scorned, and students were not trained for a vocation. Everyone took the same course of study, and there were no divisions between what we now consider to be separate disciplines. Professors were not specialists in one area of expertise but generalists who taught across the curriculum. As the second Annual Report of Oberlin College shows, the professor of Sacred Music also taught Mathematics, Natural Philosophy and Law, Rhetoric and Belles Lettres. This model of the humanist liberal arts college purified from the market place, however, was transformed and resynthesized during the rise of the Industrial Revolution.

The technological advances of the Industrial Revolution gave the sciences greater prestige in society, and research universities gained more prominence during this era. Furthermore, the agrarian social order under which the humanist liberal arts college had operated was increasingly displaced by the rise of the new urban middle class. Whereas in earlier years colleges had been insulated from the demands of the market place, they suddenly found themselves having to compete with universities for students. Because the new middle class that began entering the ranks of higher education placed a greater emphasis on the practical value of education, the Humanist "liberal studies" of the college came under direct challenge from the technological training provided by universities:

> [O]ne must recognize *the changed conditions* which we face today, as compared with those of years ago. A number of factors are here involved. First there is *no possible isolation* now, such as was possible during the early years. We stand in closer and inevitable relations to the outside world; and we stand in similar closer and inevitable relations with other institutions. We are now and must ever be a part of the world for good or for ill. [...] Our problem is further complicated by the fact that we draw our students from a much *more diverse constituency* probably than years ago. [...] We are facing a new intellectual and moral world, and we cannot help it: a new world in which the scientific convictions of *law* and *evolution* [...] have become increasingly influential. (Annual Report, 1906–1907)

As a result of these social changes, at the turn of the twentieth century the liberal arts college began synthesizing some of the contending elements of the research university. The research model of the scientific university was mimicked by splintering Humanist studies into specialized disciplines. A more practical curriculum was offered by conjoining the Humanist "liberal studies" with a scientific curriculum. The liberal arts college, which earlier had emphasized a non-professional, culturally enlightening education, began incorporating professional research. Yet even as the liberal arts college began mimicking the sciences, it never relinquished its earlier Humanist mission. Instead, the Humanist was paradoxically reconciled with the Scientific. It was during this time of social and economic transformation that English literature was institutionalized in the academy. For many college faculty members and students such as myself who went through the educational system after English literature became established as a dominant field, it is hard to believe that in the early years of professionalization, the academic merits of studying English literature were contested. In the historical context of higher education, English literature is a relatively new field that was not fully accepted as a serious discipline until fairly recently.

Unlike English literary studies, however, composition was an integral part of the college curriculum from the very beginning. According to the *Oberlin Alumni Magazine* of March 1923, "Weekly exercises in composition and declamation were a part of the work of each college from the earliest days. [...] The rhetorics of the day contained long lists of essay subjects [such as] The Ruins of Time, The Pleasures of Memory, and the Dangers of Procrastination." Although the teaching of English literature was contested because reading literature was seen as a pleasurable activity in which anybody could engage without instruction, the value of teaching writing was readily accepted and understood.

Because I was so used to writing essays in my English classes—indeed, I had come to believe that English classes were *the* place where a person learned to write essays—I was surprised to learn how recent the practice of writing papers in English classes is. In the early years, writing was not a component of literary studies; English classes were conducted using oral declamations and examinations. Essay writing was taught in composition classes, which were a part of the Rhetorics Department. Gradually, closer connections evolved between the English Department and the teaching of composition, the rationale being that both dealt with English. In 1895, Professor Tisdel, Professor of Rhetoric and Composition wrote, "It is our plan to connect the work in English Composition as closely as possible with the work in English." (Annual Report, 1895)

Three years later, in 1898, the teaching of Composition was completely assumed by the English department. During these early years of professionalization when the academic merits of English literature were being contested, composition, in effect, helped legitimize the new discipline of English literature by rendering a commodifiable value to English literary studies. The different demographics of students attending college during the Industrial Revolution placed a greater emphasis on the financial returns of education than had earlier been the case. Unlike literature, composition had an obvious practical value in the changing marketplace which was generating new managerial jobs requiring writing skills: "The stress upon accurate writing both in high school and college is no doubt due to the amazed outcries of business and professional men. [...]" (Annual Report, 1918–1919)

Yet even as the status of composition increased the value of the discipline of English literature, the professional status of English was secured within the academy through the process of specialization—specialization ironically achieved by highlighting the differences between literature and composition. Because the earlier liberal arts college had been reconceived on a scientific model, prestige could be acquired within the academy by mimicking the structural configuration of the sciences. As I noted before, this scientific model is a contradictory imposition on the Humanist liberal arts college. It circumscribes the once unified "liberal studies" of the college based on the principle of difference. Because this system operates by constructing and compartmentalizing separate disciplines, it is a structure that rewards specialization and differentiation.

Consequently, at the dawn of the twentieth century, the strategy of specialization accorded professional status to the practitioners of English, who were thereby reconfigured as trained specialists in the field of literary studies. The ironic consequence of specialization, however, was that as English began to acquire prominence, its practitioners began to insist that the teaching of composition (the very skill that had helped validate English) was extraneous to the discipline of literary studies. As the distinctions between composition and English were highlighted, the divisions between the practitioners in the now different fields were also increasingly demarcated:

> While well equipped with instructors, we are literally cramping and dwarfing our *potential* efficiency by the necessity of combining literature and composition. We should have a Professor of English Composition, a trained man who would give his undivided attention to this important instruction. (Annual Report, 1909–1910)

As this annual report shows, the specialized training required of an English professor is essentially differentiated from that required for the distinct subject matter of Composition. Yet even as the differences between composition and English were being increasingly emphasized, the teaching of composition was still relegated to the English department. Consequently, practitioners of English began to resent the burden of teaching composition because they saw it as a service duty outside the work of their true discipline:

> [A] very serious disadvantage of the union of the two departments is that full professors whose interest is not primarily in composition are required to take on required sections of Freshmen and thus reduce the number of courses of literature that the department can offer. (Annual Report, 1926–1927)

As early as 1901 (only three years after composition was integrated with English), composition is seen as "drudge" work by English professors who are quite explicit that they would rather be teaching English literature:

> I desire to call your attention to two serious needs of the Department of English. The first is an instructor to have charge of the required work in Composition. [...] I am prevented by my regular work in Literature from giving the students the individual attention that they require. [...] It would of course be possible for me to emphasize the Composition at the expense of the courses in Literature, but in the first place, I came to Oberlin with the understanding that I should have no work in Composition. [...] Moreover, the demands made upon me by the work in Composition obviously injure, to some extent, the work in the Department of Literature. [...] I desire to be released from my work in Composition in order that I may meet this class [in the history of English literature] in three sections. For these reasons, I venture to renew my appeal for an instructor to take the work in Composition that I am now doing.
> (Annual Report, 1901)

Because Composition was subsumed within the English Department, where literature was considered the primary subject matter, the teaching of composition began to be defined primarily in terms of its relation to English literature. In other words, even as the practitioners of English were emphasizing the differences between the disciplines of composition and English literature, these self-consciously positioned practitioners of English literature were simultaneously reappropriating and redefining the study of writing as essentially a means of furthering the study of English literature:

> [W]e hope to train freshmen and sophomores in correct methods of reading, to introduce them to certain fundamental books which they are not likely to read of their own motion, and above all to teach them to think of what they read. This last is the chief aim also of our required course in Freshman Composition. [...]
> (Annual Report, 1918–19)

Fifty years later, in 1969, the residual consequences of this appropriation could still be seen in the course description for the Introductory English Composition course:

101. Introductory English Composition. First Semester. The aim of the course is to *inculcate habits of accurate reading,* logical thinking, and clear, correct expression. [...] (Oberlin College Course Catalogue, 1969–1970; my emphasis)

Even in a class explicitly designated as "composition," the primary mission is to feed the literature major by "inculcat[ing] habits of accurate reading."

As I have tried to demonstrate, whether or not the high schools significantly improve, colleges will still need to familiarize new students with the specialized discourses of higher education. Despite wishful thinking, the problem of deficient student writing will not likely disappear soon. It is inevitable that writing by new students unfamiliar with scholarly discourse communities will initially be deemed "poor" by the practitioners already working within that discipline. This is where the new thinking in composition can help. Unlike in earlier years, composition no longer focuses mainly on teaching correctness. Today, expository writing is concerned with helping students make the transition to new discourse communities. This is especially evident in programs where the emphasis is on writing across the curriculum. There is advanced professional work being conducted in expository writing. What is perhaps unique about the professional work in composition is its expressly pedagogical nature. In other words, the professional claims and the service role of expository writing are not at odds. Clearly, it is time that expository writing programs and their staffs everywhere receive the full professional consideration and support that they deserve.

NOTES

All sources referenced were accessed in the Oberlin College Archives during the academic year 1995-96.

[1] In 2005 the Expository Writing Program at Oberlin College became the Rhetoric and Composition Department. Staffing has remained at three FTEs. However, the English Department no longer contributes any resources to the teaching of composition. [Editor's note]

[2] Since 2005, the Rhetoric and Composition Department has had encouragement from the College to balance its introductory courses with more advanced offerings. [Editor's note]

[3] Comment made by a faculty member at an Educational Plans and Policies Committee meeting I attended as a student representative of the Expository Writing Program (February 8, 1996).